AF848336

JUNG'S STUDIES IN ASTROLOGY

C.G. Jung had a profound interest in and involvement with astrology, which he made clear in virtually every volume of the *Collected Works*, as well as many of his letters. This ancient symbolic system was of primary importance in his understanding of the nature of time, the archetypes, synchronicity, and human fate.

Jung's Studies in Astrology is an historical survey of his astrological work from the time he began to study the subject. It is based not only on his published writings, but also on the correspondence and documents found in his private archives, many of which have never previously seen the light of day. Liz Greene addresses with thoroughness and detailed scholarship the nature of Jung's involvement with astrology: the ancient, medieval, and modern sources he drew on, the individuals from whom he learned, his ideas about how and why it worked, its religious and philosophical implications, and its applications in the treatment of his patients as well as in his own self-understanding. Greene clearly demonstrates that any serious effort to understand the development of Jung's psychological theories, as well as the nature of his world-view, needs to involve a thorough exploration of his astrological work.

This thorough investigation of a central theme in Jung's work will appeal to analytical psychologists and Jungian psychotherapists, students and academics of Jungian and post-Jungian theory, the history of psychology, archetypal thought, mythology and folklore, the history of New Age movements, esotericism and psychological astrology.

Liz Greene is a Jungian analyst and professional astrologer who received her Diploma in Analytical Psychology from the Association of Jungian Analysts in London in 1980. She holds doctorates in both Psychology and History, and worked for a number of years as a tutor in the MA in Cultural Astronomy and Astrology at the University of Wales, Lampeter. She is the author of a number of books, some scholarly and some interpretive, on the relationships between psychology and astrology, Tarot, Kabbalah, and myth, and of *The Astrological World of Jung's* Liber Novus (Routledge).

The whole universe, my friend, is a tremendous sacrament; a mystic, ineffable force and energy, veiled by an outward form of matter; and man, and the sun and the other stars, and the flower of the grass, and the crystal in the test-tube, are each and every one as spiritual, as material, and subject to an inner working.[1]

—Arthur Machen

I can only gaze with wonder and awe at the depths and heights of our psychic nature. Its non-spatial universe conceals an untold abundance of images which have accumulated over millions of years of living development and become fixed in the organism . . . And these images are not pale shadows, but tremendously powerful psychic factors . . . Beside this picture I would like to place the spectacle of the starry heavens at night, for the only equivalent of the universe within is the universe without.[2]

—C.G. Jung

Notes

1 Arthur Machen, 'The Novel of the White Powder', in Arthur Machen, *The Three Impostors* (London: John Lane, 1895), pp. 95–111. All quotations by individuals other than Jung at the beginning of each chapter of this book are by authors whose works are found in Jung's private library.

2 Jung, CW4, ¶764.

JUNG'S STUDIES IN ASTROLOGY

Prophecy, Magic, and the Qualities of Time

Liz Greene

Routledge
Taylor & Francis Group
LONDON AND NEW YORK

First published 2018
by Routledge
2 Park Square, Milton Park, Abingdon, Oxon OX14 4RN

and by Routledge
711 Third Avenue, New York, NY 10017

Routledge is an imprint of the Taylor & Francis Group, an informa business

© 2018 Liz Greene

The right of Liz Greene to be identified as author of this work has been asserted by her in accordance with sections 77 and 78 of the Copyright, Designs and Patents Act 1988.

All rights reserved. No part of this book may be reprinted or reproduced or utilised in any form or by any electronic, mechanical, or other means, now known or hereafter invented, including photocopying and recording, or in any information storage or retrieval system, without permission in writing from the publishers.

Trademark notice: Product or corporate names may be trademarks or registered trademarks, and are used only for identification and explanation without intent to infringe.

British Library Cataloguing-in-Publication Data
A catalogue record for this book is available from the British Library

Library of Congress Cataloging-in-Publication Data
Names: Greene, Liz, author.
Title: Jung's studies in astrology : prophecy, magic, and the qualities of time / Liz Greene.
Description: New York : Routledge, 2018. | Includes bibliographical references.
Identifiers: LCCN 2017041499 (print) | LCCN 2017051911 (ebook) | ISBN 9781315267371 (Master e-book) | ISBN 9781138289116 (hardback) | ISBN 9781138289123 (pbk.)
Subjects: LCSH: Astrology and psychology. | Psychoanalysis. | Jung, C. G. (Carl Gustav), 1875–1961. | Occultism.
Classification: LCC BF1729.P8 (ebook) | LCC BF1729.P8 G725 2018 (print) | DDC 133.5092—dc23
LC record available at https://lccn.loc.gov/2017041499

ISBN: 978-1-138-28911-6 (hbk)
ISBN: 978-1-138-28912-3 (pbk)
ISBN: 978-1-315-26737-1 (ebk)

Typeset in Bembo
by Apex CoVantage, LLC

For Product Safety Concerns and Information please contact our EU representative: GPSR@taylorandfrancis.com
Taylor & Francis Verlag GmbH, Kaufingerstraße 24, 80331 München, Germany.

CONTENTS

IMAGES

Figures

Plates

A NOTE ON REFERENCES

The works of C.G. Jung cited in the text are referenced in the endnotes by the number of the volume in *The Collected Works of C.G. Jung*, followed by the paragraph number. For example: Jung, CW13, ¶82–84. Full publishing information is given in the Bibliography. Cited works by Jung not included in the *Collected Works* are referenced in the endnotes by the main title, volume if applicable, and page number, with full publication details given in the Bibliography. For example: Jung, *Visions Seminars* I:23. Jung's autobiography, *Memories, Dreams, Reflections*, is referenced in the endnotes as *MDR*, with full publication details given in the Bibliography.

The works of Plato and other ancient authors cited in the text in an English translation are given in the endnotes according to the title of the work and its standard paragraph reference, with full references including translation and publication information given in the Bibliography. For example, Plato, *Symposium*, 52a–56c; Iamblichus, *De mysteriis*, I.21.

The works of Sigmund Freud cited in the text are given by the number of the volume in the *Standard Edition of the Works of Sigmund Freud*, followed by the page number of the specific edition I have used. For example: Freud, SE5, p. 155. Full translation and publishing information is given in the Bibliography.

When a cited work has a subtitle, only the main title is given in the endnotes along with publication details and page reference, but the full title is given in the Bibliography.

FOREWORD

This is a work which I have been searching for in vain for several decades, yet paradoxically, it could only have been written now. For years, I sought to locate the place of astrology in Jung's work. Like a hermetic riddle, the signs and ciphers of astrology were both abundantly evident, while their significance lay simultaneously concealed: from indications of his study of the subject in his correspondence with Freud and numerous recollections of patients and associates, to the copious references in his alchemical work, the role of his 'astrological experiment' in his paper on synchronicity, through to the overarching astrological framework of his study of the psychological significance of the precession of the equinoxes in *Aion*. Furthermore, there was little by way of a trail that linked this to the main body of his work and its process of formation. The take-up of Jung's work by astrologers in the twentieth century further complicated matters, as a complex tale of reception evidently also needed to be reconstructed. Finally, there was a dearth of secondary material on the history of astrology in the late nineteenth and early twentieth centuries that could serve as an orientation and point of departure.

The solution to this riddle came about in two ways. First, the publication of Jung's *Liber Novus* opened the way, for the first time on the basis of primary documentation, for the study of the linkages between Jung's scholarly readings: how they stimulated his dreams, visions and fantasies; how he utilised these to construct a personal cosmology in the form of a work in a literary, theological, philosophical and pictorial form, leavened by symbolic parallels; and how he attempted to distil this into the conceptual language of a new psychology in the making, which he in turn used as the hermeneutic key for the comparative study of the process of transformation in esoteric traditions. A critical documentary source was now available with which to link his life, practice, and work, which also serves as a lever to shift the rubble of the numerous myths and legends that have grown over his work. Second, a writer appeared with the necessary scholarly background in the relevant fields, able to utilise these materials to locate the place of astrology in Jung's work, and Jung's work within the history of astrology.

This work does not view psychology through an astrological lens, nor view astrology through a psychological lens – though it provides much rich material for such considerations. Rather, it tracks Jung's evolving use of astrology – or, as the work demonstrates, a number of forms and currents of astrology – in the construction of his psychology, which in turn paved the way for a psychologically inflected astrology. If the astrologies that Jung drew on were multiple, so were Jung's uses of them: in his self-understanding, his self-experimentation (in particular, in the relation of his active imagination to theurgy), as an adjunct to his practice, in his understanding of symbolism and hermeneutics, through to his later studies of astrology in his scholarly works.

Jung's psychology is marked not only by the breadth of its subject matter, but also by the range of disciplines that he drew upon. However, Jung studies have been peopled by a plethora of monocausal accounts, which, while focussing on one element, force it to stand synecdochically, *pars pro toto*, whether the source be (pre-eminently) Freud, Gnosticism, the Kabbalah, the German aesthetic tradition, or spiritualism. While a number of these works have contributed valuable insights, they have not tackled the syncretic and combinatory manner in which Jung would simultaneously draw upon a variety of fields at the same time. Till now, the role of astrology has been missing in this mix. Critically, this study does not fall into the trap of proposing yet another monocausal account, but situates Jung's uses of astrology within broader frameworks in a non-evaluative historical and contextual manner. In particular, this work is also a critical study of Jung's relation to esotericism and hermeticism, as in many ways astrology formed an inescapable element of these currents (and one which has been neglected in studies of Jung and esotericism to date). Consequently, it manages to be an instructive and essential reading in its own right, while resituating and correcting a host of other works.

Sonu Shamdasani

ACKNOWLEDGEMENTS

I would like to offer my grateful thanks to Professor Sonu Shamdasani for his careful perusal of the manuscript, and the support and helpful suggestions he offered throughout. I would also like to thank Andreas Jung and his wife Vreni for giving me their kind permission to examine the material in Jung's private archives and files of personal papers, and for their interest in and support of the writing of this book.

INTRODUCTION

The pursuit of 'wretched subjects'

> Ecstasy or vision begins when thought ceases, *to our consciousness*, to proceed from ourselves. It differs from dreaming, because the subject is awake. It differs from hallucinations, because there is no organic disturbance . . . Lastly, it differs from poetical inspiration, because the imagination is passive. That perfectly sane people often experience such visions there is no manner of doubt.[1]
>
> —William Ralph Inge

> The spirit of the depths from time immemorial and for all the future possesses a greater power than the spirit of this time, who changes with the generations. The spirit of the depths has subjugated all pride and arrogance to the power of judgement. He took away my belief in science, he robbed me of the joy of explaining and ordering things, and he let devotion to the ideals of the time die out in me. He forced me down to the last and simplest things.[2]
>
> —C.G. Jung

Some domains of knowledge are easily distinguishable from each other: archaeology, for example, or zoology. Other domains, like medicine, are also easily identified, but so broad that they require further clarification through subdivisions such as gynaecology, cardiology, and orthopaedic surgery. Still other domains are resistant to any precise definition, even with myriad subdivisions, and might be viewed as liminal. Liminal subjects tend to spread promiscuously through the interfaces between disparate spheres of study such as religion, psychology, and magic, which are themselves notoriously resistant to any universally agreed definition. It is these enigmatic borderlands of human exploration that the historian Otto Neugebauer once called 'wretched subjects'.[3] The manner in which C.G. Jung investigated, adapted, and interpreted astrology – one of the most historically significant and enduring, as well as one of the most poorly understood, of these liminal realms – forms the subject of this book.[4]

Scholars like to know the names of things and the categories to which they belong. To this end they have devised academic constructs such as 'Neoplatonism', an appellation first created in the late eighteenth century to describe the religious beliefs, philosophies, and practices of a group of individuals living between the third and sixth centuries in widely disparate areas of the Roman Empire with differing cultural denominators. These individuals never called themselves 'neo', but were attempting, in their own unique ways, to interpret Plato's work according to their personal perspectives and experiences.[5] They shared a love of Plato's ideas and a conviction that there was still a great deal within the Platonic opus that merited further elucidation. 'Neoplatonism' is a useful category because it locates these individuals within a roughly identifiable time frame, a more or less recognisable philosophical system, and a broad cultural context. But as a definitive label, 'Neoplatonism' can obscure the enormous differences between the ideas and doctrines promulgated, for example, by Plotinus (c. 204–270 CE), whose *Enneads* exercised a lasting influence on Christian theology, and Iamblichus (c. 245–325 CE), the head of the Platonic academy in Syria, whose text on theurgy, *De mysteriis*, was particularly attractive to the occultists of the late nineteenth century.[6] Likewise, 'Neoplatonism' can obscure the enormous differences in the interpretation – or, as it is currently understood, the 'reception'[7] – of these authors from the time of their writing to the present day.

Another example of an apparently precise but highly misleading academic classification is the term 'Renaissance'. From the mid-nineteenth to the mid-twentieth century, it seemed perfectly clear to historians what was meant by 'the Renaissance':[8] it spanned the period between the early fifteenth and mid-seventeenth century, fuelled by the translation from Greek into Latin of classical and late antique texts once lost to the West but made accessible through the fall of Constantinople to the Ottoman Turks in 1453.[9] The Italian Renaissance, viewed from this perspective, represents a dramatically sudden, spontaneously generated rebirth of ancient pagan philosophy and art in a Western Christian context, epitomised by the paintings of Botticelli and da Vinci; the sculptures of Michelangelo; the Platonic and Hermetic philosophical elucidations of Marsilio Ficino; the Kabbalistic explications of Pico della Mirandola; the poetry of Petrarch, Boccaccio, and Angelo Poliziano; and the scientific genius of Galileo and Copernicus.[10] It also heralded a resurgence of the three 'occult sciences' of antiquity – astrology, alchemy, and magic[11] – which were later to prove so fascinating to Jung. But this definition of 'Renaissance' has been contested within the academy for more than fifty years.[12] A period of great religious and scientific expansion between 1050 and 1250 is now referred to as the 'twelfth-century Renaissance' and, like the later Italian Renaissance, it also involved the importation of texts on magic, astrology, and alchemy, this time from the Jewish and Muslim worlds of southern Spain and the Middle East. The Italian Renaissance is now seen as the inevitable outgrowth of the twelfth-century Renaissance, enhanced by the development of printed books, which eventually led to the Reformation and what is now known as the early modern period in Western history.[13] Categories such as 'early modern' may themselves, over time, be reviewed and revised. The historiography of any place or period of human culture, and any genre of human creativity, is as revealing and complex as the history itself.[14]

Many people outside the academy have no difficulty in identifying themselves as 'religious'. But scholars continue to argue ferociously about the definition of the term 'religion' according to criteria that might mean nothing at all to those who firmly place their trust in the ineffable through direct experience, but never enter a collectively recognised place of worship or call their divinity by a conventionally acknowledged name.[15] Because many of these individuals have no intention of ever setting foot in a church, chapel, synagogue, mosque, or temple, their perspectives are deemed to be either 'New Age cults' – as is the case with many contemporary spiritualities[16] – or part of the modern process of 'secularisation': another constructed category, like 'Neoplatonism', which serves the purposes of the academy but does not faithfully reflect, and may even grossly misrepresent, the highly individual ideas, beliefs, experiences, and aspirations of those grouped under such labels.[17]

Even the term 'modern' is open to question. We might think of ourselves as 'modern', and speak of the 'modern' world, or even the 'post-modern'. Psychology is understood to be a 'modern' science; astrology, in contrast, is deemed to be 'pre-modern', and its indestructible popularity has continued to baffle sociologically inclined researchers. But is modernity a precise period of history that began at the time of the 'Enlightenment' (another academic construct) at the end of the eighteenth century? Is modernity an evolutionary step in social progress, or a regressive one? Is it the product of industrialisation, secularisation, science, or 'disenchantment'?[18] Is 'modern' a perspective that has occurred many times in history, perhaps in a cyclical fashion, reflecting a certain way of viewing reality? Or does 'modern' simply refer to a fluid category which people have used throughout history, albeit under other names, to differentiate themselves from a perceived 'primitive' past?[19]

Academically constructed categories, even when they implacably disagree or are subject to constant revision, are useful, not least because, in a scholarly work, it is advisable to make oneself understood by stating clearly what one means by a particular term. But these categories must necessarily remain hypothetical and fluid, because no two cultures, and no two individuals, will ever precisely agree about what constitutes religion, magic, or psychology. Astrology too, usually perceived by historians as a monolithic entity under the rubric of 'divination',[20] needs to be understood as a pluralistic cultural product. There have always been many astrologies in terms of the diverse cosmologies, philosophies, techniques, modes of interpretation, and material and spiritual applications developed by astrological practitioners.[21] Although the symbolic representations of Western astrology have remained relatively consistent over many centuries,[22] Jung's psychologically orientated astrological approach is very different from the Aristotelian astrology of Ptolemy in the second century, which in turn differs from the magical astrology of the adepts of the Hermetic Order of the Golden Dawn in the late nineteenth century and the Theosophical astrology of Alan Leo in the early twentieth, rooted in H.P. Blavatsky's reinterpretation of Neoplatonic and Gnostic ideas about the spiritual evolution of the soul.

In recent decades, cultural specificity has become a powerful tool within the academy for ensuring that scholarly definitions of spheres of human activity such as 'religion' remain fluid. But at the same time, these definitions are, paradoxically, expected to provide clear and stable boundaries between discrete areas of human experience that might be more subtly intertwined than at first perceived. For example, one can be a psychologist of religion, but it is not easy to be a psychologist who is overtly religious without risking a loss of credibility in the eyes of those who view psychology solely as a science.[23] Sonu Shamdasani has pointed out that much of the controversy surrounding Jung's work rests on the fact that he was 'one of the most prominent modern psychologists to affirm religious values'.[24] One can be a scholar of magic, or a scholar of astrology, yet one cannot practice ritual magic or astrology without serious questions being asked about one's academic 'empiricism'[25] – even though it is problematic, and perhaps even impossible, to discuss such fields intelligently without any direct experience of them. As Shamdasani states, Jung's 'non-derisive attention to such subjects was enough to brand him as an occultist'.[26] When non-derisiveness leads to direct experimentation (as it did with Jung), genuinely relevant questions, such as what valuable psychological insights might be gained from such experimentation, are not asked by critics. Prejudice and uninformed opinion, and even personal hostility, may replace 'methodological agnosticism' and the testimony of individual experience.[27]

Even figures from the ancient world can suffer from this kind of anachronistic imposition of present-day cultural paradigms. The reputation of Iamblichus, who was labelled a 'magician' by the religious historian E.R. Dodds in the mid-twentieth century, has never entirely recovered from the assumption that rational philosophy and theurgic mysticism are mutually exclusive; Iamblichus is still, despite recent scholarly efforts in the last two decades, viewed by some academics as a 'depraved occultist'.[28] As Zeke Mazur has pointed out in a paper on the magical roots of Plotinus' 'rational' mysticism: 'Much of the previous scholarship has consciously or unconsciously assumed that magic is a category radically distinct from both philosophy and "high" religion'.[29] And while the 'rehabilitation' of theurgically inclined Neoplatonists such as Iamblichus is finally being pursued in some quarters, this kind of common-sense neutrality does not always extend into the domain of academic psychology. The work of psychologists and psychotherapists who spend too much time exploring the liminal zones does not often meet with an unbiased reception.

In the world of 'wretched subjects', precise categories tend to dissolve, merge, and mate with each other to generate new hybrids. The insights gained from direct experience may prove as important as intellectual analyses and scientific methodologies, and blurred boundaries are the norm. However disturbing this might be, ideas with enormous agency and longevity can be seen in their most dynamic forms, while they are still in the process of transforming and creatively adapting to particular cultural milieux but have not yet been bludgeoned into codified inertia by the requirements of specific academic, socio-economic, and political concerns. 'Wretched subjects', however plentiful and important the documentary evidence, still form an academic wilderness, relatively unexplored until very recently, in which there are no neat, inarguable rules for scholastic methodology or religious ontology. This can prove uncomfortable, and the temptation to turn the wilderness into a carefully manicured garden through the application of intellectual secateurs, herbicides, and insecticides is sometimes irresistible. But it is only when these spheres are explored from within as well as without that genuinely creative thinking is possible.

Jung spent a great deal of time in the liminal interfaces between psychology and religion, psychology and magic, magic and mysticism, and mysticism and medicine. Like any individual, he was vulnerable to the dominant values of his time and his culture, and he suffered enormously each time he ventured beyond the barbed-wire fence surrounding and protecting his chosen profession of psychiatry and sought psychological insights in what are now understood to be 'esoteric' subjects. It is unclear whether the subjects Jung studied are indeed 'esoteric'; this depends on how the term is defined and in which historical period the definition has arisen.[30] Astrology is often considered an 'esoteric' sphere of study, but until the end of the eighteenth century it was 'mainstream' and, despite continuing efforts to obstruct its practice or challenge its legitimacy at various historical junctures, it has remained an intrinsic, albeit sometimes covert, aspect of the religious cosmologies of both East and West. Many of the subjects which Jung studied blend different spheres of human experience: art serves as an instrument of magic, astrological symbols yield psychological insight, dream-images open gateways to religious experiences disguised as madness, God and the unconscious become indistinguishable, medicine joins hands with shamanic ritual, and sexuality is a holy magical rite. However, the label 'esoteric' can be a comforting one for scholars because, once this term has been given fixed boundaries,[31] it is no longer necessary to tolerate the uncertainty of whether what Jung did was psychology or religion, or whether attempting to distinguish between the two might be asking the wrong question. In the view of many academics, Jung was not a proper psychologist, but rather an 'esotericist' with a 'religionist' bias whose work is rooted in the German Romanticism of the nineteenth century.[32] That, apparently, places him safely in a recognisable category where, until very recently, it was assumed that, like a tricky *jinn* in a bottle, he would quietly remain.

In the autumn of 2009, a new work by Jung titled *The Red Book: Liber Novus* was finally released for publication.[33] Close to the time of his death in 1961, Jung made the following comments about the period of his life when he was engaged in creating *Liber Novus*:

> The years when I was pursuing my inner images were the most important in my life – in them everything essential was decided. It all began then; the later details are only supplements and clarifications of the material that burst forth from the unconscious, and at first swamped me. It was the *prima materia* for a lifetime's work.[34]

Liber Novus, known as *The Red Book* because of its red leather binding, is Jung's calligraphic revision of a series of private diaries, known as the *Black Books*, covering the period from 1913 – the time of his break with Freud – to 1932. The work is both textual and pictorial. Virtually every page contains a painted image, all of them strikingly beautiful and impeccably executed, and the calligraphic writing mimics a medieval illuminated manuscript. The dominant narrative of *Liber Novus* is Jung's journey from alienation to the restoration of his soul, through the long and painful process of integrating a rift within his own nature: the seemingly irreconcilable conflict between reason and revelation, outer and inner worlds, subjectivity and objectivity, and between the scientist and the religious visionary, both of whom he experienced as authentic, demanding, and mutually exclusive dimensions of his own being.

The existence of *Liber Novus* had been an open secret once Jung's autobiographical memoir, *Memories, Dreams, Reflections*, was published in German in 1961 and in English in 1962,[35] as he described the genesis of *Liber Novus* in this work; and unpublished copies of *Liber Novus* had been circulating among Jung's close colleagues for some time. But it had never been accessible to a wider reading public, nor even to the majority of analytical psychologists outside Jung's own intimate circle. Now its publication has inspired a proliferation of books, articles, workshops, interviews, lectures, and commentaries, ranging from reviews in newspapers, internet seminars, and interpretations in analytic journals to the websites of modern pagan groups, one of which, with considerable justification, declared online that *Liber Novus* is 'the most important grimoire of our modern age'.[36]

Jung's reputation in the world of clinical psychology has always been ambiguous. Often viewed as a mystic or even, in the view of the Freudian analyst D.W. Winnicott, a schizophrenic who somehow managed to heal himself,[37] Jung's theoretical models have been deemed questionable because they are insufficiently 'scientific'. It is difficult to demonstrate through repetitive experiments the existence and location of the archetypes of the collective unconscious.[38] Current paradigms of clinical psychology tend to favour cognitive approaches to the human mind, which are more amenable to the methodologies of the natural sciences.[39] According to David Tacey, a professor of psychoanalysis at La Trobe University in Melbourne, one of the reasons why Jung has been marginalised within university psychology departments is that 'his work does not fit any specific academic discipline. Staff in psychology are likely to refer to it as religious studies'.[40]

Surprisingly, the view of Jung as 'unscientific' has also been promulgated in the academic sphere of esoteric studies, an area of scholarship that has, until quite recently, itself been marginalised, and where one might reasonably expect a more methodologically neutral and practitioner-tolerant approach. This perception of Jung suggests that, because he drew on esoteric sources in formulating his psychological models, he should be viewed as an esotericist, since esotericism and psychology are evidently mutually exclusive.[41] An example of this kind of approach is offered by Richard Noll, whose apparently scholarly treatment of Jung has been challenged in terms of its neutrality, and even its veracity. G. William Barnard, describing Noll's work, suggests:

> It also seems that underneath Noll's seemingly impeccable academic good intentions, other more emotionally charged motives are at work. Noll does not simply offer a neutral, detached depiction of Jung. Instead, in much the same way as other academics who are contemptuous of various 'lowbrow' psychology-as-a-religion perspectives, it could be argued that Noll seeks to discredit Jung, simply because of his affiliation with a number of esoteric and occult movements active at that time in Europe.[42]

It might be argued that Barnard has been excessively courteous in his evaluation of Noll. John Haule, a Zürich-trained Jungian analyst describing various biographies of Jung, simply dismisses Noll as a 'muckraker'.[43] Sonu Shamdasani, in *Cult Fictions*, likewise removes the velvet glove and highlights with impeccable scholarship the dishonesty and malice with which Noll constructed his project of Jung-bashing.[44] Jung has also been interpreted by some scholars as a philosopher of religion who covertly utilised psychological models to support metaphysical claims. This apparently renders his psychological theories dubious because he concealed his belief in the existence of God under the cloak of the psychological analysis of religious experience.[45] Religious belief, as Ann Bedford Ulinov has wryly suggested, could 'contaminate the learning process with a proselytizing fervor'.[46]

Although it has not yet been empirically demonstrated that a belief in God is mutually exclusive with the capacity to generate useful scientific research, nevertheless there seems to be an unspoken assumption that one must be an atheist or, at the very least, an agnostic in order to produce a legitimate scientific psychology. This perspective relies on particular assumptions about the nature of psychology as a science best pursued within the broader framework of medicine. These assumptions, a reflection of the early twentieth-century fixation on 'scientism', plagued Jung himself. But they are open to serious challenge today, not only by therapeutic practitioners of various persuasions, but by those historians who have remembered Thomas Kuhn's trenchant observation that science, rather than steadily accumulating incontrovertible truths, tends to lurch from paradigm to paradigm.[47] However, the tensions around Jung's position in the academy, despite the frequency of uninformed opinions and lack of direct experience of the analytic process, reflect with precision Jung's own profound conflict between scientifically demonstrable 'truths' and visionary experience.

Despite Jung's ambiguous place within the world of clinical psychology, his influence has been pervasive in the various currents of transpersonal psychology.[48] In theological circles, he has long been favoured by psychologically inclined theologians, since belief, in this context, 'is not held to be a drawback but a resource'.[49] The spiritual journey presented in *Liber Novus* is likely to enhance rather than detract from Jung's influence in this sphere.[50] In the field of literature, Jung's ideas glow like fluorescent threads within the work of novelists such as James Joyce, Hermann Hesse, and Thomas Mann,[51] and scholars of twentieth-century literature, in addition to exploring these threads, frequently utilise Jungian models as a methodology to explore the major themes in literary texts.[52] For many decades Jung's ideas also exercised an enormous influence on historians of religion such as Mircea Eliade, Gilles Quispel, Henry Corbin, and Pierre Riffard, who examined the repeating themes of myth and ritual across cultures and historical epochs and embraced Jung's idea of archetypal patterns as reflections of the deepest dynamics of the human imagination. Quispel referred to these patterns as 'basic structures of religious apperception'; Riffard called them 'anthropological structures', implying a transcultural human predisposition to generate religious ideas according to specific patterns of thought.[53] The Eranos conferences, which began in 1933 and were held annually in Ascona, Switzerland, until 1976, were inspired by Jung's work and attracted the participation of Eliade and Corbin as well as Gershom Scholem, the founder of modern scholarly research into the Jewish Kabbalah. These scholars were all variously influenced by Jung's theory of archetypes, and focused on the generic features of religions and the centrality of mystical experience rather than on culturally specific forms of worship and their social and political dimensions. For many decades their approach influenced scholarship on religion throughout the world.[54]

But all paradigms, as Kuhn wisely observed, have a finite life, and it seems that, like the heavenly bodies, they move in cycles. In zoological taxonomy, for example, the debate between 'lumpers' (those who group different subpopulations of a particular animal genus together and emphasise their similarities as a single species) and 'splitters' (those who focus on differences and give each subpopulation a separate species name) echoes the ongoing debate in historical and religious studies between 'universalist' and 'culture-specific' approaches.[55] The culture-specific approach to the history of religions now dominant within the academy has served as a necessary corrective to the dangers of grand 'metanarratives',[56] but it can sometimes be taken to extremes. From this perspective, Jung's theories are 'universalist' or 'essentialist' and are therefore unsound[57] – although Jung himself continually emphasised the cultural adaptability and fluidity of mythic themes.[58] Jung's method of 'amplification' to achieve better understanding of a symbol through comparison with other symbols is not, as is sometimes assumed, a means of abstracting universal 'categories', but rather, a way of entering into, and experiencing, the dynamic dimensions of the symbol itself:[59]

> The essence of hermeneutics . . . consists in adding more analogies to that already given by the symbol . . . The initial symbol is much enlarged and enriched by this procedure, the result being a highly complex and many-sided picture . . . Thence result certain psychological lines of development of an individual as well as collective nature. No science upon earth could prove the accuracy of these lines . . . But these lines vindicate their validity by their *value for life*.[60]

It was this approach that Jung adopted in his use of astrological symbols as a form of hermeneutics.

The tendency within contemporary esoteric circles to validate occult philosophies through Jung's psychological models has been referred to as 'Jungianism'.[61] This term is applicable to twentieth-century astrologers such as Dane Rudhyar (1895–1985) and Alexander Ruperti (1913–1998), who selected particular themes in Jung's work and used them to justify a range of Theosophically orientated interpretations.[62] Jung's influence on contemporary astrologies has certainly been potent, not least because he himself practiced astrology: the influence flowed both ways. But the object of this book is not to dismiss Jung's psychological theories as a modernisation of esoteric doctrines adapted to the requirements of a 'scientistic' modern age.[63] Jung's astrology helped to shape his psychological models from the writing of *Liber Novus* onward, and modern astrology has been profoundly reshaped by Jung's psychological concepts. This neither confirms nor denies the validity of either field of study. It simply underlines the importance of exploring both spheres as thoroughly as possible if one seeks to understand the genesis and development of a psychological system whose influence, despite the criticisms of academic psychology, continues to grow. Jung's highly eclectic library, his friendships with individuals such as the Theosophist G.R.S. Mead, and his correspondence with astrologers such as André Barbault, John M. Thorburn, and B.V. Raman, took him far beyond the boundaries of the world of the Burghölzli Clinic, allowing ideas outside that clinical environment to fertilise the development of his psychological models.[64] These models, in turn, have subsequently had enormous impact on many spheres of human exploration beyond what is academically, or even colloquially, understood as psychology.

A figure as influential as Jung in the fields of psychology, literature, philosophy, theology, history, and contemporary spiritualities will inevitably be the subject of many biographies and analyses. Some of these are hagiographic, some objectively affirmative, some conscientiously neutral, some objectively critical, and some aggressively hostile. A number of recent scholarly works on Jung, predating the publication of *Liber Novus*, have explored some of the sources that inspired his psychological models. These investigations examine Jung's early involvement in spiritualism as well as the various unconventional approaches to 'subliminal' psychology current in the early years of the twentieth century.[65] Jung's preoccupation with the Gnostics of late antiquity has been the source of further works,[66] and his links with German Romantic currents has provided fuel for a number of academic papers.[67] Various authors have noted Jung's connection with Mead, suggesting that Jung's early understanding of Gnostic, Orphic, and Hermetic materials depended largely on Mead's Theosophically inclined translations and elucidations.[68] Earlier psychological and philosophical models, such as Henri Bergson's *élan vital*, Hans Driesch's 'vitalism', and Eugen Bleuler's *die Psychoide*, have also been considered,[69] as has Jung's reliance on the philosophical explorations of Nietzsche, Schopenhauer, and Kant.[70] All these perspectives are highly relevant in understanding the genesis of Jung's ideas; he did not espouse exclusively any single current of thought or body of doctrines, but sought corroboration for his own experiences and those of his patients in an enormous variety of sources, many of them denizens of the liminal realms.

Jung's astrology has never been the subject of an in-depth investigation, even by analytical psychologists, despite an impressively large number of references in his published works and letters. Recently a welcome and much-needed compilation of Jung's references to astrology has been published, focusing for the first time on this singularly important dimension of his thought.[71] But this volume, part of a series of volumes presenting Jung's views on various subjects, is a compilation rather than a monograph, and is not intended to explore the historical sources of his interest and expertise in astrology. It is possible that some Jungian analysts, when discussing the work of their founding father, cannot easily countenance any tainting of his reputation by 'wretched subjects' that are still very much alive but treated with contempt by the scientific community – not least because such an association can be, and has been, used by hostile critics to justify their dismissal of the validity of Jung's psychology. Consequently, little attention has been paid to Jung's own statements: that he began studying astrology while he was still working with Freud 'in order to find a clue to the core of psychological truth';[72] that he used natal horoscopes to better understand the unconscious dynamics of his patients 'in cases of difficult psychological diagnosis';[73] that he recommended that any person training as a psychotherapist should learn astrology;[74] and that astrology's value 'is obvious enough to the psychologist, since astrology represents the sum of all the psychological knowledge of antiquity'.[75] These are weighty statements, yet their full significance is usually acknowledged only by astrological practitioners. Nor has any research been done on the large number of interpretations of his own horoscope that Jung requested from astrological practitioners, especially in Britain and the United States, and the numerous horoscopes of patients, friends, and family members, in both his own and Emma Jung's handwriting, that are found in his private archives.

Jung's published statements and, even more, the documentary evidence of his private papers, make clear the fact that astrology was of immense importance to him, personally and in his psychological work. Yet this importance has largely been ignored. Also ignored is the fact that the various late antique cosmologies with which Jung was preoccupied while he worked on *Liber Novus* – Gnostic, Neoplatonic, Orphic, Hermetic – were, as he himself noted, based on an astrological cosmology that focused on the celestial origin of the human soul, the dilemma of planetary fate, and the journey of the soul, assisted by theurgic ritual, toward its transformation and freedom beyond the compulsions of the planetary spheres.[76] Jung's persistent concern with astral fate as inner compulsion, his interpretation of fate in the context of 'individuation', and his use of theurgy in psychotherapy, are not subjects ordinarily discussed in works on the development and application of his ideas.

In order to fully explore Jung's astrology, this book examines these older cosmologies and the interpretations and applications Jung developed, based on what he found in the primary sources and in the later scholarly interpretations available to him. My second book, *The Astrological World of Jung's 'Liber Novus'*, focuses on *Liber Novus* itself, and the ways in which astrology infuses both the text and the images of this remarkable personal and, at the same time, mythic human journey. If, as Jung himself declared, the years he spent working on *Liber Novus* provided the raw material for all his later theories, then astrology, as Jung understood and worked with it, is unquestionably one of the most important foundation stones of analytical psychology and needs to be acknowledged as such, without prejudice and with the same methodological agnosticism that Ninian Smart recommended long ago for all scholars, whatever their domain of research.

Notes

1 William Ralph Inge, *Christian Mysticism* (London: Methuen, 1899), p. 23.
2 Jung, *Liber Novus*, p. 229. All page numbers given for citations from *Liber Novus* refer to the English translation rather than Jung's original German text, unless otherwise indicated.
3 Otto E. Neugebauer, 'The Study of Wretched Subjects', *Isis* 42 (1951), p. 111.
4 See Patrick Curry, 'The Historiography of Astrology', in Günther Oestmann, H. Darrel Rutkin, and Kocku von Stuckrad (eds.), *Horoscopes and Public Spheres* (Berlin: Walter de Gruyter, 2005), pp. 261–74.
5 For the development of the term 'Neoplatonist' in German and English, see Robert Ziomkowski, 'Neoplatonism', in Maryanne Cline Horowitz (ed.), *New Dictionary of the History of Ideas*, 6 volumes (Detroit, MI: Charles Scribner's Sons, 2005), 4:1628.
6 Iamblichus' *De mysteriis* was originally called *The Reply of the Master Abammon to the Letter of Porphyry to Anebo*. Marsilio Ficino gave it the title *De mysteriis Ægyptiorum* in the mid-fifteenth century.
7 For 'reception' as a recent academic term, see Terry Eagleton, *Literary Theory* (London: Blackwell, 1996), pp. 47–78.
8 For one of the earliest uses of the term 'Renaissance', see Jacob Burckhardt, *The Civilization of the Renaissance in Italy*, trans. Samuel George Chetwynd Middlemore (New York: Doubleday, 1878).
9 For this approach to the Renaissance, see Frances A. Yates, *Giordano Bruno and the Hermetic Tradition* (London: Routledge & Kegan Paul, 1964).
10 See Edgar Wind, *Pagan Mysteries in the Renaissance* (London: Faber & Faber, 1968); Jean Seznec, *The Survival of the Pagan Gods*, trans. Barbara F. Sessions (New York: Pantheon, 1953).
11 See Yates, *Giordano Bruno*; D.P. Walker, *Spiritual and Demonic Magic* (London: Warburg Institute, 1958).
12 See Erwin Panofsky, *Renaissance and Renascences in Western Art*, 2 volumes (Stockholm: Almqvist & Wiksell, 1960).
13 See R.N. Swanson, *The 12th-Century Renaissance* (Manchester: Manchester University Press, 1999).
14 See John Burrow, *A History of Histories* (London: Penguin, 2009).
15 For an overview of various academic definitions of 'religion', see James Thrower, *Religion* (Edinburgh: Edinburgh University Press, 1999).
16 For the use of the term 'cult' for contemporary spiritualities, see Eileen Barker and Margit Warburg (eds.), *New Religions and New Religiosity* (Aarhus: Aarhus University Press, 1998). For Richard Noll's use of the term 'cult' in reference to Jung, see Sonu Shamdasani, *Cult Fictions: C.G. Jung and the Founding of Analytical Psychology* (London: Routledge, 1998), pp. 1–12.
17 For 'secularisation', see William H. Swatos and Daniel V.A. Olson (eds.), *The Secularization Debate* (New York: Rowman & Littlefield, 2000).

18 For the concept of 'disenchantment', see Alkis Kontos, 'The World Disenchanted, and the Return of Gods and Demons', in Asher Horowitz and Terry Maley (eds.), *The Barbarism of Reason* (Toronto: University of Toronto Press, 1994), pp. 223–47.
19 See, for example, Iamblichus' idealisation of 'ancient' Egyptian theology in Iamblichus, *De mysteriis*, trans. Emma C. Clarke, John M. Dillon, and Jackson P. Hershbell (Atlanta, GA: Society of Biblical Literature, 2003), Books VII and VIII. All quotations from *De mysteriis* used in this book are from this translation, unless stated otherwise.
20 For a first-century BCE definition of astrology as divination, see Cicero, *De divinatione*, in *On Old Age, on Friendship, on Divination*, trans. W.A. Falconer (Cambridge, MA: Harvard University Press, 1970), II:44.93. For modern scholarly equations of astrology with divination, see Tamsyn Barton, *Ancient Astrology* (London: Routledge, 1994), p. 11; Sarah Iles Johnston, 'Introduction: Divining Divination', in Sarah Iles Johnston and Peter T. Struck (eds.), *Mantikê* (Leiden: Brill, 2005), p. 7. For an alternative view, see Liz Greene, 'Is Astrology a Divinatory System?', *Culture and Cosmos* 12:1 (2008), pp. 3–30.
21 For the diversity of astrologies through history, see Nicholas Campion and Liz Greene (eds.), *Astrologies* (Lampeter: Sophia Centre Press, 2011).
22 See Liz Greene, 'Signs, Signatures, and Symbols: The Language of Heaven', in Campion and Greene (eds.), *Astrologies*, pp. 17–46.
23 M. Scott Peck (1936–2005), a psychiatrist and Christian mystic, produced two best-selling books, *The Road Less Travelled* (London: Hutchinson, 1983) and *People of the Lie* (London: Rider, 1988). These books earned him the reputation of a 'self-help guru'. Although widely respected in Christian circles, the importance of his work has been neglected by the world of clinical psychology.
24 Shamdasani, *Cult Fictions*, p. 10.
25 For the questionable scholarship of the 'religionist' practitioner, see Wouter J. Hanegraff, *Esotericism and the Academy* (Cambridge: Cambridge University Press, 2012), pp. 340–70. See also Alasdair MacIntyre, 'Is Understanding Religion Compatible with Believing?', in Russell T. McCutcheon (ed.), *The Insider/Outsider Problem in the Study of Religion: A Reader* (London: Cassell, 1999), pp. 37–49.
26 Shamdasani, *Cult Fictions*, p. 3.
27 For 'methodological agnosticism', see Ninian Smart, *The Science of Religion and the Sociology of Knowledge* (Princeton, NJ: Princeton University Press, 1973).
28 For comments on this scholarly tendency, see Gregory Shaw, 'Theurgy', *Traditio* 41 (1985), pp. 1–28, esp. pp. 4–6.
29 Zeke Mazur, '*Unio Magica* Part I: On the Magical Origins of Plotinus' Mysticism', *Dionysius* 21 (2003), pp. 23–52, on p. 24.
30 For a recent academic definition of 'esoteric', see Antoine Faivre and Karen-Clare Voss, 'Western Esotericism and the Science of Religion', *Numen* 42:1 (1995), pp. 48–77. For a different definition, see Moshe Halbertal, *Concealment and Revelation* (Princeton, NJ: Princeton University Press, 2007), p. 1.
31 See Faivre and Voss, 'Western Esotericism'. For a fuller elaboration of this definition, see Wouter J. Hanegraaff, *New Age Religion and Western Culture* (Leiden: Brill, 1996), pp. 384–410.
32 See, for example, Hanegraaff, *New Age Religion*, pp. 497–501; Valentine C. Hubbs, 'German Romanticism and C.G. Jung', *Journal of Evolutionary Psychology* 4:1–2 (1983), pp. 17–24. Shamdasani relates German Romanticism to Jung's understanding of the 'prophetic and diagnostic dream'; see Sonu Shamdasani, *Jung and the Making of Modern Psychology* (Cambridge: Cambridge University Press, 2003), p. 147.
33 For the history of the publication of *Liber Novus*, see Sonu Shamdasani's Introduction in Jung, *Liber Novus*, pp. viii–xii. For Jung's own description of the genesis of *Liber Novus*, see C.G. Jung, *Memories, Dreams, Reflections*, ed. Aniela Jaffé, trans. Richard and Clara Winston (London: Routledge & Kegan Paul, 1963), pp. 194–225.
34 Jung, *MDR*, p. 225.
35 For the questionable authenticity of some of the material in this work, see Sonu Shamdasani, 'Memories, Dreams, Omissions', in Paul Bishop, *Jung in Contexts* (London: Routledge, 1999), pp. 33–50.

36 <http://wildhunt.org/blog/tag/liber-novus>.
37 See D.W. Winnicott, 'Review of C.G. Jung, *Memories, Dreams, Reflections*', *International Journal of Psycho-analysis* 45 (1964), pp. 450–55.
38 For the contrast between Jung's hermeneutical approach and the approach of the natural sciences, see William E. Smythe and Angelina Baydala, 'The Hermeneutic Background of C.G. Jung', *Journal of Analytical Psychology* 57 (2012), pp. 57–75.
39 Two exceptions in the UK are worth noting: the Centre for Psychoanalytic Studies at the University of Essex, founded in 1993, which explores both clinical and academic approaches to Freudian and Jungian models, and the postgraduate programme in Psychoanalytic Studies at University College, London, where Sonu Shamdasani, editor of *Liber Novus*, is Philemon Professor of Jung History.
40 David Tacey, 'The Challenge of Teaching Jung in the University', in Kelly Bulkeley and Clodagh Weldon (eds.), *Teaching Jung* (Oxford: Oxford University Press, 2011), pp. 13–27, on p. 15.
41 See, for example, Hanegraaff, *New Age Religion*, pp. 496–513.
42 G. William Barnard, 'Diving into the Depths', in Diane Jonte-Pace and William B. Parsons (eds.), *Religion and Psychology* (London: Routledge, 2001), pp. 297–318.
43 John Ryan Haule, 'Personal Secrets, Ethical Questions', in Bulkeley and Weldon (eds.), *Teaching Jung*, pp. 151–67, on p. 151.
44 Shamdasani, *Cult Fictions*, pp. 107–12.
45 See Robert A. Segal, 'Jung as Psychologist of Religion and Jung as Philosopher of Religion', *Journal of Analytical Psychology* 55 (2010), pp. 361–84.
46 Ann Bedford Ulinov, 'Teaching Jung in a Theological Seminary', in Bulkeley and Weldon (eds.), *Teaching Jung*, pp. 51–59, on p. 53.
47 Thomas Kuhn, *The Structure of Scientific Revolutions* (Chicago: University of Chicago Press, 1962).
48 See, for example, Ira Progoff, *The Symbolic and the Real* (New York: McGraw-Hill, 1973); Abraham Maslow, *Toward a Psychology of Being* (London: John Wiley & Sons, 1968).
49 Ulanov, 'Teaching Jung in a Theological Seminary', p. 53.
50 See, for example, John P. Dourley, *The Intellectual Autobiography of a Jungian Theologian* (Lampeter: Edwin Mellen Press, 2006); Brendan Collins, 'Wisdom in Jung's Answer to Job', *Biblical Theology Bulletin* 21 (1991), pp. 97–101.
51 For Joyce, see Hiromi Yoshida, *Joyce and Jung* (New York: Peter Lang, 2007). Joyce's daughter Lucia went into analysis with Jung in 1934. For Hesse, see Miguel Serrano, *C.G. Jung and Hermann Hesse* (Einsiedeln, Switzerland: Daimon Verlag, 1998). Hesse was the analytic patient of Jung's assistant J.B. Lang (1883–1945). For Mann, see Paul Bishop, 'Thomas Mann and C.G. Jung', in Bishop (ed.), *Jung in Contexts*, pp. 154–88.
52 See Terence Dawson, 'Jung, Literature, and Literary Criticism', in Polly Young-Eisendrath and Terence Dawson (eds.), *The Cambridge Companion to Jung* (Cambridge: Cambridge University Press, 1997), pp. 255–80; Bettina L. Knapp, *A Jungian Approach to Literature* (Carbondale: Southern Illinois University Press, 1984).
53 Gilles Quispel, *Gnosis als Weltreligion* (Zürich: Origo Verlag, 1951), p. 39; Pierre Riffard, *L'esoterisme* (Paris: Laffont, 1990), p. 135. For Jung's influence on Corbin, see Stephen Wasserstrom, *Religion After Religion* (Princeton, NJ: Princeton University Press, 1999). For more on the Eranos conferences, see Hans Thomas Hakl, *Eranos*, trans. Christopher McIntosh (Montreal: McGill-Queens University Press, 2013).
54 See Wasserstrom, *Religion After Religion*, p. 3.
55 For this debate in zoological taxonomy, see Stephen Budiansky, *The Character of Cats* (London: Weidenfeld and Nicolson, 2002), pp. 8–9.
56 For 'metanarratives' and their methodological problems, see Charlotte Aull Davies, *Reflexive Ethnography* (London: Routledge, 1999), pp. 4–5.
57 For a discussion of Jung's purported 'essentialism', see David L. Miller, 'Misprision', in Bulkeley and Weldon (eds.), *Teaching Jung*, pp. 29–50, especially pp. 36–39.
58 See, for example, Jung, CW9i, ¶¶111–147. See also Roger Brooke, 'Jung in the Academy: A Response to David Tacey', *Journal of Analytical Psychology* 42:2 (1997), pp. 285–96; James S. Baumlin, 'Reading/Misreading Jung', *College Literature* 32:1 (2005), pp. 177–86.

59 See Smythe and Baydala, 'The Hermeneutic Background of C.G. Jung'; John Beebe, 'Can There Be a Science of the Symbolic?', in Bulkeley and Weldon (eds.), *Teaching Jung*, pp. 255–68.
60 Jung, 'The Conception of the Unconscious', in Jung, *Collected Papers on Analytical Psychology*, p. 469.
61 For 'Jungianism', see Olav Hammer, *Claiming Knowledge* (Leiden: Brill, 2004), pp. 67–68.
62 See Nicholas Campion, 'Is Astrology a Symbolic Language?', in Nicholas Campion and Liz Greene (eds.), *Sky and Symbol* (Lampeter: Sophia Centre Press, 2013), pp. 9–46, on p. 22.
63 See Hammer, *Claiming Knowledge*, pp. 69–70.
64 For Jung and Mead, see Chapter 5. For the Fraternitas Saturni, see Chapter 4. For Jung's correspondence with Barbault, see Chapter 1.
65 For Jung's involvement with spiritualism, see F.X. Charet, *Spiritualism and the Foundations of C.G. Jung's Psychology* (Albany: SUNY Press, 1993). For Jung's interest in crystal-gazing, automatic writing, and hypnosis, see Wendy Swan, 'C.G. Jung's Psychotherapeutic Technique of Active Imagination in Historical Context', *Psychoanalysis and History* 10:2 (2008), pp. 185–204.
66 For Jung's interest in the Gnostics, see Robert A. Segal (ed.), *The Gnostic Jung* (Princeton, NJ: Princeton University Press, 1992); Stephan A. Hoeller, *The Gnostic Jung and the Seven Sermons to the Dead* (Wheaton, IL: Theosophical Publishing House, 1982).
67 See Hanegraaff, *New Age Religion*, pp. 496–513; Paul Bishop, *Analytical Psychology and German Classical Aesthetics* (London: Routledge, 2009).
68 For Jung's dependence on Mead for his interpretations of Gnostic and Hermetic material, see Hanegraaff, *New Age Religion*, p. 510; Noll, *The Jung Cult*, pp. 69, 326.
69 For Bergson, see Shamdasani, *Jung and the Making of Modern Psychology*, pp. 77 and 129; Beatrice Hinkle, 'Jung's Libido Theory and the Bergsonian Philosophy', *New York Medical Journal* 30 (1914), pp. 1080–86. For Driesch and Bleuler, see Ann Addison, 'Jung, Vitalism, and "the Psychoid": An Historical Reconstruction', *Journal of Analytical Psychology* 54 (2009), pp. 123–42.
70 See Lucy Huskinson, *Nietzsche and Jung* (London: Routledge, 2004); James L. Jarrett (ed.), *Jung's Seminar on Nietzsche's Zarathustra* (Princeton, NJ: Princeton University Press, 1997).
71 C.G. Jung, *Jung on Astrology*, ed. Keiron le Grice and Safron Rossi (London: Routledge, 2017).
72 C.G. Jung, Letter to Sigmund Freud, 12 June 1911, in *C.G. Jung Letters*, Vol. 1, pp. 23–24.
73 Letter to B.V. Raman, 6 September 1947, in *C.G. Jung Letters*, Vol. 1, pp. 475–76.
74 Letter from Ira Progoff to Cary F. Baynes, courtesy of Sonu Shamdasani.
75 Jung, CW15, ¶81.
76 For Jung's discussions on fate and the planetary ascent of the soul, see Chapter 5. For this theme in the religions of late antiquity, see Alan F. Segal, 'Heavenly Ascent in Hellenistic Judaism, Early Christianity and Their Environment', in *Aufstieg und Niedergang der römischen Welt* (*ANRW*), Vol. 2, ed. W. Haase (Berlin: De Gruyter, 1980), pp. 1333–94; Ioan P. Couliano, *Psychanodia I* (Leiden: Brill, 1983).

1

JUNG'S UNDERSTANDING OF ASTROLOGY

> Although I must admit the use of Astrology in foretelling the outcome of certain causes, it is not of vital moment . . . This consideration, of course, opens up the whole question of Fate versus Freewill, and it at once determines the difference between the 'exoteric' and the 'esoteric' astrologer. The former is a confirmed fatalist, who believes himself forever under the bane of Destiny . . . The esoteric astrologer has no such creed. His faith is based upon the belief that as a man sows, so he must reap; his motto is 'Man, Know Thyself'.[1]
>
> —Alan Leo

> The sun, moon and planets were the exponents, so to speak, of certain psychological or psychical constituents of the human character; and this is why astrology can give more or less valid information about character . . . The religious mysteries of later antiquity were all concerned with freeing man from the Heimarmene; in other words, with freeing him from the compulsive quality of the foundations of his own character.[2]
>
> —C.G. Jung

Astrology in the early twentieth century

As befits its liminal nature, astrology is open to many definitions. Making sense of Jung's astrology requires placing it in some kind of context: how was it viewed in the West at the time Jung began his studies? Patrick Curry has offered an admirably comprehensive description of astrology: it is 'the practice of relating the heavenly bodies to lives and events on earth, and the tradition that has thus been generated'.[3] Astronomy involves the observation and measurement of the heavenly bodies, but astrology assigns meaning to them in relation to human experience. Although a history of Western astrology during the years Jung worked on *Liber Novus* is beyond the scope of this book,[4] nevertheless the varying approaches to astrology current in the late nineteenth and early twentieth centuries are relevant to Jung's understanding of it.

Astrology as a method of predicting events was as ubiquitous in esoteric circles at the *fin de siècle* as it had been in the Middle Ages; with few exceptions, German-speaking astrologers writing at the time Jung began work on *Liber Novus* pursued astrology as a method of foretelling the future.[5] There was no specific German astrological 'movement' until the mid-1920s,[6] and the psychologically orientated astrology that subsequently began to develop in the German-speaking world relied heavily on Jung's own publications. But two other types of astrology, with antecedents in late antiquity, emerged in Britain at the turn of the century and gradually began to influence astrologers in both Europe and America. These 'new' astrologies – although they were in fact not new at all – were largely due to the work of the Theosophical Society, founded by Helena Petrovna Blavatsky in 1875, and the Hermetic Order of the Golden Dawn, founded by William Wynn Westcott, Samuel Liddell MacGregor Mathers, and William Robert Woodman in 1888.[7] Theosophical astrologers such as Alan Leo, whose work is discussed in greater detail in the next chapter, were concerned with what the natal horoscope might indicate about the individual's spiritual development, while occultist astrologers such as Frederick Hockley and MacGregor Mathers, both practicing magicians, adapted astrology to magical rituals derived from Neoplatonic texts and the Kabbalistic astral magic of the medieval period. Their application of astrology concerned the invocation of celestial potencies through the use of astrological symbols, sigils, and talismans in order to achieve individual psychological and spiritual transformation.[8] Although astrologers involved in the Golden Dawn and other occult societies used horoscopes for characterological and divinatory purposes, particularly in assessing the suitability of a neophyte for initiation and the correct timing of a magical ritual, their focus was more interior and provided a prototype for the psychological approach to astrology that Jung himself developed.[9]

Although no evidence has yet emerged indicating that Jung was acquainted with the work of Hockley and MacGregor Mathers, he was familiar with the writings of other members of the Golden Dawn, and he had acquired a range of older magical texts with a similar emphasis during the time he worked on *Liber Novus*.[10] Jung's friendship with the former secretary of the Theosophical Society, G.R.S. Mead,[11] and his reliance on Theosophically inclined astrologers for horoscopic interpretations, suggest that it was in the British esoteric community that he found the greatest inspiration for his psychological understanding of astrology. From the outset, it seems that Jung, although not immune to the desire to speculate on the future, was not primarily interested in the literal prediction of events. Instead, he concerned himself with psychological events, and sought to understand what the horoscope as a symbolic map might reveal in terms of the individual psyche and its unfoldment over time. He maintained this position throughout his life. In a lengthy letter to the French astrologer André Barbault, written in 1954, Jung declared:

> There are many instances of striking analogies between astrological constellations and psychological events . . . Astrology, like the collective unconscious

> with which psychology is concerned, consists of symbolic configurations: the 'planets' are the gods, symbols of the powers of the unconscious . . . I would say that the astrologer does not always consider his statements to be mere possibilities. The interpretation is sometimes too literal and not symbolic enough.[12]

It has always been an open secret in analytical circles that Jung was deeply involved with astrology. However, even within this knowledgeable community, considerable discomfort has been demonstrated by some analysts, and some Jungian training groups, about such an apparently questionable predilection.[13] There were times when Jung himself felt it necessary to hide the extent of his interest in astrology, even from his own colleagues. In a letter to Michael Fordham (1905–95), who founded the Society for Analytical Psychology in London in 1946 and who assisted in the English publication of Jung's *Collected Works*, Jung, defending the astrological research described in his two essays on synchronicity,[14] wrote:

> You really need not believe a word of astrology in order to make a horoscope or statistics. I am reasonably skeptical and yet I can make and try out all sorts of mantic experiments. I can even repeat some absurd alchemical procedures without the slightest conviction, for sheer curiosity. You can also attend a mass without believing in transsubstantiation [*sic*] and a communist meeting without believing in Stalin.[15]

This letter was dated 15 December 1954, just seven months after Jung's letter to Barbault describing the 'striking analogies' between astrological configurations and psychological events. It is unlikely that Jung experienced a sudden change of heart toward astrology during those months, or that he would have attempted to gratuitously flatter a professional astrologer like Barbault. Rather, Jung seems to have found it wiser to disguise his astrological research as a 'mantic experiment', while attempting at the same time to explain to Fordham in further letters, as diplomatically as possible, that the various criticisms of his experiment were due to 'a profound lack of astrological knowledge',[16] and that the statistical results were 'most complimentary to astrology'.[17] There is no indication that Fordham was ever convinced.[18] Jung's concern about keeping his astrological work under wraps is also evident in a letter written in 1953 by the American psychotherapist Ira Progoff (1921–1998), who studied with Jung in Zürich from 1952 to 1955, to Cary F. Baynes, who translated a number of Jung's works into English:

> You'll be very interested to know that Dr. J. has advised me to study Astrology when I get back . . . He says that every analyst should be equipped with it because there are borderline cases where it gives a very valuable clue. I don't think he would like it known that he holds Astrology in such respect. Altho, he did say that he doesn't feel that he needs to be as cautious about it as he used to be.[19]

Progoff's horoscope, drawn in an unknown hand, is one of the large collection of charts of patients and colleagues in Jung's private archives.

Jung's absorption in alchemical symbolism may be more acceptable in analytic circles because alchemy is safely separated from the modern world by a decent historical interval and can be viewed as a curious hiccup in the history of science. And in any event, Jung was not a practicing alchemist in any literal sense. But astrology, being part of the modern as well as the ancient and medieval worlds, is apparently not something with which a rationally inclined psychologist should become involved, particularly in the extremely simplistic forms in which it is presented in the popular press. Andrew Samuels, in his comprehensive work, *Jung and the Post-Jungians*, never mentions Jung's preoccupation with *Heimarmene*, the late antique concept of astral fate,[20] and makes only one dismissive reference to astrology.[21] Robert Segal, a prolific writer and lecturer on Jung's ideas, never discusses Jung's predilection for astral lore, even in Segal's lengthy introduction to a selection of Jung's discussions on Gnosticism – a religious current firmly rooted in an astral cosmology and deeply concerned with astrological fate as inner compulsion.[22]

Attempting to interpret an author's work selectively, according to the prejudices of the interpreter and the prevailing fashions of the academy, is hardly a new phenomenon in scholarship. The imposition of 'researcher's bias' has been going on since the Greek allegorists argued about what Orpheus 'really' meant, Iamblichus and Porphyry disagreed about the 'true' Platonic world-view, and Christian theologians insisted they had discovered the concealed 'signatures' of their own truths in both the Torah and the Jewish Kabbalah.[23] Attempting to cleanse the reputation of a great scientific thinker from the taint of 'wretched subjects' has been consistently applied by modern scholars to such figures as Galileo, who, in addition to his acknowledged contribution to the history of science, was a committed astrologer as well as an astronomer.[24] However, apart from the age-old phenomenon of 'researcher's bias' and its vagaries, and independent of the extensive and revealing astrological documents in Jung's private archives, the *Collected Works* alone, as well as Jung's published letters to Freud and others, reflect even to the lay reader, clearly and inarguably, Jung's ongoing and extremely serious concern with the philosophy, nature, and practical applications of astrology as a form of psychological exegesis.

The libido and the qualities of time

From his published correspondence, it appears that Jung began his exploration of astrology in the spring of 1911, while he was still working with Freud.[25] In a letter to Freud, dated 8 May of that year, Jung wrote:

> At the moment I am looking into astrology, which seems indispensable for a proper understanding of mythology. There are strange and wondrous things in these lands of darkness.[26]

Freud's reply was not antagonistic, but he expressed anxiety at this latest display of eccentricity in his favourite disciple:

> I am aware that you are driven by innermost inclination to the study of the occult and I am sure you will return home richly laden . . . You will be accused of mysticism.[27]

This last observation turned out to be entirely prophetic. In another letter to Freud, dated 12 June of the same year, Jung commented further on his astrological studies, revealing an increasing emphasis on the importance of astrology for psychology:

> My evenings are taken up very largely with astrology. I make horoscopic calculations in order to find a clue to the core of psychological truth . . . It appears that the signs of the zodiac are character pictures, in other words libido symbols which depict the typical qualities of the libido at a given moment.[28]

In his reply, Freud declined to comment on this deepening involvement with astrology, although he may not have been quite as disinterested as he seemed. In 1896, eleven years before he met Jung, Freud wrote a letter to his close friend and medical colleague, Wilhelm Fliess (1858–1928), commenting on Fliess' idiosyncratic theory of 'vital periodicity': the idea that astronomical cycles influence both historical periods and the organs of the human body.[29]

> You know that I do not laugh at fantasies such as those about historical periods . . . There is something to these ideas; it is the symbolic presentiment of unknown realities with which they have something in common . . . One can no longer escape from acknowledging heavenly influences. I bow before you an honorary astrologer.[30]

Whatever he might have meant by this statement, it seems that Freud was unwilling to enter into a discussion with Jung about his own views on 'heavenly influences'. In 1910, a year before Jung announced his involvement with astrology, Freud had asked Jung to help him form an 'unshakeable bulwark' against 'the black tide of mud – of occultism'.[31] Jung was understandably mistrustful of what he understood as Freud's 'flight from himself . . . from that other side of him which might perhaps be called mystical'.[32] The painful and acrimonious break between them came soon after, when Jung published his literary throwing down of the gauntlet, *Wandlungen und Symbole der Libido*, in 1911–12.[33] As Jung himself put it: 'The publication of the book marks the end of our friendship'.[34]

As important as is Jung's admission of the value of astrology in providing psychological insights, his second letter to Freud is also significant because of the way in which Jung used the term 'libido'. For him, it was not limited to the sexual instinct, as Freud had insisted, but encompassed the raw psychic energy of life, manifesting as 'the creative impulse'.[35] This widening of the concept of libido was clearly expressed when *Wandlungen* was first published and, allied with Jung's understanding of the cycle of the zodiac as an imaginal portrayal of the cycles of the libido, suggests that astrology had already begun to influence his understanding of psychological dynamics at least two years before the final break with Freud. Jung initially described astrological imagery as 'projection' – the unconscious imposition of an interior psychological content onto an external object – seemingly implying that astrology is entirely a product of the human psyche and has no actual connection with the heavens. But his letter to Freud actually reveals a much subtler view. The French philosopher Henri Bergson had developed a concept which he called *élan vital* ('vital force'), and Jung borrowed Bergson's phrase, *durée créatrice* or 'creative power', as a synonym for the libido that exists everywhere and in everything.[36] Within this framework, the symbols of the zodiac, while their specific imagery might be generated by the human psyche, find a correspondence in something inherent in reality itself, reflected in the qualities of time. 'Time and creative power', Jung insisted, 'are absolutely identical'.[37] There is, in other words, a form of 'sympathy' or resonance between what humans experience and formulate imaginally as the zodiacal images, and what actually belongs to life itself, unfolding its creative potency through the particular attributes of each individual moment. While astrological symbols, as psychic projections, might have no connection with the heavens on a physical level, the cycles of the heavens reflect temporal qualities that are 'out there' as much as 'in here'.

Jung emphasised this idea of a resonance between the human psyche and celestial cycles in one of his 'Interpretation of Visions' seminars, given in Zürich in 1932:

> Astrology may be quite unknown to you consciously, yet to your unconscious it is very intimately known . . . The qualities of the different months of the year, in other words, the signs of the zodiac, are really the projections of our unconscious knowledge of time and the qualities of time. It is as if there were profound knowledge in our unconscious, knowledge based upon unconscious experiences, that certain things originating at certain times of the year have such and such qualities.[38]

This perspective echoes Plato's declaration that time is 'the moving image of eternity', and that the heavens, along with the days, nights, months, and years generated by the cyclical motion of the heavenly bodies, 'are all parts of time'.[39] In the *Visions Seminars*, Jung elaborated further on his understanding of the qualities of time as expressed in individual zodiacal images. The time between the third week of July and the third week of August, represented by Leo, the celestial Lion, is 'passionate, fiery, dangerous, and . . . exceedingly male', and symbolises 'the idea of power'.[40] Taurus, the celestial Bull – the 'sign of May' – is 'blind unconscious creative force'.[41] As we shall see in Chapter 6, Jung's understanding of the so-called Platonic Year, the great cycle of 26,000 years that maps the movement of the vernal equinoctial point through the zodiacal constellations, was also based on perceiving the cycle of the zodiac as a symbol of the qualities of time. Jung was convinced that the collective unconscious, as well as the individual psyche, reflects these constantly shifting qualities of the libido, and that the cycles of history – particularly the formation of new religious images – mirror the great cycles of equinoctial precession.

Jung's first published reference to astrology appeared soon after his letter to Freud, in an essay titled 'The Theory of Psychoanalysis'. This essay was initially presented as a series of lectures at the medical school of Fordham University in New York in September 1912, when Jung and Freud crossed the Atlantic to deliver the message of psychoanalysis to the American psychiatric establishment.[42] At this time the relationship between Jung and his mentor was already strained to breaking point.[43] A German translation of Jung's essay was published in 1913, with the English version appearing in five issues of the American journal, *The Psychoanalytic Review*, between 1913 and 1915.[44] Discussing the dream of a female patient, Jung referred to the mythic theme of death and resurrection, and declared:

> This motif is found in countless myths all over the world . . . The meaning immediately lying behind it is astro-mythological: the sun is swallowed by the sea monster and is born again in the morning. Of course, the whole of astro-mythology is at bottom nothing but psychology – unconscious psychology – projected into the heavens; for myths never were and never are made consciously, they arise from man's unconscious.[45]

This statement was carefully phrased to prevent misunderstandings: 'astrology' has become 'astro-mythology', a term undoubtedly more appropriate for the medical students at a Jesuit-run university.[46] But it echoes Jung's letter to Freud from the previous year, in which Jung stated that the zodiac is an imaginal projection of the human psyche onto the heavens. Jung's statement to Freud that astrology is 'indispensable' to an understanding of mythology suggests that he understood 'astro-mythology' – narratives about the heavenly bodies – as the source of all myth, a perception supported by the oldest extant cosmogonic myths of the Sumerians and Babylonians.[47] In Jung's view, the most fundamental human experiences of birth, youth, maturity, and death, both physical and psychological, are 'projected' onto the cycles of the Sun, planets, and constellations, which rise, culminate, and set only to rise again in an apparently eternal round.

Jung's assumption of a mysterious, 'sympathetic' connection between psyche and cosmos may already have been firmly entrenched by the time he gave his lectures to the students at Fordham University. Robert Segal has argued that Jung was a 'modernist' following in the tradition of Sir James Frazer and Edward Burnett Tylor in the late nineteenth century, because Jung promulgated a 'clear-cut separation of the psychological from the physical and the metaphysical – the separation of the inner from the outer'.[48] But this observation is relevant only to Jung's very early statements, which may well have been worded to avoid conflict with Freud and protect himself from ridicule. What is particularly interesting about the remark Jung made at Fordham University is that he felt it necessary to make it at all. In

1912, Jung, in his official capacity as a Freudian, appeared to offer a 'scientific' explanation of astrology at Fordham: the ubiquitous human experience of birth and death is imagined as a solar narrative, which offers the promise of rebirth as well as assigning meaning to a natural celestial event. This approach, as Segal suggests, seems to echo Frazer's *Golden Bough*, which presented the cyclical journey of the Sun-god or his human surrogate, the solar hero, as an effort of the 'primitive mind' to explain the natural phenomenon of the rising and setting of the Sun as well as injecting meaning into the frightening reality of the brevity of human life. Myth is thus nothing more than bad science and an effort to escape the existential fact of human mortality. But Jung's statement was much subtler, and hinted at the psychological importance he had already begun to assign to the perception of meaning in heavenly cycles. His comment to the students at Fordham foreshadowed what emerged soon afterward in *Liber Novus*: the central significance of the astrological Sun as the symbol of an inner, transpersonal Self.

Once *Wandlungen* was published and Jung's repudiation of Freudian psychoanalysis was made public, references to astrology in the various papers included in the *Collected Works* became more frequent. These references reflect a continuing and deepening involvement with astrology, punctuated by various letters to colleagues and friends, that reveals Jung's increasing reliance on astrological symbolism as a source of insight into both his patients and himself. Despite his ongoing concern with presenting a scientific approach in his work, Jung sometimes exhibited a mischievous sense of humour: he casually dropped astrological observations into his essays, along with the traditional planetary and zodiacal glyphs – references which his professional colleagues were not likely to understand and which Jung did not bother to explain.

An example of this mischievous propensity is displayed in an essay first published in German in 1934.[49] In this paper, Jung discussed a patient whom he called 'Miss X',[50] who was 'born in the first degrees of Cancer'.[51] In a footnote to this statement, Jung casually observed that Miss X's horoscope 'shows four earth signs but no air sign'. This is not likely to mean a great deal to a reader unacquainted with astrological terminology. To an astrologer, however, 'four earth signs but no air sign' indicates that, in the birth horoscope, there are no planets placed in any of the zodiacal signs of the airy trigon (Gemini, Libra, and/or Aquarius), but four planets are placed in the signs of the earthy trigon (Taurus, Virgo, and/or Capricorn).[52] There is, in other words, an inherent overemphasis on those characterological attributes described by the symbol of earth, and an absence of those attributes described by the symbol of air. Following this information, for which Jung offered no interpretation, he then laconically declared:

> The danger coming from the animus is reflected in ☽□☿.[53]

Apart from the bewilderment this statement is likely to arouse among the astrologically uninitiated, there are three important ideas expressed in Jung's brief assessment of Miss X's horoscope. The first idea relates to his formulation of the psychological 'types' and their relationship with the four astrological elements.

The four elements and the psychological types

First published in 1921, *Psychological Types* was researched between 1913 and 1918, while Jung was steeped in the visions of *Liber Novus* and concurrently worked to deepen his astrological knowledge.[54] Jung's theory of types provides models of the individual's general orientation to the world (extravert or introvert) and the four 'functions of consciousness' (thinking, feeling, sensation, and intuition): modes of adaptation through which a person perceives and evaluates reality. It is a dynamic model in which there is constant movement, development, and change throughout life, with integration and wholeness emerging in direct proportion to the degree to which an individual makes an effort to become conscious of those aspects of the personality that are inherently 'weak' and undeveloped.

Of all Jung's models, his psychological typology has proven to be the most popular. It has been simplified, generalised, and adapted in numerous forms in both cognitive psychology and various commercial milieux – a development which Jung himself might have found highly questionable, given his deep mistrust of the 'Spirit of This Time'. The Myers-Briggs Type Indicator (MBTI), first published in 1943 by Katharine Briggs and Isabel Myers and based on Jung's work, is still widely used in vocational guidance as well as personality assessment and marital counselling, despite numerous criticisms of its ultimate accuracy and effectiveness.[55] Since 1977, the *Journal of Psychological Type* has offered a steady sequence of articles on the subject, and the Center for Applications of Psychological Type, the organisation currently promulgating the Type Indicator, offers on its website a 'quick and easy to read primer on archetypes' whose brevity and simplicity bring to mind Monty Python's 'All-England Summarize Proust Competition'.[56] It has also become a commonplace in modern astrology texts to apply Jung's theory of the four psychological function types to the astrological elements, offering interpretations of those elements based on Jung's descriptions.[57]

The astrological elements were clearly important in Jung's assessment of his patients' horoscopes, as his comments about Miss X indicate. The elements are also relevant to the characters Jung encountered in the visions he recorded in *Liber Novus*, since these figures are described in terms of particular elements: The Red One, for example, wears 'fiery red clothes'.[58] The elements, and their concomitant Aristotelian qualities of hot or cold, moist or dry, are also an essential aspect of the scenic backdrops or landscape settings in which the characters in *Liber Novus* appear. This is the 'composition of place' described in Ignatius of Loyola's *Spiritual Exercises*, a sixteenth-century work which was of considerable importance to Jung.[59] In *Liber Novus*, the Anchorite Ammonius, for example, appears in a hot, dry desert landscape, although he himself is described as dry and cold: in Aristotelian terms, he is an earthy figure inhabiting, and dependent on, a fiery landscape.[60]

These kinds of element associations in *Liber Novus* are discussed more fully in *The Astrological World of Jung's* Liber Novus.

The late antique, medieval, and early modern astrological and alchemical texts in Jung's library provided him with a rich matrix of speculations on the four elements. The first extant textual evidence of the elements appears in the writings of the philosopher Empedocles in the fifth century BCE. But despite Jung's statement that Empedocles 'attempted to impose order on the chaos of natural phenomena by dividing them into the four elements',[61] Empedocles himself referred to them as 'roots' rather than 'elements'. They are divinities, not substances, and they generate the 'forms and colours of all those mortal things'.[62] Plato was the first to call them 'elements' (*stoicheia*), after the Greek word for a letter of the alphabet; ancient Greek letters, like Hebrew, are identical with numbers, and number, for Plato, provided the archetypal foundation of all things.[63] For Jung, too, numbers were archetypal, existing both within and outside the human psyche:

> One does not know whether numbers are discovered or invented. I think counting, i.e. making use of numbers, has been invented; numbers however were found in us and outside ourselves. Numbers are like archetypes, *which are just as much outside as inside*.[64]

In the second century CE, the astrologer Claudius Ptolemy, although he did not use the term 'element', adopted Aristotle's association of hot, cold, moist, and dry in relation to the elements, which are all admixtures of those four attributes: earth is dry and cold, fire dry and hot, water moist and cold, and air moist and hot,[65] and the temperaments associated with the four astrological elements reflect these qualities in characterological and physiological terms.[66] Vettius Valens, a younger contemporary of Ptolemy, whose work, like Ptolemy's, was familiar to Jung,[67] was the first astrologer to assign the elements to four groups of three zodiacal signs each, referred to as 'triplicities' or 'trigons'. According to Valens, the element of fire comprises the triplicity of Aries, Leo, and Sagittarius; earth the triplicity of Taurus, Virgo, and Capricorn; air the triplicity of Gemini, Libra, and Aquarius; and water the triplicity of Cancer, Scorpio, and Pisces.[68] This idea of the astrological triplicities proved to be an extremely long-lived tradition, reappearing in medieval and early modern astrological texts, and eventually in the works of the modern astrologers who provided the materials from which Jung first learned to cast and read horoscopes.[69] In his descriptions of the function types – thinking, feeling, sensation, and intuition[70] – Jung did not explicitly assign them to the four elements of air, water, earth, and fire, although he made clear in *Psychological Types* that he believed the correlation existed:

> From earliest times attempts have been made to classify individuals according to types, and so to bring order into the chaos. The oldest attempts known to us were made by oriental astrologers who devised the so-called trigons of the

> four elements – air, water, earth, and fire . . . According to this age-old view, whoever is born in these trigons shares in their aerial or fiery nature and will have a corresponding temperament and fate.[71]

Jung also referred to the theories of Claudius Galen (129–216 CE), a physician, surgeon, and astrologer, whose four 'temperaments', derived from the fifth-century BCE physician Hippocrates, equated the element of air with the sanguine temperament; water with the phlegmatic; fire with the choleric; and earth with the melancholic. Jung declared that Galen merited 'the credit for having created a psychological classification of human beings which has endured for two thousand years'.[72] Jung's insistence that astrology's four elements provided the earliest form of typology can be challenged; it has been argued that theories of temperament did not begin with astrology, but that astrology acquired them from philosophy and medicine.[73] However, what is relevant in the context of Jung's astrology is what he himself believed, and it seems that he supported his theory of the ancient history behind the four function types with the assumption that astrology provided the first blueprint for them.

A comparison of Jung's descriptions of the function types with descriptions of the elements provided by contemporaneous astrological texts offers a clue to one of the routes, and possibly the primary route, by which Jung arrived at his typology. Alan Leo, whose work was published over a decade before Jung wrote *Psychological Types*, described the element of air as 'the higher mind', related to 'extension and expansion'; the airy signs abstract the 'essence' from external situations and objects and relate that essence to an 'ideal'.[74] For Jung, the thinking function is an 'intellectual process' that begins with the perception of objects and 'attempts to subordinate them to a subjective idea'.[75] Leo described the element of earth as 'the dense body of man', representing 'solidity and stability'; earth is the 'plane of action, conservation of energy, and concentrated forces'. Virgo, as one of the earthy signs, reflects the power to 'interpret sensations more or less correctly'.[76] For Jung, the sensation function, as sense perception, is entirely dependent on the evidence of material reality:

> As sensation is chiefly conditioned by the object, those objects that excite the strongest sensations will be decisive for the individual's psychology . . . Objects are valued in so far as they excite sensations, and, so far as lies within the power of sensation, they are fully accepted into consciousness whether they are compatible with rational judgments or not. The sole criterion of their value is the intensity of the sensation produced by their objective qualities.[77]

Jung's elaboration of the astrological element of earth, included in an essay he wrote in 1928 about the role of the Swiss in Europe, was not entirely complimentary.[78] But his descriptions of the psychological types were likewise not written to flatter; and his portrayal of the earth signs, which echoes his descriptions of the sensation type, followed faithfully the interpretations offered by astrologers from Ptolemy to Alan Leo in terms of the character qualities associated with this 'dry' and 'cold' element.

> From olden times the astrological sign for Switzerland was either Virgo or Taurus; both are earth-signs, a sure indication that the earthy character of the Swiss had not escaped the old astrologers. From the earth-boundness of the Swiss come all their bad as well as their good qualities: their down-to-earthness, their limited outlook, their non-spirituality, their parsimony, stolidity, stubbornness, dislike of foreigners, mistrustfulness, as well as that awful *Schwitzerdütsch* and their refusal to be bothered, or to put it in political terms, their neutrality.[79]

According to this model, Jung's patient, Miss X, born with 'four earth signs', was inherently inclined to relate to life through a well-adapted sensation function, focused on the particular rather than on the general, and on the concrete level of existence rather than on its hidden meaning or relation to broader ideas. With 'no air sign' – that is, no planets placed in any of the three airy signs at birth – her thinking function, although capable of exhibiting a high degree of intelligence, was less conscious and therefore less adapted, and consequently more vulnerable to the domination of the critical, opinionated, and divisive inclinations of the unconscious 'animus', exacerbated by that pesky Moon-Mercury configuration which Jung described in his enigmatic footnote.[80] Jung's division of the function types into polarities – extraverted and introverted expressions of each function – does not match Alan Leo's tripartite division of each element into what are known in astrology as the quadruplicities: 'cardinal' (initiating), 'fixed' (stabilising), and 'mutable' (interpreting and adapting) expressions.[81] But both Leo and Jung postulated, for each of the four personality types, a variety of modes of perception and action within a particular sphere of experience. Both also insisted that the function type, or element, needs to be viewed in relation to other factors in the individual personality in order to be properly understood and, if necessary, integrated more fully into consciousness through deliberate effort. Both men, in other words, understood their typologies to be dynamic, flexible, and evolutionary, rather than static and immovable.

Planets and complexes

The second idea expressed in Jung's description of Miss X's astrological makeup relates to his understanding that planetary configurations – the 'planetary gods' in dynamic relationship to each other – symbolise unconscious complexes, which are expressed imaginally through the mythic narratives that portray in symbolic form the structure and teleology of the complex. The animus, according to Jung, personifies the unconscious masculine aspect of the female psyche and, in the horoscope of Miss X, it is symbolised in part by the planet Mercury, which threatens the instinctual female qualities of the Moon through the tension of the difficult angle between them. This tension is in turn exacerbated by the unsophisticated quality of Miss X's thinking function.[82] Viewed in this way, an unconscious complex is not the product of either traumatic childhood events or suppressed instinctual urges; it is inherent and archetypal, although its expressions are coloured by both circumstances and conscious choice.

By the time Jung wrote *Psychology of the Unconscious*, his understanding of complexes had deviated radically from the earlier views propounded by Freud and his predecessors.[83] Freud understood complexes to be rooted in instinctual urges; within the Freudian model, the complex (and specifically the Oedipus complex) is the primary factor in psychic dynamics. Myth is secondary: a poetic and, at the same time, sublimated expression of those instinctual urges that are repressed due to social taboos. Myths can therefore be intellectually analysed and 'reduced' to the bare bones of unconscious sexual conflicts.[84] Thus, when Oedipus unknowingly murders his father Laius and marries his mother Iokasta, the mythic narrative is 'merely' a poetic portrayal of every son's unconscious desire to destroy his father in order to gain sexual possession of his mother. Behind the mythic Oedpius stands the 'Oedipus complex'.

For Freud, like his predecessors, the complex is always pathological, because it involves a repression of powerful instinctual urges that results in conflict and psychic suffering. Complexes are not 'normal', let alone creative or suggestive of a meaningful teleology, but must be overcome:

> They [neurotics] fall ill of the same complexes against which we healthy people struggle as well. The only difference is that healthy people know how to overcome those complexes without any gross damage demonstrable in practical life, whereas in nervous cases the suppression of the complexes succeeds only at the price of costly substitutive formations.[85]

Jung, in contrast, eventually came to understand that behind the 'Oedipus complex' stands Oedipus himself – not as an historical reality, but as the imaginal portrayal of a dynamic psychic energy of which the sexual urge represents only one dimension. Oedipus' destruction of his father and union with his mother might, in this context, reflect not simply a literal and forbidden incestuous desire, but a fundamental human longing to shatter the power of the rational ego (the father) in order to merge with, and be transformed by, the depths of the unconscious (the mother) – an interior process which forms the primary theme of *Liber Novus*.[86] Complexes, as Jung first developed the idea in 1912 in *Psychology of the Unconscious*, are the psychic expressions of the libido, which is not limited solely to forbidden Oedipal wishes. Complexes embody fundamental life processes, psychic and spiritual as well as instinctual, and are not merely products of the repression of the sexual instinct. Their compulsive and often destructive power arises, not from their innate malignancy, but from what Jung perceived as the failure of the individual to recognise and integrate their deeper teleology:

> For if he allows his libido to get stuck in a childish milieu, and does not free it for higher purposes, he falls under the spell of unconscious compulsion.

> Wherever he may be, the unconscious will then recreate the infantile milieu by projecting his complexes, thus reproducing all over again, and in defiance of his vital interests, the same dependence and lack of freedom which formerly characterized his relations with his parents. His destiny no longer lies in his own hands: his Τυχαι και Μοιραι (fortunes and fates) fall from the stars.[87]

For Jung, the myth came first. As he suggested at Fordham University in 1912, myths emerge from projections of fundamental psychic patterns onto the heavens, which provide an excellent 'hook' because they mirror back the same patterns through the qualities of time. These patterns are 'just as much outside as inside'. The Sun rises from an unknown darkness each morning, and sinks back into the darkness in the evening; the human being emerges out of an unknown darkness at birth and returns to that unknown darkness at death, with the hope that, like the Sun, some immortal fragment will survive death and be reborn in some form, some time, somewhere.

The myth thus embodies the complex in imaginal form. Complex and myth are the same: the former is experienced as psychic compulsion and the latter as a psychic image that can itself facilitate consciousness and the transformation of the compulsion. The individual expression of the complex, in turn, follows specific channels shaped by a unique succession of personal experiences and the responses to those experiences; but the responses themselves are rooted in inherent temperament. Typology and complex are therefore intimately related. Jung believed that collectives also have complexes, and so do religions; so, too, do the cycles of history. Everything possessing life and dynamism is thus 'fated' by the nature of its complexes, which are inherent patterns perceived by the human psyche as mythic narratives that determine both character and fate. Studies of demonic possession, the phenomenon of multiple personalities, mediumistic trances, shamanic rituals, exorcism, hypnotic healing trances, automatic writing, and visions in the crystal all contributed to Jung's increasing appreciation of the contents of the unconscious complex as mythic and transpersonal rather than personal and pathological.[88] And for Jung, the archetypes that lie at the core of every complex are symbolised by the planetary gods:

> The journey through the planetary houses . . . therefore signifies the overcoming of a psychic obstacle, or of an autonomous complex, suitably represented by a planetary god or demon.[89]

Transformation and individuation

The third idea implicit in Jung's discussion of the horoscope of Miss X is the possibility of transformation. Complexes, like planetary fate, are negotiable, in their level of expression if not in their essence. Had Jung not believed that change was possible, he would not have accepted Miss X as a patient, nor referred to 'danger' from the animus rather than an irrevocable fate. 'Danger' suggests that something can be mitigated or avoided, provided there is sufficient knowledge and insight; Jung's brief comment on Mercury in a quadrate aspect to the Moon is not described as a preordained event, but as a psychological dynamic amenable to conscious intervention. The idea of a developmental process initiated by the unconscious psyche itself – the transformation of instinct into 'higher purposes' through the power of symbols – provides the core theme of *Wandlungen*, and echoes a seminal statement made by Iamblichus in the third century CE: it is the gods themselves, of their own volition and through their own symbols, who take charge in the theurgic ritual and accomplish the transformation of the individual soul.[90] This idea is intimately linked with Jung's concept of 'individuation', which he defined as the inner process through which an individual can achieve full integration of his or her unique, inherent personality:

> Individuation means becoming an 'in-dividual', and, in so far as 'individuality' embraces our innermost, last, and incomparable uniqueness, it also implies becoming one's own self. We could therefore translate individuation as 'coming to selfhood' or 'self-realization'.[91]

But this process cannot be achieved solely through the power of the conscious will; it depends on the cooperation of the unconscious or, in Iamblichus' terms, the gods themselves.

Jung associated individuation with a degree of psychological freedom, once again comparing the unfoldment of the process with the myth of the soul's journey through the planetary spheres:

> The journey through the planetary houses boils down to becoming conscious of the good and the bad qualities in our character, and the apotheosis means no more than maximum consciousness, which amounts to maximal freedom of the will.[92]

'Maximal' freedom, it should be noted, is not the same as complete freedom. Commenting on the planetary journey of the soul as it was described in a late fifteenth-century romance by Francesco Colonna titled *Hypnerotomachia Poliphili*, Jung noted that the author created a psychological document that is 'a perfect example of the course and the symbolism of the individuation process'.[93] It seems, from Jung's equation of the soul's celestial journey with the individuation process, that he understood the natal horoscope not only as a psychological map of character and complexes, but as a meaningful narrative or, in effect, a personal mythic journey. This journey unfolds over time through a sequence of life experiences connected by meaning through a central organising principle understood as the Self, and moves toward the experience of a whole personality and a meaningful life.

In Jung's view, while this process occurs naturally in all human beings and is initiated by the unconscious psyche itself, techniques of analytic work such as active imagination deepen and enhance the process,[94] making it possible for an individual such as Miss X to work with the 'danger coming from the animus' in a conscious and more creative way. Jung never suggested that Miss X could replace her horoscope with a different one. But he seems to have developed the conviction that the relationship between consciousness and the archetypal realm needed to become a dialogue, not a monologue, and that participating in the dialogue with the appropriate receptivity could affect both the individual and the mysterious archetypal patterns that constitute individual fate.

Astrology and alchemy

In the years following the completion of *Liber Novus*, Jung's statements about astrology became more frequent in his correspondence, his lectures, and his published works. While he continued to formulate his astrological experience through terms such as 'synchronicity', which he hoped would be acceptable to a scientific community, he also deepened his understanding of astrology's relationship with other liminal spheres, particularly alchemy, whose symbolism likewise provided him with a model of the individuation process. Jung insisted that astrology and alchemy had always been intertwined:

> The alchemical figures, especially the gods of the metals, should always be thought of astrologically as well . . . The alchemical symbols are saturated with astrology.[95]

In another essay, he suggested, writing as an astrologer, that a knowledge of mythology and alchemy are both necessary for a psychological interpretation of astrological significators:

> Alchemy is inconceivable without the influence of her elder sister astrology, and the statements of these three disciplines [mythology, alchemy, astrology] must be taken into account in any psychological evaluation of the luminaries [Sun and Moon].[96]

This intimate relationship is based on the idea that astrology and alchemy, and the myths accompanying them, present the process of individuation in symbolic form. Astrology, like alchemy, is 'ceaselessly engaged in preserving the bridge to . . . the unconscious psyche'; astrology 'led the conscious mind back again and again to the knowledge of Heimarmene, that is, the dependence of character and destiny on certain moments in time'.[97] The melding of alchemical symbolism with that of its 'elder sister', astrology, led Jung to perceive a striking parallel between the stages of the alchemical *opus*, the Gnostic, Neoplatonic, and Hermetic portrayals of the journey of the soul through the planetary spheres, and the circuitous path by which the individual psyche achieves integration and wholeness.

> Astrologically . . . this process [alchemy] corresponds to an ascent through the planets from the dark, cold, distant Saturn to the sun . . . The ascent through the planetary spheres therefore meant something like a shedding of

> the characterological qualities indicated by the horoscope . . . Anyone who has passed through all the spheres is free from compulsion; he has won the crown of victory and become like a god.[98]

In later years, Jung maintained his insistence that astrology could be of immense value to psychology. In a letter to the Indian astrologer Bangalore Venkata Raman, written in 1947, he stated:[99]

> As I am a psychologist I'm chiefly interested in the particular light the horoscope sheds on certain complications in the character. In cases of difficult psychological diagnosis I usually get a horoscope in order to have a further point of view from an entirely different angle. I must say that I very often found that the astrological data elucidated certain points which I otherwise would have been unable to understand. From such experiences I formed the opinion that astrology is of particular interest to the psychologist.[100]

The planetary gods, according to Jung, are symbols of the archetypal dominants of the collective unconscious, present in every human psyche but, according to the specific moment of birth, appearing in the individual as a unique pattern of interrelationships representing 'a definite moment in the colloquy of the gods, that is to say the psychic archetypes'. Jung suggested to André Barbault that these patterns are 'expressed in a recognizable way in the horoscope' but are likewise present in life itself.[101] The idea that astrology is merely a human projection onto an inanimate sky – Frazer's understanding of myth as bad science – had, for Jung, long been superseded, if he had ever thought of it that way in the first place.

Notes

1 Alan Leo, *The Progressed Horoscope* (London: Modern Astrology Office, 1905), p. iii.
2 Jung, *Modern Psychology*, Vol. 5–6, p. 120.
3 Patrick Curry, 'Astrology', in Kelly Boyd (ed.), *The Encyclopedia of Historians and Historican Writing* (London: Fitzroy Dearborn, 1999), pp. 55–57.
4 For astrology at the *fin de siècle*, see Nicholas Campion, *A History of Western Astrology*, Vol. 2 (London: Continuum, 2009), pp. 229–39. For a history of British astrology during this time, see Patrick Curry, *A Confusion of Prophets* (London: Collins & Brown, 1992).
5 Among the German astrological astrologers writing during the 1920s and found in Jung's library are: Karl Brandler-Pracht, Adolph Drechsler, A. Frank Glahn, Alexander von Steiger, and H. von Klöckler. For Brandler-Pracht and von Klöckler, see Ellic Howe, *Urania's Children* (London: William Kimber, 1967), pp. 81–83 and 99–100. For Dreschler, see James H. Holden, *A History of Horoscopic Astrology* (Tempe, AZ: American Federation of Astrologers, 1996), p. 256. None of these astrologers had published books during the early period of Jung's studies.
6 Howe, *Urania's Children*, p. 95.
7 For the history of the Theosophical Society, see Bruce F. Campbell, *Ancient Wisdom Revived* (Berkeley: University of California Press, 1980). For the history of the Golden Dawn, see Robert A. Gilbert, *The Golden Dawn Scrapbook* (Slough: Quantum, 1997). For the social context, see Alex Owen, *The Place of Enchantment* (Chicago: University of Chicago Press, 2004).

8 For the use of astral magic in Golden Dawn rituals, and the literature produced by the members of this order, see Liz Greene, *Magi and Maggidim* (Lampeter: Sophia Centre Press, 2012), pp. 244–73 and the references given there.
9 For horoscopic astrology in the Golden Dawn, see J.W. Brodie-Innes et al., *Astrology of the Golden Dawn*, ed. Darcy Küntz (Sequim, WA: Holmes Publishing Group, 1996).
10 For a full discussion, see Chapters 2 and 3. Jung was familiar with the work of several members of the Golden Dawn and its breakaway groups, including A.E. Waite, Algernon Blackwood, Arthur Machen, and Israel Regardie.
11 See Chapter 4. Mead seems to have been involved in Kabbalistic magic; see Greene, *Magi and Maggidim*, pp. 289–92.
12 C.G. Jung, Letter to André Barbault, 26 May 1954, in Jung, *C.G. Jung Letters*, Vol. 2, pp. 175–77. For Barbault's psychological perspective, see André Barbault, *De la psychanalyse à l'Astrologie* (Paris: Seuil, 1961); André Barbault, 'L'astrologia, psicologia del profondo dell'antichità', *Ricerca '90* 48 (2001), pp. 105–13.
13 Analytic training groups vary in their attitudes toward Jung's astrology. The C.G. Jung Institute in Zürich has held courses in astrology for many decades, and in recent years the Association of Jungian Analysts in London has offered seminars on astrology and synchronicity. The Society of Analytical Psychology in London, in contrast, has never included astrology as part of its curriculum.
14 See Jung, 'Synchronicity', CW8, ¶¶816–968; Jung, 'On Synchronicity', CW8, ¶¶969–997; Jung, 'On Synchronicity', CW18, ¶1193–1212.
15 C.G. Jung, Letter to Michael S. Fordham, 15 December 1954, Wellcome Library, London, PP/FOR/C.1/1/2:Box 7. All letters cited between Fordham and Jung belong to this file of materials.
16 C.G. Jung, Letter to Michael J. Fordham, 9 November 1954.
17 C.G. Jung, Letter to Michael J. Fordham, 20 October 1954.
18 Jung's correspondence with Fordham was congenial. Fordham was helpful in suggesting that Liliane Frey, who collaborated with Jung on the 'astrological experiment', might write a brief foreword outlining the astrological traditions behind the experiment (Michael S. Fordham, letter to C.G. Jung, 20 October 1954). He also reassured Jung that, although he could not 'speak with any semblance of authority on this difficult topic', he knew what a horoscope was (Michael S. Fordham, Letter to C.G. Jung, 10 January 1955). This is confirmed by a natal horoscope drawn for Fordham in the German style in an unknown hand, accompanied by a typed analysis using both technical astrological language and Jungian terms such as 'anima-possession' (Wellcome Library PP/FOR/A.4). This horoscope bears neither date nor signature. It was not drawn by Jung; Fordham probably requested it from a Swiss or German astrologer but chose not to mention it to Jung.
19 Ira Progoff, letter to Cary F. Baynes, 18 May 1953, courtesy of Sonu Shamdasani.
20 For Jung's views on *Heimarmene*, see Chapter 5.
21 Andrew Samuels, *Jung and the Post-Jungians* (London: Routledge & Kegan Paul, 1985), p. 123.
22 See Segal (ed.), *The Gnostic Jung*, pp. 3–52.
23 For Greek allegory, see Peter T. Struck, *Birth of the Symbol* (Princeton, NJ: Princeton University Press, 2004). For Orphic texts, see Gábor Betegh, ed. and trans., *The Derveni Papyrus* (Cambridge: Cambridge University Press, 2004); W.K.C. Guthrie, *Orpheus and Greek Religion* (London: Methuen, 1952). For Christian interpretations of the Kabbalah as a 'foreshadowing' of Christian trinitarian doctrine, see Joseph Dan (ed.), *The Christian Kabbalah* (Cambridge, MA: Harvard University Press, 1997).
24 See Nicholas Campion and Nick Kollerstrom (eds.), 'Galileo's Astrology', *Culture and Cosmos* 7:1 (2003).
25 Jung may have begun his astrological explorations even earlier. He acquired an original edition of Alan Leo's essay on the planet Mars, which appeared in 1910 in Leo's journal, *Modern Astrology*. Leo later published this material as a book: *Mars the War Lord* (London:

L.N. Fowler, 1915). Jung purchased this work as well, suggesting that he had acquired the earlier version when it was first published.

26 *The Freud-Jung Letters*, ed. William McGuire, trans. Ralph Manheim and R.F.C. Hull (London: Hogarth Press/Routledge & Kegan Paul, 1977), 254J, p. 421.

27 *Freud-Jung Letters*, 255F, p. 422.

28 *Freud-Jung Letters*, 259J, p. 427.

29 See Wilhelm Fliess, *Der Ablauf des Lebens* (Leipzig: F. Deuticke, 1906). For Fliess' 'vital periodicity' – although with no specific mention of astrology – see Frank J. Sulloway, *Freud, Biologist of the Mind* (Cambridge, MA: Harvard University Press, 1992), pp. 152–58.

30 Sigmund Freud, Letter to Wilhelm Fliess, 9 October 1896, in Jeffrey Moussaieff Masson (ed. and trans.), *The Complete Letters of Sigmund Freud to Wilhelm Fliess, 1887–1904* (Cambridge, MA: Harvard University Press, 1985), p. 200. See also Nicholas Campion, 'Sigmund Freud's Investigation of Astrology', *Culture and Cosmos* 2:1 (1998), pp. 49–53; Frank McGillion, 'The Influence of Wilhelm Fliess' Cosmology on Sigmund Freud', *Culture and Cosmos* 2:1 (1998), pp. 33–48.

31 Jung, *MDR*, p. 173.

32 Jung, *MDR*, p. 175.

33 Jung, *Wandlungen und Symbole der Libido* (Leipzig: Dueticke Verlag, 1912). The first English translation, *Psychology of the Unconscious*, appeared in 1917, and was revised and reissued as Jung, CW5 in 1956. Citations from the 1917 edition will subsequently be referred to as *Psychology of the Unconscious*.

34 Jung, *Introduction to Jungian Psychology*, p. 27.

35 See Jung, *Psychology of the Unconscious*, pp. 77–86.

36 Bergson's concept of *élan vital* strongly influenced Jung's understanding of the libido. Jung acquired a German translation of Bergson's *L'energie spirituelle* (Paris: Librairie F. Alcan, 1919), and refers to *élan vital* frequently in the *Collected Works*; see Jung, CW3, ¶418; Jung, CW4, ¶568; Jung, CW6, ¶540; Jung, CW8, ¶55. Jung accused Bergson of 'cryptomnesia', insisting that Bergson had unconsciously derived his idea of *durée créatrice* from the Neoplatonist Plotinus; see Jung, *Visions Seminars*, Vol. 2, p. 325. The idea is more likely to have come from Bergson's Hasidic background; see Ben-Ami Scharfstein, *The Roots of Bergson's Philosophy* (New York: Columbia University Press, 1943).

37 Jung, *The Visions Seminars*, Vol. 2, p. 325.

38 Jung, *The Visions Seminars*, Vol. 1, p. 44.

39 Plato, *Timaeus*, 37c–e.

40 Jung, *The Visions Seminars*, Vol. 1, pp. 175–76.

41 Jung, *The Visions Seminars*, Vol. 1, pp. 39–40.

42 See Sonu Shamdasani, 'Introduction: New York, 1912', in Sonu Shamdasani (ed.), *Jung contra Freud* (Princeton, NJ: Princeton University Press, 2011), pp. vii–xxi; John Ryan Haule, 'Freud and Jung: A Failure of Eros', *Harvest* 39 (1993), pp. 147–58.

43 For Jung's description of his journey to America with Freud, see his letters to Emma in Jung, *MDR*, pp. 400–404.

44 Jung, 'Versuch einer Darstellung der psychoanalytischen Theorie', in *Jahrbuch für psychoanalytische und psychopathologische Forschungen*, V (Vienna and Leipzig, 1913); Jung, 'The Theory of Psychoanalysis', *The Psychoanalytic Review* (New York), I (1913–14), pp. 1–4 and II (1915), p. 1.

45 Jung, CW4, ¶477.

46 Fordham University was founded by the Catholic Diocese of New York in 1841, and was placed in the care of the Jesuits soon after. Although it is an independent research university, its present Board of Trustees describes it as 'in the Jesuit tradition'.

47 See the Babylonian epic, *Enuma Elish*, in which the solar deity Marduk fashions the heavens and the zodiacal constellations from the body of his slain mother Tiamat, and the opening sentences of Genesis, in which God's first creations are the Sun and Moon.

48 Robert A. Segal, 'Jung's Very Twentieth-Century View of Myth', *Journal of Analytical Psychology* 48 (2003), pp. 593–617, on p. 593.

49 'Zur Empirie des Individuationsprozesses' was first published in the *Eranos-Jahrbuch* in 1934, and was published in English as Jung, *The Integration of the Personality*, trans. Stanley Dell (New York: Farrar & Rinehart, 1939; London, 1940). The version published in CW9i is, according to Jung, a 'thoroughly revised and enlarged version'.
50 'Miss X' was Kristine Mann (1873–1945), an American medical practitioner who was Jung's patient between 1921 and 1922. See Thomas B. Kirsch, *The Jungians* (London: Routledge, 2012), p. 65.
51 Jung, CW9i, ¶606.
52 At the time Jung wrote this essay, Pluto had just been discovered and was not included in Jung's assessment. There were thus nine planets known to him.
53 Jung, CW9i, ¶606, n. 166. The glyphs indicate the Moon in a 'square' or 90° angle to Mercury.
54 C.G. Jung, *Psychologische Typen* (Zürich: Rascher Verlag, 1921). The work was first published in English as Jung, *Psychological Types, or, the Psychology of Individuation*, trans. H.G. Baynes (London: Kegan Paul, Trench, Trubner, 1923), and reappeared, with little revision but in a new translation by R.F.C. Hull, in 1959 as CW6. See 'Editorial Note' in Jung, CW6, pp. v–vi.
55 For the MBTI, see Isabel Briggs Myers, *An Introduction to Type* (Oxford: Oxford Psychologists Press, 2000 [1990]). For criticisms, see David J. Pittinger, 'Measuring the MBTI . . . and Coming Up Short', *Journal of Career Planning and Employment* 54:1 (1993), pp. 48–52.
56 <www.capt.org/research/psychological-type-journal.htm#>. The 'All-England Summarize Proust Competition', written by Graham Chapman, John Cleese, Eric Idle, Terry Jones, Michael Palin, and Terry Gilliam, was aired on TV by the BBC on 16 November 1972 as Episode 5, Season 3 of *Monty Python's Flying Circus*.
57 See, for example, Stephen Arroyo, *Astrology, Psychology, and the Four Elements* (Davis, CA: CRCS, 1975).
58 Jung, *Liber Novus*, p. 275. For more on The Red One, see Liz Greene, *The Astrological World of Jung's 'Liber Novus'* (London: Routledge, 2018), chapter 1.
59 See Chapter 2.
60 Jung, *Liber Novus*, pp. 267–73.
61 Jung, CW6, ¶960.
62 Empedocles, Frag. 71, cited in John Burnet, *Early Greek Philosophy* (London: A&C Black, 1920), pp. 215–16. Jung cited Empedocles frequently: see Jung, CW8, ¶55; Jung, CW9ii, ¶35; Jung, CW11, ¶¶62, 93, 104, 246; Jung, CW12, ¶¶109, 433, 436; Jung, CW13, ¶242; Jung, CW15, ¶11.
63 See Plato, *Timaeus*, 48b.
64 Jung, Letter to Michael J. Fordham, 20 October 1954. Italic emphasis mine.
65 See Aristotle, *On Coming-to-Be and Passing Away*, trans. Forster and Furley, in *Aristotle III* (Cambridge, MA: Harvard University Press, 1955), II:4, pp. 279–81. For the development of this idea in the work of Galen, see Peter Brain, *Galen on Bloodletting* (Cambridge: Cambridge University Press, 1986).
66 See Ptolemy, *Tetrabiblos*, I:3.27. Jung was familiar with Ptolemy's work; see Jung, CW8, ¶869; Jung, CW9ii, ¶¶128 and 149; Jung, CW14, ¶576.
67 Jung cites Valens' *Anthologiarium* in Jung, CW13, ¶412.
68 Vettius Valens, *The Anthology*, trans. Robert Schmidt (Berkeley Springs, WV: Golden Hind Press, 1993–96), Book I, pp. 7–16.
69 For the early history of the elements, see Dorian Gieseler Greenbaum, *Temperament* (Bournemouth: Wessex Astrologer, 2005), pp. 5–44.
70 For descriptions of the 'function types', see Jung, CW6, ¶¶556–671.
71 Jung, CW6, ¶933. 'Oriental' here means Mesopotamian, Babylonian, or Middle Eastern.
72 Jung, CW6, ¶¶883–84.
73 See Greenbaum, *Temperament*, p. 47.
74 Alan Leo, *The Art of Synthesis* (London: Modern Astrology Office, 1912), p. 179; Alan Leo, *How to Judge a Nativity* (London: Modern Astrology Office, 1903), p. 14.

75 Jung, CW6, ¶¶577–81.
76 Leo, *The Art of Synthesis*, pp. 177–78; Leo, *How to Judge a Nativity*, p. 14.
77 Jung, CW6, ¶¶604–5.
78 C.G. Jung, 'The Swiss Line in the European Spectrum', in Jung, CW10, ¶¶903–924, first published as 'Die Bedeutung der schweizerischen Linie im Spektrum Europas', *Neue Schweitzer Rundschau* 24:6 (1928), pp. 1–11.
79 Jung, CW10, ¶914.
80 For the propensity of the animus to express itself in critical and divisive ways, see Jung, CW7, ¶¶296–340; Jung, CW13, ¶¶57–63; Jung, CW9ii, ¶¶20–42.
81 This division comprises the astrological 'quadruplicities': three groups of four signs each, concerned with action (cardinal), stabilisation (fixed), and adaptation (mutable). Each zodiacal sign thus partakes of an element (triplicity) and a mode of response (quadruplicity). See Leo, *How to Judge a Nativity*, pp. 14–15.
82 For Jung's association of the Moon with the instinctual feminine, see Jung, CW14, ¶¶154–73; Jung, CW9i, ¶156. For descriptions of the planetary relationships (aspects) in astrology, see Leo, *How to Judge a Nativity*, pp. 39–67; Charles E.O. Carter, *The Astrological Aspects* (London: Theosophical Publishing House, 1930). Jung possessed an earlier work by this English astrologer, *An Encyclopaedia of Psychological Astrology* (London: Theosophical Publishing House, 1924).
83 These predecessors were Jean-Martin Charcot (1825–93), Pierre Janet (1859–1947), and Josef Breuer (1842–1925). For Charcot's work, see Jean-Martin Charcot, *Clinical Lectures on Diseases of the Nervous System*, ed. Ruth Harris, trans. Thomas Savill (London: Routledge, 1991 [1886]). For Janet's idea of complexes as *'idées fixes'*, see Pierre Janet, *The Major Symptoms of Hysteria* (New York: Macmillan, 1924). For Breuer, see Freud and Breuer, SE2. For Freud's understanding of complexes, see Freud, SE7.
84 See Jung, CW8, ¶¶194–219.
85 Freud, SE7, p. 188.
86 For this approach to the Oedipus myth, see Erich Neumann, *The Origins and History of Consciousness* (Princeton, NJ: Princeton University Press, 1954).
87 Jung, CW5, ¶644.
88 For works by analytical psychologists on the complex, see Erel Shalit, *The Complex* (Toronto: Inner City Books, 2002); Edward F. Edinger, *Ego and Archetype* (New York: Putnam, 1972). For complexes in collectives and historical cycles, see Thomas Singer and Samuel L. Kimbles (eds.), *The Cultural Complex* (London: Routledge, 2004); James L. Henderson, *A Bridge Across Time* (London: Turnstone, 1975).
89 Jung, CW14, ¶308.
90 For more on Iamblichus' theurgy and its importance in Jung's work, see Chapter 3.
91 Jung, CW7, ¶266.
92 Jung, CW14, ¶309. 'Houses' in this instance refer to the celestial 'abodes' or 'planetary spheres' as they appear in Gnostic and Hermetic literature. The 'apotheosis' is described in texts such as the Hermetic *Poimandres* as an experience of rising beyond the planetary spheres to a union with the deity, resulting in the transformation of the individual. Jung possessed Mead's translation of *Poimandres*: for the relevant passage, see G.R.S. Mead (ed. and trans.), *Thrice-Greatest Hermes*, 3 volumes (London: Theosophical Publishing Society, 1906), II:15–16. For a more recent translation, see Brian P. Copenhaver (ed. and trans.), *Hermetica* (Cambridge: Cambridge University Press, 1992), *CH*1:25–26.
93 Jung, CW14, ¶297. For the only complete English translation of the *Hypnerotomachia*, see Joscelyn Godwin (trans.), *Hypnerotomachia Poliphili* (London: Thames and Hudson, 1999). See also Greene, *The Astrological World of Jung's 'Liber Novus'*, conclusion.
94 Jung, CW14, ¶¶752–55.
95 Jung, CW14, ¶¶311 and 353.
96 Jung, CW14, ¶222.
97 Jung, CW12, ¶40. For a more detailed discussion of Jung's understanding of *Heimarmene*, see Chapter 5.

98 Jung, CW14, ¶308.
99 B.V. Raman (1912–98) was an influential Indian astrologer who published a number of books and articles on Hindu or Vedic astrology, and edited a journal called *The Astrological Magazine*, to which Jung referred in his letter. See B.V. Raman, *How to Judge a Horoscope*, 2 volumes (Columbia, MO: South Asia Books, 2000).
100 C.G. Jung, Letter to B.V. Raman, 6 September 1947, in Jung, *C.G. Jung Letters*, Vol. 1, pp. 475–76.
101 Jung, Letter to André Barbault, p. 176.

2

JUNG'S ASTROLOGERS

> But, if the stars announce the future . . . what explanation of the cause have we to offer? . . . We may think of the stars as letters perpetually being inscribed on the heavens or inscribed once for all and yet moving as they pursue the other tasks allotted to them; upon these main tasks will follow the quality of *signifying* . . . All teems with symbol; the wise man is the man who in any one thing can read another.[1]
>
> —Plotinus

> In the symbol there is the release of the bound human force struggling with darkness . . . One can certainly gain outer freedom through powerful actions, but one creates inner freedom only through the symbol. The symbol is the word that goes out of the mouth, that one does not simply speak, but that rises out of the depths of the self as a word of power and great need and places itself unexpectedly on the tongue.[2]
>
> —C.G. Jung

Jung's astrological sources

The astrological sources Jung cited for public consumption in the *Collected Works* are those that the passing centuries have transformed into historical artefacts. These include such works as Ptolemy's second-century *Tetrabiblos*, Abu Ma'shar's ninth-century *De magnis coniunctionibus*, published in Latin in 1515, and Jerome Cardan's seventeenth-century *Commentaria in Ptolomaeum de astrorum indiciis*.[3] Jung avoided citing any living astrological practitioners when referring to the subject in his published works, except those authors involved in statistical research. While the older texts clearly provided him with important insights, it is unlikely that Jung actually learned how to cast a horoscope from them; not only is the language obscure, but the mathematical calculations, when they are described, depend on actual observation and measurement of the heavens rather than on the ease of the published tables of planetary positions, known as ephemerides, available in Jung's own time. It seems that Jung's discomfort about revealing the extent and sources of his astrological investigations pursued him throughout his life.

In the essay, 'Synchronicity: An Acausal Connecting Principle',[4] Jung displayed considerable technical astrological knowledge. He freely referred to twentieth-century explorers into psychic phenomena, such as J.B. Rhine,[5] and he acknowledged the statistical results of astrological experiments made in the 1920s and 1930s by researchers such as the Swiss astrologer Karl Ernst Krafft and the French astrologer Paul Flambart.[6] But he cited for his horoscope interpretations only the 'big names' in ancient, medieval, and early modern astrology, along with various alchemical texts and the works of those reputable philosophers – Philo of Alexandria, Plotinus, Schopenhauer – who indicated sympathy toward the subject.[7] It is unclear from Jung's early letters to Freud whether he was 'looking into' astrology – or, to be more precise, learning to cast and interpret horoscopes – through texts he had acquired, or whether he had a private tutor. According to Jung's grandson, Ulrich Hoerni, Jung 'got his knowledge from books rather than from any personal teacher'.[8]

Richard Noll claims that 'it is thought' Toni Wolff taught Jung astrology, but precisely who 'thought' it is not mentioned; and, in any event, Jung's astrological studies predated his meeting with Wolff by at least two years.[9] Jung mentioned no sources to Freud, although in later life he enjoyed a lively correspondence with professional astrologers such as Barbault and Raman. But although the *Collected Works* include only astrological sources rendered worthy of scholarship by a respectable historical interval, Jung's private collection of modern astrology books tells another story. While he accumulated individual works published from the mid-1920s onward by German, French, British, and American astrologers, the only books in Jung's library that had been published shortly before his two letters to Freud, and which were likely modern sources for his early studies, are those by three British astrologers. Of these three, only one was of sufficient interest for Jung to acquire more than one of the author's works.

The first of these British texts, a work titled *The Text-Book of Astrology* by Alfred John Pearce (1840–1923), was originally published in 1889 as a series of volumes dealing with diverse astrological themes, including the reading of the birth horoscope, the interpretation of national charts and political events, astro-meteorology, medical astrology, and 'electional' astrology (choosing the appropriate moment to begin a venture). These smaller works appeared in a combined single volume in 1911, the edition that Jung acquired. James Holden, Research Director of the American Federation of Astrologers, which issued a reprint of Pearce's work in 2006, points out that Pearce's book is 'traditional' and 'devoid of the psychological trend set in motion by his [Pearce's] younger contemporary Alan Leo'. With a bias reflecting his own personal views in terms of what constitutes valid astrology – a debate that has been ongoing within the world of astrological practitioners for over two millennia – Holden further states that *The Text-Book of Astrology* 'precedes the complications introduced by esotericism . . . and vague psychological interpretations'.[10] Pearce was deeply antagonistic to any astrology that trailed esoteric clouds behind it, declaring categorically: 'We draw the line at magic and spiritualism'. Alan Leo's Theosophical astrology, according to Pearce, is 'superstitious nonsense'.[11]

But if Pearce was not interested in esotericism and 'vague psychological interpretations', it seems that Jung was not interested in Pearce. Although Pearce wrote numerous other astrological works, *The Text-Book of Astrology* is the only publication by this British astrologer to be found in Jung's library.[12] Nor does Jung seem to have been attracted to the journals that Pearce edited,[13] although he acquired a sizeable collection of other esoteric journals that included astrological material, such as Ralph Shirley's *The Occult Review* and Mead's own journal, *The Quest*.[14] It would appear that the 'psychological trend' emerging in British astrology at the turn of the twentieth century was more rewarding to Jung during the time he was first formulating his theories about the nature and dynamics of the human psyche.

The second work Jung acquired by a British astrologer writing during this period was Raphael's *The Key to Astrology*.[15] It was the fashion of the time for astrologers to adopt celestial pseudonyms, usually those of angels associated with specific planets. A series of astrologers editing a particular journal might use the same pseudonym in sequence, which was the case with Raphael. The angel Raphael, one of the seven archangels, is usually linked with Mercury, the planet in astrological lore most concerned with writing and the communication of ideas and thus appropriate for the editor of a journal.[16] Raphael was initially the pseudonym for an astrologer called Robert Cross Smith (1795–1832). Smith's pseudonym was then adopted by the astrologer John Palmer (1807–37) and by four subsequent astrologers before Robert Thomas Cross (1850–1923), author of *The Key to Astrology*, took up the name.[17] *The Key to Astrology* was originally published in 1896, although it later ran through a number of reprints. Jung's particular edition appeared in 1909. Like Pearce, Raphael was both traditional and prolific, publishing other volumes such as *Raphael's Horary Astrology* (1897). Also like Pearce, Raphael edited an almanac, predictably titled *Raphael's Almanac*. As with Pearce, it seems that, having read one work by this author, Jung was not sufficiently impressed to acquire more.

Alan Leo's 'modern' astrology

The third British astrologer whose work was published around the time Jung began his studies seems to have held a far higher position in Jung's estimation than Pearce and Raphael. Alan Leo, born William Frederick Allan (1860–1917), was a unique figure in the esoteric world of fin-de-siècle Britain because, virtually single-handed, he brought astrology into the modern era as a tool for insight into character rather than a method of prediction.[18] Leo displayed no erudition in any sphere of clinical psychology or classical scholarship, relying almost entirely on the works of his mentor, H.P. Blavatsky, founder of the Theosophical Society. According to Leo's wife Bessie, who produced a hagiography of her husband two years after his death, Leo studied no astrological works other than those of Raphael, and relied solely on

FIGURE 2.1 Alan Leo

Blavatsky's foundation texts of Theosophy, *Isis Unveiled* and *The Secret Doctrine*, to acquire his spiritual knowledge.[19] In a section of her biography titled 'Alan Leo's Faith', Bessie Leo cited the cosmological and religious perceptions on which her husband's understanding of astrology was based:

> I believe that the Principle which gives life dwells in us and without us comes from the Supreme Intelligence through the Rays of the Sun . . . I believe the Soul of Humanity is immortal or perpetual; and I am convinced that each individual soul or mind is symbolised by the Moon in its ebb and flow . . . also by its relation to the Planetary Spheres of Influence . . . Every man derives his will power from a Planetary Sphere of Influence which he uses, or abuses, by which he can overcome evil tendencies and control his animal nature, hence Astrology teaches that Character is Destiny.[20]

Alan Leo joined the Theosophical Society in 1890, when he became involved with G.R.S. Mead, then secretary of the Society, in the creation of a Theosophical lodge in Brixton. Bessie's biography of her husband is a treasure-trove of anecdotal information about the emergence of an early form of psychological astrology at the turn of the century that has many echoes in Jung's own work. Most important of these echoes is the central significance of the Sun in the horoscope, which was one of Leo's great innovations in modern astrology. He derived the idea from Blavatsky's quasi-Neoplatonic teachings about the invisible 'spiritual' Sun or Solar Logos as the embodiment of divinity,[21] and it is recognisable in Jung's identification of this noetic solar potency as the focus of the inner journey of *Liber Novus*.[22]

Jung acquired early editions of a number of Leo's texts, some of which were initially published as articles in Leo's own journal, *Modern Astrology*. These articles subsequently appeared as individual pamphlets, and were then compiled and reissued within a few years as revised single volumes. Leo's strong influence on Jung's astrological imagery in *Liber Novus* is discussed more fully in the appropriate chapters in *The Astrological World of Jung's* Liber Novus. But Jung's editions of Leo's books tell an interesting story in themselves. Jung was very careful with his books; he neither dog-eared the pages nor defaced them with ink. Particular sections of certain favoured books are lightly marked in pencil with vertical lines in the margins indicating a significant paragraph, or the occasional underlining of a phrase or reference. Sometimes he wrote a few words in pencil in the margin of a work that particularly interested him, or a question mark if he queried an author's opinion. Alan Leo's *Astrology for All* was originally published in two volumes in 1899.[23] The first volume discusses natal chart interpretation through the combination of Sun and Moon signs. The second volume comprises mathematical tables and detailed instructions for calculating a horoscope. A second edition of both volumes was published in 1904; it is this edition that Jung obtained. As a third, revised edition appeared in 1908 and a fourth in 1912, it is likely that Jung acquired his own copy before its third edition, suggesting that he began his exploration of astrology much earlier than the date indicated by his letter to Freud.

Jung had also begun accumulating the technical apparatus of astrology, such as ephemerides – published tables of planetary positions – five years earlier than his letter to Freud. As these planetary tables were produced each year, an ephemeris for 1906 would only be useful for that year,[24] although it is possible that Jung acquired his 1906 ephemeris at a later date in order to calculate the horoscope of his daughter Gret, who was born in that year.[25] Jung's copy of *Astrology for All, Part II* is heavily annotated; here one can see specific dates which Jung underlined with coloured pencils, and a series of mathematical calculations in pencil in the margins. It seems that Jung was learning the mechanics of setting up a birth horoscope from the instructions given in Leo's book.[26] This evidence, and an unmistakable similarity between the two men in their phrasing and ideas about particular astrological configurations, suggest that Jung was reading, and learning from, a succession of Leo's publications throughout the period he worked on *Liber Novus*.

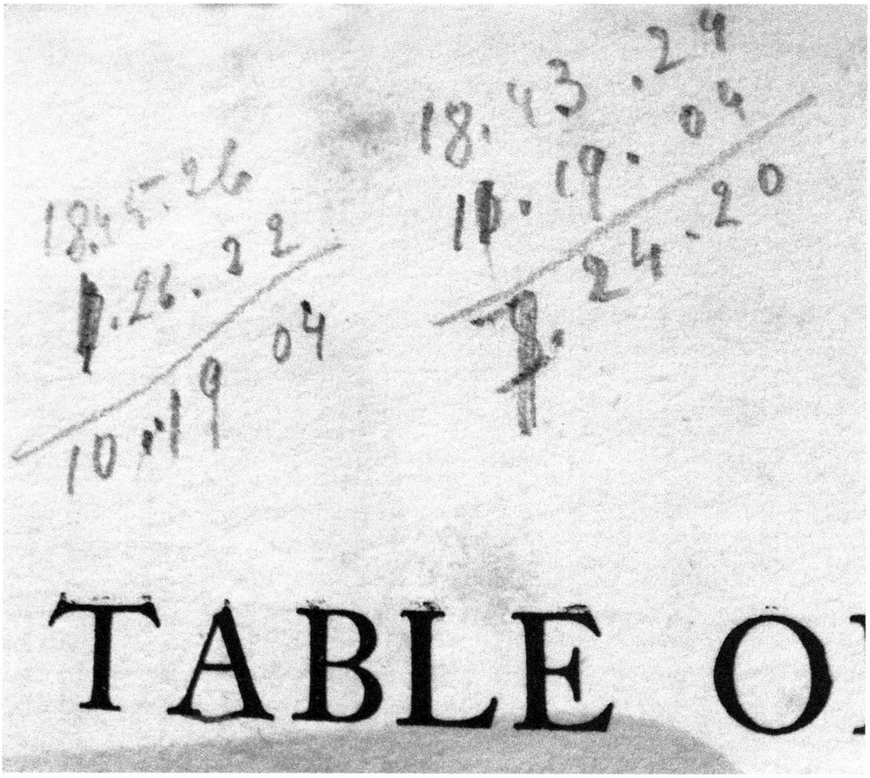

FIGURE 2.2 Jung's notations in Alan Leo's *Astrology for All, Part II*[27]

Another and far more striking indication that Jung relied on Alan Leo's astrological interpretations is provided by a document titled 'The Key to Your Own Nativity: Special Chart', which Jung received from the Dutch psychoanalyst Dr. Johan van Ophuijsen in 1911 – the year that he informed Freud that he was 'looking into' astrology. Van Ophuijsen (1882–1950), whose signature is on the document, was a disciple of Freud, and had spent time in Zürich as Jung's patient between 1911 and 1913, while Jung was still nominally part of the psychoanalytic *côterie*.[28] Van Ophuijsen became co-founder of the Dutch Psychoanalytical Society in 1917. He was one of several psychoanalysts who attempted to resolve the growing conflict between Freud and Jung, and was present at a meeting between the two men in Munich in November 1912, organised to discuss the escalation of their antipathy and architect some kind of reconciliation. After Freud and Jung parted ways, van Ophuijsen remained a staunch Freudian. However, his involvement with astrology suggests that Freud's lack of response to Jung's interest in the subject was either not shared by his followers, or did not reflect Freud's real views at the time. The 'Special Chart' provides no name and simply states 'for male' (in English), but lists all of Jung's planetary placements at the time of his birth. It was intended, as its title indicates, to be supplemented by specific paragraphs in Leo's *The Key to Your Own Nativity*, published

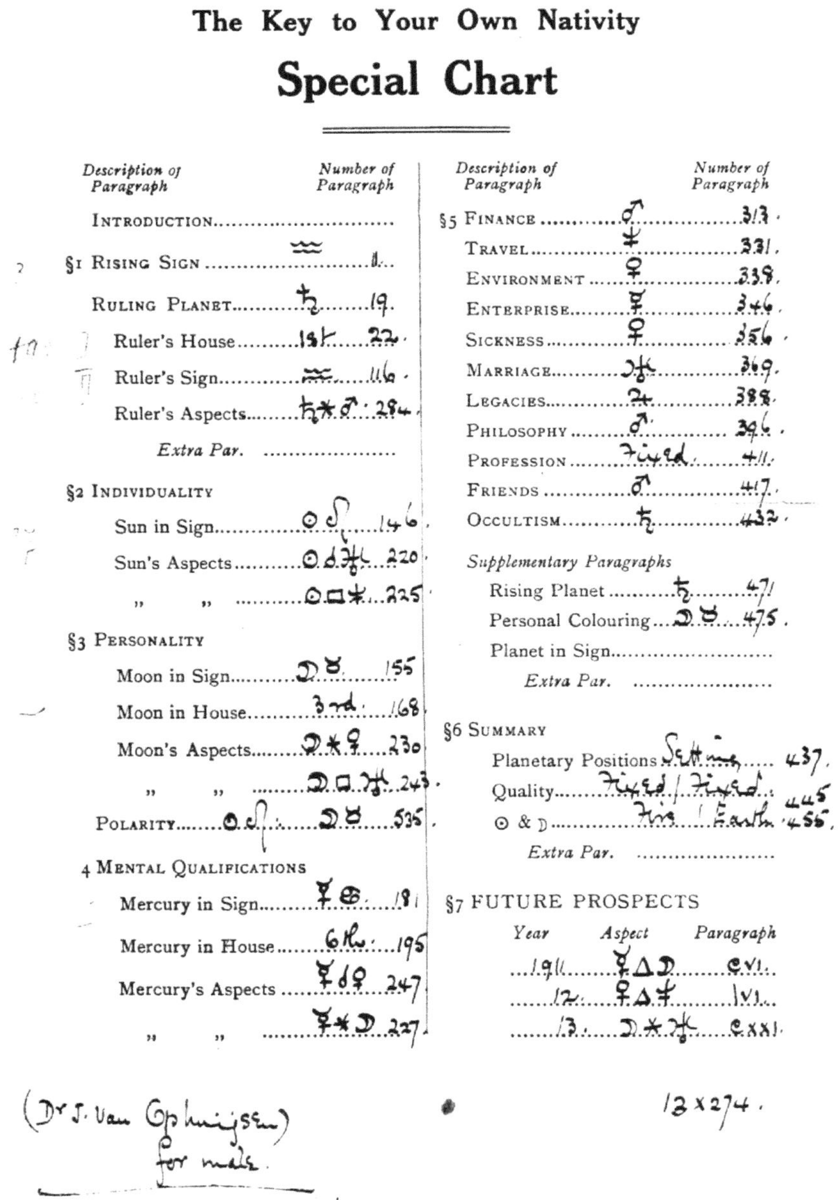

The Key to Your Own Nativity

Special Chart

Description of Paragraph	Number of Paragraph
Introduction	
§1 Rising Sign ♒	1
Ruling Planet ♄	19.
Ruler's House 1st	22.
Ruler's Sign ♒	116.
Ruler's Aspects ♄✱♂	284.
Extra Par.	
§2 Individuality	
Sun in Sign ☉♌	146.
Sun's Aspects ☉☌♅	220
" " ☉□♃	225
§3 Personality	
Moon in Sign ☽♉	155
Moon in House 3rd	168
Moon's Aspects ☽✱♀	230
" " ☽□♅	243
Polarity ☉♌ ☽♉	535
4 Mental Qualifications	
Mercury in Sign ☿♋	181
Mercury in House 6th	195
Mercury's Aspects ☿☌♀	247
" " ☿✱☽	227
§5 Finance ♂	313.
Travel ♃	331.
Environment ♀	338.
Enterprise ☿	346.
Sickness ♀	356.
Marriage ☽♅	369.
Legacies ♃	388.
Philosophy ♂	396.
Profession Fixed	411.
Friends ♂	417.
Occultism ♄	432.
Supplementary Paragraphs	
Rising Planet ♄	471
Personal Colouring ☽♉	475.
Planet in Sign	
Extra Par.	
§6 Summary	
Planetary Positions Setting	437.
Quality Fixed / Fixed	445
☉ & ☽ Fire / Earth	455.
Extra Par.	

§7 FUTURE PROSPECTS

Year	*Aspect*	*Paragraph*
1911	☿△☽	CVI.
12	♀△♃	LVI.
13	☽✱♅	CXXI.

(Dr J. Van Ophuijsen)
for male.

12 x 274.

FIGURE 2.3 'Special Chart' relating Jung's natal horoscope to specific paragraphs in Alan Leo's *The Key to Your Own Nativity*[33]

in 1910.[29] An example of the general application of the 'Special Chart' is given at the beginning of Leo's book, with the planetary placements inserted for King George V as an illustration. Each planetary position in the 'Special Chart' is assigned a paragraph number that correlates with the appropriate descriptive passage in Leo's book.

The pre-printed blank form on which Jung's astrological information was written is from Leo's Modern Astrology Office in London, suggesting that van Ophuijsen was either officially working as a tutor for Leo's school, or had obtained a form from the school. Although he may have had copies made of the blank form included at the end of *The Key to Your Own Nativity*,[30] the document in Jung's private archives is not a copy but an individual printed form, neither mimeographed nor torn from a book. Van Ophuijsen's handwritten notes are in English. It is impossible to know from the 'Special Chart' itself whether the two men discussed it in any depth, although, given van Ophuijsen's presence in Zürich for two years as Jung's colleague and patient, it would be surprising if they had not. The chart states explicitly that Saturn in Jung's horoscope is the 'ruling planet', and refers to the paragraph in Leo's book in which Saturn is described as giving 'a disposition that is sober, serious, and thoughtful' and confers the gift of 'the meditative mind'.[31] As we will see later, this Saturnine rulership of Jung's horoscope was profoundly important to him and is particularly relevant to certain figures in *Liber Novus*.

In the lower right corner of the 'Special Chart' is a section titled 'Future Prospects', in which van Ophuijsen inserted the movements of Jung's planets after birth for the years 1911, 1912, and 1913.[32] The 'Special Chart' was evidently prepared in 1911, just at the time that Jung announced his astrological studies to Freud, and it provides one of the earliest documentary indications of an important source of Jung's astrological research at the time. It also suggests that, the 'black tide of occultism' notwithstanding, Jung's introduction to Alan Leo was encouraged, if not actually initiated, by one of Freud's colleagues. It seems that, in 1911, Jung was not alone among his fellow psychoanalysts in the pursuit of 'wretched subjects'.

The 'Future Prospects' section of the 'Special Chart', which covers the precise period of Jung's break with Freud, the publication of *Psychology of the Unconscious*, and the beginning of work on *Liber Novus*, also suggests that Jung may have been seeking astrological insights to help with the growing tensions between himself and Freud. In 1911, Jung was not merely 'looking into' astrology; he was assiduously reading and learning from Alan Leo's books and had received – probably at his own request – a horoscope calculated by a psychoanalyst familiar with Leo's school and linked with the interpretative material Leo had provided in his published text. It seems likely that most, if not all, of Jung's early forays into astrology were strongly coloured by the distinctive psycho-spiritual perspective offered by Leo's extensive works.

Max Heindel's 'Rosicrucian' astrology

In 1909, a Danish esotericist named Carl Louis von Grasshoff (1865–1919), who later called himself Max Heindel, founded a school in Seattle, Washington, which he described as 'The Rosicrucian Fellowship: An Association of Christian Mystics'. The mission of Heindel's school was to prepare the public for the approaching Aquarian Age through promulgating the 'true philosophy' of the Rosicrucians. This 'true philosophy' was related to a legendary historical fellowship purportedly founded in 1313 by a Christian mystic called Christian Rosenkreutz. Like the

FIGURE 2.4 Max Heindel

foundation narrative of Freemasonry, the foundation narrative of the Rosicrucians, whose existence was first proclaimed in the early seventeenth century through a series of published pamphlets known as the 'Rosicrucian Manifestos',[34] is difficult if not impossible to confirm through historical evidence, as is the existence of any historical personage called Christian Rosenkreutz. Nevertheless, since the seventeenth century, various groups and currents linked with both early modern alchemy and Freemasonry have proclaimed themselves as 'Rosicrucian',[35] and a long sequence of works by self-proclaimed members of the 'Order' has continued into the present day. That Jung was deeply interested in the Rosicrucians is suggested by the large number of references found in the *Collected Works*,[36] and also by his familiarity with, and respect for, the works of A.E. Waite (1857–1942), a former Theosophist and member of the Order of the Golden Dawn as well as a historian of Rosicrucian, alchemical, and Grail lore, who in 1915 established his own 'Rosicrucian' group called the Fellowship of the Rosy Cross.[37]

In 1911, Max Heindel established a permanent home for his Rosicrucian organisation at Oceanside, California, where it still exists today and, even in these postmodern, multicultural times, still refers to itself as 'An Association of Christian Mystics'.[38] Heindel was strongly influenced by the work of the German esotericist Rudolph Steiner (1861–1925), who had himself originally been schooled in Blavatsky's Theosophical Society before he broke away because of Blavatsky's exclusively Eastern orientation. Steiner subsequently founded his own school, known as Anthroposophy,[39] and Jung, not surprisingly, was as familiar with this particular German esoteric current as he was with British Theosophy, and was equally critical of both. Steiner's Anthroposophical Society, like Blavatsky's Theosophical Society, was, in Jung's view, a movement 'of a genuinely religious character', but it masqueraded as 'spiritual science' and, despite Steiner's efforts, failed to develop into an organised church.[40] Something similar has, of course, been said about Jung: that his analytical psychology is 'of a genuinely religious character' but masquerades as scientific psychology.[41] Jung's criticisms of Steiner notwithstanding, although Jung found Anthroposophy, like Theosophy, unattractive in its official dogmas and organisational structure, it seems that Steiner's ideas, many of which were inspired by Goethe and were particularly amenable to being embedded in an astrological-psychological context, were not so easily repudiated.[42]

Like Blavatsky, Max Heindel believed he had received communications from highly evolved disincarnate spiritual entities. He called his spiritual guides the Elder Brothers, and it is these communications that formed the basis of the Fellowship's doctrines. Heindel was a prolific teacher and writer; his most important books were *The Rosicrucian Cosmo-conception*, a work similar in genre to Blavatsky's *The Secret Doctrine*, and *The Message of the Stars*, one of several works he produced on astrology and its applications to both healing and what he understood as spiritual growth.[43] None of Heindel's books appears in the catalogue of Jung's private library. But it seems that Jung was more interested in Heindel than this absence of published works might suggest.[44] Even if Jung never actually purchased any of Heindel's works, he actively took up a course of astrological study with Heindel's Rosicrucian Fellowship in the mid-1920s, drawing on this 'Rosicrucian' material, not only for an understanding of his own horoscope, but, as discussed more fully in Chapter 5, for certain themes in his interpretation of the Astrological Ages or Aions.

Heindel's organisation, then as now, offered correspondence courses in both 'Rosicrucian Philosophy' and astrology; Jung apparently enrolled in the latter. It is unclear for how long he pursued this course, as the materials in the archives are not dated and many appear to be missing; he might only have tried a few lessons and abandoned the effort, or he might have completed the course. The former is more likely, as Jung had little patience with dogmatic teachings filled with religious certainty, and Heindel was nothing if not dogmatically certain. The course was advertised as a study programme that taught 'the importance of astrology as a phase of religion and a Divine Science', and, following Heindel's particular understanding of astrology as spiritual knowledge rather than divination, it was open to 'anyone not engaged in fortune telling or similar methods of commercializing spiritual knowledge'.[45] The material in Jung's archives consists of several pages, and begins with a cover diagram displaying a general but comprehensive astrological scheme, including the traditional zodiacal signs divided into their triplicities (elements), quadruplicities ('cardinal', 'fixed', and 'mutable'), decans (divisions of each sign into ten-degree segments), and ruling planets, as well as the spheres of life covered by each of the twelve sectors or 'houses' of the horoscope.

Astrological Chart

The Rosicrucian Fellowship,
Oceanside, California

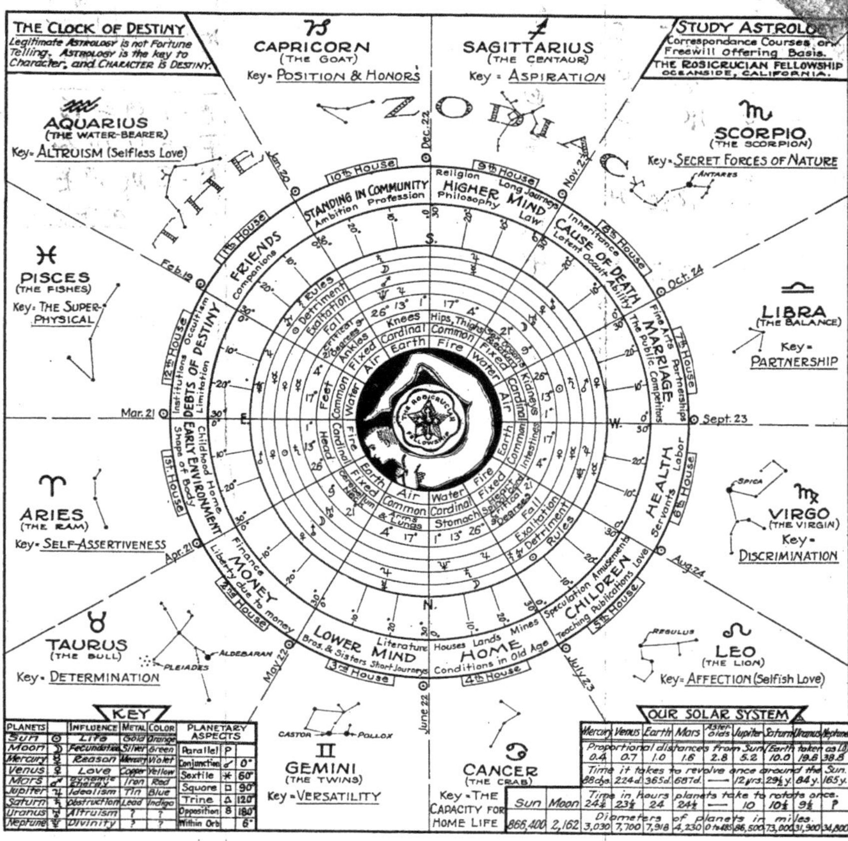

NOTICE TO STUDENTS:

This chart is designed to give you a bird's eye view of the whole subject of Astrology, including keywords, elements, metals, colors, a star map, and general astronomical information.

It should be used as a means of correlating the information which you gradually obtain from our correspondence course and books. A careful study of it will well repay you. There are no answers required in connection with it; it is merely to be kept for reference. If you have any questions about it, we would suggest that as far as possible you wait until you are able to obtain the answers from your study of the correspondence course and the text books recommended. We would call your attention to the fact that every sign, house, and planet has several keywords to describe all its various qualities. As you progress in your study of the subject, you will constantly add new keywords to your previous list.

FIGURE 2.5 Cover page for the Rosicrucian Fellowship's correspondence course in astrology[46]

Beneath the diagram is a paragraph headed 'Notice to Students'; the diagram, an original printed document and not a mimeograph, is an introduction intended for neophytes who had just enrolled in the correspondence course.

> This chart is designed to give you a bird's eye view of the whole subject of Astrology . . . It should be used as a means of correlating the information which you gradually obtain from our correspondence course and books. A careful study of it will repay you . . . If you have any questions about it, we would suggest that as far as possible you wait until you are able to obtain answers from your study of the correspondence course and the text books recommended . . . As you progress in the study of the subject, you will constantly add new keywords to your previous list.

Following this cover page is a personal 'Horoscope Data Sheet', with the name of the student left blank but cast for Jung's birth date, place, and time. The handwriting is not Jung's, and it is probable that this information was filled in by one of the tutors running the course. That the writing is by an American astrologer is indicated by the manner in which the dates are written, with the month given first and then the day. A list of transiting planets is given for various dates in 1928. A second Horoscope Data Sheet, in the same handwriting, once again presents Jung's natal chart (with the name left blank), but with the progressed planetary positions listed for 1926, 1927, and 1928. A third Horoscope Data Sheet displays the progressed planetary positions for 1929. Finally, a fourth Horoscope Data Sheet presents a list of both natal and transiting planets for 1931. All these lists of horoscopic data are drawn in the same hand on standard pre-printed blank forms with the Rosicrucian Fellowship logo at the top. It is impossible to know from the existing documents whether Jung requested all these charts at the same time or over a period of several years, as the papers are not dated. It is during this same period – the mid- to late 1920s – that Jung engaged in a lengthy correspondence with a British astrologer called John Thorburn, discussed more fully below, and requested a natal chart interpretation from him. It was also during this period that Jung completed his calligraphic transcription of *Liber Novus*.

It is possible that Jung enlisted a friend already involved with Heindel's organisation to produce these horoscopes for him. There are a number of charts in Jung's private archives that were prepared for his colleagues and patients – including Freud, Toni Wolff, and Eugen Bleuler (1857–1939), who was Jung's mentor at the Burghölzli Clinic from 1900 to 1909 – by individuals other than himself. Some were drawn by Emma Jung, who seems to have been as involved with astrology as was Jung himself; some are drawn by persons unknown.[48] A few were prepared by Jung himself, such as the one shown below in Fig. 2.7 for an unknown individual, and a calculation sheet which Jung prepared for his daughter Helene, born in 1914.

However, if the Rosicrucian charts were prepared by someone other than a tutor from the Fellowship, it is difficult to understand why the general cover sheet for students was included in the materials. Moreover, even if Jung was not enrolled in

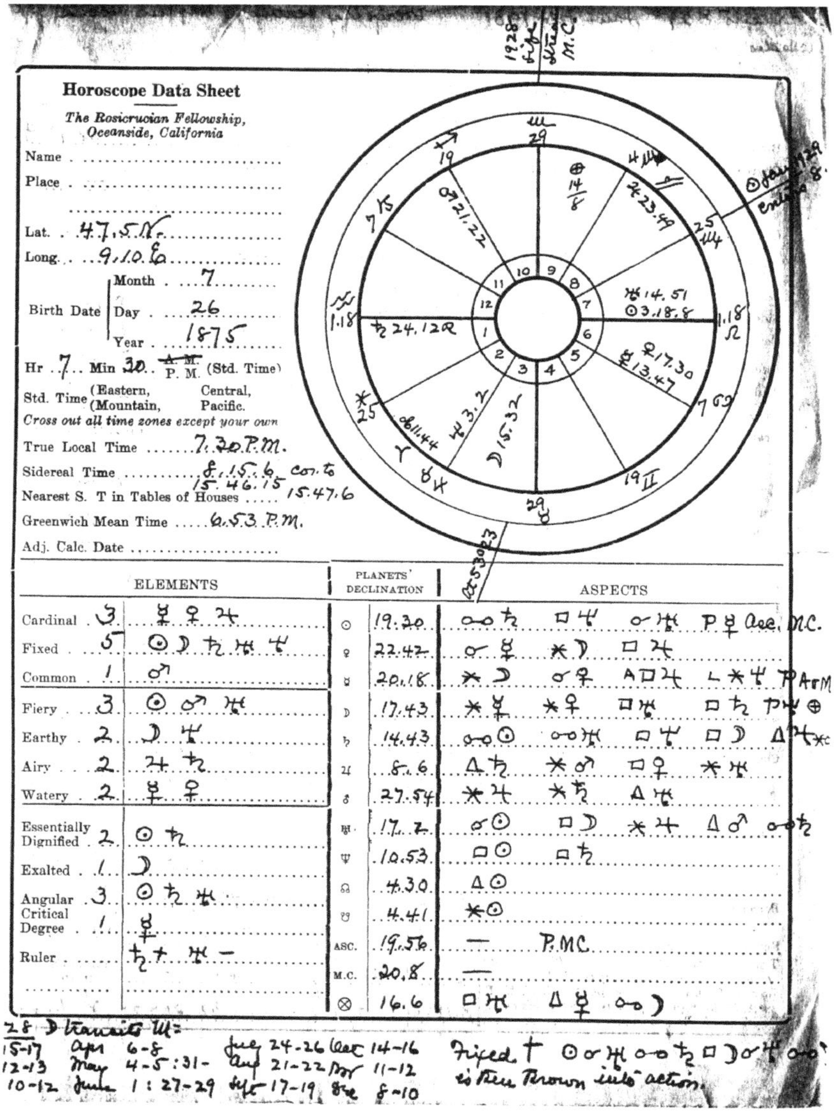

FIGURE 2.6 The Rosicrucian Fellowship 'Horoscope Data Sheet', set for Jung's birth year, date, time, and place[47]

the course, his choice of astrologer to provide the materials is, in itself, revealing: he chose an American who followed an astrology with an esoteric or spiritual overview, echoing Jung's interest in the Theosophically inclined astrologer Alan Leo. Although Jung was no more a card-carrying Rosicrucian than he was a Theosophist, it seems he found Heindel's approach to astrology more congenial than the predictive applications available at the time in both English and German, because

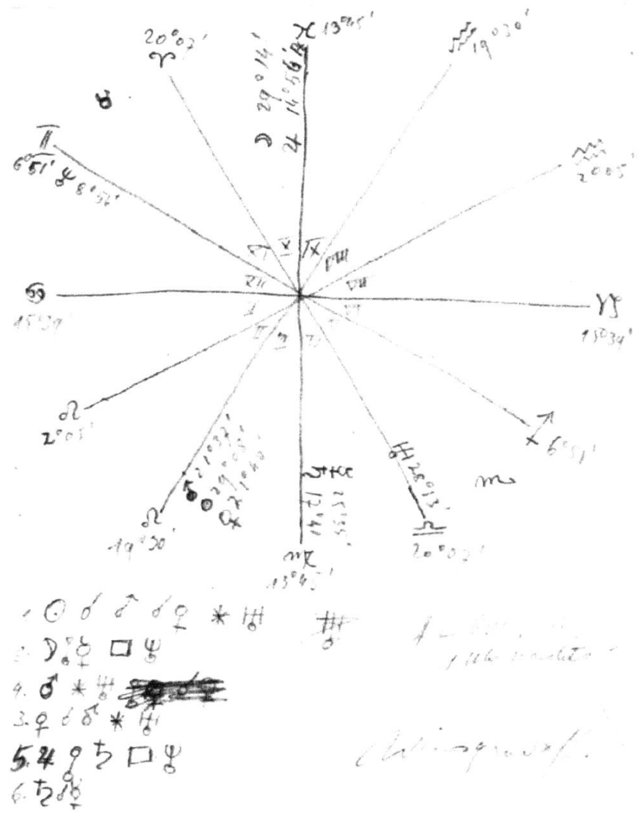

FIGURE 2.7 Horoscope drawn by Jung for an unknown individual, born 12 August 1891[49]

Heindel promulgated a process of dynamic inner transformation that could be understood psychologically as well as spiritually. Like Leo, Heindel incorporated the idea of reincarnation into his understanding of the natal horoscope:

> It should never be forgotten, however, that our horoscope shows what we have made of ourselves in past lives, and he who has the configuration that attracts friends must have been kind and obliging, while he who draws out the mean side of human nature and makes enemies is himself selfish and unfriendly. But if he will strive to turn away from his ways and make some sacrifice for others, he will also in time overcome the undesirable aspects, for the Star Angels are not maliciously bent upon scourging anyone.[51]

In its extreme moral simplicity and certitude, this could hardly be construed as a 'psychological' understanding of the natal horoscope. But Heindel's astrology was concerned with a conscious effort to transform habitual character propensities, and in this sense it was more adaptable to Jung's psychological approach than a simple description of personality traits or a prognosis of preordained future events.

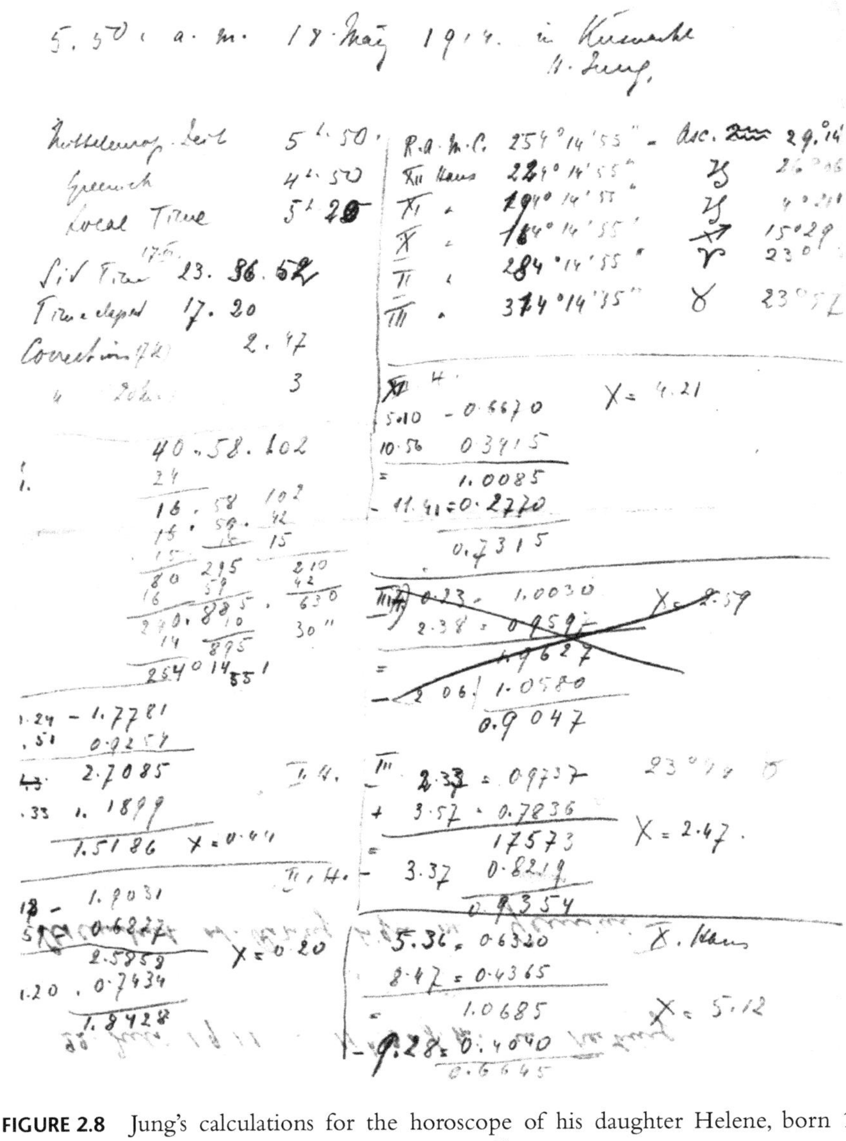

FIGURE 2.8 Jung's calculations for the horoscope of his daughter Helene, born 18 March 1914 at 5.50 am in Küsnacht[50]

Myths and astrological symbols

There are other elements in Heindel's work that merit closer scrutiny in relation to Jung's understanding of astrological configurations. The use of mythic narratives in the interpretation of astrological symbols is a hallmark of Heindel's approach, and it closely resembles Jung's concept of 'amplification': the use of mythic stories and images to elucidate the deeper meanings and associations of a symbol. Heindel was an avowed Christian and would not have considered stories about the life of

Jesus as myth, and the mythic narratives he described were usually bound up with the grand cosmological drama of human evolution presented in Blavatsky's *Isis Unveiled*. Nevertheless, some of the imagery Heindel utilised – which was often less Christian than he might have been willing to recognise – echoes the manner in which Jung also drew on mythic motifs to breathe life and teleology into otherwise static characterological descriptions of the zodiacal signs.

In *The Message of the Stars*, for example, Heindel introduced Mercury through the planet's mythic role as 'Messenger of the Gods', whose 'wisdom-teaching is symbolically represented by the caduceus or "staff of Mercury"'; he then explained the symbolism of the serpents around the caduceus as the Theosophical 'spiral path' of the 'involution' of the soul into matter.[52] Heindel's interpretation of the zodiacal sign of Virgo offers another example: unlike other astrological texts that focus on the sign's earthy, fastidious nature (as did Jung himself in his description of the Swiss), Heindel emphasised the symbolism of the 'celestial virgin' as the mother of the inner messiah waiting to be born.

> Before the Aquarian age is definitely ushered in, we will, in all probability, have made great strides, both in overcoming the lust of the flesh and the lust after the flesh. For Virgo, the immaculate celestial virgin, and the ears of wheat contained in the sign, show both these ideals as profitable to soul growth at the present time . . . By looking to the mother ideal of Virgo during the Piscean Age, and following the Christ's example of sacrificial service, the immaculate conception becomes an actual experience to each of us, and Christ, the Son of Man, Aquarius, is born within us.[53]

While Aquarius, for Heindel, is the 'Son of Man', offering the possibility of the realised spark of divinity within, Virgo is 'the vehicle of the immaculate conception':

> Yearly, at the winter solstice, the immaculate Madonna is ascendant at midnight, when the newborn Sun commences to rise to the task of growing the grain and grape . . . The Sun is therefore an apt symbol of the Savior, born to feed his flock on the spiritual bread of life.[54]

The equation of Mary with the 'celestial virgin', and Christ with the new-born Sun entering Capricorn at the winter solstice, was not Heindel's invention. Christ's solar attributes are observable in the iconography of the early Church, chiefly in the nimbate figure of the saviour with solar rays around his head, and in the choice of the winter solstice, which marked the annual rebirth of pagan solar deities such as Mithras and Sol Invictus, for the birth of the Christian messiah. It is hardly a new observation that the early Church appropriated a number of motifs from pagan religious iconography in order to make its own message more 'marketable'.[55]

Heindel seems to have availed himself of literature from the late nineteenth century regarding the intimate relationship between solar myths, religion, and celestial phenomena. As a practising astrologer, he then applied mythic images to the interpretation of individual horoscopes. The influential Orientalist scholar Friedrich Max Müller (1823–1900) gave the theme of universal solar worship scholarly respectability in 1873 with his reiteration of the already well-established claim that there had once been an original, pure religion focused on the Sun:

> This source of light and life, this silent traveller, this majestic ruler, this departing friend or dying hero, in his daily or yearly course.[56]

Müller's influence extended not only to Blavatsky and Heindel but also to Jung, who acquired Müller's *Theosophy: Or, Psychological Religion* as well as a German translation of *Lectures on the Origin and Growth of Religions*.[57] The scholarly trend toward seeing a primal, universal solar religion behind figures such as Christ and Mithras permeates Jung's work during the period he worked on *Liber Novus*. In *Psychology of the Unconscious*, references to the Sun as the central symbolic motif of the individuation process dominate the work, as well as providing one of the core themes of *Liber Novus*. If the new-born Sun at the winter solstice is equated with the messiah, the 'celestial virgin', Virgo, would necessarily be equated with Mary as the mother of the messiah. Max Heindel was not the originator of the use of myth to provide a deeper meaning for the zodiacal signs; but he was perhaps the most important astrological author, contemporary with and familiar to Jung, who appropriated the idea of the Sun as a Christ-symbol and Virgo as the 'Celestial Mother' and used it in his astrological interpretations.

Jung, like Heindel, drew on older ideas about the mythic associations of the constellations, adapting them to his understanding of the zodiacal signs and incorporating them in his interpretation of birth chart significators. It is useful to compare Heindel's description of Virgo given above with Jung's own mythically inclined interpretation of this zodiacal sign. According to Jung,

> The mother-goddess – and the star-crowned woman of the Apocalypse counts as one – is usually thought of as a virgin . . . Virgo, the zodiacal sign, carries either a wheat-sheaf or a child . . . At any rate, this woman has something to do with the prophecy of the birth of the Messiah at the end of time . . . Its [*Salvator mundi*, saviour of the world] mother is the *Sapientia Dei* [Sophia, wisdom of God] or Mercurius as Virgo.[58]

Virgo is thus not only a Mercury-ruled earthy sign whose 'parsimony, stolidity, and stubbornness' seemed discernible to Jung in the Swiss character. This zodiacal sign also carried a deeper significance for him: it symbolised that aspect of the libido that conceives and brings to birth the inner solar 'saviour' or Self. In psychological terms, Virgo spoke to Jung of mediumship and the hidden wisdom of the archetypal realm – a perception that emerges in the figure of Salome in *Liber Novus*, and was perhaps not uninfluenced by the fact that Toni Wolff, who acted as Jung's psychic guide and midwife throughout the period he worked on *Liber Novus*, was born with the Sun in Virgo.[59]

In another example, the zodiacal sign of Cancer, as Jung described it in 1934, 'signifies resurrection because the crab sheds its shell', and, as a 'feminine and watery sign' belonging to the realm of the Mother, is related to the ambiguous crablike creature called Karkinos, sent by Hera to bite the hero Herakles in the heel during his fight with the Lernaean Hydra.[60] This use of mythic themes in relation to a specific individual's horoscope – in the case of Cancer, the horoscope of his patient, Miss X, who was 'born under' this zodiacal sign[61] – may have been partly inspired by Max Heindel's approach to astrology. Whatever the source, myth seems to have provided Jung with a sense that the horoscope at birth can describe not only the nature of the individual's inherent temperament and unconscious complexes, but, more importantly, the deeper teleology of the individual's psychic life: the path of individuation. It is the unique manner in which Jung understood myth, and the ways in which he applied it to amplify astrological signatures and vice versa, that allowed him to weave horoscopic themes into his understanding of the individuation process.

John Thorburn and the 'epoch' charts

In 1928, when Jung was nearing the completion of his calligraphic transcription of *Liber Novus* and was also exploring the astrology of Max Heindel's Rosicrucian Fellowship, he and his wife Emma both engaged in a correspondence with John MacCaig Thorburn (1883–1970), a Scottish astrologer and university lecturer in philosophy who had settled in the west of England. At Jung's request, Thorburn sent him, on 19 August 1928, a lengthy written interpretation of Jung's natal horoscope. Thorburn was then teaching at University College, Cardiff, but he had spent some time with Jung in Zürich prior to their correspondence, in the capacity of a patient as well as a friend. In a letter to Emma Jung, dated 15 February 1929, Thorburn mentioned how deeply he missed David and Cary Baynes,[62] and stated that his psychotherapeutic work with a certain 'Mrs. Schwill' in England gave him 'the feeling of keeping a little bit in touch with Zürich at a time when it seems impossible to visit it any more'.

Thorburn was an early admirer of Jung's work, and produced, within three years of the English publication of Jung's *Psychology of the Unconscious*, several scholarly papers, as well as one book, that favoured Jung's analytical psychology over Freud's psychoanalytic theories. These works were written several years before the date when Thorburn produced his interpretation of Jung's horoscope.[63] Thorburn's *Art and the Unconscious*, published in 1925, presents an unabashed criticism of Freudian theory in comparison with what Thorburn viewed as the inarguable importance of Jung's unique understanding of religious symbolism and the role of the imagination in creative work.[64] Thorburn was one of the original members of the Analytical Psychology Club of London,[65] and remained a member for many years, giving a paper to the Club in 1958 titled 'Do the Gods Exist?', which was later published in the Jungian journal *Harvest*.[66] He was also active in British astrological circles, and was a participant at the first formal British astrological conference, given at Harrogate in April 1939, at which a number of astrologers (although not all), in common with many of their European counterparts, issued misguidedly optimistic predictions that there would be no European war.[67] Although Thorburn had been Jung's patient, he was also a friend, and it seems he spent a considerable amount of his time in Zürich discussing astrology with Jung. This astrology was in part characterological, but it was not the kind of predictive analysis described in so many texts available at the time. It was a quasi-psychological, quasi-Theosophical astrology, focused primarily on the teleology of the individuation process.

Thorburn's analysis of Jung's natal chart is, at first glance, a fairly conventional character study. The chart was drawn on the distinctive pre-printed horoscope form first designed by Alan Leo.[69] However conventionally characterological some of Thorburn's statements might have been, his analysis also included some pointedly psychological references, such as the interpretation of particular planetary configurations as 'complexes'. For example, Thorburn referred to Jung's Sun in Leo in a quadrate (90°) angle to Neptune in Taurus as 'a "mystical" complex' which is 'the direct astrological equivalent of your mysticism and of your mystical

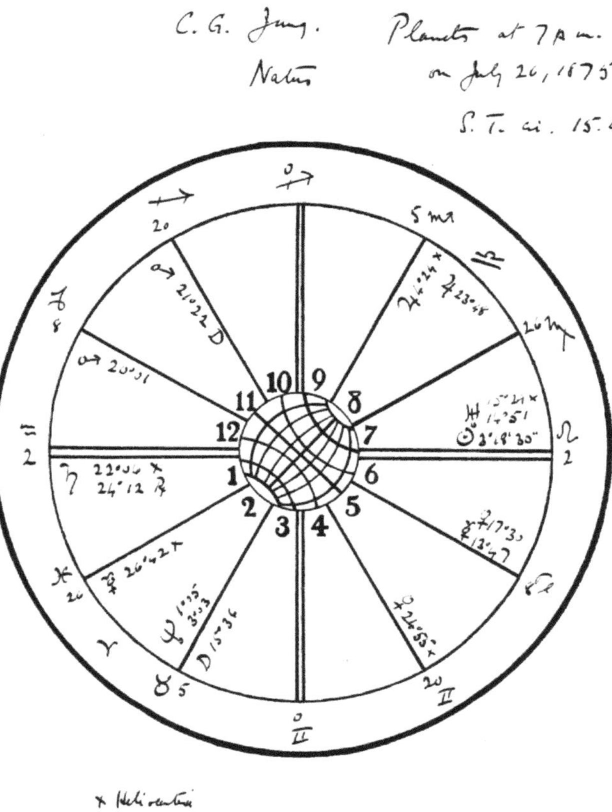

FIGURE 2.9 John M. Thorburn's drawing of Jung's natal chart, included in a letter dated 19 August 1928[68]

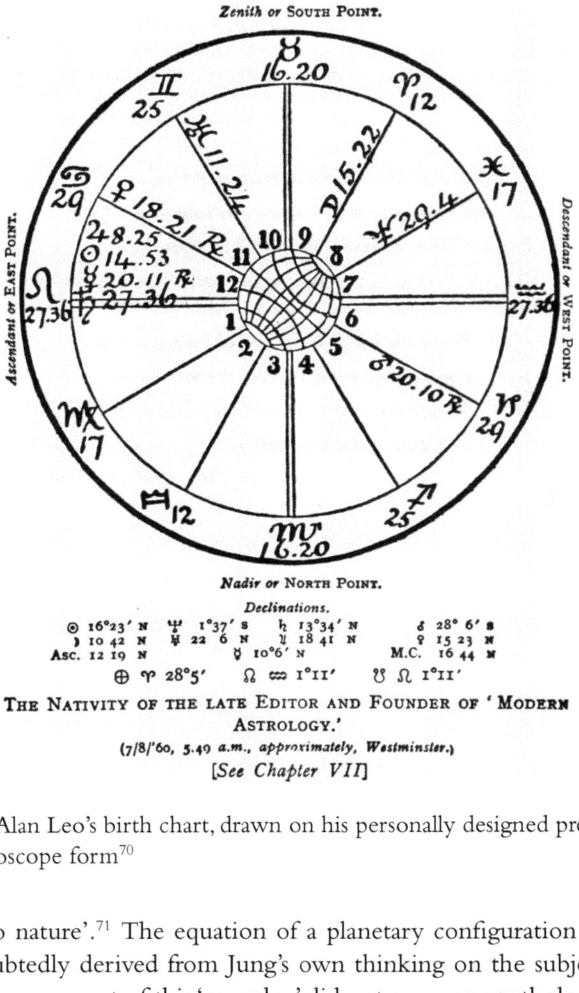

FIGURE 2.10 Alan Leo's birth chart, drawn on his personally designed pre-printed horoscope form[70]

orientation to nature'.[71] The equation of a planetary configuration with a complex is undoubtedly derived from Jung's own thinking on the subject, especially as Thorburn's assessment of this 'complex' did not carry any pathological implications. This reference in Thorburn's analysis is important in demonstrating how Jung's ideas about complexes related them to the relationships between the planets in the horoscope.

In one of his published papers, Thorburn declared Freud's psychoanalysis to be based on the function of 'sensation', in contrast to Jung, whose psychology was based on 'intuition', the opposite function.[72] In *Psychological Types*, Jung had asserted that individuals invariably perceive life through the bias of their own temperament; complete objectivity is an illusion, and the creation of any psychological 'system' is inevitably based on the psychologist's own individual psychology.[73]

> One sees what one can best see oneself. Thus, first and foremost, one sees the mote in one's brother's eye. No doubt the mote is there, but the beam sits in one's own eye – and may considerably hamper the act of seeing.[74]

Although Jung did not mention either his own or Freud's 'function type' in *Psychological Types*, he explicitly declared his typology in a letter to the German astrologer Oskar Schmitz, written in 1923: Jung considered himself 'a thinking intuitive introvert'.[75] Given the fact that the visions of *Liber Novus* were pervading his life at the time he was researching the text of *Psychological Types*, that work, without the need for specific personal revelations, also suggests how Jung understood his own temperament:

> Had this type [introverted intuition] not existed, there would have been no prophets in Israel . . . Introverted intuition apprehends the images arising from the *a priori* inherited foundations of the unconscious.[76]

Jung did not make specific equations between astrological elements and function types in his published work. But as an astrologer, he would have been fully aware of the fact that Freud was born under Taurus, an earthy sign (which Thorburn related to the function of sensation), while Jung himself was born under Leo, a fiery sign (which Thorburn related to intuition). Additionally, Jung's Ascendant, and that all-important chart ruler, Saturn, are both placed in the element of air (which Jung seems to have related to thinking). According to the logic of Jung's references to the balance or imbalance of elements in the chart of his patient, Miss X, the emphasis on air and fire in Jung's chart seems to fit with precision his assessment of his own typology as biased toward thinking and intuition. Thorburn's remarks on Freud's and Jung's respective typologies reflect an astrological perspective on the nature of the conflict between the two men – a collision between a world perceived through sensation and a world perceived through intuition – which Thorburn must have discussed with Jung himself. Thorburn's remarks thus highlight the importance of astrology in the development of Jung's typological model.

One of the most notable observations in Thorburn's interpretation of Jung's natal horoscope is his emphasis on the great importance of the planet Saturn. Thorburn's analysis opened with the bald statement: 'Saturn rises in Aquarius'. He went on to elaborate:

> We have here a strong, dignified and powerfully aspected Saturn without affliction. Now this is rather remarkable and, so far as my experience goes, very unusual . . . It must surely be a tremendous asset that 'the greater malefic' should be thus free and favoured in the natus . . . The trine[77] of Jupiter and Saturn in these signs [Libra and Aquarius respectively] is very strong evidence of life-work steadily pursued on behalf of mankind and in an unquestionable ethical and religious orientation.[78]

Thorburn's description echoes with uncanny accuracy the role that Philemon, the most important imaginal figure in *Liber Novus*, played throughout Jung's psychic life. The paradox of a planet known as the 'greater malefic', serving as a positive and creative guide of the soul's 'life-work', seems to reflect the ambiguity of Jung's archetypal 'wise old man' in *Liber Novus*. Philemon's relationship with the astrological Saturn is discussed in greater detail in *The Astrological World of Jung's* Liber Novus. Here it is sufficient to note that Jung took very seriously the idea that he was 'ruled' by Saturn. In a letter he wrote to the American author Upton Sinclair in 1955, Jung declared:

> The ruler of my birth, old Saturnus, slowed down my maturation process to such an extent that I became aware of my own ideas only at the beginning of the second half of life, i.e. exactly with 36 years.[79]

Jung was thirty-six years old in 1911, the year in which he informed Freud he was studying astrology and made public his disagreement with his mentor's theories through the publication of *Wandlungen*, the German version of *Psychology of the Unconscious*.

Thorburn's 'epoch' charts

Along with the interpretation of Jung's natal chart, Thorburn included a detailed interpretation of a chart which he titled 'Epoch'.

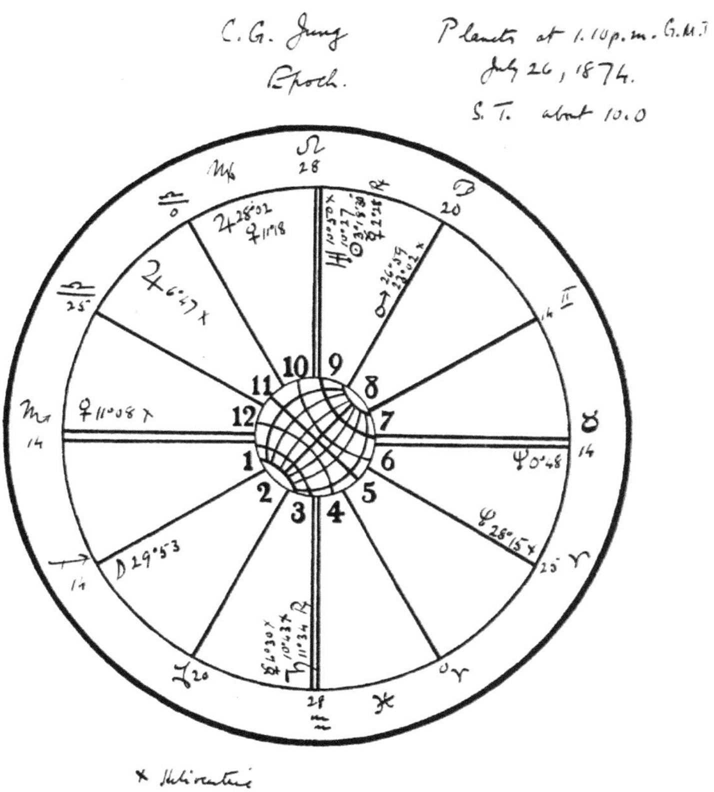

FIGURE 2.11 John M. Thorburn's drawing of Jung's 'Epoch' chart[80]

In Britain during the 1920s and 1930s, an astrological technique known as the 'Prenatal Epoch' came into fashion. It was based on an ancient theory known as the 'Trutine of Hermes', attributed to Hermes Trismegistus and mentioned in the second century CE by Vettius Valens in his *Anthologiarum Libri* and by Ptolemy in his *Tetrabiblos*.[81] The technique was fully developed in the Arab world in the tenth century, refined further in the medieval to early modern periods, and resurrected in the astrology of the early twentieth century.[82] The Prenatal Epoch is an effort to determine and interpret the horoscope for the moment of conception,[83] and was utilised by astrologers as a means of 'rectifying' or correcting a horoscope when the birth time was vague or inaccurate (a common problem in England, as the birth time is not usually recorded except in the case of twins). The Prenatal Epoch was also deemed to be useful as a means of investigating the possible causes for birth defects of various kinds. The technique is still in use today in some astrological circles, and computer software is available that will calculate it.[84]

A more esoteric interpretation of the Prenatal Epoch emerged in 1925, when the British Theosophical astrologer Walter Gorn Old (1864–1929), who wrote under the angelic pseudonym of Sepharial, published a work that transformed the technique into a means of determining the purpose of the soul's incarnation. Sepharial's underlying idea, in accord with Theosophical doctrines, was based on the belief that many successive lifetimes are required before the soul reaches its full spiritual potential. Sepharial proposed that the natal horoscope reflected the physical circumstances of a particular life; the Epoch chart, in contrast, indicated the 'astral' inheritance or soul-level of that life. The spiritual purpose of a given incarnation could be discerned in a hybrid of the Prenatal Epoch chart that Sepharial called the Solar Epoch.[85] Sepharial's book on the subject emphasised the spiritual nature of the Sun – a theme close to the heart of any Theosophical astrologer – in contrast to the biological nature of the Moon. Sepharial's work was quickly followed by other texts emphasising the spiritual potential of various forms of Epoch horoscopes.[86] In 1931, the astrologer A.E. Thierens (1875–1941) openly declared his allegiance to Madame Blavatsky and her seminal work, *The Secret Doctrine*, and called Sepharial's Solar Epoch chart a map of 'the solar nature of Man's being'.[87]

Various technical permutations of Sepharial's Solar Epoch produced a plethora of interpretative innovations. The Epoch chart that John Thorburn sent to Jung is one of these innovations. It was calculated for the moment the Sun was in the precise position it had occupied at the time and place of Jung's birth, but exactly one solar revolution earlier, in July 1874, when the other heavenly bodies were in positions entirely different from those in Jung's natal chart.[88] Drawing on the Theosophical idea of the Sun as a symbol of the divine spark in the incarnate human being, Thorburn's interpretation of Jung's Epoch chart was concerned with the 'spiritual purpose' of Jung's life. Thorburn referred to a theme that appears repeatedly in *Liber Novus*: the nature of magic.

> Hence we might regard this as the horoscope of a magician . . . These [configurations] stress philosophic reflection, religion, and, generally, spiritual masterfulness – a spirituality which also dominates within as well as without.

> Regeneration . . . might, therefore, be a better general characterisation than magic.[89]

Thorburn also identified the nature of Jung's 'life problem' in Jung's own language – the 'relation of unconscious to conscious' – and then declared that the configurations of the Epoch chart made Jung 'a prophet, a teacher, appropriating ideas from an elemental source or applying them through an elemental medium'.[90] This is not a simple character analysis, but a declaration of how Thorburn understood astrology as a psychological and spiritual tool, able to highlight the essential challenges and ultimate purpose of Jung's life and work.

Thorburn placed great value on his Epoch chart as a key to the goal of individuation. He also produced an Epoch chart for Emma Jung, who, apparently impressed by the interpretation of her husband's chart, requested it from Thorburn herself.[91] Although the Epoch chart was undoubtedly a topic of conversation between Thorburn and Jung during their various meetings in Zürich, no other charts of this kind appear in Jung's private archives; it seems that Jung did not attempt to work with the technique himself. Nevertheless, Thorburn was able to provide the kind of astrology in which Jung was most interested: an astrology of the psyche and the soul, amenable to interpretation through psychological models, and reflecting a teleology and pattern of inner development – 'individuation' – that could be facilitated and enhanced through analytic work.

Jung's influence on astrology

Jung acquired numerous interpretations of his own horoscope from other astrologers. Although the zodiacal and planetary placements were always the same in each of these versions of his natal chart (with the exception of Thorburn's Epoch chart), it seems that Jung sought a variety of approaches, as well as information on the planetary movements at specific times in his life. The natal chart provided by John Thorburn was accompanied by a written analysis. So was another horoscope, prepared for Jung by the Zürich-born analytical psychologist Liliane Frey-Rohn (1901–1991). Frey-Rohn's material consists of a detailed list of planetary movements from Jung's birth to 1945,[92] including brief interpretations of the important configurations for each successive year. Frey-Rohn was an accomplished astrologer as well as an analytical psychologist, and acted as Jung's assistant in the astrological 'experiment' that formed the basis for Jung's essays on synchronicity.[93] In an interview with the clinical psychologist Gene F. Nameche, Frey-Rohn stated that when she first met Jung, he advised her to do astrological research with schizophrenics at the Burghölzli Clinic. 'Later', she told Nameche, 'he gave dates of birth and would want to know if this person can become schizophrenic or not'.[94]

The material Frey-Rohn sent to Jung was accompanied by an undated letter but, as she included a horoscope displaying the progressed planetary placements for 1939–40 and refers in her letter to Jung's request for information on these years, it is likely that the material was prepared in 1939, at the time of the outbreak of the Second World War.[95]

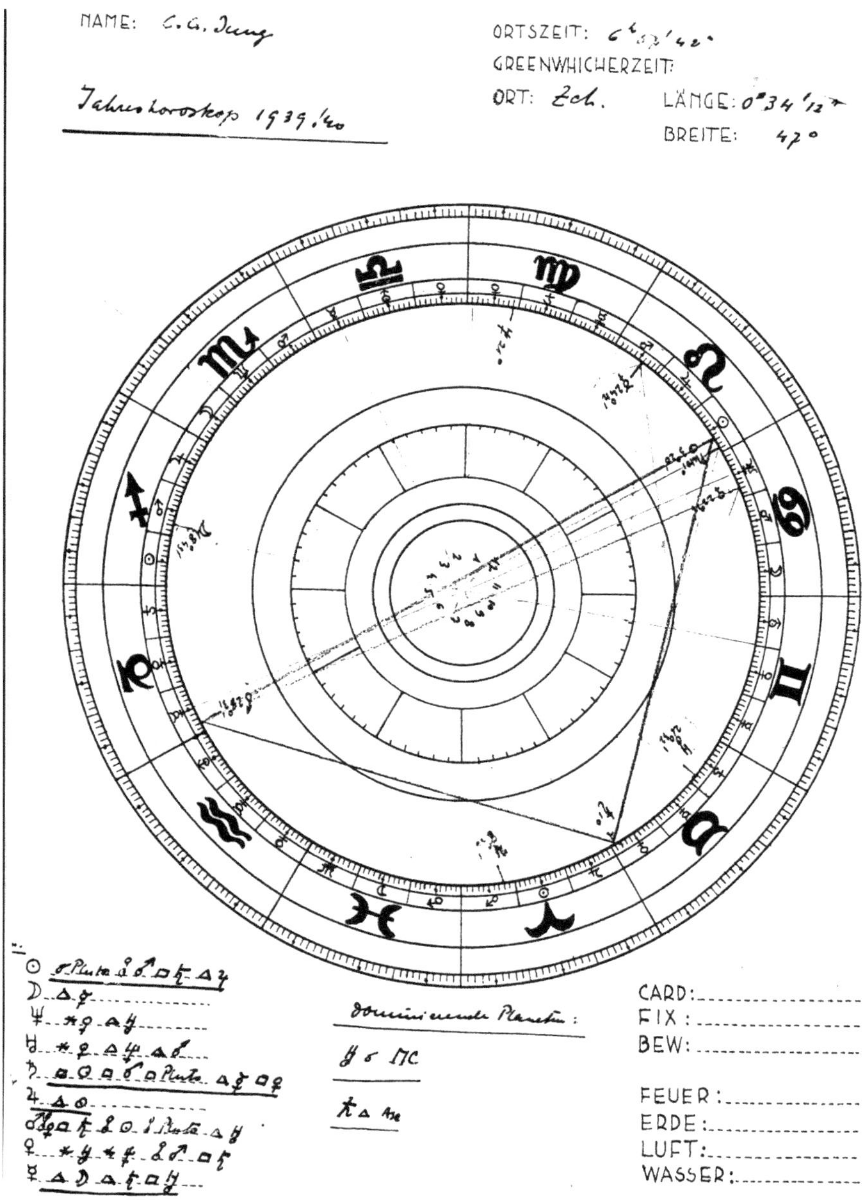

FIGURE 2.12 Progressed horoscope for Jung for 1939–40, drawn by Liliane Frey-Rohn[96]

Other versions of Jung's horoscope were apparently discussed with him in person, as no written analyses accompany the horoscopes in the archives. One of these horoscopes was, like Thorburn's, drawn on Alan Leo's distinctive pre-printed horoscope form. It includes both Jung's natal horoscope and the planetary positions for 1926, two years before Thorburn sent his own interpretation to Jung.

Accompanying this chart are several pages consisting of a 'keyword' analysis of the main configurations in Jung's birth horoscope, as well as lengthier paragraphs on the four chief astrological significators: Sun, Moon, Ascendant, and Jung's planetary ruler, 'Old Saturnus'. A further page lists important planetary movements in 1928–30 – the same period in which Jung was receiving materials from the Rosicrucian Fellowship and was corresponding with Thorburn. The individual who compiled this material signed it 'M.C. Bond'. That he or she was an American is identifiable, not only from the manner in which the dates are written, but also because Bond included his/her own horoscope along with Jung's. Although no birthplace is given, the longitude and latitude indicate that Bond was born in Washington, D.C. This individual, who was eight years older than Jung, may have been Jung's patient. But Bond was also a competent astrologer who utilised the horoscope forms associated, once again, with Alan Leo's Theosophical astrology.

Jung was evidently deeply concerned with the direction his life was taking in the late 1920s, as he approached the end of his work on *Liber Novus*. But the nature of this concern is unclear. He was travelling extensively during the mid-1920s, visiting East Africa and the Pueblo Indians in North America. In 1929 he published his commentary on Richard Wilhelm's translation of the Chinese *I Ching*, titled *The Secret of the Golden Flower*, although it was several years later that he realised the full importance of alchemical symbolism as a symbolic mapping of the individuation process.[98] Thorburn provided analyses only of Jung's natal and Epoch horoscopes, with no information about later planetary movements. Jung might have wanted insight into some personal dilemma through an interpretation of the prevailing astrological factors. He may also have noticed some approaching configuration of importance and wanted to understand its meaning. In viewing the planetary movements in his chart during this period, he might have observed, for example, a transit of the planet Saturn over the 'midheaven' or *Medium Coeli* of the natal horoscope in the late autumn of 1926. Alan Leo described this transit as bringing 'failure, scandal, trouble with superiors and loss of honour and credit' unless the individual was 'cultured and refined', in which case the transit signified 'the undertaking of great responsibilities'.[99] It is possible that Jung hoped to avoid the former and pursue the latter.

The influence of astrology on Jung's thinking was penetrating and profound, as was his own influence on modern astrologies. Despite determined efforts by more 'traditional' astrologers who, like Alfred Pearce at the end of the nineteenth century, oppose the marriage of astrology and psychology, Jung's impact on astrology shows no sign of abating.[100] This influence began, not during his later years, or during the 1970s when 'New Age' ideas were in full flower, but during the period in which Jung worked on *Liber Novus*. Jung's efforts to convince his fellow psychologists that astrology could provide an important tool for psychology, and that psychology could enrich astrology, were immediately successful in certain circles. Heinz Arthur Strauss, an astrologer and historian of astrology, and his wife Sigrid Strauss-Klöbe, a psychotherapist, worked within a uniquely German astrological current known as *Kosmobiologie*, which developed in the late 1920s and early 1930s and espoused the idea that cosmic energies influence biological processes on earth.[101] *Kosmobiologie*

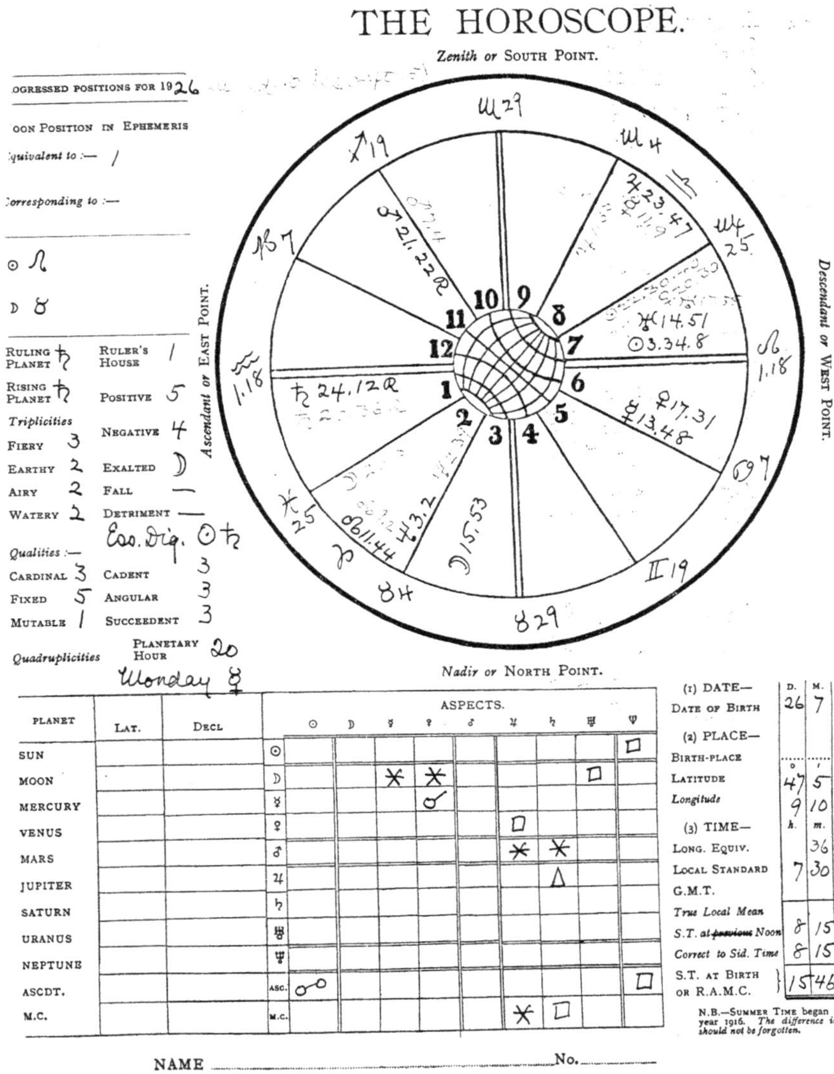

FIGURE 2.13 Natal chart for Jung by M.C. Bond, with progressed planetary placements for 1926[97]

was one of the first fields of astrology to emphasise the importance of research findings from a variety of scientific disciplines, with a particular focus on medical astrology. From 1927 to 1928, Strauss edited a journal called *Jahrbuch für kosmobiologische Forschung*, which contained papers on medical astrology and its rationale. Jung acquired both volumes of this journal.[102]

At this point, the influence seemed to be flowing one way. Jung, at the same time he was receiving astrological interpretations from John Thorburn, M.C. Bond, and the Rosicrucian Fellowship, was reading the work of Strauss and Strauss-Klöbe to deepen his own understanding of astrology. But the direction of the influence quickly changed. Strauss and his wife were both involved in the publication of Wilhelm's *The Secret of the Golden Flower*. In Jung's memorial address for Wilhelm, given in 1930, he stated that the *I Ching*, the subject of Wilhelm's book, was 'not only analogous to astrology, but essentially related to it'.[103] At the second Eranos conference, held in Ascona in 1934, Sigrid Strauss-Klöbe, who had clearly been reading Jung's writings in the interim, delivered a paper titled 'The Psychological Significance of the Symbol in Astrology'.[104] Jung, who had also delivered a paper at the conference,[105] responded to Strauss-Klöbe's presentation by declaring that she was 'the first person to think deeply about the astrological symbols in terms of psychology'[106] – perhaps a reflection, not only of Strauss-Klöbe's insights, but also of Jung's low estimation of many of the astrological texts available to him at the time. Strauss-Klöbe was already familiar with psychoanalytic theories, but in 1935, a year after the Eranos conference, she decided to work with Jung as his patient.[107] Her astrological publications in subsequent years increasingly incorporated Jung's theories of types, complexes, myths, and archetypes.[108] Deeply influenced by Jung's ideas for the remainder of her life, in 1982 Strauss-Klöbe contributed a short essay titled 'Memory of C.G. Jung' in the memorial volume, *C. G. Jung, Emma Jung, and Toni Wolff*.[109] Strauss-Klöbe and her husband are examples of a trend in German astrology that directly owed to Jung its focus on the psychological rather than the literal.

Another German astrologer, Oskar Adolf Hermann Schmitz (1873–1931),[110] considered himself Jung's pupil by virtue of his attendance at some seminars Jung gave in Zürich in 1925.[111] Although Schmitz was a great admirer of Jung's theory of psychological types and was active in disseminating Jung's ideas through his own publications,[112] Jung had little sympathy with the views propounded by the esoteric group with which Schmitz was involved. Jung compared it with Theosophy, which was itself a 'danger' because

> A new house is being erected on the old, unsatisfactory foundations and new wine poured in old bottles . . . Man must after all first be changed from the inside.[113]

According to Ellic Howe (1910–91), a British historian of twentieth-century occultism, a diversity of astrologies began to emerge in Germany during the inter-war years, including those influenced by Blavatsky's Theosophy, Steiner's Anthroposophy, and various magical groups allied with these movements. The Germans, according to Howe, were 'the first to discuss the idea of what they called "psychological astrology."'[114] Howe does not mention Strauss-Klöbe, nor the importance of the Eranos conferences in the development of this marriage of psychology and astrology. He does discuss Schmitz, whom he calls 'the enthusiastic disciple of C. G. Jung', but suggests that Schmitz' influence was minimal in the astrological community.[115] However, Howe overlooks not only Jung's pervasive influence on German astrologers such as Strauss-Klöbe, whose books were reprinted in numerous editions, but also the indirect influence on many currents of esoteric thought exercised internationally by the Eranos conferences and their speakers and attendees, virtually all of whom were sympathetic, to a greater or lesser extent, to Jung's theories on the archetypes and the psychological types.

Symbols and doctrines

Despite Jung's distaste for the doctrinal nature of Theosophy, the unexpectedly fruitful three-way union of Theosophical ideas with analytical psychology and astrology bred a number of interesting hybrids during the 1920s and 1930s. Virtually none of these hybrids enjoyed Jung's approval. He strongly opposed any effort to exteriorise the archetypal realm, insisting that the interpretations offered by Theosophy and Anthroposophy were problematic because they objectified the archetypes rather than recognising them as inner processes.

> I would never want my conception of the unconscious to be even remotely associated with parapsychology, for then the unconscious would take on a concretized form, making impossible the psychological approach that is so necessary for us . . . We must continue for quite a long time to stick to the territory of critical psychology if we want to avoid the danger of conjuring up a new Theosophy. One cannot be too careful to guard against the temptation to regard the manifestations of mysticism and parapsychology from the outside . . . The whole thrust of analytical psychology is to open up the territory from inside, that is from within the soul.[116]

Jung's understanding of the zodiacal images as imaginal projections by the human unconscious, generated through an intuitive understanding of the qualities of cyclical time, reflects his insistence on an interior approach to astrological symbols. The planetary 'gods' are found within, and can only be dealt with on a psychological level by the individual. This approach is not found in the discussions by astrologers such as Schmitz, although it is evident in Strauss-Klöbe's work and, despite the thick overlay of Theosophical language, can be discerned in a nascent form – perhaps unintentionally – in the works of Alan Leo.

The boundaries between 'spiritual' and 'psychological' realms, both of them liminal, are full of hidden doorways, unknown tunnels, and secret windows, as Jung himself was well aware. The terms themselves are a modern imposition of constructed categories that would have meant nothing to Iamblichus, Plotinus, Agrippa, or Paracelsus. *Psuche* is the Greek word for 'soul', and *logos* the word for 'speech'; and the term 'psychology', considered in the context of its etymological roots, bears little resemblance to some of the perspectives now offered in the academy. But Jung was not merely being self-protective in trying to avoid the label of 'mysticism' that Freud had prophesied he would end up having to carry. He seems to have felt deeply that any astrological insight had to be understood as a psychological dynamic, without attempts to exteriorise and concretise its symbols. In this he agreed with Plotinus, who embraced the idea of cosmic 'sympathies' but understood them as a web of symbols linked through meaning, rather than a network of 'influences' or, as the Theosophist Alice A. Bailey insisted, 'rays' emanating from deified planetary beings.[117]

Alice Bailey's approach, and the astrological currents that sprang from her teachings, achieved precisely what Jung had tried to forestall at Eranos: they incorporated his ideas into an astrology wedded to an exteriorised religious cosmology, rather than presenting astrology psychologically, as an interior process. In America, the highly influential French-born astrologer Dane Rudhyar (1895–1985), whose work remains enduringly popular in many astrological circles, trained in Alice Bailey's Arcane School, an offshoot of the Theosophical Society. Rudhyar encountered Jung's work during the 1930s.[118] He began mentioning Jung in *The Astrology of Personality*, first published in 1936 by Bailey's own press, the Lucis Trust. In this early work, Rudhyar used terms such as 'The Synchronistic Principle', and devoted an entire chapter to 'Astrology and Analytical Psychology', quoting freely from a number of Jung's *Collected Works*.

However, Rudhyar then went on to speak of a 'spiritual psychology', related to but fundamentally different from analytical psychology, that 'considers man to be essentially and in reality a spiritual being using a body for the purpose of acquiring concrete experiences and certain faculties which can be generated only in contact with matter'.[119] In this 'Jungianist' underpinning of a cosmology that assumes the ontological independence of higher spiritual powers governing a spiritually evolving universe, Rudhyar demonstrated his allegiance to his Theosophical roots.[120] Jung was aware of Rudhyar, and acquired *The Astrology of Personality* in its original edition, as well as one of Rudhyar's early works on music.[121] But Jung never mentioned this well-known astrologer in his published works or letters, nor did he purchase any of Rudhyar's later books; nor is there any evidence of any correspondence between them. Despite Rudhyar's importance in American astrological circles, Jung may have viewed Rudhyar, as he viewed Schmitz, as too concretely doctrinal in his pronouncements, despite the fact that many of Rudhyar's ideas about the teleology of the birth horoscope were inspired by Jung's own concept of individuation.

Jung's prophecy that astrology would be 'assured recognition by psychology' may seem doomed to failure. Many psychologists, particularly in the clinical sphere, are far more reluctant to acknowledge astrology than astrologers are to acknowledge psychology. But in the currents of depth and transpersonal psychologies, astrology, as Jung perceived it, has been found to be useful and enlightening.[122] The cross-fertilisation between Jung's astrology and Jung's astrologers – and between Jung's astrology and the various depth and transpersonal psychologies that have emerged from his work – is proving to be a rich and enduring one.

Notes

1 Plotinus, Ennead II.3.7.
2 Jung, *Liber Novus*, pp. 136–37, trans. p. 310.
3 For Ptolemy, see above, Chapter 1, n. 66. For Abu Ma-shar (Albumasar), see Jung, CW9ii, ¶¶128, 131–33, 153–54. For Cardanus, see Jung, CW8, ¶869; Jung, CW9i, ¶436; Jung, CW9ii, ¶¶130 and 136; Jung, CW14, ¶474.

4 Jung, CW8, ¶¶816–968.
5 J.B. Rhine, *Extra-Sensory Perception* (Boston, 1934); J.B. Rhine, *New Frontiers of the Mind* (New York: Farrar & Rinehart, 1937). See Jung, CW8, ¶833, n. 29.
6 Karl Ernst Krafft, *Le premier traité d'astro-biologie* (Paris: Wyckmans, 1939); Paul Flambart (a.k.a. Paul Choisnard), *Preuves et bases de l'astrologie scientifique* (Paris: Bibliothèque Chacornac, 1921).
7 For Philo's *De opificio mundi*, see Jung, CW8, ¶855. For Plotinus' *Enneads*, see Jung, CW8, ¶927. For Schopenhauer's *Parega und Paralipomena*, see Jung, CW8, ¶829.
8 Private letter from Ulrich Hoerni, 15 December 2012.
9 Noll, 'Jung the *Leontocphalus*', p. 67. Noll gives no source for this statement.
10 James Holden, 'Preface to the 2006 Reprint', in Pearce, *The Text-Book of Astrology*, p. vii.
11 Cited in Curry, *A Confusion of Prophets*, p. 111.
12 See, for example, Alfred J. Pearce, *The Science of the Stars* (London: Simpkin, Marshall, 1881), and *The Weather Guide-Book: A Concise Exposition of Astronomic-Meteorology* (London: Simpkin, Marshall, 1864).
13 These included *The Future*, launched in 1892 and discontinued in 1894; *Urania*; and *Star Lore*. Pearce was also editor of the popular annual *Zadkiel's Almanac*, likewise absent from Jung's library.
14 Jung's issues of *The Occult Review* comprise four volumes dated from 1920–33. The issues of *The Quest* which Jung collected extend over many years (1910–24 and 1929–30), and comprise seventeen volumes.
15 Raphael, *The Key to Astrology* (London: W. Foulsham, 1896).
16 See Kim Farnell, 'Seven Faces of Raphael', <www.skyscript.co.uk/raphael.html>.
17 See Curry, *A Confusion of Prophets*, pp. 46–60. The similarity of names between Robert Cross Smith and Robert Thomas Cross appears to be coincidental (or synchronous).
18 For Alan Leo's life and work, see Curry, *A Confusion of Prophets*, pp. 122–59; Bessie Leo, *The Life and Work of Alan Leo* (London: Modern Astrology Office/N.L. Fowler, 1919); Campion, *A History of Western Astrology*, pp. 231–34.
19 Bessie Leo, *The Life and Work of Alan Leo*, p. 43. See also Campion, *A History of Western Astrology*, p. 232.
20 Leo, *The Life and Work of Alan Leo*, pp. 11–12.
21 For Blavatsky's discussions about the 'Invisible Sun', see Blavatsky, *Isis Unveiled: A Master-Key to the Mysteries of Ancient and Modern Science and Theology*, 2 volumes (London: Theosophical Publishing, 1877), Vol. 1, p. 302; Blavatsky, *The Secret Doctrine: The Synthesis of Science, Religion, and Philosophy*, 2 volumes (London: Theosophical Publishing, 1888), Vol. 1, p. 100.
22 See Greene, *The Astrological World of Jung's 'Liber Novus'*, chapter 2.
23 Alan Leo, *Astrology for All, Parts I and II* (London: Modern Astrology Office, 1899; repr. 1904, 1912, 1921, and many subsequent editions).
24 A German ephemeris called *Planeten-Calendarium*, listing the planetary positions for 1906, is included in Jung's library.
25 Jung's first daughter, Agathe, was born on 28 December 1904; his second daughter, Gret, was born on 8 February 1906. The year 1906 was not included in the table of sidereal times given in Jung's edition of Leo's *Astrology for All*, Part II; the table ends in 1904, the date of the book's publication. Jung added the sidereal times for 1906, 1907, and 1908 in pencil at the bottom of the column on p. 182. Jung's son Franz was born in 1908.
26 Jung's copy of Leo's *How to Judge a Nativity* is also heavily marked in pencil.
27 © 2007 Foundation of the Works of C.G. Jung, Zürich.
28 For van Ophuijsen, see his listing in *The International Dictionary of Psychoanalysis*, 3 volumes, ed. Alain de Mijolla (Farmington Hills, MI: Cengage Gale, 2004), and the references given there.
29 Alan Leo, *The Key to Your Own Nativity* (London: Modern Astrology Office, 1910).
30 Leo, *The Key to Your Own Nativity*, p. 283.
31 Leo, *The Key to Your Own Nativity*, p. 21.
32 These planetary movements are known as 'secondary progressions'; for this astrological technique, see Alan Leo, *The Progressed Horoscope* (London: Modern Astrology Office, 1905).

33 Jung private archives, reprinted courtesy of Andreas Jung, © 2007 Foundation of the Works of C.G. Jung, Zürich.
34 See Frances A. Yates, *The Rosicrucian Enlightenment* (London: Routledge & Kegan Paul, 1972), pp. 294–322, for English translations of the three treatises.
35 See Joscelyn Godwin, *The Theosophical Enlightenment* (Albany: SUNY Press, 1994), pp. 216–22; Roland Edighoffer, 'Rosicrucianism: From the Seventeenth to the Twentieth Century', in Antoine Faivre and Jacob Needleman (eds.), *Modern Esoteric Spirituality* (New York: Crossroad, 1992), pp. 186–209. For literature from modern groups associating themselves with the original Rosicrucian 'order', see H. Spencer Lewis, *Rosicrucian Questions and Answers with Complete Answers* (San Jose, CA: Supreme Grand Lodge of AMORC, 1969); R. Swinburne Clymer, *The Rosy Cross* (Quakertown, PA: Beverly Hall, 1965). For an overview, see Christopher McIntosh, *The Rosicrucians* (York Beach, ME: Weiserbooks, 1998). For Theosophical and Anthroposophical interpretations, see A.E. Waite, *The Real History of the Rosicrucians* (London: George Redway, 1887); Rudolf Steiner, *The Secret Stream* (Great Barrington, MA: Anthroposophic Press, 2000).
36 See Jung, CW6, ¶¶314–16; Jung, CW7, ¶¶385, 494; Jung, CW9i, ¶652; Jung, CW10, ¶764; Jung, CW12, ¶¶99, 422; Jung, CW13, ¶391.
37 Waite wrote two books on the Rosicrucians: *The Real History of the Rosicrucians and the Brotherhood of the Rosy Cross* (London: William Rider & Son, 1924). Jung acquired the former and refers to it in Jung, CW14, ¶312, and Jung, CW16, ¶500. Jung had a number of other works by Waite, including books on the Tarot and the Kabbalah. For Waite, see R.A. Gilbert, *A.E. Waite* (Wellingborough: Crucible, 1987); Greene, *Magi and Maggidim*, pp. 301–76.
38 The Rosicrucian Fellowship can be found at <www.rosicrucianfellowship.org/>. There are other current Rosicrucian organisations, including the American AMORC (Ancient Mystical Order Rosae Crucis) and the British SRIA (Societas Rosicruciana in Anglia), both of which have their own websites.
39 For Steiner's work, see, among many other books, Rudolf Steiner, *The Way of Initiation*, trans. Max Gysi (London: Theosophical Publishing Society, 1910); Rudolf Steiner, *An Outline of Occult Science*, trans. Max Gysi (London: Theosophical Publishing Society, 1914). See also Gilbert Childs, *Rudolf Steiner* (Hudson, NY: Anthroposophic Press, 1996).
40 Jung, CW10, ¶170; Jung, CW11, ¶859.
41 See Hanegraaff, *New Age Religion*, pp. 496–513.
42 For an effort by an Anthroposophist to find common ground between Jung and Steiner, see Gerhard Wehr, *Jung and Steiner*, trans. Magdalene Jaeckel (Great Barrington, MA: Anthroposophic Press, 2002).
43 See also Max Heindel, *Simplified Scientific Astrology* (London: L.N. Fowler, 1928).
44 Books, as I was assured by Andreas Jung, tend to 'walk' from private libraries after the death of their owner, due to the claims of family members and friends; many of Jung's astrological texts found their way into the library of his daughter Gret (1906–95), who was herself a practicing astrologer. As Jung did not usually write his name in his books, it is impossible to ascertain which works in Gret's astrological library might have initially belonged to him.
45 Heindel, *Simplified Scientific Astrology*, p. 201.
46 © 2007 Foundation of the Works of C.G. Jung, Zürich.
47 © 2007 Foundation of the Works of C.G. Jung, Zürich.
48 A number of charts for Jung's patients are signed with the initials of an unknown individual, 'BW'. Two identical charts were set up for Toni Wolff, one by Emma Jung and one in another unknown hand. Some of the charts were given to Jung by the individuals themselves. Astrological glyphs, when drawn by hand, reflect the same individual peculiarities as handwriting. Identification of Jung's astrological handwriting, in contrast to Emma's, was kindly given to me by Vreni Jung, the wife of Andreas Jung; Frau Jung is well versed in graphology.
49 © 2007 Foundation of the Works of C.G. Jung, Zürich. Compare the planetary glyphs with those in the *Systema Munditotius*, discussed in Greene, *The Astrological World of Jung's 'Liber Novus'*, chapter 7.

50 © 2007 Foundation of the Works of C.G. Jung, Zürich. The handwriting for these calculations, and the name 'Jung' written across the top of the page, is identical to the first page of Jung's habilitation thesis, reproduced in Shamdasani, *Jung*, p. 43.
51 Heindel, *Simplified Scientific Astrology*, p. 160.
52 Max Heindel, *The Message of the Stars* (Oceanside, CA: Rosicrucian Fellowship, 1918), p. 192.
53 Heindel, *The Message of the Stars*, p. 28.
54 Heindel, *The Message of the Stars*, p. 10. Virgo 'ascendant at midnight' at the winter solstice refers to the relationship of the Sun to the zodiacal sign rising in the east. In northern latitudes, in the moments before midnight at the solstice, the Sun, entering the zodiacal sign of Capricorn, is about to arrive at the *Imum Coeli*, the north or 'midnight' point, associated with death and rebirth; at this time, the last few degrees of Virgo are rising in the east.
55 For a recent discussion of the solar mythology related to Christ, see David Fideler, *Jesus Christ, Sun of God* (Wheaton, IL: Quest Books/Theosophical Publishing House, 1993).
56 F. Max Müller, *Lectures on the Origin and Growth of Religions as Illustrated by the Religions of India* (London: Longmans, Green, 1878), p. 213.
57 F. Max Müller, *Theosophy* (London: Longmans, Green, 1917); F. Max Müller, *Vorlesungen über den Ursprung und die Entwickelung der Religion* (Strasbourg: Trübner, 1880).
58 Jung, CW9ii, ¶¶164–66 and 194. Jung may have derived the image of Virgo holding a child from any of the sources given above. However, in most astrological texts, the female figure representing Virgo holds an ear of wheat rather than a baby.
59 Birth data according to the two horoscopes in Jung's private archives: Antonia Anna Wolff, 18 September 1888, 2.30 pm, Zürich.
60 Jung, CW9i, ¶¶604–605.
61 By 'born under', Jung seems to have meant that Cancer was rising on the eastern horizon (the Ascendant) at the time of Miss X's birth. Alan Leo used this phrase to describe the Ascendant rather than the zodiacal sign in which the Sun was placed at birth; see, for example, Leo, *The Art of Synthesis*, p. 203.
62 John M. Thorburn, Letter to Emma Jung, 15 February 1929, Jung Private Archives. 'David' Baynes is Helton Godwin Baynes (1882–1943); he and his wife Cary Fink Baynes (1883–1977) were close friends of Jung and the translators into English of a number of Jung's works.
63 See J.M. Thorburn, 'Mysticism and Art', *The Monist* 30:4 (1920), pp. 599–617; J.M. Thorburn, *Art and the Unconscious* (London: Kegan Paul, Trench, Trubner, 1925); J.M. Thorburn, 'Analytical Psychology and the Concept of Individuality', *International Journal of Ethics* 35:2 (1925), pp. 125–39; J.M. Thorburn, A.H. Hannay, and P. Leon, 'Artistic Form and the Unconscious', *Proceedings of the Aristotelian Society* 13 (1934), pp. 119–58.
64 See Thorburn, *Art and the Unconscious*, pp. 39–80, in which Thorburn quotes and paraphrases extensively from Jung's *Psychology of the Unconscious*. See also Jung, CW15, ¶¶133–162.
65 See Diana Baynes Jansen, *Jung's Apprentice* (Einsiedeln, Switzerland: Daimon Verlag, 2003), p. 271.
66 J.M. Thorburn, 'Do the Gods Exist?', *Harvest* 6 (1959), pp. 72–87.
67 For Thorburn's participation at this conference, see 'Astrologers' Weekend', *Picture Post: Hulton's National Weekly*, 29 April 1939, pp. 3–4.
68 © 2007 Foundation of the Works of C.G. Jung, Zürich.
69 Leo was deceased by the time Thorburn drew up Jung's chart, but his printed horoscope forms remained available. Many astrology schools at the time tended to use their own unique printed horoscope forms. Leo's forms always displayed a diagram of the globe at the centre, with the horizon and meridian axes of the horoscope marked with a double line. Examples of this distinctive wheel can be found in Leo, *The Art of Synthesis*, pp. 228, 232, and 238.
70 The chart appears in Leo, *The Progressed Horoscope*, p. xvi.
71 John M. Thorburn, 'Analysis of Jung's Natal Horoscope', Jung private archives, p. 4.
72 Thorburn, 'Analytical Psychology and the Concept of Individuality', p. 128.

73 Jung, CW6, ¶601.
74 Jung, CW6, ¶9.
75 Jung, Letter to Oskar Schmitz, 26 May 1923, in 'Letters to Oskar Schmitz', p. 82. In 1955 Jung declared: 'Everybody would call me an introvert'. See Stephen Black, 'The Stephen Black Interviews', in *C.G. Jung Speaking*, p. 256.
76 Jung, CW6, ¶¶658–59.
77 A 'trine' is an angle of 120° between two planets, generally interpreted as beneficial.
78 Thorburn, 'Analysis of Jung's Natal Horoscope', p. 1.
79 Jung, Letter to Upton Sinclair, 25 February 1955, in *C.G. Jung Letters*, Vol. 2, pp. 230–32.
80 © 2007 Foundation of the Works of C.G. Jung, Zürich.
81 See Robert Zoller, *Tools & Techniques of the Medieval Astrologer* (London: New Library, 2001), Book 1, p. 17.
82 For Arabic sources, see Zoller, *Tools & Techniques*, p. 22. For a medieval discussion, see Guido Bonatti, *Liber Astronomiae* (1277), ed. Robert Hand, trans. Robert Zoller (Berkeley Springs, WV: Golden Hind Press, 1994–96), Vol. 3, pp. 45–48.
83 The calculations are based on the idea of a relationship between the Moon as ruler of the formation of the embryo, and the Ascendant as designator of the moment of birth.
84 See http://astrozet.com/Manual/trutina.html.
85 Sepharial, *The Solar Epoch* (London: W. Foulsham, 1925). For Sepharial, see Kim Farnell, 'That Terrible Iconoclast: A Brief Biography of Sepharial', at <www.skyscript.co.uk/sepharial.html>. Sepharial had previously dedicated a chapter to the Prenatal Epoch in Sepharial, *The New Manual of Astrology* (Philadelphia, PA: David McKaym, 1898), Book 3, pp. 151–74. This earlier description of the technique follows the classical Trutine of Hermes in terms of Moon-Ascendant exchanges.
86 In 1928, George H. Bailey (1896–1959), a member of the Astrological Lodge of London, founded by Alan Leo in 1915, published an article titled, 'The Descent to Birth and the Soli-Lunar Interchanges', *Modern Astrology* (1928). Bailey's technique was used for 'rectification', a means of ascertaining a precise birth time.
87 A.E. Thierens, *Elements of Esoteric Astrology* (Philadelphia, PA: David McKay, 1931), pp. 145–47. Jung seems to have been mildly interested in Thierens' work and acquired another of his books, this time on the Tarot: A.E. Thierens, *The General Book of the Tarot* (London: Rider, 1930), with an introduction by A.E. Waite.
88 This chart is, in effect, a solar return chart for the year preceding Jung's birth. For various perspectives on solar return charts – calculated for each year of life and based on the return of the Sun to the precise degree and minute of its zodiacal sign at birth – see, among others, Lynn Bell, *Cycles of Light* (London: CPA Press, 2005); J. Lee Lehman, *Classical Solar Returns* (Atglen, PA: Schiffer, 2012).
89 John M. Thorburn, Jung 'Epoch' Chart, Jung private archives, pp. 2–3.
90 Thorburn, Jung's 'Epoch' Chart, p. 5.
91 In Thorburn's letter to Emma (15 February 1929), which included both her natal and 'Epoch' charts, he indicates that Emma had asked him for these charts in the previous September, and had also inquired how astrology could be used 'for individuation'.
92 These movements are calculated as 'Primary Directions', the name given to a method of progressing the horoscope forward from birth that originates in Ptolemy's *Tetrabiblos* and is still in use today. See Sepharial, *Directional Astrology* (London: Rider, 1921).
93 See Angela Graf-Nold, 'C.G. Jung's Position at the Swiss Federal Institute of Technology Zürich', *Jung History* 2:2, at <www.philemonfoundation.org/resources/jung_history/volume_2_issue_2>. For Frey-Rohn's major work on analytical psychology, see Liliane Frey-Rohn, *From Freud to Jung*, trans. Fred E. Engreen and Evelyn K. Engreen (New York: Putnam, 1976; repr. Shambhala/Daimon Verlag, 1990).
94 Liliane Frey-Rohn, Interview with Gene Nameche, C.G. Jung Biographical Archive 1968–73, Countway Library of Medicine, Harvard University, Interview 2, p. 25.
95 Jung personal archives, kindly provided by Andreas Jung, © 2007 Foundation of the Works of C.G. Jung, Zürich.
96 © 2007 Foundation of the Works of C.G. Jung, Zürich.

97 © 2007 Foundation of the Works of C.G. Jung, Zürich.
98 Richard Wilhelm, *Das Geheimnis der goldenen Blüte* (Munich: Dorn, 1929); published in English as *The Secret of the Golden Flower*, trans. Cary F. Baynes (London: Kegan Paul, Trench, Tubner, 1931). For Jung's late realisation of the psychological significance of alchemy, see Jung, *MDR*, pp. 229–31; Jung, CW13, 'Foreward to the Second German Edition', in Wilhelm, *Secret of the Golden Flower*, p. 4; Jung, *Liber Novus*, p. 360 and p. 305, n. 232.
99 The configuration was transiting Saturn moving over the Medium Coeli (MC) or south point of the natal chart; for a description, see Leo, *The Progressed Horoscope*, p. 263.
100 The name 'traditional' can be misleading. These currents emphasise the importance of Hellenistic and/or Arabic techniques, which reflect specific traditions within astrology. For a contemporary text on this approach, see Benjamin Dykes, *Traditional Astrology for Today* (St. Paul, MN: Cazimi Press, 2011). Jung, however, relied on the traditions of late antique Neoplatonic and Hermetic works that emphasised the interior, symbolic astrology in which he was interested. There are a number of 'traditions' within astrology, all apparently valid to those who pursue them.
101 For works by these authors, see Heinz Arthur Strauss, *Astrologie* (Leipzig: Kurt Wolff, 1977); Heinz Arthur Strauss and Sigrid Strauss-Klöbe, *Die Astrologie des Johannes Kepler* (Munich: Oldenbourg, 1926). The term 'Kosmobiologie' was later incorporated into the work of the astrologer Reinhold Ebertin (1901–88), sometimes considered the founder of the school. However, Strauss was using the concept more than a decade earlier than Ebertin, and the term itself can be dated to 1914.
102 See *C. G. Jung Bibliothek Katalog* DF 16–17.
103 Jung, 'Appendix: In Memory of Richard Wilhelm', in *The Secret of the Golden Flower*, p. 144. This memorial address was originally delivered on 10 May 1930.
104 Sigrid Strauss-Klöbe, 'Über die psychologische Bedeutung des astrologischen Symbols', in *Eranos Jahrbuch 1934, Band 2* (Zürich: Rhein-Verlag, 1935).
105 Jung, 'Über die Archetypen des kollektiven Unbewussten'. This paper first appeared in *Eranos Jahrbuch 1934*, and was revised, translated, and published in Jung, CW9i, pp. 3–41.
106 Hakl, *Eranos*, p. 96.
107 See Strauss-Klöbe's own statement in Ferne Jensen and Sidney Mullen (eds.), *C. G. Jung, Emma Jung, and Toni Wolff* (San Francisco, CA: Analytical Psychology Club of San Francisco, 1982), p. 90.
108 See Sigrid Strauss-Klöbe, *Kosmische Bedingtheit der Psyche* (Oberbayern: O.W. Barth, 1968); Sigrid Strauss-Klöbe, *Das kosmopsychische Phänomen* (Freiburg: Walter-Verlag, 1977); Heinz Arthur Strauss, *Psychologie und astrologische Symbolik* (Zürich: Rascher Verlag, 1953).
109 Jensen and Mullen (eds.), *C. G. Jung, Emma Jung, and Toni Wolff*, pp. 89–90.
110 For Schmitz, see André Barbault, *From Psychoanalysis to Astrology* (Munich: Hugendubel, 1991 [1961]); Carl-Ludwig Reichert, 'Oskar Adolf Hermann Schmitz', in *New German Biography*, Vol. 23 (Berlin: Duncker and Humblot, 2007), pp. 254–55.
111 For Schmitz' attendance at the seminar, see William McGuire, 'Introduction to the 1989 Edition', in Jung, *Introduction to Jungian Psychology*, p. xxxi. See also Jung's letters to Schmitz in Jung, 'Letters to Oskar Schmitz, 1921–1931', trans. James Kirsch, *Psychological Perspectives* 6:1 (1975), pp. 79–95. Three of these letters can be found in *C. G. Jung Letters*, Vol. 1, pp. 39–41, 53–54, 82.
112 See, for example, Oskar A.H. Schmitz, *Geist der Astrologie*, 2 volumes (Munich: Müller, 1922), in which Schmitz uses the term 'astro-psychology'. Jung had other works by Schmitz in his library, but they are not astrological. For Jung's references to Schmitz in the *Collected Works*, see Jung, CW9i, ¶51; Jung, CW10, ¶¶188 and 921; Jung, CW18, ¶1825. None of these references concerns astrology, but instead focus on the relationship between psychoanalysis and folklore. Jung also wrote an introduction to Schmitz' posthumously published *Märchen aus dem Unbewussten* (Munich: Karl Hanser, 1932), a work on fairy tales rather than astrology.
113 C.G. Jung, Letter to Oskar Schmitz, 26 May 1923, in 'Letters to Oskar Schmitz', p. 82.
114 Howe, *Urania's Children*, pp. 98–99.

115 Howe, *Urania's Children*, p. 99.
116 C.G. Jung, Letter to Gustav-Richard Heyer, 4 December 1931, cited in Hakl, *Eranos*, p. 66. Hakl points out that this letter stands as eloquent testimony against Richard Noll's 'simplistic criticism' of Jung's alleged promotion of a pagan mystical cult.
117 For Bailey's theory of the seven Rays, see Alice A. Bailey, *Esoteric Astrology* (New York: Lucis, 1951). Jung was familiar with Bailey's work through his Eranos contacts, and strongly opposed it; see Hakl, *Eranos*, pp. 27–32.
118 See Dane Rudhyar, 'Preface to the Third Edition', in Dane Rudhyar, *The Astrology of Personality* (New York: Doubleday, 1970 [1936]), pp. vii–xvi.
119 Rudhyar, *The Astrology of Personality*, pp. 75–82.
120 Rudhyar was an artist as well as a prolific writer who produced novels as well as works on music and art. Many of his astrological works focus on insightful horoscope interpretations; others, such as *The Planetarization of Consciousness* (New York: Harper, 1972), reveal his enduring devotion to Bailey's cosmology.
121 Dane Rudhyar, *The Rebirth of Hindu Music* (Adyar: Theosophical Publishing House, 1928).
122 See James Hillman, 'The Azure Vault: The Caelum as Experience', in Nicholas Campion and Patrick Curry (eds.), *Sky and Psyche* (Edinburgh: Floris Books, 2006), pp. 37–58). My knowledge of Hillman's involvement in astrology is based on personal contact and correspondence.

3

ACTIVE IMAGINATION AND THEURGY

> Of the works of theurgy performed on any given occasion, some have a cause that is secret and superior to all rational explanation, others are like symbols consecrated from all eternity to the higher beings, others preserve some other image, even as nature in its generative role imprints (upon things) visible shapes from invisible reason-principles.[1]
>
> —Iamblichus

> The Professor: 'Nowadays, the imitation of Christ leads to the madhouse'.
> Jung: 'That is hardly to be doubted, professor'.
> The Professor: 'The man has wit – he is obviously somewhat maniacally aroused. Do you hear voices?'
> Jung: 'You bet! Today it was a huge throng of Anabaptists that swarmed through the kitchen'.
> The Professor: 'Now, there we have it. Are the voices following you?'
> Jung: 'Oh no, Heaven forbid, I summoned them'.[2]
>
> —C.G. Jung

The origins of active imagination

Liber Novus, and the *Black Books* that gave rise to it, are the first documented evidence of Jung's use of a psychological technique he later called 'active imagination'. He had developed the technique no later than 1913, when work on *Liber Novus* began; *Liber Novus* is, in fact, the first fruit of it. Jung published his early thoughts on active imagination in 1916,[3] and again in 1921,[4] but he did not use the term itself until a series of lectures he gave at the Tavistock Clinic in London in 1935.[5] Initially he referred to it as the 'transcendent function', and then the 'picture method'; he also described it as 'active fantasy', 'trancing', 'visioning', 'exercises', and, perhaps most revealing, 'technique of the descent'.[6] Joan Chodorow, in the introduction to her edited selection of Jung's discussions on active imagination, points out that it is 'a single method, but it is expressed through many different forms'.[7] The method involves a specific type of meditation: deep concentration on, and emotional engagement with, images that have arisen in dreams, reveries, emotional eruptions, waking fantasies, or deliberately invoked altered states of consciousness. The imagination is understood as a kind of gateway or threshold into ordinarily inaccessible psychic realms, and as a means of giving shape to otherwise inchoate psychic realities.

In 1916, Jung described the entry point for active imagination as a turbulent emotional state:

> He must make the emotional state the basis or starting point of the procedure. He must make himself as conscious as possible of the mood he is in, sinking himself in it without reserve and noting down on paper all the fantasies and other associations that come up. Fantasy must be allowed the freest possible play, yet not in such a manner that it leaves the orbit of its object, namely the [emotional] affect.[8]

This description, written three years after Jung's break from Freud, is sometimes viewed as Jung's version of the psychoanalytic technique of 'free association', which Freud first described in 1893.[9] But Jung carefully distinguished between the two, describing active imagination as 'a sequence of fantasies produced by deliberate concentration':

> It is not a question of the 'free association' recommended by Freud for the purpose of dream analysis, but of elaborating the fantasy by observing the further fantasy material that adds itself to the fragment in a natural manner.[10]

The purpose of active imagination is thus not to provide material for an intellectual analysis of repressed conflicts, but rather, to allow that which is hidden and unknown to express itself in its own language – the language of images. Active imagination may also be seen as a form of ritual, akin to the focused states of religious contemplation found in the *kavvanah* or 'directed attention' of the Jewish Kabbalah, in certain forms of Sufi meditation, in Ignatius Loyola's 'spiritual exercises', and in Neoplatonic theurgy. These older approaches to an encounter with deity involve a deliberate suspension of the rational critical faculties in order to allow a specific image, colour, or sound to reveal its hidden life in its own way.[11] It is this kinship with religious practices, often those of marginalised or 'heretical' religious currents, that, in some circles, has given active imagination an esoteric connotation. And despite Jung's numerous elaborations, ambiguity continues to surround the sources that might have inspired the technique.

A number of recent works have described active imagination in practical therapeutic terms, and are intended to provide insights for the psychotherapist. But such investigations are, understandably, not concerned with the details of Jung's historical sources.[12] Marie-Louise von Franz (1915–98), one of the best-known of Jung's students and interpreters, distinguished between the various forms of Eastern meditation, which are aimed at ignoring the flow of images in meditative practice, and Jungian active imagination: 'In contrast to all Eastern techniques we welcome this image and do not dispel or ignore it'.[13] But von Franz' essay does not explore the origins of this apparently peculiarly Western favouring of the image in inner work. Jeffrey Raff, in a book titled *Jung and the Alchemical Imagination*, states emphatically that Jung's analytical psychology is a 'spiritual process' aimed at 'promoting profound transformational experience'.[14] While many who have undergone Jungian analysis might wholeheartedly agree with this comment, there is, as ever, a problem of definition. What does Raff mean by a 'spiritual' process in contrast to a 'psychological' one, and in what context should we understand a 'transformational experience'? Is it spiritual, psychological, physiological, or perhaps all three? Raff points out that, as Jung consistently referred to older esoteric traditions such as alchemy and Gnosticism, his psychological models are clearly connected with 'earlier esoteric schools'. Although this observation has been made by other authors as well, it is not developed in Raff's discussion. Raff is, in the context of his book, more concerned with the practical applications of active imagination than in examining just what the doctrines of these 'older esoteric schools' entailed, how they differed from each other, which of their ideas Jung adapted, and in what ways he utilised them.[15]

Active imagination bears an affinity with mediumistic trance-states.[16] Jung's interest in spiritualism, which led to his doctoral dissertation, *On the Psychology and Pathology of So-Called Occult Phenomena*,[17] supports the likelihood that his observations of the altered state of the trance medium contributed to the development of his ideas about the importance of the imagination in psychological work. Jung's explorations into spiritualist phenomena did not abate after he had completed his dissertation, and he was still attending seances in 1931, well after the completion of the text of *Liber Novus*.[18] These seances were organised by the Hermetische Gesellschaft, a Swiss group founded in 1930 by Rudolf Bernoulli (1880–1948), an art historian and Tarot practitioner; Fritz Allemann (1884–1968), a banker and financier who joined the Psychology Club of Zürich in 1930; and Oskar Rudolf Schlag (1907–1990), an esoterically inclined psychoanalyst, graphologist, and Freemason, whom Jung had met at the Burghölzli Clinic when Schlag was training there.[19] The group was focused on the symbolism of the Tarot, but also held seances. Jung, according to Schlag, was usually present at these seances until his expulsion 'was made necessary' due to friction between Jung and Schlag.[20] Although the Hermetische Gesellschaft was founded after Jung's work on *Liber Novus* was completed, his involvement reflects his continuing interest in the borderland between altered states of consciousness as a spontaneous psychological phenomenon and the deliberately provoked visions and experiences of automatic writing generated by what might be understood as ritual magic.

Jung's interest in the psychology of automatic writing was intense, as he strove to understand both his own experiences and the inspirational or revelatory work of other authors.[21] F.X. Charet, in a work titled *Spiritualism and the Foundation of C.G.*

Jung's Psychology, argues persuasively that Jung's early investigations, combined with the popularity of spiritualism and hypnotic trance-states in the late nineteenth century, exercised a major influence on his later work.[22] However, Charet's suggestion that spiritualism is the 'foundation' of Jung's psychological models may overemphasise one factor over others that were equally important. Jung was an incurable morphologist. In an effort to confirm his various theories through historical evidence as well as direct observation and experience, he sought to discern similar structural patterns in widely diverse systems of thought and belief. It may therefore be unwise to assume that any single current, whether religious, philosophical, or scientific, ancient, medieval, or modern, provided the sole theoretical or practical foundation for the technique of active imagination. Astrology was of great importance to Jung, and he seems to have explored it, not only intellectually, but also through active imagination; this application of astrology forms the subject matter of *The Astrological World of Jung's* Liber Novus. But astrology, for Jung, was not a discrete entity in itself. Rather, he perceived complex relationships between astrology and alchemy, magic, ritual, symbol, individual psychological transformation, and collective shifts in religious perception, and these interconnections preoccupied him throughout his life.

Charet has also emphasised Kant's philosophical discussions on the imagination as an important element in Jung's efforts to reconcile spiritualist phenomena with science.[23] A cogent argument could also be made for a relationship between active imagination and the Jewish Kabbalistic *kavvanah*, a form of meditation intended to effect transformations both internally and within the infrastructure of the godhead.[24] And, given the number of works on practical magic in Jung's library – ancient, medieval, and modern – a persuasive case could be argued for Jung's experimentation with ritual magic as a psychological technique for inducing altered states of consciousness.[25] Jung's Christian background likewise needs to be considered in relation to active imagination; various Christian theurgic rituals – especially the kind of intentional altered states developed in Eastern monasticism as early as the fourth century CE – may have also provided important elements in the development of Jung's technique.[26] These rituals were largely derived from Neoplatonic practices, discussed more fully below, and were utilised by the early sixth-century Christian philosopher Dionysius the Areopagite ('Pseudo-Dionysius'), with whose work Jung had become familiar by 1921.[27] In a seminar given in 1939, Jung explicitly referred to the late antique Christian mystics as predecessors of the technique of active imagination, because they used directed fantasy to achieve spiritual transformation.[28]

The 'spiritual exercises' of the sixteenth-century Jesuit priest Ignatius of Loyola, which Jung placed in the same category, were sufficiently interesting to impel him to deliver an entire lecture series on them at the ETH in Zürich in 1939.[29] According to Loyola, the individual must learn to 'see with the eyes of the imagination the length, breadth and depth of hell', and to respond to these visions with all of the senses.[30] Loyola is one of the most important Christian sources that Jung applied to his ideas about active imagination. Jung also made a direct link between Loyola's *exercitia spiritualia* and the Neoplatonic theories of the imaginal world offered by Plotinus, Iamblichus, Porphyry, and Proclus.[31] He referred to Loyola's *exercitia* as a 'special technique':

> It is a transformation experience induced by technical means . . . These exercises represent special techniques prescribed in advance and intended to achieve a definite psychic effect, or at least to promote it . . . They are, therefore, technical procedures in the fullest sense of the word; elaborations of the originally natural processes of transformation.[32]

This description follows a statement about 'magical procedures' as a similar, technically induced form of psycho-spiritual transformation: 'The rite is used for the express purpose of effecting the transformation'.[33] Religion and magic, in Jung's view, were evidently not as distinct from each other as was assumed by those scholars of his time who were influenced by Frazer's view of magic as a primitive form of religion that 'commits the mistake of assuming that things which resemble each other are the same'.[34] The kind of magic that interested Jung was not concerned with material gain, nor was it based on 'mistaken' analogies. Through the use of symbols, it was focused on the transformation of the personality through a direct experience of the archetypal dominants underpinning conscious life – modern psychological terminology for what was once understood as the *unio mystica*. Describing active imagination in more prosaic terms for the members of the Society for Psychical Research (SPR) in London in 1919, Jung referred to it as 'a means to bringing unconscious contents to consciousness'.[35] In this public setting, Jung was not prepared to offer any hint of its religious and magical significance in earlier sources or, for that matter, in his own private explorations, although he was in the midst of working on *Liber Novus* when he gave his paper to the SPR.

Jung was not the only researcher at the time to cross the border into the liminal zones. In the late nineteenth and early twentieth centuries, a number of psychologists were experimenting with a wide variety of unconventional psychotherapeutic techniques, such as automatic writing, crystal-gazing, and post-hypnotic suggestion, in an effort to understand more about the nature and dynamics of the unconscious.[36] Jung himself, from his descriptions of Elijah's crystal in *Liber Novus*, evidently tried out crystal-gazing (also known as 'scrying').[37] The researchers exploring these obscure avenues included William James (1842–1910), whose work seems to have impressed Jung deeply; Herbert Silberer (1882–1923), whose book on the symbolism of alchemy was credited by Jung with providing the 'connecting-link' between analytical psychology and Greek philosophy; and F.W.H. Myers (1843–1901), a poet, classical scholar, philologist, and founding member of the Society for Psychical Research, who used automatic writing as a means of exploring the unconscious, and whom Jung quoted in his own dissertation on spiritualist phenomena.[38]

This predilection for blending the occult with the psychological was favoured in Britain, partly due to the quiet exchanges between certain psychotherapists and various esoteric currents such as the Theosophical Society and the Hermetic

Order of the Golden Dawn.[39] The short-lived but immensely influential Medico-Psychological Clinic, for example, provided the first, albeit unofficial, psychoanalytic training in the United Kingdom, but its practitioners were consistently engaged in scrying and automatic writing along with more orthodox methods of psychotherapy.[40] Jung was privy to, and happy to make use of, all of this research carried out within his own profession.[41] From a morphological perspective, a single recognisable theme is evident in Jung's sources for active imagination, expressed through numerous cultural adaptations but possessing a structural integrity. This theme rests on the idea that the human imagination, properly developed and trained, can provide a mode of passage from one dimension of consciousness – understood in psychological terms as ego-awareness – to another, more mysterious dimension, referred to as 'the unconscious' and experienced by the individual as compulsive, frightening, and, at times, numinous, transformative, and even indistinguishable from deity.

Robert Kugelman, who reviewed *Liber Novus* soon after its publication, calls the work 'visionary writing', and has suggested that its roots lie in the traditions of the German Romanticism of the early nineteenth century.[42] Wouter J. Hanegraaff, writing about 'New Age' spiritualities, likewise considers German Romanticism as the primary source of Jung's ideas about the imagination.[43] The importance of the Romantic writers for Jung's work is inarguable, especially Goethe. But German Romanticism did not spring into being full-blown through some kind of cultural spontaneous generation. It was itself the heir of those same older philosophical and religious currents – Gnostic, Hermetic, Neoplatonic, Kabbalistic – that Jung drew on directly.[44] If Jung identified with particular Romantic ideas, it may be partly due to the fact that he recognised the traces of more ancient currents in the works of Goethe, Novalis, and other authors of the Romantic movement.

Jung insisted that psychic energy, or libido, 'cannot appear in consciousness except in the form of images'.[45] This provides an apparently modern scientific understanding of such images: they are products of the deeper levels of the unconscious psyche, emerging either spontaneously in dreams and visions or through deliberate invocation, and they give shape to otherwise incommunicable psychic realities. This view was also promulgated by British occultists contemporary with Jung, such as Dion Fortune (1890–1946), who had worked at the Medico-Psychological Clinic in London before she joined the Order of the Golden Dawn:

> The uninstructed person thinks he is developing psychism when he sees elves, archangels, and elementals with the inner eye. The instructed person knows that he is using a technique of the imagination in order to clothe with visible form intangible things that would otherwise be imperceptible to his consciousness.[46]

It is the precise nature of these 'intangible things' that has been the source of the greatest controversy around Jung's ideas about the unconscious. Fortune acquired many of her concepts from Jung himself, as well as from the Freudian and Kleinian approaches offered at the Medico-Psychological Clinic. She used Jung's models to support her belief that occultism and analytical psychology were complementary modes of exploring the invisible realms.[47] But occultists such as Fortune, like Jung, were familiar with the earlier sources, including Loyola and Iamblichus.[48] The practice of 'seeing with the inner eye' long predates the psychotherapeutic experiments of Charcot, Janet, James, Myers, and Silberer in the modern era, and forms an important aspect of both alchemical and Kabbalistic theurgic techniques of the medieval and early modern periods, as well as comprising a central theme in late antique Gnostic, Hermetic, Jewish, and Neoplatonic literature.[49] Although Jung's expositions on active imagination are psychological, they often, albeit covertly, attribute the qualities of divinity to the collective unconscious, reflecting a panentheistic understanding of symbols as complex webs of associations that transcend the perceived opposites and paradoxically conjoin, in a single and apparently discrete image, object, word, number, or glyph, the inner and the outer, the material and the psychic, within an *unus mundus* or unified cosmos which Plato, in the fourth century BCE, called the World Soul.[50]

Sumpatheia, sunthemata, and *sumbola*

Jung encouraged his patients to paint the images that arose from their imaginal work, and there are numerous case studies in the *Collected Works* that present evidence of how efficacious this creative effort could be in aiding the process of psychological integration.[51] Sometimes Jung discussed his own paintings under the guise of examples done by patients.[52] This practice of painting the visual products of the unconscious is encouraged by many Jungian analysts, but it has also spread into other dynamic psychologies, especially those concerned with transpersonal themes, and it provides the basis for some forms of art therapy.[53] The enormous detail and care with which Jung executed the paintings in *Liber Novus* is testimony to how important it was to him to give concrete form to the images that emerged in his interior explorations, including those he related to astrological symbols. Yet strangely, Jung's focus on the embodied image, which is amply explicated in numerous works by analytical psychologists as a therapeutic tool, has not been sufficiently explored in terms of its history and its importance in theurgic practices.

Jung suggested that, by providing a container for the archetypal potencies, the individual might be spared the often horrific experience of being inundated by the collective unconscious, resulting in a psychosis.[54] This kind of inundation seems to have buffeted Jung during the period between 1913 and 1917, when he was experiencing uncontrollable visions and believed that his house was 'haunted' by the spirits of the dead. By providing a visual container for what he understood as the irruption of the archetypal realm, he was able to maintain a reasonably stable external life and preserve his psychotherapeutic practice. The traditions of theurgy from late antiquity not only offered ample food for Jung's hunger for a philosophical framework in which to embed his psychological insights; they also provided explicit instructions on how to avoid the disintegration of the personality that can accompany a confrontation with the divine. Neoplatonic theurgists such as Iamblichus eloquently expounded the reasons and methods for providing symbolic vehicles for the gods, and were equally eloquent about the terrifying consequences of a mortal experiencing 'possession' by a deity without the protection of the appropriate *sumbola*.[55]

Central to Jung's development of active imagination is his understanding of symbols, which differs radically from the approach currently favoured within the academy. Symbols today are understood within the fields of anthropology and sociology as human constructs relevant only within a specific cultural context.[56] Mary LeCron Foster, for example, expressing the functional perspective of many cultural anthropologists, asserts that a symbol 'is any entity that has socially participative meaning'.[57] The meaning perceived in symbols thus exists only in the concordant minds of the participants in a given culture; symbols do not contain any ontically intrinsic meaning, but are constructions that form the binding glue of societies and their customs. The potency of a symbol in a particular culture, in LeCron's view, is determined by its 'use-potential', like the logo for a company or a household product. The wider and more useful the application, the more potent is the symbol:

> Symbolism arose and evolved into human culture because of a growing appreciation and social utilization of abstract likenesses between objects and events separated in time and space.[58]

In contrast, Jung's view that the symbol 'rises out of the depths of the self as a word of power' seems to have been derived from older sources, as well as from his own direct experience.[59] The impact of German Romanticism on Jung's ideas about symbols has been examined by a number of scholars: nineteenth-century authors such as Johann Gottfried Herder (1744–1803) and Friedrich Wilhelm Joseph von Schelling (1775–1854) are usually cited as the origin of Jung's belief that symbols, and the mythic narratives that accompany them, express an ontic reality independent of the humans who articulate the symbols.[60] But Jung also seems to have directly appropriated Neoplatonic theories on the nature of symbols.[61] This view of symbols as the visible expression of an unseen reality rests on the idea of συμπαθεια (*sumpatheia*) or 'sympathies', first given this name by the Stoic-Platonic philosopher Poseidonius of Apamaea (135–51 BCE). *Sumpatheia* expresses the affinity of all the parts of the cosmos to each other and to the organic whole, resulting in mutual interdependence along 'chains' of correspondences operating at different levels of reality. As Iamblichus, borrowing from Plato's *Timaeus*, put it: 'The universe is a single living being'.[62]

Sumpatheia provides the philosophical underpinning for the Neoplatonic understanding of and emphasis on astrology, since the planets, as celestial symbols in the chain of interlinked cosmic emanations, are mirrored by, and inherent in, their correspondences within both earthly reality and the human soul. Thus the 'Chain of the Moon', in Proclus' understanding, begins with the lunar deities Athene, Artemis, and Hekate, all expressions of a specific emanation of the One. The chain continues down through the 'Moon-soul' to the physical Moon in the heavens, the metal silver, the gemstone known as selenite, the vegetative power of nature, and the fish known as 'moonfish'.[63] Although Proclus did not discuss the various dimensions of the human body and psyche as belonging to these chains, such associations appear elsewhere in antiquity, especially in the idea of melothesia, where each organ of the body is associated with a particular planet or zodiacal sign (see Plate 1),[64] and in Galen's elemental and planetary 'humours'. These kinds of specific symbolic chains abound in the images and text of *Liber Novus*.

This interlinking of the different levels and dimensions of the cosmos also provided a mode of understanding astral fate. The interaction of each part (or 'cause') on every other part results in the chain of causation called *Heimarmene*, the Stoic term for fate,[65] eloquently described by the classical scholar Gilbert Murray in 1912:

> Heimarmene, in the striking simile of Zeno [the founder of Stoicism], is like a fine thread running through the whole of existence – the world, we must remember, was to the Stoics a live thing – like the invisible thread of life which, in heredity, passes on from generation to generation of living species and keeps the type alive; it runs causing, causing forever, both the infinitesimal and the infinite.[66]

Causes, in Stoic thought, are not causes in the modern sense of 'instrumental causality',[67] in which Event A makes Event B happen, and driving at 60 mph in a 30 mph zone 'causes' the flash of the speed camera and the inevitable fate of paying a hefty fine. A Stoic 'cause' is a 'body', not an event, and causes operate on one another. The Stoic *Heimarmene* is not a sequence of events causing other events, but rather, 'a simultaneous and mutual interaction' between the different components and levels of reality. In other words, a cause is a dynamic relationship that generates further dynamic relationships.[68] Jung seems to have utilised this ancient idea when he compared the nature of a human relationship with the alchemical work: 'For two personalities to meet is like mixing two different chemical substances: if there is any combination at all, both are transformed'.[69]

Poseidonius described individual souls as the 'pieces' (αποσπασμα) or 'seeds' (σπερματα) of the 'intellectual fiery breath' of the cosmos (πνευμα νοερον και πυρωδεσ), akin to Plato's World Soul.[70] According to Poseidonius, there are sympathies between all parts of this material divinity or divine matter, and Jung would later use the term 'psychoid', referring to the 'objective psyche' or 'collective unconscious' as both physical and psychic.[71] The human soul is thus made of the same stuff as the divine, and it is through this shared substance that theurgy acquires its efficacy. Not only are human souls 'pieces' or 'sparks' of the World Soul; the gods have embedded their tokens or 'passwords' (συνθεματα = *sunthemata*) throughout existence, and this encapsulates the Neoplatonic understanding of a symbol (συμβολον = *sumbolon*).

Iamblichus and Proclus used the terms *sumbolon* and *synthema* interchangeably to describe the 'receptacles' or 'tokens' in material reality through which the gods may be contacted. The *sumbolon* operates on the basis of natural sympathies between the deity and the manifest world. It is not a human social construct, but rather, the expression of ineffable divinity in manifest reality. Rather than being created by humans as social constructs, true symbols, for these philosophers as for Jung, are discovered, because they embody divinity – or, in Jung's terminology, the realm of the archetypes – in the world, in the form of images. As Jung would later put it: 'Myths . . . consist of symbols that were not invented but happened'.[72] Symbols, for Jung, are also gateways; they both embody and facilitate passage into a liminal zone through which one may move from one dimension of reality to another.

> If one accepts the symbol, it is as if a door opens leading into a new room whose existence one previously did not know But if one does not accept the symbol, it is as if one carelessly went past this door, and since this was the only door leading to the inner chambers, one must pass outside into the streets again, exposed to everything external . . . Salvation is a long road that leads through many gates. These gates are symbols.[73]

The poet William Butler Yeats (1865–1939), a member of the Order of the Golden Dawn and also an astrologer, phrased it in a similar fashion:

> Symbols and formulae are powers, which act in their own right and with little consideration for our intentions . . . They are, indeed, personifying spirits that we had best call Gates and Gate-Keepers, because through their dramatic power they bring our soul to crisis.[74]

The word *sumbolon* is itself derived from συμβαλλειν (*sumballein*), meaning 'to join together'. A symbol thus expresses two aspects: it functions as the visible half of a whole object, and it is a perceptible entity hinting at a pre-existing imperceptible entity of which the symbol is an expression. In ancient Greek divinatory practice, the term *sumbolon* also carried the notion of a meeting, an encounter, or a 'bumping into' something.[75] Proclus used the term *sumbolon* to describe a particular kind of relationship between a visible object (a planet, plant, flower, metal, or gemstone) and unseen reality. Divine potencies 'appear by concealing themselves in form to us who have been endowed with form',[76] and these forms are symbols that both conceal and reveal. Thus the physical Sun and the physical planets are the forms that both conceal and reveal celestial divinities: the Sun conceals and reveals Apollo and Helios, while the Moon conceals and reveals Athene, Artemis, and Hekate.

In the *Collected Works*, Jung offered many definitions of a symbol, usually preferring an ontologically neutral context;[77] but he also referred to symbols as 'god-images'.[78] In *Liber Novus* he presented a perspective very close to that of Proclus:

> Sun and moon, that is, their symbols, are Gods. There are still other Gods; their symbols are the planets.[79]

The effects of reciting certain kinds of myth, according to Proclus, are similar to those of religious or magical ritual. Myth is itself symbol, and every symbol embodies a mythic narrative. Symbol and sympathy are complementary notions; only where a bond of sympathy links together the unseen and the visible are symbols possible.

> There is sympathy between all things, the derivative existing in the primal, the primal reflected in the derivative . . . There are . . . myths which are addressed to a more inspired state of soul and join together the lowest to the highest by means of analogy alone and place the highest possible value on that universal sympathy which joins effects with the causes that give birth to them.[80]

For Proclus, the symbol is both the image and the embodiment of the god or daimon, and inherently possesses the power to awaken the bond between human and divine:

> To those few whose intellects have been awakened, they [Plato's myths] reveal sympathy and afford proof, by means of the workings of the sacred art [theurgy], that the power they possess shares its nature with the gods. For the gods, when they hear such symbols as these, rejoice and readily heed those who call upon them; they also reveal their special character through these tokens [*sunthemata*] because they are their own, appropriate to them, and most familiar.[81]

This perspective is so close to Jung's own perception of the potency of symbols that Neoplatonic theurgy as one of the major contributors to this most seminal of his ideas cannot be ignored. It is unclear just when Jung encountered Iamblichus' *De mysteriis*, as he did not cite this Neoplatonist in *Psychology of the Unconscious*, as he did Plotinus and Proclus. But there are a number of references to Iamblichus in Reitzenstein's *Poimandres* as well as in his *Die hellenistiche Mysterienreligionen*, which Jung referred to in 1912. Reitzenstein was convinced that Hermetic treatises, rather than ancient Egyptian religious practices, provided the basis for Iamblichus' theurgy.[82] Mead, citing Reitzenstein's comments, echoed this conviction, and offered his own translation of sections of *De Mysteriis* in *Thrice-Greatest Hermes*, published in 1906, declaring that Iamblichus

> is of prime importance seeing that it was he who put the Later Platonic School, previously led by the purely philosophical Ammonius, Plotinus and Porphyry, into conscious touch with those centres of Gnosis into which he had been initiated.[83]

It would be surprising if Jung had overlooked these references, especially as they link Iamblichus' theurgic practices to the Hermetic texts, with which Jung was already preoccupied while working on *Liber Novus*. It is more likely that he had already acquired at least one of his editions of *De mysteriis* by 1912, although it is unclear why he did not refer to it – perhaps because, unlike Plotinus, Iamblichus – despite Ficino's efforts to 'rehabilitate' him during the Renaissance – was not viewed by the scholars of the early twentieth century as a proper philosopher, but as a proponent of magic and divination.[84] Yet even Plotinus, although Mead called him 'purely philosophical', was not averse to the practice of theurgy to achieve a direct experience of the divine. Plotinus, however, preferred the term 'contemplation', defining its fruit as 'a vision' stirred by 'an object of contemplation' (in other words, a symbol), and suggesting that the Platonic 'Ideal Forms' – or what Jung later understood as the archetypes – could be experienced through such visions:

> All the forms of Authentic Existence spring from vision and are a vision. Everything that springs from these Authentic Existences in their vision is an object of vision . . . All that springs from vision exists to produce Ideal Form, that is a fresh object of vision, so that universally, as images of their engendering principles, they all produce objects of vision, Ideal Forms.[85]

Although some scholars credit the writers of the German Romantic movement with promulgating in modern times the idea that symbols express an ontic reality independent of human consciousness, Jung turned to the Neoplatonic texts directly, and did not rely solely on their later Romantic interpreters. These texts emphasised the independent power of the symbol, which, according to Iamblichus, wields its transformative influence, not through human agency, but through the gods themselves.[86]

Anyone familiar with Jung's later concept of 'synchronicity' – the 'acausal connecting principle' that mysteriously links apparently unrelated outer events with inner psychic events – will recognise in this idea the underpinnings of *sumpatheia*, renamed and shorn of its overtly religious connotations. In his letter to the French astrologer André Barbault, Jung, responding to Barbault's question about the *modus operandi* of astrological configurations, was explicit about the equation between synchronicity and sympathy:

> It seems to me that it is primarily a question of that parallelism or 'sympathy' which I call *synchronicity*.[87]

The World Soul has been renamed the collective unconscious, and the gods have become archetypes. But the idea that all things in the universe are secretly interconnected through invisible chains of symbolic correspondences remains unchanged, as does the perception that the gods (or archetypes) themselves, through their 'tokens', are amenable to, and even desirous of, a dynamic interaction with human consciousness that, for Jung, led toward some unknown goal:

> There are other processes which bear within them a hidden meaning, processes which are not merely derived from something but which seek to become something, and are therefore symbols.[88]

Notes

1 Iamblichus, *De mysteriis*, I.11.
2 Jung, *Liber Novus*, p. 295.
3 Jung, 'New Paths in Psychology', in Jung, *Collected Papers on Analytical Psychology*, pp. 352–77. This paper is now included in Jung, CW7, ¶¶407–441.
4 Jung, CW6, ¶¶711–722.
5 The 'Tavistock Lectures' are included in Jung, CW18, ¶¶1–415. Jung's discussion of active imagination is found in Lecture V, ¶¶390–406.
6 See Joan Chodorow, 'Introduction', in Joan Chodorow (ed.), *Jung on Active Imagination* (Princeton, NJ: Princeton University Press, 1997), p. 3.
7 Chodorow, 'Introduction', p. 4.
8 Jung, CW8, ¶167.
9 For the earliest description of Freud's 'free association' technique, first published in 1893, see Freud, SE2, p. 112. For a fuller description, see Freud, SE5, pp. 176–78.
10 Jung, CW9i, ¶101. The essay in which this description occurs was first published in 1936.
11 For *kavvanah*, see Gershom Scholem, 'The Concept of Kavvanah in Early Kabbalah', in Alfred Jospe (ed.), *Studies in Jewish Thought* (Detroit, MI: Wayne State University Press, 1981), pp. 162–80; Elliot R. Wolfson, *Through a Speculum That Shines* (Princeton, NJ: Princeton University Press, 1994), pp. 270–325. For Loyola's 'exercises', see George E. Ganss (trans.), *The Spiritual Exercises of Saint Ignatius* (Chicago: Loyola Press, 1992). For Sufi visionary practices, see Henry Corbin, *Avicenna and the Visionary Recital* (Princeton, NJ: Princeton University Press, 1960). For Neoplatonic theurgy, see Chapter 3.
12 For therapeutically orientated works on active imagination, see Marie-Louise von Franz, *Alchemical Active Imagination* (Boston, MA: Shambhala, 1997); Benjamin Sells (ed.), *Working with Images* (Woodstock, CT: Spring, 2000). Chodorow's *Jung on Active Imagination* presents a compilation of passages from Jung's own work, with a commentary and discussion as well as a comprehensive list of 'post-Jungian' references on pp. 177–79.
13 Marie-Louise von Franz, 'On Active Imagination', in Ian Baker (ed.), *Methods of Treatment in Analytical Psychology* (Fellbach: Verlag Adolf Bonz, 1980), p. 88.
14 Jeffrey Raff, *Jung and the Alchemical Imagination* (York Beach, ME: Nicholas-Hays, 2000), pp. 4–5.
15 In support of the idea that Jung belongs to an 'esoteric tradition', Raff cites Gerhard Wehr, 'C.G. Jung in the Context of Christian Esotericism and Cultural History', in Faivre and Needleman (eds.), *Modern Esoteric Spirituality*, pp. 381–99.
16 See Leon Hoffman, 'Varieties of Psychoanalytic Experience', *Journal of the American Psychoanalytic Association* 58 (2010), pp. 781–85, on p. 783.
17 Jung, 'On the Psychology and Pathology of So-called Occult Phenomena', in Jung, CW1, pp. 3–92. This paper was first published in English in 1916, in Jung, *Collected Papers on Analytical Psychology*, pp. 1–93. This collection of papers was the first work by Jung available in English, published a year before *Psychology of the Unconscious*. The dissertation was published in Leipzig in 1902 as *Zur Psychologie und Pathologie sugennanter occulter Phänomene*.
18 Charet, *Spiritualism and the Foundations of C.G. Jung's Psychology*, p. 283. See also Jung, *C.G. Jung Letters* I, p. 511.
19 For Bernoulli, Allemann, and Schlag, see W.P. Mulacz, 'Oscar R. Schlag', *Journal of the Society for Psychical Research* 60 (1995), pp. 263–67; Hakl, *Eranos*, pp. 93–95; Riccardo Bernardini, *Jung a Eranos* (Milan: FrancoAngeli, 2011), pp. 176–78.
20 See Hakl, *Eranos*, p. 93. For the purported disturbances at the séances caused by Jung's inner 'psychogogue' Philemon, see Peter-Robert Koenig, 'Did You Know Oscar R. Schlag?', at <www.parareligion.ch/sunrise/schlag1.htm>. See also Charet, *Spiritualism and the Foundations of C.G. Jung's Psychology*, p. 283 nn. 230–31; Roderick Main, 'Introduction', in Roderick Main (ed.), *Jung, Synchronicity, and the Paranormal* (London: Routledge, 1997), pp. 6–7; Nandor Fodor, *Freud, Jung and Occultism* (New Hyde Park, NY: University Books, 1971); Roderick Main, *The Rupture of Time* (London: Routledge, 2013), p. 71.

21 For Jung's own experiences, see Jung, *MDR*, pp. 215–17.
22 See also James Hillman, 'Some Early Background to Jung's Ideas: Notes on C.G. Jung's Medium by Stephanie Zumstein-Preiswerk', *Spring* (1976), pp. 123–36.
23 See Michael Thompson, *Roots and Role of Imagination in Kant* (unpublished PhD dissertation, University of South Florida, 2009); Janet Kaylo, 'Imagination and the Mundus Imaginalis', *Spring* 77 (2007), pp. 107–24.
24 Jung made numerous references to the Kabbalah in the *Collected Works*, and also acquired a number of Kabbalistic works for his library, including Christian Knorr von Rosenroth, *Kabbala denudata* (Sulzbach/Frankfurt: Abraham von Lichtenthal, 1677–84); Christian D. Ginzburg, *The Kabbalah* (London: Longmans, Green, 1863); A.E. Waite, *The Holy Kabbalah* (London: Williams & Norgate, 1929); Ernst Müller (ed. and trans.), *Der Zohar* (Vienna: Heinrich Glanz, 1932); Harry Sperling and Maurice Simon (ed. and trans.), *The Zohar* (London: Soncino Press, 1949).
25 See the discussion and references to Jung's collection of magical works in Chapter 4.
26 For this tradition of Christian theurgy, see Gregory of Nyssa, *On the Soul and Resurrection*, trans. Catherine P. Roth (Yonkers, NY: St. Vladimir's Seminary Press, 1993); Basil of Caesarea, *Hexaemeron*, trans. Blomfield Jackson (Amazon CreateSpace, 2014); John F. Callahan, 'Greek Philosophy and the Cappadocian Cosmology', *Dumbarton Oaks Papers* 12 (1958). Jung was familiar with both Gregory and Basil, and refers to them in various volumes of the *Collected Works*.
27 Jung referred to Dionysius many times in the Collected Works; see, for example, Jung, CW6, ¶62, first published in 1921. For Dionysius' theurgy, see Gregory Shaw, 'Neoplatonic Theurgy and Dionysius the Areopagite', *Journal of Early Christian Studies* 7:4 (1999), pp. 573–99; Sarah Klitenic Wear and John M. Dillon, *Dionysius the Areopagite and the Neoplatonist Tradition* (Farnham: Ashgate, 2007). Jung's German edition was Max Remmerich (trans.), *Was mir das Jenseits mitteilte* (Diessen: C. Hubers Verlag, Diessen vor München, 1928).
28 Jung, *Modern Psychology*, Vol. 3–4, p. 154. This transcription of Jung's ETH lectures was privately published and never edited by Jung himself. A new edited edition of the ETH lectures is currently being prepared by the Philemon Foundation; see <www.philemon-foundation.org/forthcoming/eth_lectures>.
29 See Jung, 'Exercitia spiritualia of St. Ignatius of Loyola', in *Modern Psychology*, Vol. 3–4, pp. 153–57. This lecture was originally given in 1939. See also Ken L. Becker, *Unlikely Companions* (Leominster: Gracewing/Inigo, 2001); Dan Merkur, *Crucified with Christ* (Albany: SUNY Press, 2007), pp. 47–68.
30 St. Ignatius of Loyola, 'The Spiritual Exercises', in *Personal Writings*, trans. J. Munitiz and P. Endean (London: Penguin, 1996), p. 298, cited by Shamdasani in Jung, *Liber Novus*, p. 200, n. 62.
31 Jung, *Modern Psychology*, Vol. 3–4, pp. 178–79.
32 Jung, CW9i, ¶232.
33 Jung, CW9i, ¶231.
34 James Frazer, *The Golden Bough* (New York: Macmillan, 1922), 3:1–2.
35 Jung, CW8, ¶599. The paper in which this definition is found, 'The Psychological Foundations of Belief in Spirits', was originally translated by H.G. and C.F. Baynes from Jung's German manuscript and first published in *Proceedings of the Society for Psychical Research* 31 (1920). Both Freud and Jung were members of the SPR.
36 See Shamdasani's comments in *Liber Novus*, p. 196. For crystal-gazing in the early twentieth century, see Sepharial, *How to Read the Crystal* (London: Foulsham, 1922); Theodore Besterman, *Crystal-Gazing* (London: Rider, 1924), p. 160. See also Greene, *Magi and Maggidim*, pp. 177–81.
37 See, for example, Jung, *Liber Novus*, pp. 239, 248, 252.
38 Among Jung's many references to James' *The Varieties of Religious Experience* (London: Longmans, Green, 1902), see Jung, CW5, ¶¶18–19; Jung, CW6, ¶¶506–509, 864–66; Jung, CW18, ¶1144. For Myers, see William James, 'Frederic Myers's Service to Psychology', *Popular Science Monthly* (August 1901), pp. 380–89. For Silberer, see Letter from C.G. Jung to Erich Neumann, 22 December 1935, in *C.G. Jung Letters*, 1:206; Herbert

Silberer, *Hidden Symbolism of Alchemy and the Occult Arts* (New York: Dover, 1917). For Myers' own work, see F.H.W. Myers, *Human Personality and Its Survival of Death* (London: Longmans, 1903). For Myers' interest in 'automatic writing', see Ann Casement, *Carl Gustav Jung* (London: Sage, 2001), pp. 46–47. Jung quotes from Myers' essay, 'Automatic Writing', published in 1895, in CW1, ¶91.

39 For a general background on the roots of modern dynamic psychiatry and psychology, see Henri Ellenberger, *The Discovery of the Unconscious* (New York: Basic Books, 1970), pp. 53–109. For the occult antecedents of psychoanalysis in the late nineteenth century, see James Webb, *The Occult Establishment* (London: Richard Drew, 1981), pp. 347–81.

40 For the Medico-Psychological Clinic, see Suzanne Raitt, 'Early British Psychoanalysis and the Medico-Psychological Clinic', *History Workshop Journal* 58 (2004), pp. 63–85; Philippa Martindale, 'Against All Hushing Up and Stamping Down', *Psychoanalysis and History* 6:2 (2004), pp. 177–200.

41 See Swan, 'C.G. Jung's Psychotherapeutic Technique of Active Imagination'.

42 Robert Kugelman, 'Review of *the Red Book*', *Journal of the History of the Behavioral Sciences* 47:1 (2011), pp. 101–4, on p. 101.

43 Wouter J. Hanegraaff, 'Romanticism and the Esoteric Connection', in van den Broek and Hanegraaff (eds.), *Gnosis and Hermeticism*, pp. 237–68. For a similar perspective from an analytical psychologist, see Gilbert Durand, 'Exploration of the Imaginal', in Sells (ed.), *Working with Images*, pp. 53–68.

44 For these origins of German Romanticism, see Ernst Benz, The *Mystical Sources of German Romantic Philosophy*, trans. Blair R. Reynolds and Eunice M. Paul (Eugene, OR: Pickwick, 1983).

45 Jung, CW6, ¶722.

46 Dion Fortune, 'Types of Mind Working', in Dion Fortune and Gareth Knight, *An Introduction to Ritual Magic* (Loughborough: Thoth, 1997), pp. 32–39, on p. 22.

47 For Fortune's adaptation of Jungian models, see Greene, *Magi and Maggidim*, pp. 283–363.

48 For Fortune's references to Iamblichus, and her own coupling of this Neoplatonist with Loyola, see Dion Fortune, *The Goat-Foot God* (London: Norgate, 1936), p. 49. Fortune produced her novel in 1936, three years before Jung described Loyola's exercises in CW9i.

49 For the practice in various late antique currents, see Dan Merkur, *Gnosis* (Albany: SUNY Press, 1993); Gregory Shaw, *Theurgy and the Soul* (University Park: Penn State University Press, 1971); Dan Merkur, 'Stages of Ascension in Hermetic Rebirth', *Esoterica* 1 (1999), pp. 79–96; Rebecca Macy Lesses, *Ritual Practices to Gain Power* (Harrisburg, PA: Trinity Press, 1998).

50 For the Platonic World Soul, see Plato, *Timaeus*; Proclus, *Commentary on Plato's Timaeus*, trans. Dirk Baltzly (Cambridge: Cambridge University Press, 2010), Book 3.

51 See the case material on 'Miss Miller' in Jung, *Psychology of the Unconscious*; the sequence of painted images in Jung, CW12; the visual material in Jung, CW9i; and the case material in Jung, CW18, ¶¶1–415.

52 See, for example, the description of the anima image attributed to 'a dream-series' ostensibly communicated by an unnamed patient in Jung and Kerényi, *Essays on a Science of Mythology*, p. 176. 'Dream xi' is in fact Jung's own painting from *Liber Novus*. See also Sonu Shamdasani's note 283 in Jung, *Liber Novus*, p. 317.

53 See Liesl Silverstone, *Art Therapy Exercises* (London: Jessica Kingsley, 2009); Joy Schaverien, *The Revealing Image* (London: Jessica Kingsley, 2009).

54 Among Jung's many references to psychosis as inundation by the unconscious, see Jung, CW18, ¶1159.

55 See Iamblichus, *De mysteriis*, III.4–8. For a late antique Jewish version of the dangers involved in celestial visions, see *The Book of Enoch, or 1 Enoch*, trans. R.H. Charles (Oxford: Clarendon Press, 1912), a corpus of late antique Jewish texts that Jung acquired for his library.

56 For an overview of contemporary theories of symbolism, see Dan Sperber, *Rethinking Symbolism*, trans. Alice L. Morton (Cambridge: Cambridge Univerity Press, 1974).

57 Mary LeCron Foster, 'Symbolism: The Foundation of Culture', in Tim Ingold (ed.), *The Companion Encyclopedia of Anthropology* (London: Routledge, 1994), pp. 366–95, on p. 366.

58 Foster, 'Symbolism', p. 370.
59 Jung, *Liber Novus*, p. 311.
60 See Alexander Altmann, 'Myth and Symbol', *Philosophy* 20:76 (1945), pp. 162–71.
61 For the Neoplatonic understanding of symbols, see Struck, *Birth of the Symbol*, pp. 204–53; Shaw, *Theurgy and the Soul*.
62 Iamblichus, *De mysteriis*, 4:12. See Plato, *Timaeus*, 30a–e.
63 See the diagram of Proclus' 'Chain of the Moon', in Struck, *Birth of the Symbol*, p. 230, and his discussion on pp. 230–32.
64 For melothesia in antiquity, see Mladen Popovic, *Reading the Human Body* (Leiden: Brill, 2007); Roelof van den Broek, *Studies in Gnosticism and Alexandrian Christianity* (Leiden: Brill, 1996), pp. 67–85.
65 For more on *Heimarmene* and Jung's understanding of astral fate, see Chapter 4.
66 Gilbert Murray, *Four Stages of Greek Religion* (Oxford: Oxford University Press, 1912), 115. Zeno of Citium (c. 334–262 BCE) was the founder of the Stoic school of philosophy.
67 For 'instrumental causality', see Wouter J. Hanegraaff, 'How Magic Survived the Disenchantment of the World', *Religion* 33 (2003), pp. 357–80.
68 Peter Struck, 'A World Full of Signs', in Patrick Curry and Angela Voss (eds.), *Seeing with Different Eyes* (Cambridge: Cambridge Scholars Press, 2008), pp. 3–20, on p. 12.
69 Jung, CW16, ¶163.
70 See I.G. Kidd (trans.), *Poseidonius* (Cambridge: Cambridge University Press, 2004).
71 For Jung's discussions on the 'psychoid' nature of the collective unconscious, see Jung, CW8, ¶¶419–20; Jung, CW14, ¶788; Jung, CW10, ¶¶851–52.
72 Jung, CW18, ¶568.
73 Jung, *Liber Novus*, pp. 136–37.
74 William Butler Yeats, Letter to Florence Farr, cited in Kathleen Raine, *Yeats, the Tarot, and the Golden Dawn* (Dublin: Dolmen Press, 1972), p. 44. Jung acquired a copy of Yeats' quasi-astrological work of automatic writing, *A Vision: An Explanation of Life Founded upon the Writings of Giraldus and upon Certain Doctrines Attributed to Eusta Ben Luka* (Private Publication, 1925; repr. New York: Macmillan, 1939). Only 600 copies of this limited edition were published.
75 See Struck, *Birth of the Symbol*, pp. 90–94.
76 Proclus, *On the Sacred Art*, trans. Stephen Ronan (Chthonios Books, 1998), at <www.esotericism.co.uk/proclus-sacred.htm>, 150.
77 See, for example, Jung, CW6, ¶817; Jung, CW8, ¶88.
78 Jung, CW6, ¶202.
79 Jung, *Liber Novus*, p. 371.
80 Proclus, *The Elements of Theology*, 83:26–84.12.
81 Proclus, *The Elements of Theology*, 83:12–22.
82 See Reitzenstein, *Poimandres* (Leipzig: Teubner, 1904), p. 108; Reitzenstein, *Hellenistic Mystery-Religions*, trans. John E. Steely (Pittsburgh, PA: Pickwick Press, 1978), pp. 100 n. 72, 104 n. 96, 383.
83 Mead, *Thrice-Greatest Hermes*, III:285. In 1879, Mead published a long article on the Neoplatonists, including Iamblichus: G.R.S. Mead, 'The Lives of the Later Platonists', *Lucifer* 18 (March–August 1896), pp. 185–200, 288–302, 368–80, 456–69; *Lucifer* 19 (September 1896–February 1897), pp. 16–32, 103–13, 186–95. See also G.R.S. Mead, 'Hermes the Thrice-Greatest According to Iamblichus an Initiate of the Egyptian Wisdom', *The Theosophical Review* 25 (September 1899–February 1900), pp. 9–19. Given Jung's assiduous acquisition of Mead's work, it is unlikely that he was unaware of these articles.
84 See John Dillon, 'Iamblichus' Defence of Theurgy', *International Journal of the Platonic Tradition* 1 (2007), pp. 34–35; Shaw, *Theurgy and the Soul*, p. 7.
85 Plotinus, Ennead III.8.7.
86 See Iamblichus, *De mysteriis*, 96: 13.97.9. See also Shaw, *Theurgy and the Soul*, p. 84.
87 Jung, Letter to André Barbault, in *C.G. Jung Letters*, Vol. 2, p. 175.
88 Jung, CW6, ¶822.

4

SUMMONING THE DAIMON

> The personal daimon of each of us does not in any case come to us on the basis of the configuration prevailing at our birth, but there is a yet more primordial causal principle of him than this . . . Who after all, would take this figure as a guide to freeing oneself from fate, if he has been given to us only for the purpose of fulfilling the dispensations of fate? . . . It is the emanation from the stars that allots us our daimon, whether we comprehend this or not.[1]
>
> —Iamblichus

> I prefer the term 'the unconscious', knowing that I might equally well speak of 'God' or 'daimon' if I wished to express myself in mythic language . . . I am aware that 'mana', 'daimon', and 'God' are synonyms for the unconscious . . . A creative person has little power over his own life. He is not free. He is captive and driven by his daimon.[2]
>
> —C.G. Jung

The chain of hieratic Platonism

During the time Jung worked on *Liber Novus*, a number of sources – astrology, spiritualism, scrying, hypnosis, German Romanticism, and Christian mysticism, along with liberal helpings of Aristotle's *De anima* and Plato's *Timaeus*, Gnostic and Hermetic texts,[3] and the experimental researches of his fellow psychiatrists – contributed major insights to Jung's ever-deepening speculations on the agency and transformative power of the imaginal world. As we have seen, an equally strong case can be made for the influence of the Neoplatonists, as well as those works belonging to what John Dillon has referred to as the 'underworld' of Platonism: the magical rituals of the *Chaldaean Oracles* and the so-called *Mithras Liturgy*.[4] These works of late antiquity, in various translations, made up an important part of Jung's private library.[5] He even went to the trouble of obtaining a rare Latin first edition of Iamblichus' *De mysteriis*, translated from the Greek by Marsilio Ficino and published in Venice in 1497,[6] although it is unclear when he acquired it. The influence of Neoplatonism on the philosophy and art of the Italian Renaissance has been discussed in depth by numerous scholars, as has its impact on the 'occult revival' of the late nineteenth and early twentieth centuries.[7] Jung availed himself not only of texts from late antiquity, but also the works of Renaissance and early modern interpreters such as Marsilio Ficino and Henry Cornelius Agrippa, as well as occultist writings from his own time. In order to make sense of Jung's approach to astrology, it is important to understand in what ways he took up this current of ideas and applied it to active imagination, particularly in relation to astrological symbols.

The chain of 'hieratic' or 'priestly' Platonism[8] – Platonic philosophical ideas translated into ritual action – runs from Plotinus and Porphyry through Iamblichus to the later Neoplatonists: Proclus, Olympiodorus, and Damascius, the last head of the Platonic Academy in Athens before the Christian Emperor Justinian closed it down in 529 CE in an effort to rid his empire of the taint of pagan heresy.[9] All of these authors produced commentaries on Plato's dialogues; all incorporated astrology as a central component in their cosmological speculations as part of the web of *sumpatheia*; and all were preoccupied with the more enigmatic elements in Plato's work, which they believed hinted at magical applications of philosophical truths. Recent scholarship has begun to focus more carefully and with less prejudice on the elements of ritual magic presented by this enormously influential current in late antique philosophy and religion.

The magical 'underworld' of Platonism, which permeated various currents of Gnostic thought as well as the Greek Magical Papyri, might appear very different from the apparently purely philosophical and daimon-free Christianised Platonism of Church fathers such as Origen and Gregory of Nyssa.[10] Nevertheless, these less reputable texts espoused a world-view that Jung seemed to find relevant for his psychological models. The world of hieratic Platonism valorised the imagination, the ontological autonomy of symbols, and the importance of inner experience. The borders between philosophy and religion are blurred in this liminal world, as are the borders between religion, psychology, and magic. Jung seems to have been very fond of Plotinus,[11] generally considered the 'founder' of Neoplatonism, who, in contrast to his successors, has usually been viewed by scholars as a mystical philosopher rather than a theurgist.[12] But Plotinus may have been important to Jung for reasons other than the purportedly 'rational' mysticism of the *Enneads*. In recent times a number of scholarly papers have explored the overtly magical elements in Plotinus' work. Jung credited Plotinus with being 'an earlier witness to the idea of the *unus mundus*' because this Greco-Egyptian philosopher declared that all individuals 'are merely one soul'. Jung thus viewed him as a predecessor, along with Plato himself, of the idea of the collective unconscious.[13]

Jung also perceived Plotinus' description of the soul's natural movement 'around something interior, around a centre' as a foreshadowing of his own concept of the

FIGURE 4.1 Head of Plotinus, late third century CE, Museo Ostia Antica[14]

Self, the centre around which the various components of the psyche circle.[15] In *Memories, Dreams, Reflections*, Jung emphasised the importance of this centrifugal movement in the development of his idea of individuation:

> During those years, between 1918 and 1920, I began to understand that the goal of psychic development is the self. There is no linear evolution; there is only a circumambulation of the self. Uniform development exists, at most, only at the beginning; later, everything points toward the centre.[16]

Plotinus' *Enneads*, written around 250 CE and edited by his student Porphyry, were first published in English as a series of volumes between 1917 and 1930.[17] An earlier German translation with a lengthy commentary appeared in 1907,[18] and Jung seems to have acquired this edition during the period in which he wrote *Psychology of the Unconscious* and began work on *Liber Novus*. He later obtained Stephen MacKenna's English translation as well as a modern critical edition of the Greek text.[19] Jung cited liberally from the *Enneads* in *Psychology of the Unconscious*, placing particular emphasis on Plotinus' description of the World Soul, which, in Jung's paraphrase, is 'wholly energy' and 'a living organism of ideas': a mirror of the concept of libido as universal psychic energy generating, and expressing through, the archetypes.[20] Jung also referred to Plotinus' equation of the primal creative principle with 'light in general', symbolised by the Sun:[21]

> The dynamic of the gods is psychic energy. This is our immortality, the link through which man feels inextinguishably one with the continuity of all life . . . The psychic life-force, the libido, symbolizes itself in the sun.[22]

Equally important for Jung was Plotinus' Fourth Ennead, titled *On the Nature of the Soul*, in which the philosopher expounded his views on the primary importance of the imagination as the gateway between visible and invisible realms. The power of magic, according to Plotinus, depends on *sumpatheia*, 'like a musical string which, plucked at one end, vibrates at the other also'.[23] The third tractate of the Second Ennead, titled *Are the Stars Causes?*, was especially relevant to the development of Jung's ideas about astrology. In this work Plotinus dismissed the idea that the planets 'produce' effects in a material manner. They 'signify' rather than cause events; they are 'letters perpetually being inscribed on the heavens'.[24] They are, in fact, *sumbola*:

> All teems with symbol . . . All things must be enchained; and the sympathy and correspondence obtaining in any one closely knit organism must exist, first, and most intensely, in the All . . . And in this order the stars, as being no minor members of the heavenly system, are co-operators contributing through their radiance to its symbolic function. Their symbolic power extends to the entire realm of sense.[25]

This might be understood as the Plotinian version of what Jung later referred to as synchronicity, through which he explained in neutral, scientific language the efficacy of astrology. In Plotinus' seminal text, astrology is the interpretation of the divine *sumbola* of the heavens, which embody and reflect, in their cyclical motions, the ever-changing patterns inherent in the World Soul or, in Jung's terminology, the libido. This Plotinian understanding of the symbolic nature of the heavenly configurations appears to underpin Jung's observation, made in his letter to Freud, that the zodiacal signs 'depict the typical qualities of the libido at a given moment'. For Jung, as for Plotinus, the planets and zodiacal signs are not material causes, but symbols.

Jung's interest in Orphic ideas, demonstrated by the importance of the Orphic primal god Phanes in *Liber Novus* and the description of Phanes as the 'cosmogenic principle' in *Psychology of the Unconscious*,[26] may have been sparked by the Orphic poems cited by later Neoplatonists such as Damascius and Olympiodorus, which were translated into English as *The Mystical Hymns of Orpheus* by the Platonic scholar Thomas Taylor in 1824.[27] Richard Reitzenstein likewise discussed the Orphics in

Die hellenistischen Mysterienreligionen,[28] as did Isaac Preston Cory in *Ancient Fragments*, and Erwin Rohde in *Seelencult und Unsterlichkeitsglaube der Griechen*;[29] Jung acquired all three of these works, the first two (and possibly the third) by the time he began work on *Liber Novus*.[30] Mead had produced his own commentary on what he called the Orphic 'theology' in 1896, frequently citing Taylor's translation of the *Hymns*;[31] and, given the importance of Mead's work for Jung's understanding of late antique religious currents, Mead's views on the continuity of Orphic ideas in Neoplatonism may also have captured Jung's interest. Taylor, who believed the Orphic *Hymns* to be faithful to ancient Presocratic originals, declared, in the introduction to his translation:

> That this theology, indeed, was derived from Orpheus is clearly testified by those two great philosophic luminaries Iamblichus and Proclus.[32]

Jung found Proclus interesting too, and, in addition to the many translated passages offered by Mead in his work on the Orphics, acquired a treatise by this late Neoplatonist titled *Select Theorems in Proof of the Perpetuity of Time*, translated by Taylor and embedded in a compilation that included other authors writing on the great astrological cycles.[33] Proclus' writings on time provided another useful source for Jung's explorations into the paradoxical, qualitative, and cyclical nature of time as reflected in the symbols of the zodiac and the movements and interrelationships of the planets. This matrix of materials emphasises the central importance of astrology as a demonstration of the laws of *sumpatheia*, the nature of planetary 'influence' as symbolic, and the validity of magic as a means of breaking the chains of astral fate. These ideas seem to have preoccupied Jung's reading and research from the time of the inception of *Liber Novus* if not earlier, reflected in the various themes found in *Liber Novus* as well as in the references in *Psychology of the Unconscious*, published in German a year before work on *Liber Novus* had begun.

The 'Divine' Iamblichus

Although Jung referred more often to Plotinus in the *Collected Works*, the 'Divine' Iamblichus may be one of the most significant sources from antiquity on which Jung drew for his ideas about active imagination and his use of astrological hermeneutics to comprehend its products.[35] Iamblichus, like Plotinus, embraced the importance and veracity of astrology, but he distinguished between ordinary predictive astrology as a humanly constructed form of divination subject to human error, and theurgic astrology, which employs images and symbols to contact the astral potencies and receive direct knowledge from them.[36] Surprisingly, despite the strong similarities between Iamblichus' descriptions of the philosophy and practice of theurgy and Jung's descriptions of active imagination, this Syrian Neoplatonist is usually overlooked when scholars explore earlier contributions to Jung's most important analytic technique.[37] That Jung was fully aware of the relationship between active imagination and magic is evident in a comment he made about his

FIGURE 4.2 A seventeenth-century engraver's conception of Iamblichus Chalcidensis[34]

patients in a lecture given at the Tavistock Clinic in 1935. He was also describing his own experiences while writing *Liber Novus*.

> I have patients who, evening after evening, work at these images, painting and shaping their observations and experiences. The work has a fascination for them; it is the fascination which the archetypes always exert upon consciousness . . . It is a sort of 'magical' effect, that is, a suggestive influence which goes out from the images to the individual, and in this way his unconscious is extended and is changed.[38]

The 'suggestive influence' emanating from the image echoes Iamblichus' declaration that the transformations of the soul achieved through theurgy rest on 'secret symbols' sent by the gods:

> Beings beyond form brought under the control of form, things superior to all image reproduced through images.[39]

The word 'theurgy' has a long history and, like so many other terms connected with the human religious imagination, it is subject to ongoing scholarly debate, particularly around its distinction from, or identity with, magic. There is, as yet, no agreed scholarly consensus on precisely what the term describes.[40] The original Greek *theurgos* (θεοργος) is a neologism – *theos* + *ergon* (θεος + εργον), or 'god-work' – which first appeared in the late antique ritual text known as the *Chaldaean Oracles*, a work with which Jung was familiar and which exercised a powerful influence on Iamblichus' interpretation of hieratic Platonism.[41] The *Oracles*, known primarily through fragments cited by other authors, are usually considered magical rather than philosophical. Nevertheless, the philosophy underpinning the text is unmistakably Neoplatonic. The extant fragments concern the invocation of various celestial gods and daimons, an approach presented in ample detail in that large and diverse body of magical literature stretching from the late antique Greek Magical Papyri through the grimoires of the medieval and early modern periods and on to the occult texts of modern magi such as Aleister Crowley, Dion Fortune, and Israel Regardie in the early twentieth century.

Theurgy is often described by its practitioners as a 'higher' form of magic, concerned with communion or even union with the gods rather than with the imposition of the magician's will on everyday life. Theurgy does not involve the coercion of higher powers, but relies on the gods' willingness to respond to their own symbols or *sunthemata*.[42] It is thus viewed as closer to the idea of prayer, a theme on which Iamblichus himself expounded:

> Prayer establishes links of friendship between us and the gods, and secures for us the triple advantage which we gain from the gods through theurgy, the first leading to illumination, the second to the common achievement of projects, and the third to perfect fulfilment (of the soul) . . . No sacred act can take place without the supplications contained in prayers.[43]

Some of the debate around theurgy centres on this interface between magic and prayer. If Iamblichus is understood to be describing a serious religious practice, then it is difficult to ignore the parallels with Christian performative events such as the Mass, which is then difficult to define as anything other than theurgy: a combination of ritual action and recitation, symbolic objects, focused imagination, and prayerful supplication. A close reading of Jung's *Liber Novus* likewise renders it difficult to consider the operations that led to the text and images as anything other than theurgy. *Liber Novus* also combines ritual action and recitation, symbolic objects in the form of paintings, focused imagination, and prayerful supplication, including a lengthy incantation to facilitate the birth of the Sun-god from the cosmic egg.[44]

Jung was ambiguous in his discussions about prayer, and seems to have shifted over the years in his understanding of its meaning and effectiveness. In *Psychological Types*, he was concerned with the psychology of prayer rather than its ontology. Citing Paul Deussen's German translation of and commentary on Hindu sacred texts,[45] Jung pointed out that the word 'prayer' derives from the Hindu *barh*, meaning 'to swell'; prayer is thus 'the upward-striving will of man towards the holy, the divine'. Jung then stated that this etymological root

> indicates a particular psychological state, a specific concentration of libido, which through overflowing innervations produces a general state of tension associated with the feeling of swelling. Hence, in common speech, one frequently uses images like 'overflowing with emotion', 'unable to restrain oneself', 'bursting' when referring to such a state . . . This accounts for all those sun, fire, flame, wind, breath similes that from time immemorial have been symbols of the procreative and creative power that moves the world.[46]

However, the 'creative power that moves the world' was already evidencing itself in the images of *Liber Novus* as something rather more potent than a 'feeling of swelling'. It is likely that, even in 1920, when he wrote the passage cited above, Jung never assumed the effects of prayer to be solely a form of emotional 'overflowing' projected onto an imagined deity.

The carefully revised and rewritten material of the *Collected Works* was Jung's legacy to a public in general, and a psychiatric profession in particular, whose derision he feared. In an essay on the archetypes first published in German in 1936,[47] Jung discussed the differences between the often 'heretical' visions that contain the raw archetypal dominants behind religious ideas, and the more conventional visions which 'agree with the dogma' and are 'visualizations of conscious contents, evoked through prayer, autosuggestion, and heterosuggestion'.[48] Prayer, in this latter context, is merely a form of autosuggestion that follows collectively acceptable formulae and produces collectively acceptable religious 'experiences'.[49] However, nearly twenty years later, in a letter to the Roman Catholic priest Père William Lachat, Jung wrote:

> I do not for a moment deny that the deep emotion of a true prayer may reach transcendence, but it is above our heads.[50]

Prayer, for Jung, could thus open the gateway to a transcendent mystery that defies psychological explanations.

Iamblichus, like Jung, was concerned with distinguishing between images produced through deliberate human agency and images arising from the true gnosis experienced through theurgy. Book III of *De mysteriis* is dominated by descriptions of 'true' divination, dreams, and prophecy initiated and inspired by the divine, in contrast to the 'turbulent and false' visions artificially produced through technical means. Imagination, as distinct from mere fantasy,

> is inspired because it is not roused by itself, but by the gods, to modes of imagination when normal human behaviour has been completely displaced.[51]

Paraphrased according to Jung's terminology, the imagination is roused by the archetypes themselves, when their intrusions 'displace' the 'normal' functioning of the conscious ego. Iamblichus insisted that the theurgist achieves his or her object – absorption into the divine – through the correct ritual performance of certain magical actions which may be incomprehensible to the theurgist, but whose significance is known to the gods.[52] The ritual was understood to be a kind of dialectic between the human soul and the god or daimon; divine willingness to participate is set in motion by the symbols of the ritual act, which are the *sunthemata* of the divine embedded in the manifest world, and which ensure that the deity participates in the theurgic process. Transformation results, not through the power of the human will, but through the autonomous power of the divine symbols.

Iamblichus also distinguished between theurgy and ordinary magic or sorcery (γοητεια = *goeteia*):

> Do not, furthermore, compare the clearest visions of the gods to the images produced artificially from magic, for these have neither the energy, nor the essence of things seen, nor truth, but present mere images, reaching only as far as appearance.[53]

While theurgy is concerned with divine things, *goeteia* is 'readily accessible and widespread among the vulgar throng', employs 'falsehood and deceit', and 'enjoys the presence of no god'. Its practitioners, moreover, 'overlook the whole procedure of effective contemplation'.[54] Jung, in contrast, did not offer any comments on the distinction between theurgy and 'lower' magic. The word 'theurgy' does not appear in the *Collected Works*, although, not surprisingly, Jung had a great deal to say about magic.[55] He described magic as encompassing both light and dark dimensions, since its potency arises from those primordial levels of the psyche that predate 'splitting':

> The magician has preserved in himself a trace of primordial paganism, he possesses a nature that is still unaffected by the Christian splitting, which means he has access to the unconscious, which is still pagan, where the opposites still lie in their original naive state, beyond all sinfulness, but, if assimilated into conscious life, produce evil and good with the same primordial and consequently daimonic force.[56]

The British occultists of the late nineteenth and early twentieth centuries used the words 'magic' and 'theurgy' interchangeably, to dignify the kind of magic they practiced and to provide an ancient pedigree stretching back to hieratic Platonism. Iamblichus is frequently acknowledged in their work.[57] Israel Regardie (1907–85), a member of an offshoot of the Order of the Golden Dawn known as the Stella Matutina, produced a work on Kabbalistic magic called *The Tree of Life*, which Jung acquired along with another of this author's works. Regardie made the debt to Iamblichus explicit:

> I hope to show that the technique of Magic is in closest accord with the traditions of highest antiquity, and that it possesses the sanction, expressed or

implicitly, of the best authorities. Iamblichus, the divine Theurgist, has much to say in his various writings about Magic.[58]

Jung's hieratic paintings

A comparison of Iamblichus' views with Jung's reveals the immense relevance of the Syrian Neoplatonist's ideas about theurgy to Jung's technique of active imagination. It is difficult to avoid the conclusion that active imagination is not only a psychological technique; viewed within a different linguistic framework, it is a carefully structured theurgic ritual, albeit an 'inner ritual' that does not require concrete *sumbola* such as incense, plants, or gemstones.[59] However, the paintings in *Liber Novus* can themselves be viewed as hieratic *sumbola*, as could the stone Jung carved at Bollingen, with its planetary glyphs surrounding the figure of Telesphoros at the centre.[60] Jung incorporated precise details in the images of *Liber Novus*, such as a certain type of tree or animal, and may have intended to achieve the same end as Iamblichus' material *sumbola*.[61] The image of the grove of date-palms in Jung's painting of Philemon, for example, can serve the same theurgic purpose as an actual branch of the tree. This raises questions about the complex relationship between a physical object and its image in a dream, vision, or magical invocation, and between the object and the image as it appears in an artistic work. If Jung's paintings are intentional *sumbola* in Iamblichus' sense, just how spontaneous were they?

Jung's original visions were recorded in a series of diaries known as the *Black Books*, which he began writing in December 1913.[62] He continued writing entries in the *Black Books* until 1932. But these diaries, which Jung referred to as 'my most difficult experiment',[63] were selectively revised, edited, honed, chiselled, and ornamented to produce the single volume we now know as *Liber Novus*. Images such as that of Philemon, whose initial appearance Jung claimed to have seen in a dream, were painted with immense thought, care, and detail; there are earlier 'draft' versions, such as one that he painted in 1914, reproduced in Gerhard Wehr's biography of Jung published in 1987.[64] In this earlier painting, Philemon appears as Jung described him in *Memories, Dreams, Reflections*: he is crowned with a solar halo, bears bull's horns, and, like Mithraic statues of the god Aion, holds a ring of keys in his right hand.[65] In the final version of the painting produced for *Liber Novus*, the bull's horns are missing and the keys have vanished, replaced by a glowing stone, although the solar halo remains. In these different presentations of Philemon, what John Thorburn referred to as 'the selective meditation of the artist' has resulted in a synthesis of the fluid and the formal, or, as both Thorburn and Jung described it, a synthesis of the unconscious and consciousness.[66]

The deliberate inclusion of detailed symbolic references in Jung's paintings does not preclude their potency as genuine spontaneous visions. Instead, it transforms them into works of art. A similar question about spontaneity might be raised around the material generated in automatic writing, which is inevitably subjected to the filter of the individual's conscious selectivity when it is transcribed, edited, and prepared for publication.[67] Likewise, the descriptions, both verbal and visual, that follow in the wake of a 'mystical' experience, now referred to as a 'unitive' experience or 'religiously altered state of consciousness', partake of the individual's selective awareness the moment they are communicated.[68] Both automatic writing and 'religiously altered states of consciousness' are terms that might justifiably be applied to *Liber Novus*, which describes encounters that Jung perceived as transpersonal, and which reflects ideas and images that he experienced as coming from an autonomous, unknown source.

Late antique ritual texts such as the *Chaldaean Oracles* have been described as automatic writing, akin to the trance-utterances of spiritualist mediums. E.R. Dodds, one of the most influential classical scholars of the mid-twentieth century, described the *Oracles* as originating 'in the "revelations" of some visionary or trance medium'.[69] The most vivid example of Jung's 'automatic writing' is the third section of *Liber Novus*, titled 'Scrutinies', completed in the winter of 1917. Jung attributed his revelations to the 'voice' of Philemon. The scholarly debate on whether such experiences are entirely culturally determined, or whether they contain some kind of essential, ineffable core, continues without any resolution as to the precise nature and origin of the experience.[70] As with astrology itself, the conflict between direct experience and lack of scientific 'proof' seems irreconcilable. Although Jung's visionary material appears to have been genuinely spontaneous initially, there may be no such thing as complete spontaneity in terms of the process by which this type of experience is translated into words, images, or any other medium through which an artist works. That the paintings may have also been intentional talismanic *sunthemata* does not preclude the power, authenticity, and genuine autonomy that Jung attributed to them.

Epitedeiotes: 'fitness', 'aptitude', or 'receptivity'

Jung emphasised the magical power of the unconscious by citing the great medieval magus, Albertus Magnus (c. 1206–80):

> A certain power to alter things indwells in the human soul and subordinates the other things to her, particularly when she is swept into a great excess of love or hate or the like. When therefore the soul of a man falls into a great excess of any passion . . . it [the excess] binds things [magically] and alters them in the way it wants.[71]

Jung suggested that the images that arise from the unconscious during such states of intense emotional affect 'present themselves spontaneously'.[72] He was in complete accord with Iamblichus' insistence that it is the god or daimon who initiates the encounter: 'The god acts by himself'.[73] For Jung, it was the archetypes of the collective unconscious that act by themselves and require a respectful and receptive response:

> You must enter into the process with your personal reactions . . . as if the drama being enacted before your eyes were real . . . It is as real as you – as a psychic entity – are real.[74]

The lines of communication are thus opened between seen and unseen worlds, and between the individual psyche and the collective unconscious or, in Neoplatonic terms, the World Soul.[75] Jung described the magical process of opening the portal as a necessary aspect of engagement with the unconscious, in order to 'receive or invoke the messenger'.[76] His emphasis on respectful attentiveness to the images echoes Iamblichus' idea of επιτεδειοτες (*epitedeiotes*): 'fitness', 'aptitude', or 'receptivity'. Iamblichus understood the 'soul-vehicle' or 'astral body' – the quasi-spiritual, quasi-corporeal intermediary binding the soul to the body – as the locus of the image-making faculty or *phantasia*. During the theurgic ritual, the *phantasia* is emptied of all personal images and becomes receptive to the images sent from the gods.[77]

Iamblichus used the idea of *epitedeiotes* to explain why not everyone could achieve the highest mystical states during theurgy.[78] Although the gods were everywhere, they could not be 'received' by those who, intentionally or not, lacked receptivity.[79] In the fifth century CE, the Neoplatonic philosopher Hermias, a contemporary of Proclus, applied the same idea to the prophetic inspiration conferred by the personal daimon:

> Not everyone is aware of his daimon; for one to be conscious of its care, there needs to be great suitability [*epitedeiotes*] . . . For, just as all things are subject to the providence of the gods, though not all have consciousness of this, unless they have the natural ability to see and are purified, so it is also with regard to the supervision of the daimon.[80]

Jung believed that the ego needs to possess both willingness and the capacity to endure a confrontation with the deeper levels of the unconscious. Like Iamblichus' *epitedeiotes*, this involves fitness as well as receptivity. If consciousness is too fragile, psychosis can ensue through the overwhelming of the ego by the archetypal dominants of the collective unconscious.[81] But if consciousness is too rigidly defended, the unconscious may somatise its irruptions, or express itself through compulsions experienced as 'fate'.[82]

Equally, the individual cannot simply summon the archetypal dominants by an act of will, but must await the significant symptom, dream, vision, or life crisis, expressed as *kairos*, the 'right moment'. The capacity to discern this 'right moment' would seem to depend partly on the appropriate qualities of time (in other words, the correct astrological configuration), and partly on *epitedeiotes*. Both Iamblichus and Jung emphasised a dynamic relationship between the individual and the universal. In this relationship, human consciousness is an active recipient, not a passive, unwilling victim. The images of the gods, according to Iamblichus, then take possession of the *phantasia*, allowing an experience of true revelation.[83] The psychological and philosophical implications of the idea of *epitedeiotes* are profound. The human being, properly prepared and protected by the appropriate *sumbola*, is able to meet the archetypal realm, not as the powerless subject of astral or psychic fate, but as a respectful co-creator.

The 'master of the house'

Theurgy, in Iamblichus' view, moves hand in hand with astrology, although it is not the astrology of horoscopic prediction. Following a tradition originating with Plato and taken up by Plotinus and Porphyry,[84] Iamblichus spoke of a 'personal daimon' (οικειος δαιμων or ιδιος δαιμων), the 'overseer and leader of our soul', who directs the individual's life and acts as 'the fulfiller of the various levels of life of the soul'.[85]

> The daimon does not guide just one or another part of our being, but all of them at once, and it extends to us the whole administration of us, even as it has been allotted to us from all the regions of the universe.[86]

Plotinus had earlier described the personal daimon as 'the power which consummates the chosen life', insisting that it is 'not entirely outside of ourselves . . . it belongs to us as belonging to our Soul'.[87] Following this idea of the daimon as an intensely individual, interior potency, Iamblichus, in a letter to an unknown recipient, referred to this divine being as 'the daimon allotted to each in life'.[88] In *De mysteriis*, he was more specific. The soul has only one ruling daimon in a particular lifetime; in order to fulfil its requirements, one must first recognise and develop a rapport with it.[89] This can be fully achieved only through theurgy, during which the daimon 'reveals his particular mode of worship as well as his name', and 'teaches the particular manner of invoking him'.[90] The personal or guardian daimon is synonymous with the individual's destiny, the 'suprarational personality that controls the whole of our lives'.[91] Rapport with the 'personal daimon' seems to be precisely what Jung intended in his invocation of Philemon.

Iamblichus enumerated two means of discovering and experiencing this celestial intermediary who facilitates the unfolding of the destiny of the individual life. The 'technical' method involves the natal horoscope, as the personal daimon was believed by most late antique astrologers to be reflected by the dominant planet at the moment of birth. Porphyry, in his *Letter to Anebo*, discussed the idea of finding the personal daimon through an examination of the natal horoscope.[92] The astrological significator of the personal daimon was given the designation οικοδεσποτης (*oikodespotes*) or 'Master of the House'.[93] In his *Introduction to the Tetrabiblos*, Porphyry gave precise technical instructions to ascertain the *oikodespotes* in the horoscope, but conceded that 'there is much dispute about this'.[94] The dispute continued for centuries, reflecting individual religious as well as astrological predilections.[95]

In Iamblichus' view, such technical methods of revealing the *oikodespotes* are useful, but inferior to true gnosis. They operate on the 'merely human level', and therefore involve guesswork and potential mistakes:

> Following the former [theurgic] procedure, one summons the daimon down from the higher causal principles, while according to the latter [technical], one resorts to the visible cycles of the generated realm [the natal horoscope] . . . The former operates on a more universal basis, transcending the

> realm of nature, while the latter conducts its worship on an individual level, following the dictates of nature.[96]

Theurgic invocation of the daimon thus reflects its archetypal (universal) nature, while its representation in the horoscope reflects its expression in the particular conditions of an individual life. The two methods can be combined: revelation of the daimon through theurgy can sometimes be achieved through meditation on the images associated with the planet signifying the *oikodespotes*. Equally, the planetary *sunthemata*, such as a specific flower or gemstone, may be helpful in the ritual work, as these *sunthemata*, in Iamblichus' view, are, like other 'natural' symbols, divine 'tokens' that the gods have embedded in the world of form.[97]

It is unlikely that Jung utilised the complex array of techniques offered by late antique astrologers to determine the *oikodespotes*;[98] there is no evidence that he had access to any of their texts.[99] Nor is it certain that he would have attempted the techniques even if he had possessed an entire library of Hellenistic astrological works, as he disliked the mathematical aspects of casting a horoscope and later recruited his daughter Gret to do the calculations for him.[100] Gregory Shaw, discussing Iamblichus' approach to the *oikodespotes*, suggests that the Master of the House was usually considered the planetary lord of the natal Ascendant – the zodiacal sign rising in the east at the moment of birth – providing that planet was strong and well-related to the other planets. The idea of the Ascendant ruler as the 'lord' of the entire nativity reappeared, shorn of its daimonic and theurgic associations, in the new, 'modern' astrology initiated by Alan Leo at the beginning of the twentieth century. This undoubtedly made everything much simpler for Jung.[101]

The Ascendant ruler in Jung's natal chart is Saturn, as he was born when that 30° segment of the ecliptic known as Aquarius was rising due east of his birthplace, and Saturn is traditionally the lord of this zodiacal sign. Jung's natal Saturn does in fact fulfil Porphyry's more detailed requirements for the *oikodespotes*,[102] as it is strong by virtue of being placed in its own sign of Aquarius as well as rising in the east and forming benign relationships to several other planets.[103] Not surprisingly, Saturn figured prominently in Jung's writing throughout his life. Saturn is constantly mentioned in the *Collected Works* due to its overwhelming importance in alchemy. Here it was said to 'reign' during the initial phase of the alchemical work, known as the *nigredo* or 'blackening'[104] – a process which Jung associated with the necessary breaking down of the ego's defences prior to any authentic engagement with the unconscious – and was understood to be the primal substance or matrix out of which eventually emerged the 'Philosopher's Stone', the chief alchemical symbol of the Self.[105]

In *Liber Novus*, a number of figures reveal unmistakably Saturnine *sumbola*, culminating in Philemon, whose relationship to this planet is indicated by his age, his lameness, his function as a generator of 'order' and 'law', and his central role as magician and 'Wise Old Man'.[106] That Jung deliberately invoked Philemon through active imagination is explicitly stated in *Memories, Dreams, Reflections*;[107] that this daimonic figure is Saturnine in nature is evident from Jung's various descriptions of him; that he was Jung's personal inner guide was also clearly stated by Jung himself. These references, in addition to Jung's mention of 'old Saturnus' as his ruler, strongly suggest that Philemon's close family resemblance to the ancient Neoplatonic 'Master of the House', invoked through theurgy as well as defined by the horoscope, is not coincidental.

There is more than one interpretation of the nature of the daimon offered in ancient texts. Gábor Betegh, the translator of the Orphic fourth-century BCE *Derveni Papyrus*, has observed: 'The semantic field of the word δαιμων is distressingly wide in Greek usage'.[108] The term 'daimon' is derived from the Greek *daiomai*, meaning 'to allot' or 'to divide',[109] and the daimon is thus related to the idea of *moira*, which means 'allotment' and is one of the Greek representations of fate, conceived of as both an allotted span of life and its teleology. *Moira* is in turn etymologically related to *Heimarmene*, a term which, as we will see in the next chapter, Jung used repeatedly as a synonym for astral fate. This complex of ideas – daimon, allotment, and astrological fate – forms a core theme in late antique theurgy and astrology, as well as in Jung's ideas about individuation as fate.

Daimons may be understood as 'lesser' gods; as semi-divine messengers or intermediaries, similar to the mediating angels in Jewish, Islamic, and Christian religious thought; and as the souls of the deceased, who mediate between celestial and terrestrial realms but who can also vengefully impede the soul from pursuing its ascent to freedom. In the *Derveni Papyrus*, the unknown author noted that the daimons 'are called assistants of the gods'.[110] The *Derveni Papyrus* also presents the idea of a 'personal daimon' assigned to each soul. As the Orphic poem on which the text is based predates Plato by at least a century, it is likely that Plato acquired this idea, like so many others, from Presocratic Orphic currents.[111] The daimon could be inborn, or it could exist independent of the person it accompanied. It was not always perceived as ontologically 'outside', but could also be interior. As Heraclitus suggested in the sixth century BCE, two and a half millennia before the German Romantics took up the idea: 'Man's character is his daimon'.[112]

James Hillman (1926–2011), whose school of archetypal psychology relies heavily on Jung but differs in its overtly declared debt to the pagan polytheism of the Neoplatonists, devoted a work to the ancient idea of the daimon, titled *The Soul's Code*. Hillman defined the daimon as an 'individualised soul-image':[113]

> The soul of each of us is given a unique daimon before we are born, and it has selected an image or pattern that we live on earth. This soul-companion, the daimon, guides us here . . . The daimon remembers what is in your image and belongs to your pattern, and therefore your daimon is the carrier of your destiny.[114]

The individual's physical body, parents, and place and time of birth – in other words, not only environment and genetic inheritance but also the natal horoscope – are all 'chosen' because they belong to the necessity of the daimon, who is both 'outside' the configurations of the horoscope and 'inside' because the seminal moment of birth reflects the soul's own choice. Discussing the nature of Jung's daimonic visitations, Hillman noted:

> He [Jung] did call up voices from the deep, and these are daimons, in the Greek sense of the word ... These were figures from the middle world. They were not necessarily only from the underworld. They were the mediators in a way but they were living figures.[115]

The 'holy guardian angel'

The 'personal daimon', in Jewish, Christian, and Islamic adaptations, eventually merged into the figure of the 'guardian angel'.[116] The word 'angel' is derived from the Greek *angelos*, meaning 'a messenger', divine or human, and the term was sometimes used for gods who served as messengers, such as Hermes and Iris.[117] Jung used the term 'messenger' in *Liber Novus* to describe such a being:

> We need magic to be able to receive or invoke the messenger and the communication of the incomprehensible.[118]

But the Abrahamic guardian angels are not, in traditional theological currents, understood as interior, nor are they concerned with the teleology of the horoscope. They are, quite literally, messengers sent from heaven by God to protect the individual. This applies especially to the Christian angels, who, after the official 'de-animation of the heavens' that occurred in 1277 at the request of Pope John I, lost their ancient astral associations and became obedient servants of God in a celestial world that was now perceived as a gigantic clockwork mechanism designed, created, and managed, but no longer inhabited by, divinity.[119]

Guardian angels are thus usually understood as ontologically separate from the human soul. It is only in the borderlands of Jewish and Islamic esoteric currents that the interior nature of this personal angel is described as an aspect of the divine spark within the human being. In the twelfth and thirteenth centuries there emerged within the Jewish communities of the diaspora, influencing and influenced by Islamic mystical speculation, explicit descriptions of the guardian angel or *maggid* as an image of the highest aspect of the soul. These exegeses drew on a syncretic base that adapted, within a Jewish religious framework, a number of Neoplatonic and Greco-Egyptian magical ideas and rituals from late antiquity,[120] and combined them with an already well-developed Jewish magical tradition believed to stretch back to Solomon and Moses.[121] The texts emerging from these Jewish esoteric currents acknowledged the astral nature of the angels and their responsiveness to ritual invocation.[122] As magic was international in the late antique world and tended to cross religious boundaries, the guardian angel in Jewish magic bears a close family resemblance to the personal daimon of the Neoplatonists.[123]

Although ontically autonomous, the guardian angel may also be found within, constituting that element of the human being consubstantial with divinity, and capable of being theurgically invoked through the organ of the imagination. Such speculations and rituals were taken up by heterodox Christians whose work was well known to Jung, such as Dionysius the Areopagite in the late sixth century and Henry Cornelius Agrippa in the late 16th.[124] These theurgic practices provided the basis of most of the medieval and early modern grimoires: the foundation texts of the Western magical tradition, replete with angelic and demonic forms whose gifts, coaxed or coerced, could sometimes lead to the angelification of the human being. The invocation of an angelic 'higher Self' also appeared in the currents of Jewish esotericism in the medieval period. Abraham ibn Ezra (1089–1164), a Jewish polymath, astrologer, and philosopher of the twelfth century, whose work was known to Jung,[125] described the angelic upper worlds in a manner closely resembling the *mundus imaginalis* presented by Iamblichus, in which, through theurgic ritual, the human can experience a 'natural and indivisible' connection with the divine.[126] The imagination, through which these celestial worlds may be perceived, is the 'spiritual body' or 'spirit vehicle' of the soul.[127]

Ibn Ezra proposed that the human soul derives originally from this celestial realm.[128] Each of the stars and planetary spheres likewise has its own soul and strives to return to its source, in the same manner that the human soul does. Ibn Ezra specifically referred to these planetary and stellar souls as angels, making a direct link to the astral daimons described by Porphyry and Iamblichus.[129] The human being seeking an experience of the higher realms must learn to see through 'the pupils of your heart'.[130] Through knowledge of one's own soul, the individual as microcosm can discover knowledge of the universe as macrocosm; the angels can be accessed from within because they *are* within. Ibn Ezra's idea of the goal of the inner journey echoes that of late antique theurgy: the individual is transformed through a direct experience of the divine. In Jung's psychological terminology, individual consciousness is transformed through a direct experience of the Self.

In medieval Jewish esoteric circles, complex theurgic rituals were developed, intended to facilitate a vision of the divine that might culminate in the angelification of the human.[131] The work of Eleazar of Worms (1176–1238) continued to resonate into and beyond the early modern period through magical compilations such as the *Sefer ha-Raziel* ('Book of the Angel Raziel'), yet another work with which Jung was familiar.[132] Eleazar, like ibn Ezra, adopted the idea of the Neoplatonic 'spirit-vehicle', made of the same substance as the angels and itself an angelic form; through this image of divinity within the human, called the *tselem*, the upper worlds could be accessed.[133] Eleazar understood this interior angel to rule the zodiacal sign under which the individual is born:

> Every angel who is an archon of the zodiacal sign of a person when it is sent below has the image of the person who is under it . . . And this is the meaning of 'And God created man in his image'.[134]

Each individual thus has an inner astral angel when he or she is born into the physical world. Eleazar's 'archon of the zodiacal sign of a person' mirrors the Neoplatonic idea of the *oikodespotes* in the natal horoscope, as it refers, not to the sign in which the Sun was placed, but to the planetary ruler of the Ascendant. This is a profoundly psychological understanding of the angelic entity: the form of the angel is the imaginal expression of a psychic dimension of the individual, which in turn incarnates in human shape a celestial complex of astral qualities and meanings embodied in the soul and its fate in mortal life.

Jung's grimoires

One of the most important magical texts of the medieval period is known in Latin as *Liber Razielis* or 'Book of Raziel'.[135] This work is especially relevant for any discussion of Jung's ritualistic use of the imagination.[136] *Liber Razielis* is a Latin translation of the Hebrew *Sefer ha-Raziel*.[137] It contains large portions of the work of Eleazar of Worms, and was also the chief source for the early modern grimoire known as *Sixth and Seventh Books of Moses* – a text in Jung's library that, in *Liber Novus*, he described as the property of the magician Philemon.[138] Because *Moses*, like a number of other grimoires, involves dialogues with daimonic beings related to planetary and zodiacal significators, it is a work of astral magic, rooted in an astral cosmology which can be traced back to Gnostic, Hermetic, early Jewish, and Neoplatonic origins. Not surprisingly, *Moses* was not the only grimoire that Jung acquired. There are a number of other texts of this kind in his library, and they might be better understood as theurgic because they deal with an ascent of the soul to a form of gnosis or unitive experience, and are not primarily concerned with 'lower' *goeteia*. It seems that, by the time he commenced work on *Liber Novus*, Jung was already intrigued by magic and the psychological transformations that could result from ritually performed techniques utilising the imagination as a gateway.

The magical work perhaps best known to those outside the circle of scholars of medieval and early modern magic is Henry Cornelius Agrippa von Nettesheim's sixteenth-century bible for aspiring magicians: *De occulta philosophia*, a three-volume comprehensive treatise on astrology, alchemy, and Kabbalistic magic. Agrippa, like the author of *Moses*, relied on the *Sefer ha-Raziel* for his source material.[139] Jung possessed two editions of Agrippa's text in German, one published in 1855 and the other in 1916,[140] as well as two rare early Latin editions, published respectively in 1584 and 1653, of another of Agrippa's works, *On the Vanity of All Arts and Sciences*.[141]

Equally significant in relation to *Liber Novus*, Jung also acquired a grimoire published in German in the early eighteenth century, purportedly by a medieval Jewish magus called Abraham of Worms,[142] titled *Buch der wahren Praktik in der uralten göttlichen Magie und in erstaunlichen Dingen*.[143] This book, divided into four parts, is the first printed version of a work known in English as *The Book of Abramelin*. According to Lon Milo DuQuette, who wrote the foreword for a new English translation published in 2006, the original manuscript was written between 1387 and 1427.[144] A large portion of Book Three of *Abramelin*, concerned with the invocation of various astral angels and spirits, is duplicated in the *Sixth and Seventh Books of Moses*.[145] *Abramelin* was first translated into English at the end of the nineteenth century by Samuel Liddell MacGregor Mathers, one of the founders of the Order of the Golden Dawn.[146] Through Mathers' translation and the publicising of the book's rituals by Aleister Crowley, as well as the publication of two new twenty-first-century editions in English and German, *Abramelin* remains a popular work in contemporary occult circles.[147]

Abramelin presents a specific astrological and angelogical ritual that its author claimed was taught to him by a Jewish-Egyptian mage called Abramelin. The object of the *Abramelin* ritual, which requires eighteen months of arduous preparation involving fasting, abstinence, and various psycho-spiritual exercises, is a form of gnosis resulting in the transformation of the magus and the power to command 'unredeemed' spirits. According to Mathers, the book's first English translator, the purpose of the ritual is

> By purity and self-denial to obtain the knowledge of and conversation with one's Guardian Angel, so that thereby and thereafter we may obtain the right of using the Evil Spirits for our servants in all material matters.[148]

Following the long period of ritual preparation, according to Abraham,

> I experienced this vision in humility and bliss for three continuous days. I was addressed lovingly and with friendship by my guardian angel. He explained the godly wisdom and Kabbalah and later completely explained the complete truth about this magic.[149]

Something very similar could be said about Jung's Philemon, who, according to *Liber Novus*, taught Jung the secrets of magic. In DuQuette's view, the Holy Guardian Angel of *Abramelin* 'is a divine entity uniquely linked to each individual – in essence the magician's personal spiritual soul mate'.[150] Although DuQuette proposes antecedents in Indian yogic practices, the source of this idea in Western magical currents in the medieval period is more likely to lie in the Neoplatonic concept of the *oikodespotes* and the Jewish idea of the *maggid* – although both were generally invoked for the transformation of the soul, rather than as a means through which 'unredeemed' demons could be summoned.[151]

Although it is unlikely that Jung concerned himself with summoning unredeemed spirits except in the psychological context of his concept of the 'shadow' – the problematic or unacceptable elements of the personal unconscious[152] – it is not difficult to understand why he was interested in *Abramelin* from a psychological perspective. Philemon, in Judaeo-Christian religious contexts, might be understood as a form of guardian angel as well as an archetypal image of the wisdom of the collective unconscious. It is also unlikely that Jung would have missed the parallels between the 'Holy Guardian Angel' of *Abramelin* and the Neoplatonic *oikodespotes*. Both enjoy a liminal status that is inner and psychological as well as objective and celestial; both are denizens of the *mundus imaginalis*; and both act as a bridge between individual microcosm and universal macrocosm. It is possible that Jung may have attempted the *Abramelin* ritual in a form adapted to his psychological understanding of Iamblichean theurgy, the Neoplatonically inspired astral magic developed by Marsilio Ficino in the late fifteenth century,[153] and Loyola's *exercitia*, and experienced the presence of an imaginal inner guide whom he referred to as 'my psychagogue', and whom he called Philemon.[154]

That Jung was deeply interested in ritual magic is hardly surprising, as the boundary between magical practices and psychological explorations is a fragile and constantly shifting one. Jung's investigations moved beyond the late antique, medieval, and early modern grimoires to the literature of contemporary magical orders such as the Fraternitas Saturni, whose journals he acquired for a brief period in the late 1920s, and which promulgated the idea of an imminent new 'Age of Aquarius' governed by the planet Saturn.[155] Sonu Shamdasani notes that a work was published in 1912 by Ludwig Staudenmaier, a German professor of chemistry, titled *Magic as an Experimental Science*; this book describes Staudenmaier's experiments with 'automatic writing' and deliberately induced visual hallucinations. The aim of Staudenmaier's efforts was, according to Shamdasani, to 'provide a scientific explanation of magic'.[156] Jung possessed a copy of this work and marked several passages in it. Restricted by the conventions and cultural expectations of his time and his profession, Jung nevertheless found the courage to acknowledge the importance of this liminal zone where psychological insights could be found in the applications of ritual magic to the development of human consciousness through the imagination, that 'organ of the soul' through which invisible worlds could be accessed.

Evidence that Jung practiced as well as read about magic – or, perhaps more accurately, theurgy – does not automatically indicate that he was a 'believer' in the sense that Agrippa and MacGregor Mathers were, or that he invoked astral entities every evening before bedtime. For Jung, everything, in the end, needed to be understood within the context of human psychology. Magic is a theme that unquestionably looms large in *Liber Novus*. And astral magic – those rituals concerned with invoking and navigating an ascent of the soul through the planetary spheres, in order to break the compulsive chains of astral fate – likewise features prominently as a psychological theme in various volumes of the *Collected Works*. A magical ritual to invoke the Sun-god appears in *Liber Novus*, inspired in part by the ritual invocation in the *Mithras Liturgy*; a similar type of invocation, echoing a number of themes in Thomas Taylor's English translation of the hieratic Orphic *Hymn to Protogonos*, appears in one of the *Black Books*, dedicated to the new god of the Aion, the Orphic primal deity Phanes.[157] As for the 'real' nature of whatever it is that responds to such invocations, Jung viewed these entities as imaginal personifications of the archetypal potencies of the collective unconscious. That, however, is not an explanation likely to comfort those who expect to find rigorous scientific verification in the liminal zones.

Notes

1 Iamblichus, *De mysteriis*, IX:3.
2 Jung, *MDR*, pp. 369 and 391.

3 For Jung's involvement in Gnostic texts, see Chapter 5.

4 See John Dillon, *The Middle Platonists* (Ithaca, NY: Cornell University Press, 1997), pp. 384–96. Jung acquired G.R.S. Mead's English translations of the *Mithras Liturgy* (G.R.S. Mead, *The Mysteries of Mithra* [London: Theosophical Publishing Society, 1907]) and the *Chaldean Oracles* (G.R.S. Mead, *The Chaldean Oracles* [London: Theosophical Publishing Society, 1908]), as well as Albercht Dieterich's German translation, *Ein Mithrasliturgie* (Leipzig: Teubner, 1903) and Franz Cumont's discussion of the text, *Die Mysterien des Mithra* (Leipzig: Teubner, 1903). Jung refers to all these texts in *Psychology of the Unconscious*. For more recent English translations and commentaries, see Hans Dieter Betz, *The Mithras Liturgy* (Tübingen: Mohr Siebeck, 2003); Hans Lewy, *Chaldaean Oracles and Theurgy* (Paris: Institut d'Études Augustiniennes, 2011 [1956]).

5 According to *MDR*, p. 186, during this period Jung 'read like mad' a work by Georg Friedrich Creuzer, *Symbolik und Mythologie der alten Völker* (Leipzig: K.W. Leske, 1810–12). Creuzer had also translated into Latin the works of Plotinus and Proclus. For Creuzer's Neoplatonic translations, see Georg Friedrich Creuzer (trans.), *Plotini Enneades cum Marsilii Ficini Interpretatione Castigata* (Paris: Dübner, 1855). For the relationship between Jung's ideas and those of the Neoplatonists, see James Hillman, 'Plotino, Ficino, and Vico as Precursors of Archetypal Psychology', in James Hillman, *Loose Ends* (Zürich: Spring, 1975), pp. 146–69; Bruce MacLennan, 'Evolution, Jung, and Theurgy', in Robert Berchman and John F. Finamore (eds.), *History of Platonism* (New Orleans, LA: University Press of the South, 2005).

6 Another edition of *De mysteriis* that Jung acquired was Pierre Quillard (trans.), *Le livre de Jamblique sur les mystères* (Paris: Libraire de l'art indépendant, 1875). Jung referred to Iamblichus' *De mysteriis* in CW9i, ¶573 and his *Vita Pythagorica* in CW18, ¶1521, indicating familiarity with both works, although he never discussed Iamblichus' theurgy in the *Collected Works*.

7 For Neoplatonism in the Renaissance, see Yates, *Giordano Bruno*; Michael J.B. Allen, Valery Rees, and Martin Davies (eds.), *Marsilio Ficino* (Leiden: Brill, 2002); Moshe Idel, 'The Magical and Neoplatonic Interpretations of the Kabbalah in the Renaissance', in Bernard Dov Cooperman (ed.), *Jewish Thought in the Sixteenth Century* (Cambridge, MA: Harvard University Press, 1983), pp. 186–242; Lenn E. Goodman (ed.), *Neoplatonism and Jewish Thought* (Albany: SUNY Press, 1992). For Neoplatonism in the British occult revival of the late nineteenth century, see Hanegraaff, *New Age Religion*, pp. 386–92. For the Theosophists' acknowledgement of their debt to Neoplatonism, see Anonymous, 'Ancient Landmarks', *Theosophy* 28:2 (1939), pp. 53–57.

8 For the term 'hieratic Platonism', see Lewy, *Chaldaean Oracles*, p. 464.

9 For the late Neoplatonists, see Crystal Addey, 'Oracles, Religious Practices, and Philosophy in Late Neoplatonism' (2007), <www.practical-philosophy.org.uk>, pp. 31–35; Sebastian R.P. Gertz, *Death and Immortality in Late Neoplatonism* (Leiden: Brill, 2011).

10 For Christian Platonism, see Andrew Louth, *The Origins of the Christian Mystical Tradition* (Oxford: Oxford University Press, 1983); I.P. Sheldon-Williams, 'The Greek Christian Platonist Tradition from the Cappadocians to Maximus and Eriugena', in A.H. Armstrong (ed.), *Later Greek and Early Medieval Philosophy* (Cambridge: Cambridge University Press, 1967), pp. 421–534.

11 References to Plotinus in the *Collected Works* include Jung, CW6, ¶21; Jung, CW9ii, ¶342; Jung, CW14, ¶761; Jung, CW5, ¶198; Jung, CW8, ¶927. There are also numerous citations in Jung, *Psychology of the Unconscious* and Jung, *Modern Psychology*.

12 For the various perspectives on Plotinus' involvement in magic, see Wendy Elgersma Helleman, 'Plotinus and Magic', *International Journal of the Platonic Tradition*, 4 (2010), pp. 114–46. For Plotinus' influence on Christian thought, see John M. Rist, 'Plotinus and Christian Philosophy', in Lloyd P. Gerson, *The Cambridge Companion to Plotinus* (Cambridge: Cambridge University Press, 1996), pp. 386–413; Henry J. Blumenthal and Robert A. Markus (eds.), *Neoplatonism and Early Christian Thought* (Farnham: Ashgate, 1981). Plotinus was not entirely averse to magic; see Philip Merlan, 'Plotinus and Magic', *Isis* 44:4 (1953), pp. 341–48; A.H. Armstrong, 'Was Plotinus a Magician?', *Phronesis* 1:1 (1955), pp. 73–79; Zeke Mazur, 'Unio Magica: Part I: On the Magical Origins of

Plotinus' Mysticism', *Dionysius* 21 (2003), pp. 23–52; Zeke Mazur, 'Unio Magica: Part II; Plotinus, Theurgy, and the Question of Ritual', *Dionysius* 22 (2004), pp. 29–55.

13 Jung, CW14, ¶761.

14 Head of Plotinus from Museo Ostia Antica, Inv. 436. This head is one of four replicas all of which were discovered at Ostia. The identification as Plotinus is probable but not proven.

15 Jung, CW9ii, ¶342, citing Plotinus, Ennead VI, in Stephen MacKenna (trans.), *Plotinus* (London: Medici Society, 1917–30), originally published in six volumes, later reissued in one volume (London: Faber & Faber, 1956). See below, n. 17.

16 Jung, *MDR*, p. 222.

17 The standard older English translation is MacKenna's *Plotinus*. A more recent English translation is A.H. Armstrong, trans., *Plotinus*, 7 volumes (Loeb Classical Library, 1966–88). The Greek word *enneas* (εννεας) means a collection of nine objects or entities, from εννεα, meaning nine. Porphyry edited his master's writings into fifty-four treatises of varying lengths, setting each of these into an *enneas* or group of nine dealing with a specific theme; there are thus six of these groups, providing the basis for MacKenna's six-volume translation.

18 Arthur C. Drews (trans.), *Plotin und der Untergang der antiken Weltanschaunng* (Jena: E. Diederichs, 1907). Drews published a work in 1910, *Die Christusmythe* (Jena: E. Diederichs, 1910), which related ancient astrological speculations to the origins of religion and the hidden structure of the Gospels. Not surprisingly, Jung acquired this work as well as Drews' translation of Plotinus.

19 Paul Henry and Hans-Rudolf Schwyzer (eds.), *Plotini opera, Porphyrii vita Plotini, Enneades I–III, IV–VI* (Paris: Desclée de Brouwer, 1951–59).

20 Jung, *Psychology of the Unconscious*, p. 82, citing Plotinus, Ennead II.5.3. By 'ideas', Jung is referring to Plotinus' concept of the Platonic Ideas or archetypal forms.

21 Jung, *Psychology of the Unconscious*, p. 81.

22 Jung, CW5, ¶¶296–97.

23 Plotinus, Ennead IV.4.41.

24 Plotinus, Ennead II.3.7.

25 Plotinus, Ennead II.3.7–8.

26 Jung, *Psychology of the Unconscious*, p. 81. For more on Phanes in *Liber Novus*, see Greene, *The Astrological World of Jung's 'Liber Novus'*, chapter 6.

27 Thomas Taylor (trans.), *The Mystical Hymns of Orpheus* (London: Robert Triphoon, 1824). Jung seems to have obtained his copy of this work before 1912. He cited one of the Orphic Hymns in *Psychology of the Unconscious* (p. 544, n. 34), but without any reference to the translator; but in Jung, CW5, the revised version of *Psychology of the Unconscious*, the reference is the same, and this time Taylor's translation is cited (¶528, n. 62).

28 See Reitzenstein, *Hellenistic Mystery-Religions*, pp. 90 n. 2, 241, 279.

29 Isaac Preston Cory, *Ancient Fragments of the Phoenician, Chaldean, Egyptian, Tyrian, Carthaginian, Indian, Persian, and Other Writers* (London: Reeves and Turner, 1876); Erwin Rohde, *Seelencult und Unsterlichkeitsglaube der Griechen* (Tübingen: Mohr, 1903).

30 For Jung's reliance on Cory during the writing of *Liber Novus*, see Shamdasani's note in Jung, *Liber Novus*, p. 301, n. 211.

31 G.R.S. Mead, *Orpheus* (London: Theosophical Publishing Society, 1896).

32 Taylor (trans.), *The Mystical Hymns of Orpheus*, p. 1. Taylor based his statement in part on Iamblichus, who declared that Pythagoras derived all his doctrines from Orpheus. See Iamblichus, *On the Pythagorean Life*, trans. Gillian Clark (Liverpool: Liverpool University Press, 1989), 28.146, 28.147, and 28.151.

33 Thomas Taylor (trans.), *Ocellus Lucanus, On the Nature of the Universe* (London: John Bohn, 1831).

34 The provenance of this engraving is unknown, and there are no extant late antique busts of Iamblichus.

35 The epithet 'divine' (θεοις) is used to describe Iamblichus in a number of late antique sources. See Shaw, *Theurgy and the Soul*, p. 26, n. 13.

36 See Iamblichus, *De mysteriis*, IX:1–3. See also Crystal Addey, 'Oracles, Dreams, and Astrology in Iamblichus' *De mysteriis*', in Curry and Voss (eds.), *Seeing with Different Eyes*, pp. 35–58; John Dillon (ed. and trans.), *Fragments of Iamblichus' Commentary on the Timaeus* (Leiden: Brill, 1973).
37 Iamblichus' theories on the mediating role of the imagination are explained in a still highly respected work by Murray Wright Bundy that Jung acquired at some point after its publication in 1927: *The Theory of Imagination in Classical and Medieval Thought* (Urbana: University of Illinois Press, 1927).
38 Jung, CW18, ¶407. The lecture, originally given in 1935, appeared first in published form in C.G. Jung, *Analytical Psycholoy* (London: Routledge & Kegan Paul, 1968).
39 Iamblichus, *De mysteriis*, I.21. Clarke, Dillon, and Hershbell (*De mysteriis*, p. 79, n. 112), suggest that the term *sunthemata* here describes 'the various magical substances and combinations of substances that form the basis for theurgic practice'.
40 For the history of the term 'theurgy', see Lewy, *Chaldaean Oracles*, pp. 461–66; E.R. Dodds, *The Greeks and the Irrational* (Berkeley: University of California Press, 1957), pp. 283–310.
41 See Shaw, *Theurgy and the Soul*, pp. 40–42; Garth Fowden, *The Egyptian Hermes* (Princeton, NJ: Princeton University Press, 1993), pp. 1–2, 86–87. A translation of and commentary on the *Chaldaean Oracles* was published in two volumes by G.R.S. Mead (London: Theosophical Publishing Society, 1908). Jung naturally acquired this work.
42 See Helleman, 'Plotinus and Magic'.
43 Iamblichus, *De mysteriis*, V.26.
44 See Jung, *Liber Novus*, pp. 284–85, discussed in greater detail in Chapter 7.
45 Paul Deussen, *Allgemeine Geschichte der Philosophie*, 2 volumes (Leipzig: F.A. Brockhaus, 1894–1917).
46 Jung, CW6, ¶336.
47 Jung, 'Über den Archetypus mit besonderer Berücksichtigung des Animabegriffes', translated in Jung, CW9i, ¶¶111–155.
48 Jung, CW9i, ¶130, n. 19.
49 Jung was concerned with the question of the degree to which cultural context shapes religious experience. This debate is ongoing in the academy; see the references given below, n. 70.
50 Jung, CW18, ¶1536.
51 Iamblichus, *De mysteriis*, III.14.
52 Iamblichus, *De mysteriis*, II.11.
53 Iamblichus, *De mysteriis* III.25.
54 Iamblichus, *De mysteriis*, III.14. See also Shaw, 'Theurgy', p. 1.
55 References to magic in Jung's *Collected Works* are too numerous to list here; see the entries in Jung, CW20, 'magic'.
56 Jung, CW6, ¶316.
57 Gregory Shaw has emphasised that the work of these modern occultists 'should not be ignored by scholars', because it provides useful evidence of modern appropriations of Iamblichean theurgy; see Shaw, 'Theurgy', p. 4, n. 12.
58 Israel Regardie, *The Tree of Life* (London: Rider, 1932), p. 36. The second of Regardie's works that Jung acquired was *The Philosopher's Stone* (London: Rider, 1938).
59 For the idea of theurgy as 'inner ritual', see Mazur, '*Unio Magica*: Part II'.
60 For the stone, see Greene, *The Astrological World of Jung's 'Liber Novus'*, chapter 2.
61 See Jung's use of the salamanders shaped like the astrological glyph of Leo in the painting of the solar giant Izdubar, discussed in Greene, *The Astrological World of Jung's 'Liber Novus'*, pp. 37–39.
62 For the genesis of the material, see Shamsasani, 'Introduction', in *Liber Novus*, pp. 198–203.
63 Jung, *Black Book* 2, cited in Jung, *Liber Novus*, p. 200, n. 67.
64 Gerhard Wehr, *An Illustrated Biography of Jung*, trans. M. Kohn (Boston, MA: Shambhala, 1989), p. 72. The later Shambhala reprint of this work, *Jung* (Boston, MA: Shambhala, 2001), does not contain the image. See also Jay Sherry, *A Pictorial Guide to The Red Book* (Archive

for Research in Archetypal Symbolism, ARAS Connections, 2010). Sherry has reproduced Jung's 1914 'draft' version of Philemon, and points out the similarity between this image and that of William Blake's painting, *The Elohim Creating Adam*. Shamdasani has also commented on Blake's influence on Jung's paintings; see Scott Horton, 'Inside Jung's *Red Book*: Six Questions for Sonu Shamdasani', *Harpers Magazine*, 12 July 2014, at <http://harpers.org/blog/2009/10/inside-jungs-_red-book_-six-questions-for-sonu-shamdasani/>.

65 For these Roman images of Aion, see Chapter 5.

66 See Thorburn, *Art and the Unconscious*, pp. 3–38; Jung, CW15, ¶¶155–162.

67 Examples are the works of H.P. Blavatsky, Alice A. Bailey, and Max Heindel, all of whom attributed their work to highly evolved disincarnate entities. For Jung's views on 'automatic writing' or 'psychography', see Jung, CW1, ¶¶28, 45, 49, 88, 96; Jung, CW18, ¶¶725–26, 731, 795.

68 For 'unitive' experiences, see Dan Merkur, *Mystical Moments and Unitive Thinking* (Albany: SUNY Press, 1999). For the term 'RASC', see Alan F. Segal, *Life After Death* (New York: Doubleday, 2012), p. 402. See also Jung, CW11, ¶¶474–487.

69 E.R. Dodds, 'Theurgy and Its Relationship to Neoplatonism', *Journal of Roman Studies* 37:1–2 (1947), pp. 55–69, on p. 58. Jung was familiar with the *Oracles* through Mead's translation as well as Cory's *Ancient Fragments*, which notes on p. 355 the equation in the *Oracles* of the primal power with fire.

70 The wealth of scholarly literature on this theme ranges from cognitive science to theological speculation. Jung was strongly influenced by James' *The Varieties of Religious Experience*. For Jung's own discussions, see the essays in Jung, CW11. For more recent discussions, see Jensine Andresen (ed.), *Religion in Mind* (Cambridge: Cambridge University Press, 2001); Steven T. Katz (ed.), *Mysticism and Language* (Oxford: Oxford University Press, 1992); F. Samuel Brainard, 'Defining "Mystical Experience"', *Journal of the American Academy of Religion*, 64:2 (1996), pp. 359–93; Ralph W. Hood, Jr., 'The Construction and Preliminary Validation of a Measure of Reported Mystical Experience', *Journal for the Scientific Study of Religion* 14 (1975), pp. 29–41.

71 Albertus Magnus, *De mirabilibus mundi* (1485), cited in Jung, CW8, ¶859.

72 Jung, CW9i, ¶334.

73 Iamblichus, *De mysteriis*, 115.3–7. See also Gregory Shaw, 'The Talisman', in Angela Voss and Jean Hinson Lall (eds.), *The Imaginal Cosmos* (Canterbury: University of Kent, 2007), pp. 25–34.

74 Jung, CW14, ¶753. For more of Jung's many discussions on 'active imagination', see Jung, CW8, ¶¶166–175; Jung, CW9i, ¶621; Jung, CW14, ¶¶752–755. See also Chodorow (ed.), *Jung on Active Imagination*; Marie-Louise von Franz, *Alchemical Active Imagination* (Irving, TX: Spring, 1979; repr. New York: Shambhala, 1997).

75 For Jung's associations between the *unus mundus* of alchemy, the Platonic World Soul, and the collective unconscious, see Jung, CW8, ¶393; Jung, CW11, ¶448.

76 Jung, *Liber Novus*, p. 314.

77 See Crystal Addey, 'In the Light of the Sphere', in Geoffrey Samuel and Jay Johnston (eds.), *Religion and the Subtle Body in Asia and the West* (London: Routledge, 2013), pp. 149–67. For the soul-vehicle and the imagination as intermediary, see also John F. Finamore, *Iamblichus and the Theory of the Vehicle of the Soul* (Chico, CA: Scholars Press, 1994).

78 See Shaw, *Theurgy and the Soul*, pp. 86–87. See also E.R. Dodds (ed. and trans.), *Proclus: The Elements of Theology* (Oxford: Clarendon Press, 1963), pp. 222–23 and 344–45.

79 See Shaw, *Theurgy and the Soul*, p. 87. For examples, see Iamblichus, *De mysteriis*, 105.1; 125.5; 127.9. On 'receptivity' as a critical factor in theurgy, see Crystal Addey, 'Divine Possession and Divination in the Graeco-Roman World' *On the Mysteries*', in Bettina E. Schmidt and Lucy Huskinson (eds.), *Spirit Possession and Trance* (London: Continuum, 2010), pp. 171–81.

80 Hermias, *Commentary on Plato's Phaedrus*, 65.26–69.31, cited in D.A. Russell, 'Some Texts Similar to *De genio*', in Plutarch, *On the Daimonion of Socrates*, p. 204.

81 For Jung's understanding of psychosis as the result of the inundation of the unconscious, see, for example, Jung, CW3, ¶¶317–87; CW18, ¶¶594 and 1159; CW5, ¶474; CW16, ¶196.

82 See Jung, CW5, ¶644.
83 Iamblichus, *De mysteriis*, 3:14. See also Addey, 'In the Light of the Sphere', p. 155.
84 Plato, *Republic*, 617d, describing the soul's choice of a personal daimon before incarnating in a physical body. The personal daimon also appears in Plato, *Phaedrus*, 248c. See also Plotinus, *Ennead* III, 4.3.18–20; Porphyry, *Letter to Anebo* 2, 14–17.
85 Iamblichus, *De mysteriis*, IX.6.
86 Iamblichus, *De mysteriis*, IX.7.
87 Plotinus, Ennead III.4.5.
88 Iamblichus, *Iamblichus of Chalcis: The Letters*, trans. John M. Dillon and Wolfgang Polleichtner (Atlanta, GA: Scholars Press, 2009), p. 95.
89 Iamblichus, *De mysteriis*, 282.1–5. See also Plato, *Timaeus*, 90a–c, and the discussion in Shaw, *Theurgy and the Soul*, p. 218.
90 Iamblichus, *De mysteriis*, 283:19–284:10, cited in Shaw, *Theurgy and the Soul*, pp. 218–19.
91 Dodds, *The Greeks and the Irrational*, p. 42. See also Georg Luck, *Arcana Mundi* (Baltimore, MD: Johns Hopkins University Press, 1985), p. 171.
92 Porphyry, *Letter to Anebo*, 14a-d, 15a-b. See also Dorian Gieseler Greenbaum, *The Daimon in Hellenistic Astrology* (Leiden: Brill, 2015), pp. 266–75.
93 For the nature of the Neoplatonic personal daimon and an analysis of the methods utilised by Hellenistic astrologers to calculate the *oikodespotes*, see Greenbaum, *The Daimon*, pp. 236–75.
94 Porphyry, *Introduction to the Tetrabiblos*, in *Porphyry the Philosopher, Introduction to the Tetrabiblos*, trans. James Holden (Tempe, AZ: American Federation of Astrologers, 2009), pp. 22–25.
95 For example, Macrobius, a fifth-century author with whose work Jung was familiar, maintained in his *Saturnalia* that the personal daimon is always represented by the Sun in the horoscope. See Macrobius, *The Saturnalia*, trans. Percival Vaughan Davies (New York: Columbia University Press, 1969), I.19.16–18, p. 136. For Jung's references to the *Saturnalia*, see Jung, CW5, ¶425; Jung, CW14, ¶¶154–155, 173, 701.
96 Iamblichus, *De Mysteriis* IX.1, 273.2–9.
97 Iamblichus did not offer a list of these *sunthemata* in *De mysteriis*. But see Proclus, *Commentary on Plato's Timaeus*, I.3.10, in which the plant called *heliotropius* (whose flower turns its head following the Sun) and the gemstone known as bloodstone (a form of green jasper mottled with red) are described as *sunthemata* of the Sun.
98 In medieval Arab astrology, the *oikodespotes* was called *alcocoden*, the 'Guardian Angel' or 'Giver of the Years'. For the *alcocoden*, see James R. Lewis, *The Astrology Book* (Canton, MI: Visible Ink Press, 2003), pp. 18–19, 346–47.
99 Although Iamblichus, Plotinus, Porphyry, and Proclus were well represented in Jung's library, Jung does not seem to have acquired Porphyry's introduction to the *Tetrabiblos*, nor any manuscripts from other Hellenistic astrologers concerned with the *oikodespotes*, mainly found in the *Catalogus Codicum Astrologorum Graecorum* published between 1898 and 1953.
100 Personal communication from Gret Baumann-Jung, July 1985, Stoos, Switzerland. See the calculation sheet Jung prepared for his daughter Helene in Chapter 2.
101 See, for example, Leo, *The Key to Your Own Nativity*, pp. 10–14.
102 Birth data: Carl Gustav Jung, 26 July 1875, 7.27 pm, Kesswil, Switzerland. For Porphyry's requirements, see Porphyry, *Introduction to Ptolemy's Tetrabiblos*, pp. 23–24. For modern explanations of Hellenistic astrological terms, see Joseph Crane, *Astrological Roots* (Bournemouth: Wessex Astrologer, 2007).
103 See Chapter 2 for John Thorburn's comments on the unique strength and beneficence of Jung's natal Saturn.
104 Michael Maier, *Symbola aureae mensae duodecim nationum* (Frankfurt: Julius Ägidius von Negelein, 1617), cited in Jung, CW14, p. 229, n. 585.
105 For Saturn as the matrix of the Philosopher's Stone, see Jung, CW13, ¶401; Jung, CW14, ¶703.
106 For a detailed examination of the Saturnian elements in Philemon, see Greene, *The Astrological World of Jung's 'Liber Novus'*, Chapter 5.

107 Jung, *MDR*, p. 207.
108 Betegh, *The Derveni Papyrus*, p. 86.
109 See Dorian Gieseler Greenbaum, 'Allotment and Fate', *The Astrological Journal* 56:2 (2014), pp. 27–31.
110 Betegh, *The Derveni Papyrus* Col. 3, p. 9. This text also reveals the daimon's more ambiguous face: see Betegh, *The Derveni Papyrus*, Col. 6, p. 15.
111 For the 'personal daimon' in this Orphic text, see Betegh, *The Derveni Papyrus*, Col. 3, p. 9. For the 'guardian spirit' of each soul in Plato, see Plato, *Phaedrus*, 107d.5–7; Plato, *Republic*, 617d. See also Betegh's comments in *The Derveni Papyrus*, p. 87; K. Tsantsanoglou, 'The First Columns of the Derveni Papyrus and their Religious Significance', in André Laks and Glenn W. Most (eds.), *Studies on the Derveni Papyrus* (Oxford: Oxford University Press, 2001), pp. 93–128, on pp. 96 and 105.
112 Heraclitus, DK B119, in Charles H. Kahn (trans.), *The Art and Thought of Heraclitus* (Cambridge: Cambridge University Press, 1981), CXIV, p. 81. The Greek word used in this fragment, δαιμων, is usually translated into English as 'fate'. Jung cited Heraclitus frequently in the *Collected Works*; see Jung, CW8, ¶¶99, 278, 916; Jung, CW12, ¶¶157, 182, 333, 435.
113 James Hillman, *The Soul's Code* (New York: Warner Books, 1997), p. 10.
114 Hillman, *The Soul's Code*, p. 8.
115 James Hillman, 'Jung's Daimonic Inheritance', *Sphinx* 1 (1988), pp. 9–19. See also James Hillman and Sonu Shamdasani, *Lament of the Dead* (New York: W.W. Norton, 2013), p. 119.
116 This being is known in Islamic angelology as the *Hafaza*; in Hebrew, any angel, including one guarding an individual, is *mal'akh*, a 'messenger'. See Saul M. Olyan, *A Thousand Thousands Served Him* (Tübingen: Mohr Siebeck, 1993), p. 4 and the references given on that page in n. 10.
117 For Hermes as *angelos*, see Homer, *Odyssey* 5:29; for Iris, see Homer, *Iliad* 2:786. For Greco-Roman divine *angeloi*, see Rangar Kline, *Ancient Angels* (Leiden: Brill, 2011).
118 Jung, *Liber Novus*, p. 314.
119 See D. Piché (ed. and trans.), *La condamnation parisienne de 1277* (Paris: Vrin, 1999); Henrik Wels, 'Late Medieval Debates on the Location of Angels After the Condemnation of 1277', in Isabel Iribarren and Martin Lenz (eds.), *Angels in Medieval Philosophical Inquiry* (Aldershot: Ashgate, 2008), pp. 113–27.
120 For Neoplatonic elements in late antique and medieval Jewish magic, see Idel, 'The Magical and Neoplatonic Interpretations'; Goodman (ed.), *Neoplatonism and Jewish Thought*. For the syncretism of Jewish and Greco-Egyptian magical rituals in the Greek Magical Papyri, see Hans Dieter Betz, *The Greek Magical Papyri in Translation* (Chicago: University of Chicago Press, 1986), pp. xliv–xlviii.
121 For the magical traditions surrounding Solomon and Moses, see Pablo A. Torijano, *Solomon the Esoteric King* (Leiden: Brill, 2002); Andreas Kilcher, 'The Moses of Sinai and the Moses of Egypt: Moses as Magician in Jewish Literature and Western Esotericism', *Aries* 4:2 (2004), pp. 148–70.
122 For angelic invocation in late antique Jewish literature, see Rebecca Macy Lesses, 'Speaking with Angels', *Harvard Theological Review* 89:1 (1996), pp. 41–60; Peter Schäfer, 'Jewish Magic Literature in Late Antiquity and the Early Middle Ages', *Journal of Jewish Studies* 41:1 (1990), pp. 75–91.
123 The guardian angel also resembles the parados or 'spirit helper' of the Greek Magical Papyri; see Betz, *The Greek Magical Papyri*, p. 160. Jung had access to Dieterich's references to and comments on the Magical Papyri in *Das Mithrasliturgie*.
124 For Dionysius' angelic theurgy, see Wear and Dillon, *Dionysius the Areopagite*, pp. 117–29; Gregory Shaw, 'Neoplatonic Theurgy and Dionysius the Areopagite', *Journal of Early Christian Studies* 7 (1999), pp. 573–99.
125 See Jung, CW9ii, ¶169.
126 Iamblichus, *De mysteriis*, I.3. See also Henry Corbin, 'Mundus Imaginalis, or, the Imaginary and the Imaginal', trans. Ruth Horine, *Cahiers internationaux de symbolisme* 6 (1964), pp. 3–26.

127 See Finamore, *Iamblichus and the Theory of the Vehicle of the Soul*. For the transmission of the idea into the fifteenth and sixteenth centuries, see D.P. Walker, 'The Astral Body in Renaissance Medicine', *Journal of the Warburg and Courtauld Institutes* 21:1/2 (1958), pp. 119–33, on p. 123. For alchemical references to the 'spiritual' or 'astral' body, see Agrippa, *De occulta philosophia*, I:5, III:50; Martin Ruland, *A Lexicon of Alchemy or Alchemical Dictionary* (York Beach, ME: Samuel Weiser, 1984 [1893]), p. 182; Paracelsus, *Sämtliche Werke*, ed. Karl Sudhoff, 14 volumes (Munich and Berlin: Oldenbourg, 1922–33), VIII:161–70.

128 Abraham ibn Ezra, *Commentary to Exodus* 3:15, cited in Aaron Hughes, 'The Three Worlds of ibn Ezra's Hay ben Meqitz', *Journal of Jewish Thought and Philosophy* 11:1 (2002), pp. 1–24, on p. 5.

129 Abraham ibn Ezra, *Pirqei rabbi 'Eli'ezer* (Chapters of Rabbi Eliezer), MS HUC 75ff. 4b and 6b, cited in Elliot R. Wolfson, 'Merkavah Traditions in Philosophical Garb', *Proceedings of the American Academy for Jewish Research* 57 (1990–91), pp. 179–242.

130 Hughes, 'The Three Worlds', p. 14.

131 See Elliot Wolfson, 'Theosis, Vision, and the Astral Body in Medieval German Pietism and the Spanish Kabbalah', in Nicholas Campion and Liz Greene (eds.), *Sky and Symbol* (Lampeter: Sophia Centre Press, 2013), pp. 119–42.

132 See Jung, CW14, ¶572, n. 106.

133 For a detailed discussion of the tselem, see Gershom Scholem, *On the Mystical Shape of the Godhead*, trans. Joachim Neugroschel, ed. Jonathan Chipman (New York: Schocken Books, 1991), pp. 251–73.

134 Eleazar of Worms, *Hokhmat ha-Nefesh* (Benei Beraq, 1987), Ch. 48:80, cited in Wolfson, 'Theosis and the Astral Body', p. 131.

135 For the importance of this work, see Sophie Page, 'Uplifting Souls: The *Liber de essentia spirituum* and the *Liber Razielis*', in Claire Fanger (ed.), *Invoking Angels* (University Park: Penn State University Press, 2012), pp. 79–112. See also Don Karr, *Liber Salomonis*, at <www.digital-brilliance.com/kab/karr/Solomon/LibSal.pdf>. The original Hebrew version is known as *Sefer ha-Raziel*; see Joseph Dan, 'Book of Raziel', in *Encyclopaedia Judaica* 13:15691–93. For an English translation, see Steve Savedow (ed. and trans.), *Sepher Rezial Hemelach* (York Beach, ME: Samuel Weiser, 2000).

136 See Jung, CW13, ¶173.

137 For the various MS versions of *Sefer ha-Raziel*, which long predated its publication in 1701, see François Secret, 'Sur quelques traductions du Sefer Raziel', *REJ* 128 (1969), pp. 223–45. For a further discussion, see also Ioan P. Couliano, *Eros and Magic in the Renaissance*, trans. Margaret Cook (Chicago: University of Chicago Press, 1987), p. 167.

138 According to Joseph Peterson, *Moses*' work's most recent translator, the core of this grimoire was provided by *Liber Razielis*; see Joseph Peterson (ed. and trans.), *The Sixth and Seventh Books of Moses* (Lake Worth, FL: Ibis Press, 2008), p. ix. Jung's edition of *Moses* was Johann Scheible (ed.), *Das sechste und seibente Buch Mosis* (New York: William Radde, 1865).

139 Peterson (ed. and trans.), *Sixth and Seventh Books of Moses*, p. ix.

140 Heinrich Cornelius Agrippa von Nettesheim, *Die Cabbala des E.C.A. von Nettesheim* (Stuttgart: Johann Scheible, 1855); *H.C. Magische Werke samt den gehimnisvollen Schriften des Petrus von Abano* (Berlin: Hermann Bardsdorf, 1916).

141 Heinrich Cornelius Agrippa von Nettesheim, *De incertidome & vanitate omnium scientiarum & artium liber* (Hagae-Comitum: A. Ulacq, 1653).

142 For the identity of Abraham of Worms, see Raphael Patai, *The Jewish Alchemists* (Princeton, NJ: Princeton University Press, 1995), pp. 272–88; Bernd Roling, 'The Complete Nature of Christ', in Jan N. Bremmer and Jan R. Veenstra (eds.), *The Metamorphosis of Magic* (Leuven: Peeters, 2002), pp. 231–66, on pp. 245–46.

143 Abraham von Worms, *Die egyptischen großen Offenbarungen, in sich begreifend die aufgefundenen Geheimnisbücher Mosis* (Cologne: Peter Hammer, 1725).

144 Lon Milo DuQuette, 'Foreword', in Abraham von Worms, *The Book of Abramelin*, ed. Georg Dehn, trans. Steven Guth (Lake Worth, FL: Nicolas-Hays, 2006), p. xiii.

145 It is probable that both works drew on the *Sefer ha-Raziel*. *Moses* is likely to have been based on the Latin version, *Liber Razielis,* while *Abramelin* may rely directly on the older Hebrew version.
146 S.L. MacGregor Mathers (ed. and trans.), *The Book of the Sacred Magic of Abramelin the Mage* (London: John M. Watkins, 1897). Mathers used an incomplete French version of the text.
147 The new German edition is *Buch Abramelin das ist Die egyptischen großen Offenbarungen* (Leipzig: Editions Araki, 2001).
148 Mathers (ed. and trans.), *The Book of the Sacred Magic of Abramelin*, xxvi.
149 *The Book of Abramelin*, I.7, p. 28.
150 DuQuette, 'Foreward', in *The Book of Abramelin*, p. xv.
151 As well as the printed version of *Abramelin* that Jung acquired, manuscript versions exist in German, Hebrew, and Italian, all dating from the early seventeenth century. See Gershom Scholem, *Kabbalah* (New York: Meridian, 1978), p. 186.
152 For Jung's theory of the 'shadow', see, among many references, Jung, CW10, ¶¶444–57; Jung, CW9ii, ¶¶13–19. For Jung on demons as psychological compulsions, see Chapter 2.
153 Jung was familiar with Ficino's work; see the many references in Jung, CW20. For discussions of Ficino's use of planetary images as *sunthemata* to invoke celestial potencies, see Couliano, *Eros and Magic*, pp. 32–34.
154 For Jung's description of his first encounter with Philemon, see Jung, *MDR*, pp. 207–10. According to Shamdasani, Philemon first appeared in the *Black Books* on 27 January 1914; see Shamdasani, 'Introduction', in Jung, *Liber Novus*, pp. 200–201.
155 Jung acquired five volumes of the journal of the Fraternitas Saturni, *Saturn Gnosis*, dated between July 1928 and March 1930. For the only publication in English on this highly secretive order, see Stephen E. Flowers, *The Fraternitas Saturni or Brotherhood of Saturn* (Smithville, TX: Rûna-Raven Press, 2006 [1990]); see aso Hakl, *Eranos*, p. 38. For German publications by those involved with the order, see Aythos, *Die Fraternitas Saturni* (Munich: ARW, 1979); Frater V.D., *Die Fraternitas Saturni heute* (Büllingen: Verlag Ralph Tegtmeier Nachf, 1994). The Order still exists today and can be found at <www.fraternitas.de>.
156 Ludwig Staudenmaier, *Die Magie als Experimentelle Narurwissenschaft* (Leipzig: Akademische Verlagsgesellschaft, 1912). See Shamdasani's notes on Staudenmaier in Jung, *Liber Novus*, p. 200.
157 See Greene, *The Astrological World of Jung's 'Liber Novus'*, chapters 2 and 6.

PLATE 1 An example of melothesia, from a calendar by Stegmüller von Wiesensteig, 1443, Furstliche Furstenbergische Hofbibliotek, Donauschingen, Cod. 494

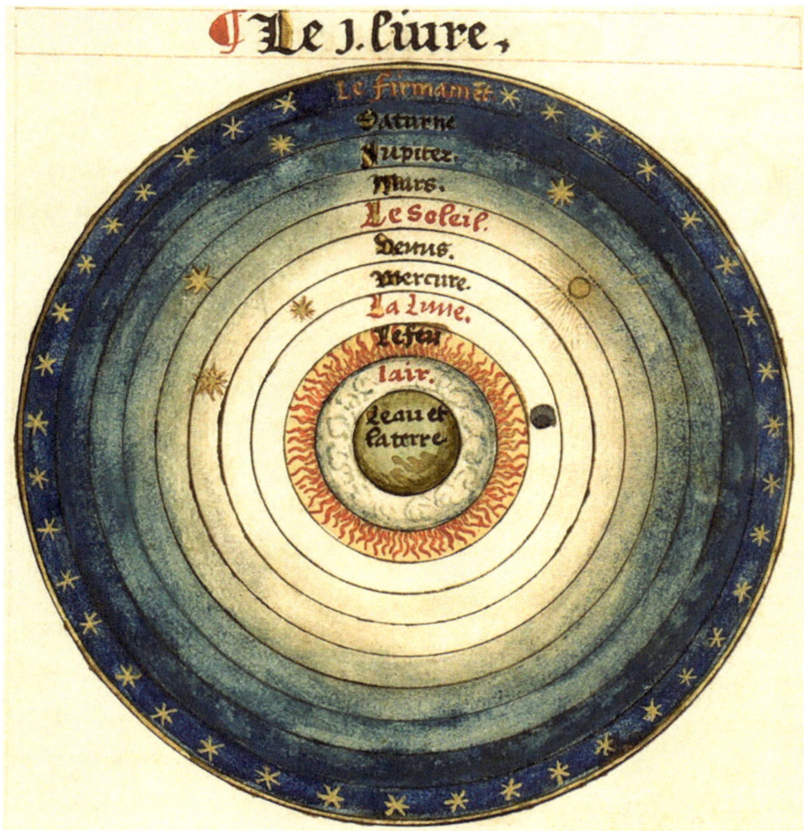

PLATE 2 The Aristotelian cosmos, showing the planetary spheres with the corruptible sublunar realm of the four elements below that of the Moon. Oronce Finé, *De mundi sphaera sive cosmographica* (Paris: Michael Vascosanus, 1549), Folio 8 verso, Houghton Library, Harvard University

PLATE 3 The lion-headed solar deity Chnoubis or Chnoumis, which Jung used in the cosmological painting titled *Systema Munditotius*. Intaglio, Kelsey 26118, Bonner 91, © Genevra Kornbluth

PLATE 4 Frontispiece for *Aion*: the Mithraic lion-headed god Aion, Roman, second to third century CE, Museo Gregorio Profano, Vatican

PLATE 5 'The Way of What Is to Come', in Jung, *Liber Novus*, p. 229, ©2007 Foundation of the Works of C. G. Jung, used by permission of W. W. Norton & Co., Inc.

FRONTISPICE.

PLATE 6 Frontispiece for Dupuis, *Origines de tous les cultes* (Paris: H. Agasse, 1795)

5

'THE GREAT FATE'

> Man's character is his fate.[1]
>
> —Heraclitus

> Fate and soul are but two names for the same principle.[2]
>
> —Novalis

> The ancients devised magic to compel fate. They needed it to determine outer fate. We need it to determine inner fate and to find the way that we are unable to conceive.[3]
>
> —C.G. Jung

A rose by any other name

Like the roads that lead to Rome, any discussion of Jung's astrology leads, sooner or later, to the question of how he understood fate. Astrology and philosophical speculations about fate have been cohabiting intimately since the origins of both. A number of modern astrological texts have addressed in more contemporary language the question of whether an individual's fate is described by the horoscope. Sometimes other words with different nuances are used, such as 'destiny'.[4] Many astrologers in the second half of the twentieth century began to reject the idea of fated circumstances altogether, and referred to 'trends' rather than the ancient idea of *Heimarmene*, the 'compulsion of the stars'. An example of this modernising of astral fate was offered by the British astrologer Jeff Mayo (1921–98), who declared categorically:

> An astrological aspect with regard to the future can correspond with any one of a variety of possibilities, mostly dependent upon the 'freedom of choice'

> of the individual concerned, yet the aspect still foretells the actual *trend* of circumstances, or the *nature* of the individual's reaction to the situation.[5]

Other astrologers accepted the idea of astral fate in principle, but suggested that it involves only the physical circumstances of the individual, and not the soul. This quasi-Platonic, quasi-Gnostic approach was expressed by the British astrologer Margaret Hone (1892–1969) in 1951:

> Inasmuch as a man identifies himself with his physical self and the physical world about him, so he is indissolubly part of it and subject to its changing pattern as formed by the planets in their orbits. Only by the recognition of that which he senses as greater than himself can he attune himself to what is beyond the terrestrial pattern. In this way, though he may not escape terrestrial happenings, by the doctrine of free and willing 'acceptance' he can 'will' that his real self is free in its reaction to them.[6]

This perspective allows a form of freedom as well as an acknowledgement of fate; but it reflects a dualism of spirit and matter that was alien to Jung's own view of their unity.

In antiquity, the ways in which astral fate was understood varied among different philosophical and religious systems. Certain Hermetic fragments claimed that astral fate acts upon the body, or on the lower dimensions of the soul, but the higher soul or *nous* remains free from its influence:

> We have the power to choose; it is within our power to choose the better, and in like way [to choose] the worse, according to our will. And if [our] choice clings to the evil things, it doth consort with the corporeal nature; [and] for this cause Fate rules o'er him who makes this choice. Since, then, the intellectual essence in us is absolutely free . . . on this account Fate does not reach it.[7]

This is the view echoed by the astrologer Margaret Hone in the mid-twentieth century. Certain Gnostic treatises, such as the *Apocryphon of John*,[8] present the idea that each planetary archon places a kind of psychic membrane over the human soul as it descends into incarnation, resulting in a soul-vehicle of seven layers, each under the governance of one of the seven archons.[9] These layers, collectively called the 'counterfeit spirit', were perceived as malign, reflecting the idea that the planetary archons bind the soul to matter through libidinous compulsions, and obstruct the soul's recollection of its divine source.[10]

Within early Christian contexts, the idea of *Heimarmene* remained an important theme in theological discourse, but astral fate was viewed as powerless against those who had undergone Christian baptism. In the medieval period, largely due to the teachings of the Dominican priest and Aristotelian philosopher, Thomas Aquinas (1225–74), the dualist approach presented in Hermetic and Gnostic treatises resurfaced as an acceptable Christian concept. A fate dictated by the stars was understood to pertain to physical desires and needs, since the body belonged to the corruptible 'sublunar' realm in the context of Aristotelian cosmology (see Plate 2). But the soul belonged to God and was beyond the reach of astral influences.[11]

Modern philosophers have come to no more inclusive agreement than their ancient predecessors.[12] The term 'fate' has been replaced by 'determinism', a word less prone to religious associations and adaptable to economic, climatic, social, and political rather than astral powers. Astrology has naturally been dropped from these modern philosophical discourses. But Jung remained profoundly concerned with the problem of fate in relation to the heavenly bodies. He looked to Kant, Schopenhauer, and Nietzsche for philosophical illumination, but he turned to the Neoplatonists, Stoics, Hermeticists, and Gnostics for more practical insights into the dilemma – not least because, in these older currents, astral fate lies at the centre of the discourse. Modern psychologies and psychiatries are also concerned with the question of fate. However, in cognitive and behavioural schools of psychology, as in philosophy, astrological discourse has largely vanished,[13] and fate is usually called by other names. In the field of organic psychiatry, it is increasingly enmeshed with the study of genetics, and is now referred to as 'genetic fate-mapping'.[14]

Nature, nurture, and reincarnation

The role of causality in human psychic suffering invariably leads back to that mystery surrounding fate, whatever synonyms might be adopted to replace the word. For example: are people born inherently 'bad' – genetically programmed (and thus fated) to do 'bad' deeds – or do they become 'bad' (and thus equally fated) through the pressure of external circumstances they did not choose? And if it is the latter, do they have any choice later or, given the right social and clinical resources, the possibility of healing? Two general approaches have arisen which form the backbone of the so-called nature-nurture debate in modern psychologies. The first conclusion, rooted in the theory of 'classical conditioning' developed by the Russian physiologist Ivan Petrovich Pavlov in the early twentieth century, embraces a perception of the human being as a *tabula rasa* ('blank slate') influenced entirely by environmental conditioning. Psychotherapeutic approaches based on this view are now known under the general umbrella of 'behavioural' therapies.[15] The second conclusion, also causal, is based on a purely biological view, in which the chemistry of the brain determines the psycho-physical future of the individual.[16] A middle way between these two extremes may also be adopted, in which physiology (nature) and environment (nurture) are both implicated, in varying degrees, in the formation of personality. In his early psychiatric work, it seems that Jung attempted this kind of compromise, declaring:

> The endless dilemma of culture and nature is always a question of too much or too little, never of either-or.[17]

By the time he began work on *Liber Novus*, however, Jung seems to have adopted a third approach. It was favoured in late antiquity but is unpopular today within the fields of medicine and organic psychiatry because it is acausal and resistant to demonstration through scientific methodologies. This approach involves a perception of the fate of the human being as embodying an *a priori* inherent character, Self, or soul-constellation that mysteriously expresses itself through the outer circumstances of an individual's life. The source and nature of this inherent 'essence' remains hidden, hinting at a more intuitive mode of speculation or, at the very least, the admission that 'proving' its existence is impossible within current research paradigms. The idea of an inherent temperament independent of, but complementing, both genetic inheritance and environment suggests a meaningful teleology of inner development, rather than static bondage to preordained circumstances. It may also be accompanied by the understanding that the intent of this essence – personified by the daimon – is reflected in the qualities of time described by the patterns of the natal horoscope.

This approach eventually seems to have dominated Jung's thinking on fate. In antiquity, the idea was usually accompanied by belief in successive incarnations of the soul; each human lifetime, its individual daimon, and its specific fate are shaped by the choices made in the previous lifetime.[18] The greater the individual's awareness of this fact, the more he or she is able to make conscious choices and develop creatively within the limits of that which cannot be changed. This results in greater harmony between the individual and the intent of the daimon. The idea of a series of incarnations, in which the 'karma' or psychic substance accrued in a given lifetime generates the challenges and rewards of the next lifetime, has had a very long life in Western esoteric currents, resurrected in modern times by Blavatsky and her followers through assimilating Hindu and Buddhist thought to Platonic and Neoplatonic concepts and lacing both with a distinctively Christian morality. Alan Leo, who embraced the idea wholeheartedly and incorporated it into his astrological writings, insisted that astrology 'has no permanent value' without incorporating the reality of former lives.[19]

That Jung was receptive to the idea of reincarnation, in later life and possibly earlier, is indicated by a statement in *Memories, Dreams, Reflections*:

> Somewhere 'out there' there must be a determinant, a necessity conditioning the world . . . This creative determinant . . . must decide what souls will plunge again into birth . . . It is possible that any further spell of three-dimensional life would have no more meaning once the soul had reached a certain stage of understanding; it would then no longer have to return . . . But if a karma still remains to be disposed of, then the soul relapses again into desires and returns to life once more, perhaps even doing so out of the realisation that something remains to be completed.[20]

Jung also speculated on what 'remains to be completed' in his own life:

> It must have been a passionate urge toward understanding which brought about my birth . . . I could well imagine that I might have lived in former centuries

> and there encountered questions I was not yet able to answer; that I had to be born again because I had not fulfilled the task that was given to me.[21]

Jung referred to reincarnation in the context of the Eastern concept of karma, and he also recognised its importance in Platonic and Neoplatonic literature; moreover, he was fully aware that modern Theosophical speculations borrowed from both. The link between the natal horoscope and the cycle of rebirth was described explicitly by Annie Besant (1847–1933), who became president of the Theosophical Society in 1907:[22]

> The karma of past lives, mental, emotional, and in relation to others, demands materials capable of the most varied expressions . . . According to this temperament will be the time of the birth of the body; it *must* be born into the world at a time when the physical planetary influences are suitable, and it thus is born under its astrological 'star'. It is not the star that imposes the temperament, but the temperament that fixes the epoch of birth under that star.[23]

Jung insisted that the idea of rebirth 'is inseparable from that of karma'.[24] He repeatedly encountered in Alan Leo's books the conviction that rebirth and karma are themselves inseparable from the moment of physical birth and the horoscope based on it. Although Jung did not relate rebirth and karma to astrology in any published work, it seems to have underpinned much of his understanding of his own horoscope, particularly in terms of what he viewed as 'what remains to be completed'.

Fate and individuation

Jung embraced the older, acausal view of fate during, or soon after, his break with Freud. In *Psychology of the Unconscious*, he indulged in one of his favourite pastimes: etymological associations, in this case connecting the Greek word for fate, *Moira*, with various words related to the Indo-European root *mer* or *mor*, meaning 'to die'. He related these words in turn to the Roman divine 'mothers', the *Matres* or *Matronae*, who are both the Teutonic Norns and the Greek Moirai.[25] This kind of imaginative association of words, word roots, and symbols is an aspect of Jung's thought that can be challenging to those who think of language as a purely semantic, culturally constructed instrument of communication. But whether or not Jung's analogical digressions comprise a 'scientific' method,[26] by the time he began work on *Liber Novus* he had already made the equation between fate and soul.

This may reflect the influence of German Romantic writers such as Novalis. It may also reflect Jung's study of astrology, especially the kind of astrology presented by Alan Leo, which led him to what he perceived as a clear demonstration of the a priori existence of a character structure mirrored by, or synchronous with, the natal horoscope. The inseparable intertwining of fate and character was presented by Leo in a work titled *Saturn: The Reaper*, which Jung seems to have acquired soon after its publication in 1916. In the foreword to this work, Leo declared: 'Character is destiny'.[27] For Jung, the qualities of time itself, reflected in astrological symbols, constitute astral fate, since time, as Jung declared, 'is often the symbol of fate'.[28] The moment of birth is thus a kind of snapshot, incarnated in flesh, of those 'typical qualities of the libido at a given moment'. Jung's deep and ongoing concern with the nature of fate might be expected in someone whose work was dedicated to understanding and healing psychic suffering. There are many references to the conundrum of fate and free will in the *Collected Works*, as well as in *Memories, Dreams, Reflections* and *Dream Analysis*. In 1912, a year before he began work on *Liber Novus*, Jung identified fate with the archetypes:

> The effect of the unconscious images has something fateful about it. Perhaps – who knows – these eternal images are what men mean by fate.[29]

In *Psychology of the Unconscious*, Jung called fate the 'driving force of the libido':

> The power of fate makes itself felt unpleasantly only when everything goes against our will; that is to say, when we no longer find ourselves in harmony with ourselves . . . The power of fate reveals itself at closer range as a compulsion of the libido.[30]

This observation is a profoundly interior perception of fate, expressed not in terms of external events, but as those inner compulsions that thwart every good intention of consciousness and result in unconscious choices which entangle the individual in painful external circumstances that have no easy resolution. Astral fate is described in this manner in a number of Gnostic and Hermetic texts, which Jung believed provided him with 'the historical counterpart of my psychology of the unconscious'.[31]

In an essay titled 'Psychology and Religion', first given as a series of lectures in 1937, Jung expressed succinctly his conviction that the individual's experience of free will is severely limited by the 'principalities and powers' of the unconscious psyche:

> Each of us is equipped with a psychic disposition that limits our freedom in high degree and makes it practically illusory . . . We do not enjoy masterless freedom; we are continually threatened by psychic factors which, in the guise of 'natural phenomena', may take possession of us at any moment . . . 'Principalities and powers' are always with us; we have no need to create them even if we could.[32]

Much later in his life, in an interview given to *The Daily Mail*, Jung expressed his understanding of the unity of fate and psyche, echoing Novalis' declaration that 'fate and soul are but two names for the same principle' by stating:[33]

> What happens to a person is characteristic of him. He represents a pattern and all the pieces fit. One by one, as his life proceeds, they fall into place according to some predestined design.[34]

Fate and soul, as presented in *Liber Novus*, are indeed two different names for a single principle. Addressing his Soul, Jung declared:

> You took away where I thought to take hold, and you gave me where I did not expect anything and time and again you brought about fate from new and unexpected quarters.[35]

Jung also equated fate with the Self, the goal of the individuation process, 'because it is the most complete expression of that fateful combination we call individuality'.[36] What happens to any individual – excluding those experiences that are part of the 'fate of the peoples' and can subsume individual unfoldment[37] – is therefore a reflection of this mysterious inner process, which can only be transformed (although neither avoided nor eradicated) through consciousness. 'If we do not see a thing', Jung commented in one of his ETH lectures, 'Fate does it to us'.[38]

The Stoic *Heimarmene*

Jung seems to have adopted some of his ideas about fate from the Stoics, in particular the concept of *Heimarmene*, which he described as 'the compulsion of the stars'.[39] He also defined *Heimarmene* as 'the dependence of character and destiny on certain moments in time'.[40] The term 'destiny' is subtly different from the idea of fate as either karmic retribution or pathological compulsion, and suggests something more akin to Neoplatonic ideas of the teleological nature of the personal daimon. Fate is not only astral compulsion, but also astral teleology: the broad outline of the path or personal myth an individual must follow in life in order to fulfil the requirements of the soul and, ultimately, the intelligent design of the 'Primal Light' or 'Primal Fire', the universal deity of Stoic philosophy.[41] Jung's various references to *Heimarmene* in the *Collected Works* reveal a fascination with this ancient Stoic idea of celestial fate, which he articulated in psychological language in his various analogies between the planetary configurations, the complexes of the unconscious, and the archetypal patterns that constitute the meaningful fate of the individual.

Stoicism emerged in the third century BCE, and exercised an enormous influence on the philosophy and practice of astrology for many centuries.[42] The Stoic *Heimarmene* may be understood as both 'fate' in the broadest sense, and 'compulsion by the stars' in a specifically astrological sense. The word *Heimarmene* is derived from the same root as *Moira*, the Greek word for 'allotment' and also the name of the goddess of Fate. In the Orphic *Derveni Papyrus*, *Moira* represents the wisdom of Zeus permeating all manifest creation; this wisdom or 'breath' (*pneuma*) of the god is presented as the 'allotment' or essential purpose of each individual thing within the whole.

> Orpheus named this [divine] breath Moira . . . For before Zeus received his name, Moira was the wisdom of the god always and through everything.[43]

Heimarmene encompasses the thread of genetic inheritance that passes from generation to generation and provides the underlying template for each species of living thing. But genetic inheritance determines the physiological aspect of the template. Jung seems to have been more concerned with the psychological aspect – the archetypes – and with the acausal or synchronistic nature of astral *Heimarmene* as a reflection of *sumpatheia*. The Stoics understood God as the fiery, animating life-force behind all creation.[44] *Heimarmene* in this context is not the 'evil compulsion of the star', but is indistinguishable from *Pronoia* or Providence: divine will or intent. The Stoic philosopher Poseidonius, discussed earlier in Chapter 3, referred to this life-force as the 'intellectual fiery breath of the cosmos'.[45] Echoing the ancient Orphic idea of *Moira* as the divine breath of Zeus, Poseidonius declared: 'God is the intellectual breath diffused throughout all matter'.[46]

In *Psychological Types*, Jung compared this Stoic divine fiery breath with the Hindu concept of *rta*, the source of all cosmic energy. He then equated *rta* with *Heimarmene*. Fate, astral compulsion, divine will, and the fiery cosmic libido are different ways of describing the same matrix of life:

> It [*rta*] is, therefore, a kind of philosophical libido-symbol that can be directly compared with the Stoic concept of *heimarmene*. For the Stoics *heimarmene* had the significance of creative, primal heat, and at the same time it was a predetermined, regular process (hence its other meaning: 'compulsion of the stars').[47]

Jung suggested that this 'predetermined, regular process' is experienced in the human psyche through the spontaneous generation of archetypal images, symbolised by the 'planetary gods'. These images are the self-portraits of the libido in its cyclical movement. The process of transforming 'raw libido' (*concupiscentia*, which Jung equated with *Heimarmene*)[48] into symbolic images is not due to any deliberate effort on the part of consciousness, but is inherent in the libido itself, and 'derives from a spiritual source: in other words, the determining factor is the numinous primordial images'.[49] Thus the unconscious itself seeks consciousness through the medium of the symbol, which alone can provide the bridge between individual and universal: an idea which Iamblichus articulated a millennium and a half before Jung did.

According to Jung, the 'primordial images' are also fate:

> These fantasies are primarily self-representations of energic transformation processes, which follow their specific laws and keep to a definite 'path' . . . This path is also fate, in so far as a man's fate depends on his psychology. It is the path of our destiny and of the law of our being.[50]

Moreover, the experience of fate as inner compulsion can be understood as magical:

> Magic exercises a compulsion that prevails over the conscious mind and will of the victim: an alien will rises up in the bewitched and proves stronger than

> his ego. The only comparable effect capable of psychological verification is that exerted by unconscious contents, which by their compelling power demonstrate their affinity with or dependence on man's totality, that is, the self and its 'karmic' functions.[51]

The intimate relationship between magic, inner compulsion, and the predetermined journey of the soul is made clear in *Liber Novus*, particularly in Jung's dialogues with his Soul and with Philemon. In these various connections between fate, astral compulsion, magic, libido, and the collective unconscious, Jung's profound and unorthodox understanding of astrology begins to emerge more clearly, as does the manner in which he translated Theosophical ideas such as 'karma' into psychological concepts. Astrological images are 'projections' generated by the unconscious human psyche onto the heavens. But these symbols, according to Ernst Gombrich's still relevant definition, unite 'mystic significance and magic effect'.[52] They portray the innate qualities of time, which unfolds through a cyclical, orderly, and 'predetermined' process initiated by the archetypes themselves and experienced by the human being as fate. As a psychologist concerned with individual development, Jung made many references to the ways in which an individual can allow his or her 'untamed', unconscious libido 'to get stuck in a childish milieu', resulting in the compulsive recreation of the original parental relationships.[53] In Jung's approach to *Heimarmene*, the value of careful clinical work was never underestimated. But behind the suffering patient lies the greater realm of the collective unconscious with its 'eternal images' – which, like the gods in Iamblichus' *De mysteriis*, seek their own transformation through the medium of the individual psyche.

The fabric of the universe, in Stoic philosophy, is simultaneously spiritual and material, a union of opposites that Jung encapsulated in his concept of the 'psychoid' unconscious.[54] Jung may have derived the term 'psychoid' from Eugen Bleuler, but it seems that the Stoics had the idea two millennia earlier. This Stoic psycho-physical universe is itself the essence of deity; there is no transcendent god 'outside' the Stoic system. It is often described in late antique texts as a web, or a cloth woven of twisted threads spun by the three Moirai.[55] In Apuleius' *Metamorphoses*, a work Jung seems to have been particularly fond of, Lucius, in his prayer to Isis, Queen of Heaven, refers to her saving hand,

> by which thou dost unravel the inextricably entangled threads of the fates, and dost assuage the tempests of fortune and restrain the malignant influences of the stars.[56]

Although Lucius understood astral influences as 'malignant', this view was not always shared by other authors, nor by Jung himself; the anti-cosmic feelings displayed in this passage of *Metamorphoses* represent only one perspective in an ongoing discourse in antiquity about the nature of astral fate. Sometimes *Heimarmene* was envisaged as a chain under the guardianship of divine providence. The Roman

Stoic philosopher, politician, and dramatist Seneca (4 BCE–65 CE), another author Jung seems to have favoured, declared:[57]

> We are all fastened to fortune. In the case of some the chain is of gold and extended, with others it is short and mean. But what does it matter? The same guardianship has enveloped all; those who have strung the cable are themselves attached . . . All life is dependence.[58]

The image of *Heimarmene* as a web, chain, tangle of threads, or woven cloth was taken up by later writers such as the eighteenth-century Swiss jurist and anthropologist Johann Jacob Bachofen (1815–1887), whose best-known work, *Das Mutterrecht*, was of considerable interest to Jung.[59] According to Bachofen,

> The web of tellurian creation becomes the web of destiny, the thread becomes the carrier of human fate . . . The loom, carrier of the supreme law of creation written in the stars, was assigned to the uranian deities in their sidereal nature . . . human life and the entire cosmos were seen as a great web of destiny.[60]

This motif of the spinning of the cloth of fate appears in *Liber Novus*. Jung, referring to the fateful power of the 'spirit of the depths', declared:

> Lost and swallowed by the streams of procreating life, we approach the overpowering, inhuman forces that are busily creating what is to come. How much future the depths carry! Are not the threads spun down there over millennia?[61]

The metaphor has also been used by Jungians such as Erich Neumann (1905–60), who described 'the primordial mystery of weaving and spinning' in relation to the archetype of the Great Mother, who 'weaves the web of life and spins the thread of fate':

> It is not by accident that we speak of the body's tissues, for the tissue woven by the Feminine in the cosmos and in the uterus of woman is life and destiny. And astrology, the study of a destiny governed by the stars, teaches that both begin at once, at the temporal moment of birth.[62]

The threads of fate are the same as the planetary compulsions, since the universe, to the Stoics, was a living thing, emanating from and infused with the 'Artificer's Fire', generating everything and forming the essence of both *Pronoia* (divine intent) and *Heimarmene* (astral fate), itself the embodiment of *Pronoia* expressed through the cycles of time.[63]

Although different Stoics approached the paradox of fate and free will with different arguments that evolved over time, the central question remained: what kind of universe do humans inhabit, and how can they learn to live in it harmoniously? The Stoically inclined Roman emperor Marcus Aurelius, another author whose work Jung acquired, phrased the options eloquently in the second century CE:[64]

> The universe must be governed either by a fore-ordained destiny – an order that no one may step beyond, or by a merciful providence, or by a chaos of chance devoid of a ruler.[65]

If the universe is entirely fated by an impersonal power, then choice cannot exist, for good or for evil. But if God is good and, as Marcus Aurelius suggested, divine providence 'watches over all', the individual can exercise free will and consciously choose to align himself or herself with *Pronoia*, struggling against evil irrational impulses, even if the struggle ultimately fails.

Jung seems to have understood this conundrum as the dilemma of individual character responding to events in accord with its own unique nature. An event might be 'predetermined' by the compulsions of a complex and 'attracted' by the law of *sumpatheia*, understood as the 'psychoid' expression of the archetype. But the individual's response depends on inherent character. Like the woven cloth of *Heimarmene*, inherent character is complex, comprised not only of conscious values and unconscious complexes underpinned by archetypal patterns, but also those values and complexes arising from family, ancestors, and culture long before the individual's birth. Although one might be compelled by unconscious compulsion to perform actions against one's wishes, one can, with the help of increased consciousness, strive to understand and avoid the destructive act. Jung referred to the configuration of Moon square Mercury in Miss X's horoscope as 'danger' rather than a preordained fate. In his view there is room for a limited degree of free will, arising from a dialectic between conscious and unconscious. Jung clearly found it difficult to reject the sense of fate at work in his own and others' lives. But his concept of individuation – the evolution of the personality into what it was always 'fated' to become – may be understood as an effort to reconcile the paradox that plagued the Stoics for so many centuries. Jung's solution was both succinct and elegant:

> Free will is doing gladly and freely that which one must do.[66]

The Gnostic *Heimarmene*

In recent years there has been considerable scholarly discussion about Jung's so-called Gnostic propensities.[67] Richard Noll, viewing every aspect of Jung's ideas in the context of his assumption that Jung was attempting to found a solar cult, declares: 'By 1916 Jung began to link his self-identity and personal destiny with Gnosticism'.[68] Lance Owen asserts something similar, although without the hostile personal agenda: 'At the very beginning of his journey, Jung most closely associated his experience with Gnosticism'.[69] Even the ring Jung wore – a purportedly

'Gnostic' ring bearing 'an ancient motif' and inscribed with the word 'Abraxas'[70] – suggests a personal identification with this late antique religious current.

Jung's own assertion that Gnostic ideas, surviving in the alchemy of the medieval and early modern periods, were the predecessors of his own psychological theories, has added to the scholarly assumption of the 'Gnostic' Jung.[71] So has the pseudonym 'Basilides', based on an Alexandrian Gnostic teacher of the second century CE, which Jung utilised in the published version of 'Scrutinies' that he titled *Septem sermones ad mortuos*.[72] Certain Gnostic concepts also found their way into the text of 'Scrutinies', and appear in the cosmological diagram Jung called *Systema Munditotius* or 'System of All Worlds'.[73] But 'Gnosticism', if it was ever an 'ism', has proven exceedingly difficult to confine to a discrete, homogenous category. If attempting to define magic is a 'maddening task',[74] attempting to define 'Gnosticism' generates a similar sort of confusion. Jung's highly individual interpretation of the Gnostics, based on the limited sources available to him in the first decades of the twentieth century and filtered through the lens of his psychological understanding, differed radically from the increasingly culture-specific perspectives of many scholars today.

Literature on the Gnostics, scholarly and otherwise, is vast, and a bibliography could easily fill hundreds of volumes. The series of monographs on Gnostic texts titled *Nag Hammadi and Manichaean Studies*, published by Brill, has already reached nearly ninety volumes and is still growing.[75] Much of this literature has attempted to clarify whether the Gnostic movement originated with Christians, Jews, or pagans; which Gnostic 'system' was the 'true' exemplar of this religious current; and whether Gnostic mythic cosmologies were rooted in Platonic, Hermetic, Zoroastrian, or Abrahamic soil, or a combination of all of them. Concepts often attributed to Gnostic groups, such as 'dualism' – the stark distinction between a 'good' transcendent deity and an 'evil' material world – are often simplistic, and depend on which Gnostic text or teacher is being investigated. Likewise, the idea that all Gnostics were 'heretical' Christians, or even Christian at all, is problematic; there were Gnostic currents within Judaism, and some Gnostics were not affiliated with Christianity in any form.[76] Moreover, 'heresy' is a religious category, not an historical one; and it may not even be possible any longer, given the increasing sophistication of scholarly research, to define any 'mainstream' Christianity of the second century CE against which Gnostic currents can be contrasted.[77]

Robert Segal, attempting to answer the question of whether Jung was a Gnostic, describes Gnosticism as 'the belief in an antithetical dualism of immateriality, which is good, and matter, which is evil'.[78] But Gnostic currents were never homogenously 'dualistic'. Even when it is clear that a particular text posits such a polarity between spirit and matter, material reality is not necessarily viewed as evil. The polarity was described by Plato, who did not understand material existence as evil, but perceived it as the emanation of the World Soul, whose divine nature, in contrast to its fluctuating reflections in the natural world, requires a different kind of consciousness to perceive.[79] The influence of Plato's benign vision of material reality on many Gnostic texts was even noted by the Christian heresiologists Irenaeus and Hippolytus, as well as by Plotinus, in late antiquity.[80]

At one end of the Gnostic spectrum is the ferociously anti-cosmic polemic of the Manichaean movement, which promulgated the idea of two eternal and irreconcilable cosmic powers: the heavenly realm of light and the earthly realm of darkness.[81] At the other end of the spectrum is the pro-cosmic approach of the Platonising Gnostics. The treatise known as *Marsanes*, for example, declared:

> I have deliberated and have attained to the boundary of the sense-perceptible world. (I have come to know) part by part the entire place of the incorporeal being, and (I) have come to know the intelligible world. (I have come to know), when I was deliberating, that in every respect the sense-perceptible world is (worthy) of being saved entirely.[82]

Jung's psychological models invariably espouse a goal of integration rather than transcendence, perfection, or repudiation of material reality. As a result of the transformations occurring through a direct encounter between consciousness and the archetypal dominants of the unconscious, the individual 'approaches wholeness but not perfection':[83]

> There is a considerable difference between *perfection* and *completeness* ... Where the archetype predominates, completeness is forced upon us against all our conscious strivings ... The individual may strive after perfection ... but must suffer from the opposite of his intentions for the sake of his completeness.[84]

This statement suggests that, although Jung perceived psyche and matter as two poles of a spectrum, he was not sympathetic to more radical Gnostic ideas of an irreconcilable division of corrupt body and incorruptible spirit. Nor does Jung's astrology reflect the Gnostic idea of the 'evil' nature of the planetary archons. Jung understood the grand cosmological dramas of Gnostic myths to be imaginal portrayals of unconscious human psychological processes. He declared that 'the idea of an unconscious was not unknown to them [the Gnostics]',[85] and that the Gnostic celestial *anthropos* or 'Original Man' – a cosmic redeemer-figure and, at the same time, the spark of divinity in every human being – 'expresses the presence of a transconscious centre which . . . must be regarded as a symbol of wholeness'.[86]

There is no 'essential' or 'typical' Gnostic work against which all others can be compared.[87] Simple views of the Gnostic 'heresy' changed radically from the mid-twentieth century onward, once the discovery in 1945 of the extraordinary cache of Gnostic and Hermetic texts at Nag Hammadi in Egypt had transformed earlier perceptions based on Christian heresiologists such as Irenaeus, Hippolytus, and Epiphanius.[88] But even in today's scholarly works, the astrological nature of Gnostic cosmology is not explored in any depth. Jung had to rely on the heresiologists and the limited number of Gnostic treatises translated by Mead,[89] as well as on early researchers such as Wilhelm Bousset and Richard Reitzenstein, whose work reflected the academic and religious fashions of their time.[90] And Mead's view of the Gnostics was filtered through a Theosophical lens, just as the views of the heresiologists were filtered through the lens of their understanding of 'true' Christianity. Jung's own elision of Gnostic, Hermetic, and Mithraic currents, evident in *Psychology of the Unconscious* as well as in *Liber Novus*, seems to be based in part on these sources. But perhaps more importantly, he expressed his personal understanding of the Greek word *gnosis*, which does not necessarily accord with either older or current scholarly definitions. Jung's focus, as always, was on gnosis as a direct psychological experience of that 'matrix and organizing principle of consciousness',[91] the archetype of the Self.

Saturn and Abraxas

In the many discussions about Jung's Gnostic predilections, the astrological core present in virtually every Gnostic treatise, to which Jung paid careful attention in his various discussions about fate, has been largely overlooked. According to Jung, astral fate or *Heimarmene* was central to both Gnostic texts and alchemy, and both currents were concerned with breaking the chains of fate by a mythic journey of the soul through seven stages or spheres. In Gnostic treatises, this ascent is planetary and celestial; in alchemical writings, it is planetary and metallurgical. Citing the third-century alchemist Zosimos, Jung referred to the Anthropos or 'Son of God' as a 'Gnostic Christ', and stated:

> As in later Christian alchemy, the Son of God is a sort of paradigm of sublimation, i.e., of the freeing of the soul from the grip of Heimarmene.[92]

For Jung, alchemy was gnosis projected onto the seven planetary metals of the earth, rather than onto the seven planetary archons of the celestial world.[93]

In his discussion of an early medieval alchemical text, Jung described a 'crown of victory' awarded by Hermes:

> This refers to the synthesis of the planets or metals with the sun, to form a crown which will be 'within' Hermes. The crown signifies the kingly totality; it stands for unity and is not subject to Heimarmene. This reminds us of the seven- or twelve-rayed crown of light which the Agathodaimon serpent wears on Gnostic gems.[94]

This 'crown of victory', which is not susceptible to astral fate, belongs to the individual who has managed to integrate into consciousness the archetypal patterns inherent in the complexes of the unconscious, and who has thus become free from astral compulsion:

> Anyone who has passed through all the [planetary] spheres is free from compulsion; he has won the crown of victory and become like a god.[95]

In Book II of *Liber Novus*, the crown is given by the Serpent to Jung as he hangs on the cross 'between sky and earth', undergoing that suffering which must inevitably accompany any effort at psychic integration.[96] The crown is also the alchemical *prima materia* or 'primal substance', the raw unconscious libido that contains the hidden spark of divinity, and which Jung described as belonging to Saturn. It is 'the most despised and rejected thing, thrown out into the street'; the more the conscious ego is 'bound by time and space', the more this hidden daimon feels like fate.[97] In these associations, Jung presented his understanding that the symbolism of the Gnostic ascent of the soul, which ultimately breaks the inner compulsion of astral *Heimarmene* through a direct encounter with the transpersonal centre of the personality, must begin with the unconscious darkness within the human being: that which is most despised and 'inferior', which Jung defined astrologically as Saturn. The highest and most obstructive of the Gnostic planetary archons, called Ialdabaoth, is 'identical with Saturn'.[98] But for Jung, this archon was not evil; he secretly contains the unknown, unconscious Self.

In the late antique iconography of magical amulets, the solar crown was worn by the serpent-bodied, lion-headed deity Chnoumis (see Plate 3), and Jung's own 'Gnostic' ring, according to his own description, displays a typical late antique Greco-Egyptian carving of this solar cosmocrator.[99] Jung tended to conflate Chnoumis with the so-called Gnostic deity Abraxas. But Abraxas was not exclusively Gnostic; rather, the name is a magical 'Name of Power' associated with several deities in the syncretic milieux of late antiquity, including Chnoumis. The cock-headed, serpent-legged being who appears on so many late antique amulets, sometimes assumed to be Abraxas, is usually designated by the name IAO, the Greek transliteration of the Hebrew YHVH.[100] Jung, following the scholarly research of the time, assumed both these figures to be Gnostic.[101] But he also understood Abraxas as a symbol of the libido in its annual solar cycle, representing 'fullness and emptiness, generation and destruction':[102]

> The Gnostic symbol Abraxas, a made-up name meaning three hundred and sixty-five . . . the Gnostics used it as the name of their supreme deity. He was a time god. The philosophy of Bergson, *la durée créatrice*, is an expression of the same idea.[103]

Jung expanded further on this perception of Abraxas as a libido-symbol – symbolised astrologically by both Saturn as the matrix and the Sun as the light born from it – in the *Visions Seminars*:

> That figure of Abraxas means the beginning and the end, it is life and death, therefore it is represented by a monstrous figure. It is a monster because it is the life of vegetation in the course of one year, the spring and the autumn, the summer and the winter, the yea and nay of nature.[104]

For Jung, Abraxas was a symbol of the collective unconscious in its cyclical movement, also portrayed by the symbolic circle of the zodiac as the pathway of the Sun in its yearly round. Abraxas unites the darkness of Saturn's earthly, mortal domain with the immortal spiritual light of the Sun:

> Comparison with the sun teaches us over and over again that the gods are libido. It is that part of us which is immortal . . . Its springs, which well up from the depths of the unconscious, come, as does our life in general, from the root of the whole of humanity . . . The divine in us is the libido.[105]

Abraxas is both the *demiurgos* or 'world-creator' and the libido as World Soul.[106] Jung's discourses on Gnostic *Heimarmene* do not reflect a personal belief in a dualistic cosmos animated by ontically independent and inimical planetary beings. They describe a psychic process that he observed in human beings and called 'individuation', and for which he was convinced the astral ascent in the Gnostic treatises provided one of the earliest and richest models.

G.R.S. Mead and *Pistis Sophia*

Between 1890 and 1891, G.R.S. Mead published, in the Theosophical journal *Lucifer*, the first English translation of a Gnostic text of the second to third centuries CE, known as *Pistis Sophia*. The translation, issued as a series of articles, was accompanied by commentaries by H.P. Blavatsky, who, predictably, attempted to correlate Gnostic and Hindu concepts and claim that the former derived from the latter.[107] The entire translation was published as a book in 1896, and in 1900 a summary of the text was included in Mead's lengthy exegesis of the Gnostics, *Fragments of a Faith Forgotten*.[108] *Pistis Sophia* is perhaps the most important of the Gnostic texts available to Jung during the years he worked on *Liber Novus*. At the time, it alone existed as a complete manuscript free of the interference of the Christian heresiologists, and its elaborate cosmology is entirely astrological.[109] So important to Jung was Mead's translation of *Pistis Sophia* that, according to Gilles Quispel, a good friend of Jung and a respected scholar of Gnostic currents, Jung made a special journey to London to thank Mead for the work.[110]

Although Mead never wrote a book on astrology, he was familiar with it through his friendship with Alan Leo and the numerous astrological articles that Leo contributed to *The Quest*. *Pistis Sophia* employs astrological concepts and imagery as the basis of its message: the Saviour-God or celestial Anthropos, sent from the upper spiritual realms by his father Jeu,[111] enters the 'Fate-sphere' of the seven planetary archons and breaks 'a third of their power' by turning the cosmic pole 'for the salvation of all souls'.[112] This idea can be seen, translated into psychological terms, in Jung's insistence that the expanded consciousness resulting from a direct individual experience of the Self, the 'organizing principle of consciousness', can, at least partially, transform the compulsive expression of the archetypes that stand behind complexes.

In the text of *Pistis Sophia*, the zodiacal constellations are called aeons:

> And after these things, when the sphere turns . . . the Good, he of the Midst, who is called Zeus [Jupiter] in the world, comes; and he comes to the eighth aeon which is called Scorpion. And Bubastis, who is called Aphrodite [Venus], comes, and she comes to the second aeon of the sphere which is called the Bull. Then the veils which are between those of the left and those of the right are drawn aside.[113]

The word 'aeon' (also spelled 'aion') is rarely used in modern astrological works as a synonym for a zodiacal sign or constellation. But Jung's application of the term to describe an astrological 'age', or 2,165-year segment of the great cycle of equinoctial precession through the zodiacal constellations, is very specific, as we will see in the next chapter, and his concept of the approaching new aion of Aquarius was clearly influenced by *Pistis Sophia.*[114]

Fate appears in the text of *Pistis Sophia* as the allotment of the span of a human life:

> And also the destiny, whose name is Moira, leadeth the man until it hath him slain through the death appointed unto him.[115]

Pistis Sophia also uses the term *Heimarmene*. However 'the great Fate', as it is called, does not concern predetermined external events such as wealth, poverty, illness, marriage, or length of life. Imposed by the planetary archons, it is expressed as individual suffering in the face of an overwhelming compulsion to sin:

> All men who shall receive the mysteries of the Ineffable and moreover the mysteries of the First Mystery, *sin every time through the compulsion of the Fate.*[116]

The idea of fate as inner compulsion appears in the much earlier Orphic fragments, which describe the 'circle of wearying heavy grief' – the zodiacal constellations – as an interior experience of compulsive, repetitive suffering.[117] The idea that a certain type of gnosis – the recollection or rediscovery of one's divine origin – can free the soul from the compulsive inner torment of astral fate can also be found in the *Hermetica*, where the zodiacal constellations 'torture the inward person with the sufferings of sense'.[118] Gnostic and Hermetic currents, like Platonic philosophy, owed a great deal to Orphic conceptions; Jung was not mistaken in perceiving parallels between them.[119] Nor, it seems, was he mistaken in understanding these interiorised astrological portrayals as 'the sum of all the psychological knowledge of antiquity'.[120]

Mead and Jung

Mead's knowledge of Gnostic texts was immensely useful to Jung, and Jung's own interpretations of Gnostic cosmology might therefore be assumed to be Theosophical.[121] But it is more likely that the importance of Mead's translations and commentaries for Jung lay, not in any specific system of beliefs imposed on the material, but in the vitality and intuitive insight that Mead brought to his work. Like Thomas Taylor a century earlier, Mead was personally sympathetic to the most important aspects of the world-view presented in Hermetic, Neoplatonic, and Gnostic writings; and this genuine love of and receptivity to the material and its poetic mode of expression was not typical of the offerings of the German scholars of Jung's time, however accurate and thorough their translations might be. Mead made his materials come alive in ways that may perhaps be insufficiently appreciated in the context of today's scholarship; and for Jung these materials were already alive, filled with visions and ideas that were immediately recognisable to him as characteristic expressions of the human psyche.

Jung was not a card-carrying Theosophist in any doctrinal sense, any more than he was a card-carrying Gnostic. His ongoing interest in Theosophical literature, reflected by the presence of a number of seminal Theosophical works in his private library, was balanced by a profound distaste for what he viewed as the Theosophists' serious lack of psychological awareness.[122] A number of Theosophical concepts, such as the 'central spiritual Sun', were attractive to him when interpreted within a psychological framework; but the idea of the noetic Sun can be found in the various Platonic, Neoplatonic, and Hermetic currents of late antiquity, which, as Jung was well aware, Blavatsky had adapted for her own purposes. Where Blavatsky saw these enduring ideas as indications of the secret transmission of a primal wisdom-religion of which she herself was the latest recipient, Jung saw them as archetypal.

Jung never underestimated the collective appeal of Theosophy's 'pseudo-Gnostic intuitions',[123] viewing them as the inevitable, if dangerously misguided, eruption of an unconscious collective need for counteracting the extreme materialism of the 'spirit of this time'.[124] But he saw Theosophical doctrines as a 'primitive projection of psychological factors',[125] full of 'pompous jargon',[126] and comparable with the determined dogmatism of Freud, which, Jung felt, 'comes very close to the attitude of religious conviction that characterizes these movements [Theosophy and Christian Science]'.[127] Mead, although he had served as private secretary to Blavatsky from 1884 to 1891 and continued his membership in the Theosophical Society until 1909, was, by the time Jung met him, as sceptical of the organisation and its ideology as Jung was. Mead joined the Theosophical Society when he was twenty-one years old, fresh from completing a degree in Classics at Cambridge, but by the time of Blavatsky's death in 1891 he had already outgrown her influence, if he was ever entirely under it:

> I had never, even while a member, preached the Mahatma-gospel of H.P. Blavatsky, or propagandized Neo-theosophy and its revelations. I had believed that 'theosophy' proper meant the wisdom-element in the great religions and philosophies of the world.[128]

Mead parted ways with the Theosophists in 1909, along with seven hundred other members of the Society, due to the sexual scandal surrounding a prominent member, C.W. Leadbeater, between 1906 and 1908.[129] But Mead had deeper ongoing problems with the Society, not least with its assumption of blind obedience to Blavatsky's spiritual 'Masters' and those who claimed to channel their wisdom. For many years he had been drawn to the traditions of Gnostic and Hermetic currents, rather than to the doctrines of the East which Blavatsky and her politically ambitious successors assiduously promulgated. Mead had the temperament of a scholar rather than a disciple, and could not tolerate the Society's 'innumerable dogmatic assertions, its crooked methods and reprehensible proceedings', which he felt marred the goals and ethics of the Society.[130]

Mead was probably the finest scholar of ancient religions the British occult revival produced, and it is easy to see why his learning, independent spirit, and inspired translations appealed to Jung. Several authors have noted Mead's impact on Jung, partly based on the eighteen volumes of Mead's work found in Jung's private library, and partly because of the number of references to Mead's books in Jung's *Psychology of the Unconscious*. Mead was certainly an inspiration for Jung's understanding of the religious currents of late antiquity throughout the period Jung worked on *Liber Novus*; but Jung was entirely capable of developing his own psychological interpretations independent of any Theosophical 'influence'.

Richard Noll has commented that Mead's influence on Jung is 'still unacknowledged', and that 'documents concerning the nature of their personal relationship have not yet come to light'.[131] But Mead's importance has been acknowledged for some time by a number of Jung scholars. And one letter *has* 'come to light', from Mead to Jung, dated 19 November 1919.[132] It is clear from the rather gossipy content of the letter that the two men had met just prior to its writing, and had enjoyed more than one meeting in the past.[133] Their relationship was that of friends and equals, rather than of mentor and disciple, and they enjoyed talking about books and their authors. In the letter, Mead mentioned an author they had apparently been discussing at their previous meeting: the Austrian novelist Gustav Meyrink (1868–1932). Meyrink, who was of great interest to Jung,[134] was a major player on the European occult 'scene' in the first decades of the twentieth century. He had been initiated into the Order of the Golden Dawn in 1889, a year after its creation, and had also founded the 'Blue Star' Theosophical Lodge in Prague in 1891.[135] Jung had assumed that Meyrink's 'occult' novel, *Der Golem*, published in 1915, was a piece of inspirational or 'automatic' writing, a spontaneous product of the unconscious similar to his own *Septem sermones ad mortuos*. Mead corrected this assumption by declaring that Meyrink had in fact laboured for many years to produce *Der Golem*.

In his letter, Mead also recommended to Jung the writings of Robert Eisler (1882–1949), a Jewish historian of ancient mystery religions and of astrology, who had contributed articles to Mead's journal, *The Quest*, before the Great War, and whose prolific work Jung later assiduously collected for his own library.[136] It is likely that Mead arranged an introduction between the two men. Jung used the image of a bas-relief of the primal god Phanes – identified by Eisler as Orphic and thus contradicting Franz Cumont's assumption of its Mithraic origin – as the frontispiece for *Aion*, citing Eisler's authority as his source.[137] Eisler, in turn, wrote a work on the history and psychology of lycanthropy that included an appendix supporting Jung's theory of the archetypes and the collective unconscious.[138]

Clare and Nicholas Goodrick-Clarke, in their biography of Mead, have asserted that Mead's focus on complex chains of symbolic correspondences, linking 'states of divine being and inner states of consciousness', became Mead's 'major legacy to Carl Gustav Jung and his psychoanalytical theory'.[139] Although Jung had already encountered this psycho-cosmological model in the writings of the Neoplatonists and Hermeticists, there is no doubt that Mead's enthusiastic articulation of the ideas in modern language appealed to him. Mead's translations included two other books that proved relevant to Jung's work on both *Psychology of the Unconscious* and *Liber Novus*. These were *A Mithraic Ritual*, based on a late antique text originally titled *Eine Mithrasliturgie* by its German editor and translator, Albrecht Dieterich;[140] and *The Mysteries of Mithra*, which included Mead's translated fragments of various late antique writings describing the Mithraic cult.[141] The so-called *Mithras Liturgy* is neither Gnostic nor Mithraic.[142] It refers to itself as a 'Ritual of Immortalisation',[143] and is, in fact, a theurgic ritual aimed at individual transformation through a direct experience of the central spiritual Sun, called Helios-Mithras. The *Mithras Liturgy* has more in common with Hermetic treatises than with the Mithraic 'mysteries',[144] a fact of which Jung was well aware, as he had acquired Franz Cumont's translation of the text as well as another work by Cumont in which the Belgian archaeologist and religious historian discounted any relationship between the *Liturgy* and Mithraism.[145] Not surprisingly, this theurgic ritual relies on an astrological framework. Along with the *Orphic Hymns*, the *Mithras Liturgy* seems to have provided inspiration for Jung's own theurgic hymns to the Sun and to Phanes in *Liber Novus* and the *Black Books*.

Mead's understanding of gnosis, which allowed him to include texts such as the *Mithras Liturgy* under its umbrella, was not limited to the anti-cosmic dualism often associated with Gnostic currents in late antiquity. He perceived the experience of gnosis as a union of all opposites, synthesising intellect and emotion, male and female, and the individual with the 'All Self':[146]

> If I believe rightly, the very essence of Gnosis is the faith that man can transcend the limits of the duality that makes him man, and become a consciously divine being.[147]

Mead equated astral fate with 'karma', as it was called in Theosophical literature: the astrological configurations at birth reflect not only the individual's pattern of unfoldment, but also the fruits of choices made in former incarnations.[148] But the power of the planets is only partial; 'Nature', or inherent genetic structure, also plays a part in the individual's unfoldment, along with free will. As Mead put it, each of these factors 're-acts on each, none is absolute'.[149] It is unlikely that Jung would have disagreed.

Astral fate and the 'subtle' body

The idea of the *ochêma pneuma* or 'spirit-vehicle', known to the Theosophists as the 'astral' or 'subtle body', seems to have interested Jung deeply.[150] He encountered the idea in various sources, including Iamblichus, Proclus, Stoic physics,[151] Gnostic texts such as *Apocryphon of John* and *Pistis Sophia*, the *Hermetica*, the Tibetan *Book of the Dead*,[152] alchemical treatises, and the Christian *corpus glorificationis*: the incorruptible 'subtle body' given to the righteous after resurrection.[153] Jung believed he had also discovered the concept in the Native American tale of Hiawatha, who, in Henry Wadsworth Longfellow's poem, receives 'a breath-body or subtle body not subject to corruption' as a reward for his victory over the Northwest Wind.[154]

Hiawatha's 'subtle body' does not resemble the unpurified planetary 'counterfeit spirit' of Gnostic texts, but seems to be the carrier of the divine spark in each individual, which Jung understood to be the Self. But these two perceptions – the 'subtle body' as an intermediary organ linking planets, soul, and body, and as a purified spirit-vehicle free of mortal corruption – often overlapped, depending on whether a particular author viewed the celestial bodies as evil or as emanations of the divine. Jung understood the 'subtle body' to represent the interconnection between the psyche and the material world, reflecting his concept of the psychoid nature of the archetypes and the secret unity of spirit and matter:

> In view of the intimate connection that exists between certain psychic processes and their physical parallels we cannot very well accept the total immateriality of the psyche . . . Spirit and matter may well be forms of one and the same transcendental being.[155]

Mead produced a work on the 'subtle body' in 1919, which Jung later cited when he suggested a parallel between this 'psychoid' intermediary and the unconscious psyche.[156] Mead's book explored the ancient 'ladder of ascent from the earth to the light-world' in Neoplatonism, Christian Gnosticism, Hermetic alchemy, and the *Mithras Liturgy*. All these late antique religious approaches, according to Mead, shared a concern with 'the soul-freeing doctrine of regeneration', which could also be understood as the purification of the subtle body.[157] Mead's short volume seems to have contributed valuable insights to Jung's equation of the soul's planetary ascent with the individuation process. Mead understood the 'regeneration' sought through theurgic rituals as the 'bringing to birth of man's perfected subtle body': an 'inner transmutation and heightening of consciousness' which bears a close parallel to Jung's idea of individuation.[158] The purification of the subtle body, as Jung described it later in relation to the alchemical process, is the purification – or integration through the mediation of consciousness – of the unconscious itself.

> The *mundificatio* (purification) means . . . the removal of the superfluities that always cling to merely natural products, and especially to the symbolic unconscious contents which the alchemist found projected into matter . . . The alchemist undertakes to produce a new, volatile (hence aerial or 'spiritual') entity endowed with *corpus, anima, et spiritus*, where *corpus* is naturally understood as a 'subtle' body or 'breath body'; the analyst tries to bring about a certain attitude or frame of mind, a certain 'spirit' therefore.[159]

The ultimate aim of alchemy, according to Jung, was 'to produce a *corpus subtile*, a transfigured and resurrected body'.[160] These comments on the subtle body do not refer directly to astrological factors, and Jung's discussions of alchemy and the projection of unconscious contents on the alchemical metals were written long after he had completed work on *Liber Novus*. But his remarks need to be understood in the context of his assertion that 'the gods of the metals should always be thought of astrologically as well . . . The alchemical symbols are saturated with astrology'.[161] The purified subtle body that provides the goal of the alchemical *opus* is not, after all, so very different from the purified soul-vehicle of the Gnostics and Hermeticists, which sheds the compulsions of its planetary 'appendages' only when the individual is transformed through gnosis.

The idea of the subtle body continued to preoccupy Jung over the years, especially as it was described by Galen and by alchemists such as Paracelsus (1493–1541) and Martin Ruland (1569–1611). According to these authors, the subtle body is not merely a 'counterfeit spirit' that generates evil desires, as described in *Pistis Sophia*. Galen called the subtle body a 'shining and aethereal' body through which the soul receives communion with the celestial bodies.[162] In the early sixteenth century, Paracelsus, following Galen, understood the 'shining' body with its planetary essences to be the intermediary between the human soul and the World Soul or *lumen naturae* ('light of Nature');[163] the *lumen naturae* is in turn the '"star" in man', and thus astrology is 'a mother to all the other arts'.[164] Martin Ruland, following Paracelsus, equated the 'shining' body with the imagination, which he called 'the celestial or supercelestial body'.[165] The influence of Iamblichus, direct or indirect, on Paracelsus and Ruland is evident in this identification of the Neoplatonic *phantasia* with the subtle body as an intermediary between body and spirit, supporting Jung's conviction that active imagination was the optimum means through which psychological transformations could be achieved. In alchemy, the spirit Mercurius is the mysterious 'volatile' agent that precipitates both the material transformation of the metals and the spiritual transformation of the alchemist.[166] Mercurius, according to Jung, is itself the subtle body: the World Soul that seeks its own transformation.[167]

Fate and compulsion

Heimarmene – the 'compulsion of the stars' – operates through the subtle body or, in Jung's understanding, 'unconscious contents': the complexes and their archetypal foundations. Although Freud was not predisposed to discuss astrological factors in relation to compulsion – at least not in print – nevertheless he used the term 'daemonic force' to describe the repetitive quality of unconscious compulsions and their disturbing 'otherness':

> The manifestations of a compulsion to repeat . . . exhibit to a high degree an instinctual character and, when they act in opposition to the pleasure principle, give the appearance of some 'daemonic' force at work.[168]

Jung also had a great deal to say about compulsion, but unlike Freud – and unlike the Gnostics – he did not view it as essentially pathological. He understood compulsiveness to be a quality inherent in all instinctual impulses, most of which, including the instinct to individuate, are life-enhancing, although sometimes experienced as inimical to conscious goals: 'Compulsion is the unconscious wish'.[169] Thus the compulsions exerted by the subtle body – those pesky 'unconscious contents' – are ultimately signs of meaning rather than of illness, and are generated by 'man's totality, that is, the self'.[170]

Jung also understood compulsion as the sudden eruption of 'conscience', an inner 'moral reaction' unfamiliar to the individual's consciously adopted values:

> The moral reaction is the outcome of an autonomous dynamism, fittingly called man's daemon, genius, guardian angel, better self, heart, inner voice, the inner and higher man, and so forth. Close beside these, beside the positive, 'right' conscience, there stands the negative, 'false' conscience called the devil, seducer, tempter, evil spirit, etc.[171]

It is this latter, 'false' conscience that *Pistis Sophia* seems to emphasise in the idea of the planetary 'counterfeit spirit', which 'contriveth and senseth all sins and the evil which the rulers of the great Fate have commanded for the soul'.[172] The Gnostic teacher Basilides referred to the 'counterfeit spirit' as seven planetary 'appendages' that lure the soul into evil.[173] This idea, stripped of its overt astrological cosmology, has remained in Christian theology to the present day in the form of the Seven Cardinal Sins, which seem to have begun their life as aspects of the soul's descent into incarnation *via* the hostile spheres of the planetary archons.[174] In a religious context in which instinctual desires were viewed as inherently evil, the suppressed compulsions of the instincts, symbolised by the planets and zodiacal constellations, would, in Jung's view, inevitably be experienced as demonic;[175] and the astrological 'great Fate' would be experienced as entirely malevolent. Although Jung learned a great deal about *Heimarmene* from *Pistis Sophia*, it seems he found a more congenial model of planetary compulsion in the world of the *Hermetica*.

The Hermetic *Heimarmene*

The earliest known examples of the body of late antique literature known as the *Hermetica* date to the first century BCE.[176] Although most extant Hermetic texts were produced later, they predate Gnostic currents as well as overlapping with them. These texts were as fascinating to Jung as those of the Gnostics. The *Hermetica*, like Gnostic treatises, emerged within the syncretic cultural matrix of Greco-Roman Egypt,[177] and are similarly concerned with astral fate, gnosis, individual transformation, and the eventual 'bliss of the soul'.[178] Some scholars consider the Hermetic treatises to be Neoplatonic.[179] Others view them as Gnostic, in the sense that some of the texts – such as *CH* XIII, cited above – express a distinctly anti-cosmic worldview. In this treatise, the interior, compulsive nature of astral fate is clearly expressed.

The mix of Gnostic and Hermetic materials found at Nag Hammadi suggests that a vigorous interchange occurred between these two religious currents.[180] The defining characteristic of the *Hermetica* is that, unlike so many Gnostic treatises, no Christian affiliation is displayed, although Jewish elements are evident in a number of the texts.[181] In the Hermetic world, the redeemer-figure is not Christ, but the mythic semi-divine teacher of the 'occult sciences' of alchemy, astrology, and magic: Hermes Trismegistus or 'Thrice-Greatest Hermes', also known by the name of his divine Egyptian counterpart, the god Thoth.

The *Hermetica* have been discussed at length by many scholars, and the literature on this extraordinary collection of texts has been growing since Marsilio Ficino first translated fourteen of the treatises from Greek into Latin in 1471.[182] By 1913, when Jung began work on *Liber Novus*, he had collected virtually all of the scholarly works on the *Hermetica* available at the time.[183] He often, and with good reason, elided Hermetic and Gnostic ideas, referring to the third-century CE alchemist Zosimos as both a Hermeticist and a Gnostic.[184] Jung was convinced that both currents were deeply psychological; both depended on individual revelation rather than obedience to doctrine, and both involved theurgic rituals and an astrologically based cosmology. Both currents also influenced the writings of Iamblichus and Proclus. And both Hermeticists and Gnostics were preoccupied with freeing of the soul from the bondage of the inner compulsions of astral *Heimarmene*.

Jung was familiar with the Hermetic texts through Marcellin Berthelot's compilation, *Collection des anciens alchemistes greques*, published in 1887, and Mead's English translations of the corpus, published in 1906. He cited both authors in *Psychology of the Unconscious*. Although he did not recognise the full psychological significance of alchemy until several years after he had completed work on *Liber Novus*,[185] the Greco-Egyptian Hermetic materials were highly relevant to Jung's early astrological and magical explorations. Their importance is indicated by their presence in *Liber Novus*, where 'the wisdom of ΕΡΜΗΣ ΤΡΙΣΜΕΓΙΣΤΥΣ [Hermes Trismegistus]' is secreted in the cupboard of the magician Philemon.[186] One of the most important treatises in terms of Jung's astrological understanding is *CH* I, known as *Poimandres*.[187] In this work, the liberation of the soul toward freedom from *Heimarmene* is presented as a journey through the planetary spheres to the divine realms beyond. The soul is progressively purified of its seven 'garments' and 'surrenders' the vices of the seven planets. Finally, it enters the sublime eighth sphere of the fixed stars.[188] The object of the Hermetic ascent, like that of the *Mithras Liturgy*, is the divinisation of the initiate. *Poimandres* echoes the words of one of the Orphic gold funerary tablets, written some seven centuries earlier: 'Out of a human, you will become a god'.[189] Hermetic initiation offered gnosis as a form of freedom from the compulsions of astral fate.[190] Although the planetary vices of *Poimandres* are not intrinsically evil as are those portrayed in *Pistis Sophia*, each planet nevertheless imposes a compulsion whose grip can be loosened only through theurgic ritual.[191]

Mead noted the echoes of the ascent of *Poimandres* in an influential fifth-century CE work by the Roman author Macrobius, titled *Commentary on the Dream of Scipio* – yet another work with which Jung was familiar, and which he cited in

Psychology of the Unconscious. But the planetary 'vices', in Macrobius' hands, were transformed into virtues; Macrobius described seven luminous 'envelopes' conveying positive attributes to the soul, such as the 'bold spirit' conferred by Mars.[192] The spectrum of vices and virtues attached to each planet by the range of authors described by Mead provided Jung with a rich psychological portrayal of astrological dynamics far more complex than the static descriptions of 'benefic' and 'malefic' planets inherited from Ptolemy.[193] In *Poimandres* and the literature that it inspired, both good and evil are presented as attributes of each planet, and the responsibility for dealing with this polarity depends, not on the intervention of a redeemer-god sent from celestial realms, but on the consciousness of the individual.

The technical astrology included in the *Hermetica* seems to have disturbed some modern scholars, and the critical edition and translation of fifteen treatises by Sir Walter Scott, published between 1924 and 1936, omitted most of this astrological material because Scott deemed it to be 'rubbish'.[194] Like Gnostic literature in the hands of the Christian heresiologists, the *Hermetica* in the hands of researchers such as Scott have been seriously distorted by personal agendas. The texts were artificially divided by Scott and a French translator, the Dominican friar and philologist André-Jean Festugière, into 'higher' or 'philosophical' *Hermetica* and 'lower', 'popular', or 'magico-religious' *Hermetica*.[195] This arbitrary division, unlikely to have been meaningful to the authors of the texts, reflects the discomfort generated in modern times by confrontation with a late antique world in which magic, astrology, and alchemy were an integral part of a highly sophisticated philosophical and religious world-view. Many of the technical *Hermetica* mentioned in other late antique texts have been lost;[196] other texts still await modern critical editions and translations.[197] However, the obvious astrological content of 'philosophical' *Hermetica* such as *Poimandres* was readily available to Jung through Mead's translations.

According to one of these treatises, the 'tent' of the earthly body is formed as the soul descends through the circle of the zodiac, rather than through the planetary spheres. The body is thus subject to *Heimarmene* through the zodiacal signs.[198] Hermeticists, like Gnostics, took up the idea of a subtle body through which planetary and zodiacal influences operated. However, *Heimarmene* was not viewed as irrevocable; it could be overcome when *kairos*, the right astrological moment, arrived and the spark of divinity could be theurgically 'freed from its bodily prison and thus removed from the control of fate'.[199] The idea of an astrologically propitious moment of time for confronting *Heimarmene*, described by both the *Hermetica* and Iamblichus' *De mysteriis* as well as the writings of Zosimos and various Gnostic texts, suggests that Jung's preoccupation with the movements occurring in his horoscope at various times in his life – particularly in the late 1920s and early 1930s – reflects not merely a concern about external events, but also a quest for the 'right moment' for some kind of inner breakthrough or illumination.[200]

Since the publication of *Liber Novus*, a number of astrologers have assessed the transits and progressions in Jung's horoscope to ascertain what was 'happening' to him during the time he worked on the book.[201] These analyses are often highly insightful, but they do not address the question of whether some of the figures appearing in *Liber Novus* might have been deliberately invoked according to what a Hermeticist would deem the astrologically appropriate moment. Sadly, no specific instructions for finding that pregnant moment are given in the extant Hermetic texts. But something resembling this type of astrological advice is offered by the *Mithras Liturgy*, with which Jung was deeply familiar. Given his understanding of astrological configurations as symbolic reflections of dynamic psychological processes, and his perception of the breaking of the chains of *Heimarmene* as an individual experience of the integration of unconscious archetypal potencies, it would be surprising if he did not avail himself of the instructions offered by the *Liturgy*.

Jung seems to have viewed fate as an integral dimension of the individuation process, and astrological symbolism as a reflection of the unfolding of that process. The various currents of late antique religious thought that Jung was studying during the time he worked on *Liber Novus* present fate as intimately linked to the cyclical movements of the heavenly bodies, which Jung understood as symbols of the archetypal dominants of the collective unconscious, expressing themselves through the qualities of time. Fate, time, and the movements of the heavens are inextricably bound up with Jung's concept of individuation. Freedom from fate, in late antique approaches, involved a form of gnosis or inner realisation that could break the compulsions of the planetary daimons. There is no mention of altering external circumstances through theurgic practices, since fate was understood as an interior structure imposed on the soul during its time in incarnation. Freedom from *Heimarmene* required an alteration in consciousness, allowing the individual to be liberated from the compulsive actions that brought about suffering, and encouraging the embrace of those dimensions of fate that reflected divine teleology. The matrix of Orphic, Neoplatonic, Hermetic, and Gnostic thought, centred on an astrological cosmology, seems to have provided Jung with a powerful form of hermeneutics to help him interpret the spontaneous visions described in *Liber Novus*, as well as presenting a symbolic model of his most important psychological concept: that inner process by which the individual becomes what he or she was always intended to be.

Notes

1 Heraclitus, DK B119, in Kahn (trans.), *The Art and Thought of Heraclitus*, p. 81.
2 'Schicksal und Gemut sind Namen eines Begriffes'. Friedrich von Hardenberg [Novalis], *Heinrich von Ofterdinge*, trans. John Owen (Cambridge: Cambridge Press, 1842), Part Two, p. 84, at <www.gutenberg.org/files/31873/31873-h/31873-h.htm>.
3 Jung, *Liber Novus*, p. 311.
4 See, for example, Dane Rudhyar, *The Astrology of America's Destiny* (New York: Random House, 1974). *The Astrology of America's Fate* would not have been in keeping with the spirit of the time.
5 Jeff Mayo, *Astrology* (London: Teach Yourself Books, 1964), p. 6.
6 Margaret Hone, *The Modern Textbook of Astrology* (London: L.N. Fowler, 1951), p. 17.
7 Stobaeus, Excerpt XX, in Mead, *Thrice-Greatest Hermes*, III:XX:2, pp. 84–85.
8 Jung's sources for the *Apocryphon of John*, the chief Gnostic exponent of this approach to astral fate, were Irenaeus, *Irenaei episcopi lugdunensis contra omnes haereses* (Oxford: Thomas Bennett, 1702), and Mead, *Fragments*, pp. 580–82. Two further redactions of the *Apocryphon* were found at Nag Hammadi in Egypt in 1945; see *Apocryphon of John*, trans.

Frederick Wisse, in James McConkey Robinson (ed.), *The Nag Hammadi Library in English* (Leiden: Brill, 1977), pp. 98–116.

9 For the seven-layered 'soul-vehicle' in the *Apocryphon*, see Roelof van den Broek, 'The Creation of Adam's Psychic Body in the *Apocryphon of John*', in Roelof Van den Broek and M.J. Vermaseren (eds.), *Studies in Gnosticism and Hellenistic Religions* (Leiden: Brill, 1981), pp. 38–57.

10 For the malign qualities of the 'counterfeit spirit' in Gnostic doctrines, see van den Broek, 'The Creation of Adam's Psychic Body'; Couliano, *The Tree of Gnosis*, pp. 102–5.

11 See Thomas Aquinas, *Summa Contra Gentiles*, trans. Anton C. Pegis, James F. Anderson, Vernon J. Bourke, and Charles J. O'Neil (New York: Hanover House, 1955–57), III.84–87, 91–92. See also Campion, *A History of Western Astrology*, pp. 49–51.

12 For discussions on free will and determinism relevant to Jung, see Arthur Schopenhauer, *Prize Essay on the Freedom of the Will*, trans. Eric F.J. Payne, ed. Günter Zöller (Cambridge: Cambridge University Press, 1999 [1839]); Immanuel Kant, *Critique of Practical Reason*, trans. Lewis White Beck (Upper Saddle River, NJ: Prentice-Hall, 1993 [1788]).

13 It has not vanished entirely. See Hans Jurgen Eysenck and David K.B. Nias, *Astrology: Science or Superstition?* (New York: St. Martin's Press, 1982).

14 See, for example, J.C. Kim and S.M. Dumecki, 'Genetic Fate-Mapping Approaches', *Methods in Molecular Biology* 493 (2009), pp. 65–85; Stanley Fields and Mark Johnston, *Genetic Twists of Fate* (Cambridge, MA: MIT Press, 2010).

15 For the work of Pavlov (1849–1936), see Ivan Petrovich Pavlov, *Conditioned Reflexes*, trans. G.V. Anrep (Oxford: Oxford University Press, 1927). See also Barbara R. Saunders, *Ivan Pavlov* (Berkeley Heights, NJ: Enslow, 2006).

16 For this perspective, see Bernardo J. Carducci, *The Psychology of Personality* (Chichester: John Wiley & Sons, 2009); Susan Hart, *Brain, Attachment, Personality* (London: Karnac, 2008).

17 Jung, CW7, ¶41.

18 For this theme in Plato, see Plato, *Republic*, 617e–6620b.

19 Alan Leo, *Esoteric Astrology* (London: Modern Astrology Office, 1913), p. vii.

20 Jung, *MDR*, pp. 353–54.

21 Jung, *MDR*, pp. 350 and 354.

22 For more on Besant and her work, see Anne Taylor, *Annie Besant* (Oxford: Oxford University Press, 1991). For Jung's dismissive references to Besant, see Jung, CW10, ¶176; Jung, CW10, ¶90; Jung, CW11, ¶859.

23 Annie Besant, *A Study in Consciousness* (London: Theosophical Publishing Society, 1904), pp. 98–100.

24 Jung, *MDR*, p. 349.

25 Jung, *Psychology of the Unconscious*, p. 155.

26 For Jung's early explorations into this type of analogical thinking, see Jung, CW2, trans. Leopold Stein (London: Routledge & Kegan Paul, 1969), originally published in German as a series of papers in *Journal für Psychologie und Neurologie* 3–16 (1904), and in English as *Studies in Word-Association*, trans. M.D. Eder (London: William Heinemann, 1918). See also Jung, 'Concerning the Two Kinds of Thinking', in Jung, *Psychology of the Unconscious*, pp. 4–21.

27 Alan Leo, *Saturn, The Reaper* (London: Modern Astrology Office, 1916), p. 5.

28 Jung, *Psychology of the Unconscious*, p. 173.

29 Jung, CW7, ¶183.

30 Jung, *Psychology of the Unconscious*, p. 42 and n. 30.

31 Jung, *MDR*, p. 205.

32 Jung, CW11 ¶143. The lectures, given at Yale University, were published by Yale University Press and Oxford University Press in 1938, and were later translated into German and published as *Psychologie und Religion* in 1940.

33 For the importance of Novalis as an influence on Jung, see Hanegraaff, *New Age Religion*, p. 513; Hanegraaff, *Esotericism and the Academy*, p. 286. For Novalis' interest in astrology, see Brian W. Kassenbrock, *Novalis and the Two Cultures* (unpublished PhD dissertation, Department of Germanic Languages and Literatures, New York University, 2009), p. 19.

34 C.G. Jung, 'Men, Women, and God', *The Daily Mail* (London), 29 April 1955.
35 Jung, *Liber Novus*, p. 233.
36 Jung, CW7, ¶405.
37 For 'the fate of the peoples', see Jung, *Liber Novus*, pp. 239 and 241. The doctrine of 'subsumption' – the ways in which an individual horoscope can be superseded or 'subsumed' by 'greater causes' – can be found in Ptolemy, *Tetrabiblos*, II:1, 117–119 and in Abraham ibn Ezra, *The Book of the World* (Leiden: Brill, 2010), p. 283.
38 Jung, *Modern Psychology*, Vol. 1 & 2, p. 223.
39 Jung, CW15, ¶31.
40 Jung, CW12, ¶40.
41 Jung, *Psychology of the Unconscious*, p. 42, n. 30.
42 For Stoic philosophy, see John M. Rist, *The Stoics* (Berkeley: University of California Press, 1978); Mauro Bonazzi and Christoph Helmig (eds.), *Platonic Stoicism, Stoic Platonism* (Leuven: Leuven University Press, 2007). For the Stoic influence on astrology, see Robert Zoller, *Fate, Free Will and Astrology* (New York: Ixion Press, 1992), pp. 94–115.
43 Betegh, *The Derveni Papyrus*, Col. XIX.
44 See Zoller, *Fate, Free Will, and Astrology*, p. 101.
45 νευμα νοερον και πυρωδες. Poseidonius, *The Fragments*, Vol. 1, ed. L. Edelstein and I.G. Kidd (Cambridge: Cambridge University Press, 1972), Frag. 101, p. 104 (translation mine).
46 θεοʃ εστι πνευμα νοερον διηκον δι απασηʃ ουσιας. Poseidonius, *The Fragments*, Vol. 1, p. 104 (translation mine).
47 Jung, CW6, ¶355.
48 For Jung's use of Tertullian's term, concupiscience, as 'untamed libido', which he equates with *Heimarmene*, see Jung, CW6, ¶33.
49 Jung, CW5, ¶223.
50 Jung, CW6, ¶355.
51 Jung, CW9ii, ¶216.
52 Ernst H. Gombrich, 'Icones Symbolicae', *Journal of the Warburg and Courtauld Institutes* 11 (1948), pp. 163–92, on p. 175.
53 Jung, CW6, ¶33, n. 9; Jung, CW5, ¶644.
54 See Chapter 1.
55 See Zoller, *Fate, Free Will, and Astrology*, p. 103.
56 '*Qua fatorum etiam inextricabiliter contorta retractas licia et Fortunae tempestates mitigas, et stellarum noxios meatus cohibes*'. The translation is from Jung, *Psychology of the Unconscious*, p. 42, n. 30. See Apuleius, *The Golden Ass*, trans. Thomas Taylor (Frome: Prometheus Trust, 1997), 11.25.
57 Jung acquired three volumes of Seneca's work in the original Latin: *L. Annaei Senecae opera, quae exstant* (1673); *L. Annaei Senecae operum tomus secundus* (1672); *L. Annaei Senecae rhetoris opera, quae existant Integris Nicolai Fabri, Andr. Schotti, accuratissimo aucta* (1672).
58 Seneca, *De tranquillitate animi* 10.3, cited in Thomas G. Rosenmeyer, *Senecan Drama and Stoic Cosmology* (Berkeley: University of California Press, 1989), p. 72.
59 Johann Jacob Bachofen, *Das Mutterrecht* (Stuttgart: Krais und Hoffmann, 1861), published in English as *Myth, Religion and Mother Right*, trans. Ralph Manheim (Princeton, NJ: Princeton University Press, 1967). See Jung, CW15, p. 84; Jung, CW5, Fig. 43.
60 Bachofen, *Myth, Religion and Mother Right*, p. 18.
61 Jung, *Liber Novus*, p. 308.
62 Erich Neumann, *The Great Mother* (Princeton, NJ: Princeton University Press, 1955), p. 230.
63 See Jung, CW5, ¶423.
64 Jung's German translation of the *Meditations* was Marc Aurel, *Selbstbetrachtungen*, trans. Otto Kiefer (Leipzig: E. Diederichs, 1903).
65 Marcus Aurelius, *Meditations,* 12:14.
66 Jung quoted by his patient, Mary S. Howells, in Jensen (ed.), *C.G. Jung, Emma Jung, and Toni Wolff*, p. 119.
67 For yet more discussions about Jung's 'Gnosticism' see Alfred Ribi, *The Search for Roots* (Los Angeles, CA: Gnosis Archive Books, 2013); E.M. Brenner, 'Gnosticism and Psychology:

Jung's *Septem Sermones ad Mortuos'*, *Journal of Analytical Psychology* 35 (1990), pp. 397–419. Further references are given by Shamdasani in Jung, *Liber Novus*, p. 346, n. 81.

68 Richard Noll, 'Jung the Leontocephalus', in Bishop (ed.), *Jung in Contexts*, pp. 51–91, on p. 72.

69 Lance Owens, 'Jung and Aion', *Psychological Perspectives* 54:3 (2011), pp. 253–89, on p. 260.

70 For this ring, see Hakl, *Eranos*, p. 45; Paul Bishop, 'Introduction', in Bishop, *Jung in Contexts*, pp. 1–30, on p. 6. For more on Jung's view of Abraxas, see the discussion in Greene, *The Astrological World of Jung's 'Liber Novus'*, chapter 7.

71 For Jung's belief that medieval alchemy perpetuated ancient Gnostic ideas, see Jung, CW9ii, ¶¶267 and 368; Jung, CW11, ¶160; Jung, CW12, ¶¶234–35; Jung, CW14, ¶¶104, 759, and 763–64.

72 For Basilides, see Birger A. Pearson, 'Basilides the Gnostic', in Antii Marjanen and Petri Luomanen (eds.), *A Companion to Second-Century Christian 'Heretics'* (Leiden: Brill, 2008), pp. 1–31. Charles William King, *The Gnostics and Their Remains* (London: Bell & Dalby, 1864), provided an important source for Jung's understanding of Basilidian doctrines.

73 See Greene, *The Astrological World of Jung's 'Liber Novus'*, chapter 7, for the astrological content of 'Scrutinies' and Jung's diagram of the *Systema Munditotius*.

74 Owen Davies, *Magic* (Oxford: Oxford University Press, 2012), p. 1.

75 For some useful (and often contradictory) texts, see Hans Jonas, *The Gnostic Religion* (Boston, MA: Beacon Press, 1958); Roelof van den Broek, *Gnostic Religion in Antiquity* (Cambridge: Cambridge University Press, 2013); Kurt Rudolph, *Gnosis*, trans. P.W. Coxon, K.H. Kuhn, and R. McL. Wilson (San Francisco, CA: HarperCollins, 1987); Birger A. Pearson, *Gnosticism, Judaism, and Egyptian Christianity* (Minneapolis, MN: Fortress Press, 1990).

76 For Gnostic currents within Judaism, see Gershom Scholem, *Jewish Gnosticism, Merkabah Mysticism, and Talmudic Tradition* (New York: Jewish Theological Seminary, 1970).

77 See Nicola Denzey Lewis, *Cosmology and Fate in Gnosticism and Graeco-Roman Antiquity* (Leiden: Brill, 2013); Couliano, *The Tree of Gnosis*, p. 23.

78 Segal, *The Gnostic Jung*, p. 3.

79 See, for example, Plato, *Symposium*, 201d–212b.

80 For Plato's influence on Gnostic texts, see Irenaeus, *Haer.* 2:14; Hippolytus, *Refutatio* 1:11; Plotinus, Ennead 2.9.6. See also Pearson, *Gnosticism, Judaism, and Egyptian Christianity*, pp. 148–64, and the essays in Richard T. Wallis and Jay Bregman (eds.), *Neoplatonism and Gnosticism* (Albany: SUNY Press, 1992).

81 On Manichaean radical dualism, see Jonas, *Gnostic Religion*, pp. 206–38; Johannes van Oort, 'Manichaeism', in van den Broek and Hanegraaf (eds.), *Gnosis and Hermeticism*, pp. 37–51.

82 *Marsanes*, NHC X.5.24–26, trans. Birger A. Pearson, in *The Nag Hammadi Library*, p. 418.

83 Jung, CW14, ¶616.

84 Jung, CW9ii, ¶123.

85 Jung, CW9ii, ¶298.

86 Jung, CW9ii, ¶308; Jung, *Liber Novus*, p. 363. For the idea of the 'Original Man', Jung relied heavily on the Manichaean texts cited in Reitzenstein's *Das iranische Erlösungsmysterium* and *Die hellenistiche Mysterienreligionen*; see Jung, CW14, ¶450.

87 See Robert McLachlan Wilson, 'Gnosis and the Mysteries', in van den Broek and Vermaseren (eds.), *Studies in Gnosticism and Hellenistic Religions*, pp. 451–66, on p. 451. For the various hypotheses on the origins of Gnosticism, see Ioan P. Couliano, 'The Angels of the Nations and the Origins of Gnostic Dualism', in *Studies in Gnosticism and Hellenistic Religions*, pp. 79–80.

88 For these heresiologists, see Gérard Vallée, *A Study in Anti-Gnostic Polemics* (Waterloo, ON: Wilfrid Laurier University Press, 1981). Jung possessed Latin and German versions of Irenaeus: *Irenaei episcopi lugdunensis contra omnes haereses* (1702) and *Des heiligen Irenäus fünf Bücher gegen die Häresine* (1912). He also acquired a German translation of Epiphanius, *Ausgewählte Schriften* (1919), and cites Hippolytus' *Elenchos* regularly in Jung, CW9ii, ¶¶287–346.

89 Mead published two collections on the Gnostics: *Fragments of a Faith Forgotten* (London: Theosophical Publishing Society, 1900) and *Echoes from the Gnosis* (London: Theosophical Publishing Society, 1906–8). Jung acquired both collections soon after they were published.
90 Wilhelm Bousset, *Hauptprobleme der Gnosis* (Göttingen: Vandenhoeck & Ruprecht, 1907); Richard Reitzenstein, *Poimandres* (Leipzig: Teubner, 1904); Richard Reitzenstein, *Mysterionreligionen nach ihren Grundgedanken und Wirkungen* (Leipzig: Teubner, 1910). Jung cited all three works frequently in *Psychology of the Unconscious.*
91 Jung, CW9ii, ¶310.
92 Jung, CW13, ¶457.
93 For Jung's discussion of this theme, see Jung, CW12, ¶461.
94 Jung, CW14, ¶6. The 'Agathodaimon' or 'good daimon' appears frequently on late antique magical amulets; the seven-rayed crown suggests the planetary order, while the twelve-rayed crown may be zodiacal.
95 Jung, CW14, ¶308.
96 Jung, *Liber Novus*, p. 325.
97 Jung, CW13, ¶¶209–10.
98 Jung, CW9ii, ¶128. For Jung's equation of Saturn with the lion-headed Ialdabaoth, see also Jung, CW9ii, ¶325; Jung, CW13, ¶275.
99 Jung described the ring in detail in McGuire and Hull (eds.), *C.G. Jung Speaking*, p. 468. Photos of the ring appear on <http://gnosticwarrior.com/the-gnostic-ring-of-carl-jung.html> and <http://gnosis.org/jung.ring.html>, but no reference is given for these images.
100 For the syncretic nature of Abraxas, see Gilles Quispel, *Gnostica, Judaica, Catholica*, ed. Johannes van Oort (Leiden: Brill, 2008), pp. 40–65, 243–60. Numerous late antique gemstone amulets show the name Abraxas combined with the figure of Chnoumis. Jung was familiar with many of these amulets through the illustrations in King, *The Gnostics and Their Remains*. See Greene, *The Astrological World of Jung's 'Liber Novus'*, chapter 7.
101 See the editors' comments in Jung, *Liber Novus*, p. 349, n. 93. Jung based much of his understanding of Abraxas on Albrecht Dieterich's *Abraxas* (Leipzig: Teubner, 1891); he studied this work closely in 1913, and his copy is annotated. The etymology of the name Abraxas can also be found in King, *The Gnostics and Their Remains*, p. 37.
102 Jung, *Liber Novus*, p. 349.
103 Cited by Shamdasani in Jung, *Liber Novus*, p. 349, n. 93. For Jung's equation of Bergson's *durée créatrice* with the libido, see Chapter 1.
104 Jung, *Visions Seminars*, Vol. 2, pp. 806–7.
105 Jung, *Psychology of the Unconscious*, p. 125.
106 For Jung's equation of Abraxas with the *demiurgos* or 'world-creator', see Jung, *Liber Novus*, p. 349, n. 93.
107 G.R.S. Mead, 'Pistis-Sophia', *Lucifer* 6 (March 1890–August 1890), pp. 107–13, 230–39, 315–23, 392–401, 489–99; *Lucifer* 7 (September 1890–February 1891), pp. 35–43, 139–47, 186–96, 285–95, 368–76, 456–63; *Lucifer* 8 (March 1891–August 1891), pp. 39–47, 123–29, 201–4. Blavatsky's commentaries can be found in Blavatsky, CW13, pp. 1–81.
108 G.R.S. Mead (trans.), *Pistis Sophia* (London: Theosophical Publishing Society, 1896); Mead, *Fragments*, pp. 459–506.
109 Portions of *Pistis Sophia* had been translated by King in *The Gnostics and Their Remains*. See Jung, CW6, ¶396, and his use of King's illustrations of 'Gnostic' gems in CW12 (Figs. 45, 52, 203, 204, 205, and 253).
110 See Clare Goodrick-Clarke and Nicholas Goodrick-Clarke, *G.R.S. Mead and the Gnostic Quest* (Berkeley, CA: North Atlantic Books, 2005), p. 31; Stephan A. Hoeller, 'C.G. Jung and the Alchemical Revival', *Gnosis* 8 (1988), pp. 34–39; Stephan A. Hoeller, *Gnosticism* (Wheaton, IL: Theosophical Publishing Society, 1982), p. 169.
111 The name 'Jeu' or 'Ieu' seems to be a Greek corruption of the Hebrew IHVH, similar to IAO, and is a magical name used to connote a god; see Betz, *The Greek Magical Papyri*, p. 335.

112 Mead, *Pistis Sophia*, 1:20.
113 Mead, *Pistis Sophia*, 4:140. It is unclear to what, if any, configuration between Jupiter and Venus this text might refer.
114 See Chapter 6.
115 Mead, *Pistis Sophia*, p. 345.
116 Mead, *Pistis Sophia*, p. 256. Italics mine.
117 For this passage, see M.L. West, *The Orphic Poems* (Oxford: Oxford University Press, 1983), p. 23. For discussions, see Roy Kotansky, 'Incantations and Prayers for Salvation on Inscribed Greek Amulets', in Christopher A. Faraone and Dirk Obbink (eds.), *Magika Hiera* (Oxford: Oxford University Press, 1991), pp. 114–16; E. Bikerman, 'The Orphic Blessing', *Journal of the Warburg Institute* 2:4 (1939), pp. 370–71. The first compilation of the Orphic fragments, Otto Kern's *Orphicorum fragmenta* (Berlin: Weidmann, 1922), was published while Jung was still working on *Liber Novus*; he eventually became familiar with this work (see Jung, CW13, ¶412, n. 11), but it had not yet appeared when he wrote *Psychology of the Unconscious*. At that time he relied on Taylor's *The Mystical Hymns of Orpheus*, Mead's *Orpheus*, and Wilhelm Heinrich Roscher's *Ausführliches Lexikon der griechischen und römischen Mythologie Lexicon* (Leiden: Teubner, 1884).
118 *Hermetica*, *CH* XIII.
119 See, for example, *The Gospel of Philip*, in *The Apocryphal New Testament*, trans. and ed. M.R. James (Oxford: Clarendon Press, 1924), 12; the ritual pronouncements that enable the soul to bypass the planetary archons are almost identical to those of the Orphic funerary tablets. Jung possessed copies of James' work in both English and German, along with other earlier English and German translations of apocryphal texts. These included Alexander Walker's *Apocryphal Gospels, Acts, and Revelations* (Edinburgh: T&T Clark, 1911), which contains the *Gospel of Philip*.
120 Jung, CW15, ¶81.
121 See Noll, *The Jung Cult*, for an example of this assumption.
122 Jung owned several works by Blavatsky, including an English edition of *The Secret Doctrine*, 2 volumes (London: Theosophical Publishing House, 1888) and *The Theosophical Glossary*, ed. G.R.S. Mead (London: Theosophical Publishing House, 1892).
123 Jung, CW8, ¶59.
124 See Jung, CW7, ¶118.
125 Jung, CW18, ¶756.
126 Jung, CW7, ¶339. For further comments, see Jung, CW7, ¶494; Jung, CW10, ¶176; Jung, CW6, ¶279.
127 Jung, CW4, ¶749; Jung, CW6, ¶594.
128 G.R.S. Mead, *'The Quest' – Old and New* (London: John M. Watkins, 1926), pp. 296–97.
129 For details on Mead's life, see Goodrick-Clarke and Goodrick-Clarke, *G.R.S. Mead*, p. 32. For the Leadbeater episode, see Campbell, *Ancient Wisdom Revived*, pp. 114–18.
130 Mead, 'The Quest', pp. 296–97.
131 Noll, *The Jung Cult*, p. 69.
132 G.R.S. Mead to C.G. Jung, 19 November 1919, ETH-Bibliothek Zürich, Archives Hs 1056:29826.
133 Stephan Hoeller states that Jung and Mead visited each other, attributing his information to a private conversation with the historian of religion, Gilles Quispel, who knew Jung well through their attendance at the Eranos conferences. Mead's letter confirms this statement. See Hoeller, 'C.G. Jung and the Alchemical Revival', p. 35, n. 1.
134 Jung acquired all of Meyrink's 'occult' novels, including *Der Engel vom westlichen Fenster* (1927), *Fledermäuse: Sieben Geschichten* (1916), *Der Golem* (1915), *Das grüne Gesicht* (1916), and *Walpurgisnacht* (1917). For his references to Meyrink, see Jung, CW6, ¶¶205, 426, and 630; Jung, CW7, ¶153; Jung, CW7, ¶¶153 and 520; Jung, *Dream Analysis*, pp. 276–94; Jung, *Modern Psychology*, I:110.
135 Nicholas Goodrick-Clarke, *The Occult Roots of Nazism* (London: Tauris Parke, 2004), p. 28.
136 These include: *Orpheus the Fisher* (1921); *Weltenmantel und Himmelszeit*, 2 volumes (1910); *L'origine babylonienne de l'alchimie* (1926); 'Pistis Sophia und Barbelo', *Angelos*

3:12 (1928), pp. 93–110; *Nachleben dionysischer Mysterienriten* (1928); and *Orphisch-dionysische Mysteriengedanken in der christlichen Antike* (Leipzig: Teubner, 1925). Jung's many published references to Eisler include Jung, CW14, ¶610; Jung, CW9i, ¶553; CW12, ¶177 and Figs. 174 and 202.

137 See Jung, CW9ii, ¶¶147, 162, 178, and 186.

138 Robert Eisler, *Man into Wolf* (London: Routledge & Kegan Paul, 1951).

139 Goodrick-Clarke and Goodrick-Clarke, *G.R.S. Mead*, pp. 15–16 and 27.

140 G. R S. Mead, *A Mithraic Ritual* (London: Theosophical Publishing Society, 1907). Mead relied heavily on Dieterich's *Ein Mithrasliturgie* to produce his own work. Jung cited both in *Psychology of the Unconscious.*

141 Mead, *The Mysteries of Mithra.*

142 The text, known as *PGM IV*, is part of the Great Magical Papyrus of Paris, a codex found in Egypt in the early nineteenth century and dated to the early fourth century CE.

143 See Betz, *The "Mithras Liturgy"*, p. 37.

144 See Betz, *The "Mithras Liturgy"*, p. 35; Fowden, *The Egyptian Hermes*, pp. 82–87 and 168–72.

145 Franz Cumont, *Die orientalischen Religionen im römischen Heidentum* (Leipzig: Teubner, 1910), p. 217, n. 5.

146 Mead, *Fragments*, pp. 10, 16.

147 Mead, *Fragments*, p. 23.

148 See Mead, *Fragments*, p. 398, citing a text attributed to the Gnostic teacher Bardaisan of Edessa (154–222 CE) to illustrate the Gnostic idea of *Heimarmene*. See also Tim Hegedus, 'Necessity and Free Will in the Thought of Bardaisan of Edessa', *Laval théologique et philosophique* 69:2 (2003), pp. 333–44.

149 Mead, *Fragments*, p. 403.

150 For the 'subtle body' in various historical contexts, see above, nn. 9 and 77. For Theosophical works on the 'subtle' body, see C.W. Leadbeater, *Man, Visible and Invisible* (London: Theosophical Publishing Society, 1902); Annie Besant, *Man and His Bodies* (Los Angeles, CA: Theosophical Publishing House, 1917).

151 For the Stoic gradations of material substance, see A.A. Long and D.N. Sedley, *The Hellenistic Philosophers*, Vol. 1 (Cambridge: Cambridge University Press, 1987), pp. 266–343; F.H. Sandbach, *The Stoics* (London: Duckworth, 1975), pp. 69–94.

152 See Jung, CW11, ¶848. Jung's source for the Tibetan idea of the *Bardo* body was W.Y. Evans-Wentz (ed. and trans.), *The Tibetan Book of the Dead* (London, 1927).

153 See Jung, CW9i, ¶202.

154 Jung, CW5, ¶513. See Henry Wadsworth Longfellow, *The Song of Hiawatha* (Boston: Ticknor and Fields, 1855).

155 Jung, CW9i, ¶392.

156 Jung, CW13, ¶137, n. 8.

157 G.R.S. Mead, *The Doctrine of the Subtle Body in Western Tradition* (London: J.M. Watkins, 1919); quotations on pp. 12–13 and p. 20.

158 Mead, *The Doctrine of the Subtle Body*, p. 41.

159 Jung, CW16, ¶486.

160 Jung, CW12, ¶511.

161 Jung, CW14, ¶¶311 and 353.

162 Galen, *De Placitis Hippocratis et Platonis, VII, Opera Omnia*, ed. Kühn, V.643, cited in Walker, 'The Astral Body in Renaissance Medicine', p. 123.

163 Paracelsus, *Sämtliche Werke,* VIII:161–70. Jung cited Paracelsus' reliance on Galen in Jung, CW13, ¶150; Jung, CW15, ¶¶19, 54.

164 Paracelsus, *Sämtliche Werke*, XII:3 and 23. Jung cited these references in CW8, ¶390.

165 Ruland, *A Lexicon of Alchemy*, p. 182. See Jung, CW13, ¶¶188, 194.

166 Jung, CW11, ¶160. For 'spiritual' alchemy, see Mircea Eliade, *The Forge and the Crucible* (Chicago: University of Chicago Press, 1956), p. 8; Lindsay, *Origins of Alchemy*, pp. 101–3. For a Platonic/Neoplatonic basis for alchemy, see Stanton J. Linden, *The Alchemy Reader* (Cambridge: Cambridge University Press, 2003), p. 3. For Plato's own passages,

see Plato, *Timaeus*, 27c–31b, 32c–34c, 36d–e, 47e–51b, 59b–c. For a nineteenth-century work on 'spiritual' alchemy that influenced Jung, see Mary Anne Atwood, *A Suggestive Inquiry into 'The Hermetic Mystery'* (London: Trelawney Saunders, 1850).

167 Jung, CW13, ¶¶262–63.
168 Freud, SE18, p. 29.
169 Jung, *Psychology of the Unconscious*, p. 454. See also Jung, CW5, ¶185.
170 Jung, CW9ii, ¶216.
171 Jung, CW10, ¶843.
172 Mead, *Pistis Sophia*, 111.384.
173 Cited in Clement of Alexandria, *Stromata*, in *St. Clement of Alexandria*, ed. and trans. Alexander Roberts, James Donaldson, and Arthur Cleveland Cox (Buffalo, NY: Christian Literature Publishing, 1885), II.20.372.
174 See Morton W. Bloomfield, *The Seven Deadly Sins* (East Lansing: Michigan State College Press, 1952).
175 For Jung's idea that cultures as well as individuals can suffer from lopsided development and compensatory unconscious compulsions, see Jung, CW7, ¶¶283, 285, 287; Jung, CW10, ¶¶250, 295.
176 For the dating of the *Hermetica*, see Fowden, *The Egyptian Hermes*, p. 3.
177 On the syncretic nature of the *Hermetica*, see Brian P. Copemhaver, 'Introduction', in *Hermetica*, pp. xxvi–xxix; Peter Kingsley, *Ancient Philosophy, Mystery, and Magic* (Oxford: Clarendon Press, 1995), pp. 233–49; Fowden, *Egyptian Hermes*, pp. 14–22, 36–37, 91, 144, 178, 188–95.
178 Van den Broek, *Studies in Gnosticism and Alexandrian Christianity*, p. 1.
179 See, for example, Christopher Lehrich, *The Occult Mind* (Ithaca, NY: Cornell University Press, 2007), p. 4.
180 For example, one of the 'technical' Hermetic treatises on astrology – the *Book of the Configurations of Heimarmene which are Beneath the Twelve* – is cited by name in the Nag Hammadi rescensions of the Gnostic *Apocryphon of John*; see Lewis, *Cosmology and Fate*, p. 107. See also Pearson, *Gnosticism, Judaism, and Egyptian Christianity*, pp. 29–34.
181 For Jewish contributions to *Poimandres* and other *Hermetica*, see Pearson, *Gnosticism, Judaism, and Egyptian Christianity*, pp. 136–47; Birger A. Pearson, 'Jewish Elements in *Corpus Hermeticum* I (*Poimandres*)', in Roelof van den Broek and Cis van Heertum (eds.), *From Poimandres to Jacob Böhme* (Leiden: Brill, 2000), pp. 336–48.
182 Marsilio Ficino (trans.), *Mercurii Trismegisti: Pimander sive de potestate et sapientia Dei* (Treviso: Gerardus de Lisa, 1471). Jung acquired a rare 1574 edition based on Ficino's Latin translation: *Mercurii Trismegisti: Pimandras utraque lingua restitutus* (Bordeaux: Simon Millanges, 1574).
183 In addition to Berthelot's collection and Mead's three-volume English translation of the then extant Hermetic treatises, *Thrice- Greatest Hermes*, Jung also acquired Reitzenstein's *Poimandres*.
184 Jung, CW12, 408–10.
185 See Jung, *MDR*, p. 230, and Jung, *Liber Novus*, pp. 218 and 360.
186 Jung, *Liber Novus*, p. 312.
187 For the history and historiography of *Poimandres*, see Peter Kingsley, 'Poimandres', *Journal of the Warburg and Courtauld Institutes* 56 (1993), pp. 1–24; Hans Dieter Betz, 'Hermetism and Gnosticism: The Question of the "Poimandres"', in Søren Giversen, Tage Petersen, and Podemann Sørensen, *The Nag Hammadi Texts in the History of Religions* (Copenhagen: Royal Danish Academy of Sciences and Letters, 2002), pp. 84–94.
188 CH I.25–26, in *Hermetica*, p. 6.
189 For this funerary tablet or *lamella* from Thurii, see Alberto Bernabé and Ana Isabel Jiménez San Cristóbal, *Instructions for the Netherworld* (Leiden: Brill, 2008), p. 81.
190 See Fowden, *The Egyptian Hermes*, p. 108; Merkur, 'Stages of Ascension', pp. 79–96.
191 For Mead's translation of the planetary compulsions in *Poimandres*, see Mead, *Thrice-Greatest Hermes*, I:413.

192 Macrobius, *Commentary on the Dream of Scipio*, trans. William Harris Stahl (New York: Columbia University Press, 1990 [1952]), XII:13. See Jung, *Psychology of the Unconscious*, p. 125.

193 The myth of the soul-journey is described by Plato in *Republic*, X.614a–621d. For examples of a Platonic-Gnostic ascent, see *Trimorphic Protennoia* (NHC XIII, 1), trans. John D. Turner; *Zostrianos* (NHC VIII, 1), trans. John H. Sieber; both in *The Nag Hammadi Library*.

194 Walter Scott (ed. and trans.), *Hermetica*, 4 volumes (Oxford: Clarendon Press, 1924–36), I:1–2. See Lewis, *Cosmology and Fate*, p. 106, n. 10.

195 André-Jean Festugière, *La révélation d'Hermès Trismégiste,* 4 volumes (Paris: Bibliothèque des textes philosophiques, 1946–54), I:30. For the questionable validity of this division, see Copenhaver, *Hermetica*, p. xxvii; Fowden, *The Egyptian Hermes*, pp. 1–4, 140–41, 161–213. Jung does not seem to have acquired either Scott's or Festugière's translations.

196 For these lost works, see Copenhaver, Hermetica, pp. xxxiv–xxxv; Lewis, *Cosmology and Fate*, p. 107.

197 For two exceptions, see Robert Zoller (trans.), *Liber Hermetis*, 2 volumes (Golden Hind Press, 2000); *Kyranides* (London, 1685; repr. New York: Renaissance Astrology, 2010.) For Jung's familiarity with *Kyranides*, see Jung, CW9ii, ¶138. See also Fowden, *The Egyptian Hermes*, pp. 87–89; David Bain, 'Μελανιτις γη in the *Cyranides* and Related Texts', in Todd Klutz (ed.), *Magic in the Biblical World* (Edinburgh: T&T Clark, 2003), pp. 191–213.

198 *CH* XIII.12.

199 Fowden, *The Egyptian Hermes*, p. 109. For *kairos*, the 'right moment', see Jung, CW10, ¶585.

200 During this period, Jung emerged from his voluntary seclusion. In 1928, he collaborated with Wilhelm on *The Secret of the Golden Flower*, and in the following year he published his first essay on Western alchemy, 'Paracelsus' (Jung, CW15, ¶¶1–17). In 1930 he became vice president of the General Medical Society for Psychotherapy, and was awarded the Literary Prize of the City of Zürich in 1932. In the same year, he completed his entries in the *Black Books*. In 1933, the Eranos conferences began at Ascona, where Jung delivered the first of many papers he was to give at these events in subsequent years: 'A Study in the Process of Individuation' (Jung, CW9i, ¶¶525–626). Also in 1933, Jung began lecturing at the ETH, and in 1934 he founded the International General Medical Society for Psychotherapy and became its first president and editor of its journal, *Zentralblatt für Psychotherapie und ihre Grenzgebiete*. In 1935, he became titular professor at the ETH, and founded the Swiss Society for Practical Psychology.

201 See Lynn Hayes, 'The astrology of Carl Jung and His Red Book' (2009), <www.beliefnet.com/columnists/astrologicalmusings/2009/09/carl-jung-and-the-astrology-of.html>; 'Carl Jung's "Red Book"', < http://heavenlytruth.typepad.com/heavenly-truth/2009/09/carl-jungs-red-book-the-astrology-behind-the-publication-of-jungs-most-personal-work.html>.

6

'THE WAY OF WHAT IS TO COME'

> When we speak of the new Aquarian type of person, we are actually referring to human beings through whom will be released . . . the energies, the faith, the downflowing enthusiasm and revelations of the new Age . . . These true 'Aquarians' . . . are mouthpieces for the new spirit, and many of them may almost be called born 'mediums' for the release of that spirit at the beginning of the new cycle.[1]
>
> —Dane Rudhyar

> When the month of the Twins had ended, the men said to their shadows: 'You are I' . . . Thus the two became one, and through this collision the formidable broke out, precisely that spring of consciousness that one calls culture and which lasted until the time of Christ. But the fish indicated the moment when what was united split, according to the eternal law of contrasts, into an underworld and upperworld . . . But the separated cannot remain separated forever. It will be united again and the month of the fish will soon be over.[2]
>
> —C.G. Jung

The idea of the 'New Age'

In the last two decades, a considerable amount of scholarly literature has been dedicated to Jung's influence on so-called New Age beliefs and practices.[3] Olav Hammer, following Richard Noll, uses the term 'Jungianism' to describe a form of 'modern psycho-religion' based on the cult-like role assigned to Jung as a New Age guru.[4] Paul Heelas has identified Jung as one of three key figures in the development of New Age thought, the other two being H.P. Blavatsky and Georges Ivanovich Gurdjieff (1866–1949), whose spiritual system, referred to as the 'Fourth Way', focuses on the development of higher states of consciousness.[5] Wouter Hanegraaff, also following Noll, views Jung as a 'modern esotericist, who represents a crucial link between traditional . . . esoteric worldviews and the New Age movement'.[6]

There are certainly broad parallels between Jung's psychological models and those currents of 'New Age' thought that emphasise the enlargement of consciousness. This can be explained, in part, by the fact that both Jung and the late nineteenth-century occult revival, which provided the basis for many of the most potent New Age ideas, drew on the same pool of sources: Hermetic, Platonic, Neoplatonic, Gnostic, and Jewish esoteric speculations and practices, along with liberal dashes of Hindu and Buddhist thought. Many New Age religious approaches had thus already been fully formed by the end of the nineteenth century. Roderick Main, in a paper on the relationship between Jung's ideas and New Age thought, comments:

> It is possible to construe that Jungian psychology, even as originally expounded by Jung, may itself have been influenced by New Age thinking . . . While Jung certainly influenced the New Age movement, he may himself have been influenced by New Age religion or was even one of its representatives.[7]

The idea of the New Age as an astrologically defined epoch – assumed, in modern times, to be the incoming 'Aquarian Age' – began to take shape in the late eighteenth century, crystallised in the nineteenth, and is still popular today. Dane Rudhyar believed that the Aquarian Age would commence in 2060, although he thought that its 'seed period' had begun between 1844–46.[8] Wouter Hanegraaff, in his important work, *New Age Religion and Western Culture*, refers to the New Age '*in sensu strictu*': those currents of ideas which focus on the expectation of an imminent Aquarian Age and an accompanying radical shift in consciousness reflecting the meaning of the astrological constellation. Hanegraaff then discusses the New Age '*in sensu lato*': an innovative movement 'in a general sense' which does not necessarily bear a specifically astrological connotation.[9]

This is a useful heuristic approach through which to explore many current spiritualities. But it is difficult to find agreement among authors about just what constitutes New Age in the broad sense. Many of the ideas that form the basis of New Age thought are very ancient, and have not been significantly altered by another exceedingly ambiguous term, 'modernity'. They might equally be viewed as 'Old Age', as they reflect certain consistent cosmological and anthropological themes that possess great agency and are immensely culturally adaptable, while maintaining a structural integrity for more than two millennia. These ideas have not necessarily been 'secularised' in the sense that their present-day adherents have become 'irreligious', nor in the sense that they eschew a specific organised form of religion. Jung viewed such ideas as archetypal: they belong to the 'Spirit of the Depths', and not, as might be assumed, the 'Spirit of This Time'.

New Age ideas – particularly the conviction that self-awareness and God-awareness are indistinguishable, and that God can be found within – are assumed by some scholars to be unique to 'modern' spiritualities. This assumption is not supported by textual evidence. The equation of 'god-knowledge' with 'self-knowledge' is clearly expressed in Hermetic, Neoplatonic, Gnostic, and early Jewish esoteric literature.[10] In this sense, Hanegraaff's assumption of the modernity of New Age thought may be misleading, creating sharp artificial divisions between historical periods, cultures, and spheres of human expression in which a more nuanced perspective might be more helpful. But however problematic the definitions of New Age *in sensu lato* might be, Jung's thinking about the incoming New Age clearly belongs in the category Hanegraaff calls '*in sensu strictu*'; for it seems that Jung believed wholeheartedly that a new epoch reflecting the symbolism of the constellation of Aquarius was about to dawn, and that his psychology might make a significant contribution to the conflicts inevitably arising in the face of such a profound shift in collective consciousness.

The god in the egg

In 1951, following two heart attacks, Jung wrote a work called *Aion*.[11] For the frontispiece, he chose a Roman sculpture of the Mithraic god known to scholars variously as Aion, Aeon, Kronos, Chronos, or Zervan (see Plate 4).[12]

While he worked on *Liber Novus*, Jung relied in large part on Dieterich's German and Mead's English translations of the *Mithras Liturgy*. He also acquired Franz Cumont's two books on Mithraism: *Die Mysterien des Mithra* and the earlier, much lengthier *Textes et monuments figurés relatifs aux mystères de Mythra*.[13] Jung referred to Cumont as 'the foremost authority on the Mithraic cult'.[14] But Cumont rejected the central importance of astrology in Roman Mithraic worship, viewing its astrological iconography as properly belonging to the earlier, 'Chaldaean' form of the cult, and blaming this older 'Oriental' religious current for infecting Western beliefs with astrology's 'long train of errors and terrors'.[15] It seems that Jung did not agree.

In recent years, Roger Beck and David Ulansey have challenged Cumont's assumptions, focusing specifically on the astrological foundations of Roman Mithraism.[16] Mithraic archaeological finds have provided the chief source for these examinations; the cult's initiations were a well-kept secret, and no body of literature exists produced directly by its members. Only references have survived, often based on hearsay, in the writings of late antique authors such as Origen and Porphyry.[17] But numerous images of Aion have survived the centuries, discovered in Roman Mithraea throughout Europe. They typically present a winged lion-headed male figure holding a staff and a key, enveloped in the coils of a serpent, and usually – although not invariably – surrounded by, or bearing on his body, the signs of the zodiac.[18]

The Greek word *aionos* has a number of different meanings and usages, all of which are relevant to Jung's understanding of the imminent collective psychic change he envisioned in *Liber Novus*.[19] Homer and Herodotus used the word to describe the lifetime of an individual.[20] Euripides, in common with some Hermetic treatises, personified Aion as a divine being, calling him the 'child of time' who 'brings many things to pass'.[21] Aeschylus and Demosthenes used the word to describe both an epoch and a generation.[22] Sophocles understood it as one's destiny or lot, akin to the idea of *moira*.[23] Hesiod used it to define an age or era, such as the Age of Gold or the Age of Iron.[24] Paul used it to refer to the present world, as well as an era or epoch.[25] In Plato's *Timaeus*, *aionos*, in contrast to *chronos*, constitutes eternity, while *chronos* expresses *aionos* temporally through the movements of the heavenly bodies:

> Now the nature of the ideal being was eternal, but to bestow this attribute in its fullness upon a creature was impossible. Wherefore he resolved to have a moving image of eternity [*aionos*], and when he set in order the heaven, he made this image eternal but moving according to number, while eternity itself rests in unity; and this image we call time [*chronos*].[26]

Jung seems to have favoured the idea of an aion as both an astrological epoch – lasting roughly 2,165 years, or one-twelfth of what he believed to be the great 'Platonic Year' of 26,000 years – and a god-image, emerging out of the human religious imagination and embodying the specific qualities of that epoch. These astrological epochs are reflected by the astronomical phenomenon of the precession of the equinoxes: the gradual backward movement of the spring equinox (the moment each year when the Sun enters the zodiacal sign of Aries) through the stars of the twelve zodiacal constellations.[27]

Pistis Sophia describes the aions as both celestial powers ruling over specific regions of the cosmos, and the regions themselves: zodiacal constellations with doorways or gates through which the redeemer-god passes as he accomplishes his task of salvation.[28] In contrast, the *Mithras Liturgy* presents Aion, not as a zodiacal constellation, a planetary archon, or an epoch of time, but as a fiery primal divinity, also called Helios-Mithras: as Jung understood it, an image of the libido or life-force.[29] A vision of this eternal being is the goal of the ritual, leading to the temporary 'immortalisation' of the initiate.[30]

> For I am to behold today with Deathless Eyes – I, mortal, born of mortal womb, but [now] made better by the Might of Mighty Power, yea, by the Incorruptible Right Hand – [I am to see today] by virtue of the Deathless Spirit the Deathless Aeon [αθανατον Αιωνα], the master of the Diadems of Fire.[31]

Later in the ritual, prayers are offered to the 'seven Fates of heaven', the planetary divinities governing *Heimarmene*. An invocation is then addressed to Aion that names his primary attributes and functions:

> Light-giver [and] Fire-sower; Fire-loosener, whose Life is in the Light; Fire-whirler, who sett'st the Light in Motion; Thou Thunder-rouser; O Thou Light-glory, Light-increaser; Controller of the Light Empyrean; O Thou Star-tamer![32]

Aion the 'star-tamer' emanates and controls the heavenly spheres, and the vision vouchsafed the initiate in the *Mithras Liturgy* allows an identification with divinity that, at least for a time, breaks the power of *Heimarmene*.[33] As we have seen, Jung associated this freedom from the bonds of astral compulsion with the integrating potency of a direct experience of the Self; like the *Liturgy*, he stipulated no guarantee of the permanence of the state. A comparison of Aion in the *Liturgy* with the words of the giant Izdubar in *Liber Novus*, who rises out of the fiery egg revealed as the Sun-god, suggests how profoundly the *Mithras Liturgy* affected Jung's understanding of the astrological symbol of the Sun.

> Streams of fire broke from my radiating body –
> I surged through the blazing flames –
> I swam in a sea that wrapped me in living fires –
> Full of light, full of longing, full of eternity –
> I was ancient and perpetually renewing myself . . .
> I am the sun.[34]

Jung's description of Aion included the name Kronos (Saturn), but he elided it with *chronos* (time) and emphasised the leonine attributes of the figure:

> We come across in the Mithraic religion, a strange God of Time, Aion, called Kronos or Deus Leontocephalus, because his stereotyped representation is a lion-headed man, who, standing in a rigid attitude, is encoiled by a snake . . . In addition to that, the figure sometimes bears the Zodiac on his body . . . He is a symbol of time, most interestingly composed from libido-symbols. The lion, the zodiac sign of the greatest summer heat, is the symbol of the most mighty desire.[35]

Paradoxically, Jung associated this 'Deus Leontocephalus' not only with the Sun, but also with the Gnostic archon Ialdabaoth and the archon's planet, Saturn.[36] Aion was many things for Jung: a fiery libido-symbol embracing all opposites; a symbol of time expressed through the solar pathway of the zodiacal round; and a personification of the planetary deity Saturn-Kronos, his own horoscopic ruler. Aion may thus also be understood as the universal or collective aspect of Jung's 'personal daimon' Philemon, the 'Master of the House'.[37] And Aion, for Jung, embodied an astrological age – that of Aquarius – which combines, in its imagery and meaning, the human form of the Water-bearer with its opposite constellation of Leo, the Lion. In one of the early paintings in *Liber Primus*, the symbols of the polarity of the new Aion, Aquarius and Leo, are presented: the Lion stands at the top left of the image with a red solar disk over his head, while the Water-bearer, dressed in a blue robe rather than in the harlequin pattern of the later 'Caster of Holy Water', stands at the top right of the image pouring his water from a red urn, with the glyph of Saturn by his left shoulder.[38] William Butler Yeats, preoccupied with the same zodiacal polarity, described his own vision of the approaching New Age in his poem, *The Second Coming*, written just after the Armageddon of the Great War, with a prophetic pessimism not unlike Jung's own: a terrifying being with a lion's body and the head of a man, that 'slouches toward Bethlehem to be born' in the midst of chaos and the disintegration of social order.[39]

In *Liber Novus*, Jung described his own transformation into a leontocephalic deity encircled by a serpent, with 'outstretched arms like someone crucified'.[40] Later, he explicitly related this vision to the Mithraic iconography of Aion:[41]

> The animal face which I felt mine transformed into was the famous [Deus] Leontocephalus of the Mithraic mysteries. It is the figure which is represented with a snake coiled around the man, the snake's head resting on the man's head, and the face of the man that of the lion.[42]

This allusion suggests a deeply personal significance underlying Jung's choice of the frontispiece for *Aion*. The vision in *Liber Novus*, like that of the *Mithras Liturgy*, describes a transient, although profoundly transformative, inner experience resulting in an enlarged consciousness and, in Jung's terminology, a fuller integration of the personality. In Jung's natal horoscope, as he was well aware, the opposites of Aquarius and Leo dominate. Aquarius was rising at the moment of Jung's birth, and the Sun was placed in Leo. It is not surprising that he felt the symbolism of Aion was relevant, not only for the collective psyche, but for his own.

The age of Aquarius

The first image on the first page of *Liber Novus* incorporates the letter D, illuminated in the style of a medieval German manuscript, and introduces the opening sentence of the work: *Der Weg des kommenden* ('The Way of What Is to Come').

An astrological 'strip' can be seen at the top of the image (see Plate 5); it is painted in a blue lighter than that of the sky with its heavenly bodies.[43] The zodiacal constellations, represented by their traditional glyphs, run in counterclockwise order, beginning with Cancer at the far left, followed by Gemini, Taurus, Aries, and Pisces, and concluding with Aquarius at the far right. The large four-rayed star in the 'strip' is placed at the precise meeting-point between the constellation represented by the glyph of Pisces and the constellation represented by the glyph of Aquarius. The star evidently represents the Sun at the moment of the annual spring equinox.[44] This equinoctial point, slowly creeping backward through the constellations over the centuries, has, according to Jung, now reached the end of the constellation of Pisces and is about to enter its 2,165-year journey through the constellation of Aquarius. Jung referred to this astronomical event as the new Aion, the 'Way of What Is to Come'. He later called it 'καιρος – the right time – for a "metamorphosis of the gods"'.[45]

The major theme of *Aion* is the shift in human consciousness, and a simultaneous shift in the God-image, reflected by the ending of the Piscean Aion. Pisces is associated with the Christian symbols of Jesus and Satan as the two Fish, and the advent of the Aquarian Aion is associated with a new symbol: humanity as the Water-bearer. Lance Owens has suggested that it is necessary to cross-reference

Aion with *Liber Novus* in order to understand both: *Aion* is Jung's effort, late in life, to provide a rational exegesis of the revelations of *Liber Novus*, and the two works are 'fundamentally wed'.[46] *Aion* appears to offer a more impersonal involvement with astrology than Jung's preoccupation with his own horoscope. But his approach to collective cycles incorporated the same psychological models as his perception of psychic dynamics in the individual: archetypes, typologies, complexes, and astrological significators as symbols of the qualities of time. Jung believed that each of the great shifts represented by a new astrological Aion is reflected in the imagery of the presiding zodiacal constellation and its planetary ruler:

> Apparently they are changes in the constellations of psychic dominants, of the archetypes, or 'gods' as they used to be called, which bring about, or accompany, long-lasting transformations of the collective psyche. This transformation started in the historical era and left its traces first in the passing of the aeon of Taurus into that of Aries, and then of Aries into Pisces, whose beginning coincides with the rise of Christianity. We are now nearing that great change which may be expected when the spring-point enters Aquarius.[47]

While *Aion* discusses the historical nature of these transformations as they are expressed in religious representations, *Liber Novus* reveals Jung's understanding of his own role in the imminent shift, in accordance with his conviction that every individual is part of the collective, and that the future of the collective depends on the consciousness of the individual.[48]

There has been considerable speculation as to where Jung acquired the idea of a New Age in relation to the movement of the vernal equinoctial point. This seems to be particularly important because Jung has been credited with being the first person in modern times to disseminate the idea that the long-anticipated New Age would be Aquarian. The idea of an Aquarian Age is rooted in the late eighteenth-century Enlightenment, when a number of scholarly works were produced that focused on the Christian figure of Jesus as one of a long line of solar deities.[49] According to Nicholas Campion, the ideas presented in these works can be divided into three distinct categories. First was the attempt to establish a common origin for religions. Second came the theory that this shared origin lay in the worship of the celestial bodies, especially the Sun. Third was the use of the precession of the equinoxes to establish the dating of the Indian sacred texts known as the Vedas.[50] Although none of the authors of these eighteenth-century works provided the kind of interpretations offered by astrologers contemporary with Jung, all of them emphasised the importance of the precessional cycle in the historical development of religious images and ideas.

In 1775, the French astronomer and mathematician Jean Sylvain Bailly (1736–93) proposed an astral origin for all religious forms.[51] Bailly was followed by a French lawyer and professor of rhetoric, Charles François Dupuis (1742–1809), who, in his *Origine de tous les cultes*, argued that all religions sprang from Sun-worship, and that Christianity was simply another form of solar myth.[52] Dupuis, like Max Heindel and Jung himself over a century later, noted the parallels between the astrological constellation of Virgo and the mother of the solar messiah. Describing the engraving he commissioned for the frontispiece of his book, Dupuis noted: 'A woman holding a child, crowned with stars, standing on a serpent, called the celestial Virgin . . . She has been successively Isis, Themis, Ceres, Erigone, the mother of Christ'.[53]

Dupuis' frontispiece (see Plate 6) combines the idea of a universal solar religion with religious themes related to the precession of the equinoxes. At the upper left corner, in the heavens, are the zodiacal constellations of Aries and Taurus, with the Sun shining on the midpoint between them. The vernal equinoctial point is thus crossing from Taurus to Aries, reflected in the shift from various Taurean religious forms represented in the engraving (Mithras slaying the cosmic bull, the Egyptian Apis-bull, the Golden Calf) to those of Aries (Zeus enthroned as the god of heaven, the Israelite High Priest before the Ark of the Covenant). At the top centre of the frontispiece are the symbols of the Christian dispensation: the four Apostles with their symbolic animals, the 'celestial virgin' crowned with stars, and the Christ-child as the new-born Sun. Although Dupuis focused on the shift from Taurus to Aries rather than from Pisces to Aquarius, there is a striking parallel between Dupuis' illustration of the Sun at the midpoint between the constellations of Taurus and Aries and Jung's four-pointed solar star at the midpoint between the constellations of Pisces and Aquarius on the opening page of *Liber Novus*. Jung never mentioned Dupuis in his published work, nor is a copy of *Origines* listed in his library catalogue. But it is probable that he was familiar with Dupuis' book.

Speculations on a link between the precession of the vernal equinoctial point and the changing of religious forms continued throughout the late eighteenth and nineteenth centuries. François-Henri-Stanislas de l'Aulnaye (1739–1830), who authored two books on Freemasonry, produced a text in 1791 called *L'histoire générale et particulière des religions et du cultes*.[54] Campion states that this work was the first to consider the implications of the precession of the vernal equinoctial point into Aquarius, which de l'Aulnaye believed had taken place in 1726.[55] Godfrey Higgins (1772–1833), a religious historian whose work exercised a major influence on Blavatsky,[56] declared in his *Anacalypsis*, published in 1836, that the equinoctial shift from Taurus into Aries was the time when 'the slain lamb' replaced 'the slain bull'.[57] In the late nineteenth century, Gerald Massey (1828–1907), an English poet and self-educated Egyptologist, offered a detailed scheme of the evolution of religious forms according to the precession of the equinoxes through the zodiacal constellations.[58] It is in one of Massey's papers, 'The Historical Jesus and the Mythical Christ', privately published in 1887, that the first reference to the Age of Aquarius appears in the English language:[59]

> The foundations of a new heaven were laid in the sign of the Ram, 2410 BC; and again, when the Equinox entered the sign of the Fishes, 255 BC. Prophecy that will be *again* fulfilled when the Equinox enters the sign of the Waterman about the end of this [nineteenth] century.[60]

All of these authors – Dupuis, Delaunaye, Higgins, and Massey – utilised myths to illustrate vast collective changes in religious forms and perceptions, and linked the myths to particular zodiacal constellations in the cycle of precession. Although Jung did not cite any of their writings in his own published work, nevertheless the same ideas are central to *Aion*. That no one seems to have agreed on the date for the start of the new Aquarian Aion is not surprising. As Jung himself stated: 'The delimitation of the constellations is known to be somewhat arbitrary'.[61]

Ancient sources for the New Age

Texts explicitly relating the dawning of a New Age to the precession of the equinoxes may only have begun in the modern era. But Jung believed that earlier sources supported his belief that a new astrological Aion was about to begin. His quest for historical evidence of the idea of the incoming Aquarian Age sometimes led him to assume connections that a twenty-first-century scholar, nervous of speculation of a 'universalist' kind, might well avoid. However, refusal to acknowledge the longevity and universality of certain ideas can itself reveal a powerful agenda, and Jung's intuitive leaps seem to have been valid more often than they were misguided. An example of Jung's search to find validation for the Aquarian Age in alchemical texts is provided by the sixteenth-century alchemist and physician Heinrich Khunrath (1560–1605),[62] who declared that an 'age of Saturn' would begin at some point in the not too distant future, and that it would usher in a time when alchemical secrets would become available to everyone:

> The age of Saturn is not yet, in which everything that is private shall become public property: for one does not yet take and use that which is well meant and well done in the same spirit.[63]

Khunrath does not mention either the precession of the equinoxes or the zodiacal constellation of Aquarius anywhere in his text. Nor does the idea appear in any other alchemical literature of the early modern period, steeped in astrology though it was. But Jung believed that Khunrath was referring to the Age of Aquarius because this constellation is traditionally ruled by Saturn. In a lecture given at the ETH in 1940, Jung cited Khunrath's statement, and then commented:

> Khunrath means that the age of Saturn has not yet dawned . . . Obviously the question is: what does Khunrath mean by the age of Saturn? The old alchemists were of course also astrologers, and thought in an astrological way. Saturn is the ruler of the sign of Aquarius, and it is quite possible that Khunrath meant the coming age, the age of Aquarius, the water carrier, which is almost due now. It is conceivable that he thought mankind would be changed by that time, and would be able to understand the alchemists' mystery.[64]

> restlessness and longing for the fulfilment of the times . . . When the confusion is at its height a new revelation comes, i.e. at the beginning of the fourth month of world history.[76]

The 'fourth month of world history' is the Aion of Aquarius; 'world history' in Jung's context began with recorded history in the Aion of Taurus, which Jung believed had occurred between 4300 and 2150 BCE. The imminent collective transformation will, in Jung's view, require a long and potentially dangerous process of integration, as it would in an individual. *Liber Novus*, with its opening image of the movement of the equinoctial point into Aquarius, and its frequent references to Phanes-Abraxas, the androgynous, dark-light god of the new aion, might be understood as a highly personal narrative of precisely that integrative process within Jung himself. Jung's interest in Nietzsche's work is likely to have contributed to the idea that the celestial Water-bearer – one of only three zodiacal images bearing a human form[77] – might be a symbol of the *Übermensch*, the 'Beyond-Man' who transcends the opposites. Nietzsche's conviction that humanity was progressing toward a goal that lay 'beyond good and evil' hints at the idea of the fully individuated human being whom Jung hoped would emerge in the new Aion.[78] But Nietzsche never associated his *Übermensch* with Aquarius.

An obvious modern source for Jung's expectations of a transformation of consciousness based on the precession of the equinoxes might seem to be the Theosophists, who certainly promulgated the idea of an imminent New Age. Blavatsky was familiar with authors such as Higgins and Massey. But she did not equate her New Age with the entry of the vernal equinoctial point into the constellation of Aquarius, preferring to use what she referred to as 'the Hindu idea of cosmogony' (the concept of the Yugas) combined with certain fixed stars in relation to the equinoctial point.[79] According to Blavatsky, twelve transformations of the world will occur, following a partial destruction by water or fire (a lift from the Stoics) and the generation of a new world with a new twelvefold cycle. She identified this idea as 'the true Sabaean astrological doctrine', which describes these twelve transformations as reflections of the twelve zodiacal constellations.[80] But this approach does not involve precession, and the twelve transformations do not comprise a precessional cycle of 26,000 years; they comprise the entire history of the planet over many millions of years.

In an article on the history of the idea of the New Age, Shepherd Simpson points out that Jung, whom he credits with the first promulgation of the idea of an 'Aquarian Age' in modern times, could not have got the idea from Blavatsky.[81] The German esotericist Rudolf Steiner, whose Anthroposophical Society rejected the Eastern inclinations of the Theosophists but retained many of their ideas, likewise subscribed to the idea of a New Age, and referred to it as the 'Age of Christ's Second Coming'. But this New Age, which, in Steiner's view, began in 1899, is not Aquarian.

> There is much talk about periods of transition. We are indeed living just at the time when the Dark Age has run its course and a new epoch is just

> beginning, in which human beings will slowly and gradually develop new faculties . . . What is beginning at this time will slowly prepare humanity for new soul faculties.[82]

These 'new soul faculties' do indeed belong to the Aquarian Age, but they are only in preparation. According to Steiner's idiosyncratic reckoning, the Age of Aquarius will not begin until 3573, and the world at present is still living in the Piscean Age, which began in 1413.[83] Steiner wrote extensively about the problem of evil; like Jung, he believed evil to be a reality rather than a mere 'deprivation of good', and, also like Jung, he was fascinated with but also repelled by Nietzsche's ideas.[84] Steiner also understood the necessity for humans taking responsibility for evil:

> Until now, the gods have taken care of human beings. Now, though, in this fifth post-Atlantean epoch, our destiny, our power for good and evil, will increasingly be handed over to us ourselves. It is therefore necessary to know what good and evil mean, and to recognize them in the world.[85]

But Steiner was much closer to Gnostic perceptions than Jung was, and understood evil to belong to the incarnate world and the spiritual potencies (Lucifer and Ahriman) who, like the Gnostic archons, work to inflame the innate selfishness and destructiveness of the human being. Nor did Steiner associate the integration of good and evil with an imminent Aquarian Age. Steiner was no more likely a source for Jung's understanding of the new Aion than Blavatsky was.

In 1906, Mead offered his own version of the New Age:

> I too await the dawn of that New Age, but I doubt that the Gnosis of the New Age will be new. Certainly it will be set forth in new forms, for the forms can be infinite . . . Indeed, if I believe rightly, the very essence of the Gnosis is the faith that man can transcend the limits of the duality that makes him man, and become a consciously divine being.[86]

This idea of a resolution of the problem of duality is much closer to Jung's formulation, and Mead may have contributed important ideas to Jung's vision of 'The Way That Is to Come'. In *Aion*, Jung elaborated on Mead's description in a psychological context:

> The approach of the next Platonic month, namely Aquarius, will constellate the problem of the union of opposites. It will then no longer be possible to write off evil as the mere privation of good; its real existence will have to be recognized. This problem can be solved neither by philosophy, nor by economics, nor by politics, but only by the individual human being, via his experience of the living spirit.[87]

Jung's view of the incoming new Aion was full of foreboding, and bears little resemblance to the sentimentalised presentations of the 'Age of Aquarius' that emerged during the 1960s, exemplified by Broadway's first 'concept' musical, *Hair*, in which the dawning New Age will be one of 'harmony and understanding, sympathy and trust abounding'.[88] The romantic idealism of these lyrics, and their cultural context, belong to a more optimistic and less cynical era. It is not surprising that Jung – who, in 1913, a year before the outbreak of the Great War, experienced a terrifying vision of 'rivers of blood' covering the whole of northern Europe[89] – initially anticipated the opening of the new Aion as a mortal struggle requiring recognition of the 'real existence' of evil. But although Mead referred to the 'cycles of the Aeon',[90] he did not link these cycles with the precession of the equinoxes in his published work. The New Age, whatever it might be, was apparently not, for Mead, an Aquarian Age. While Jung turned to Mead's work for insights into many of the texts of late antiquity, it seems he looked elsewhere for ideas about the meaning of the Water-bearer.

Two likelier sources for Jung's ideas about the Age of Aquarius were the two Theosophically inclined astrologers who provided Jung with much of his knowledge of astrology: Alan Leo and Max Heindel. Leo embraced Blavatsky's idea that humanity was at the midpoint of its millennia-old evolutionary cycle. But he could not ignore the significance of the precession of the equinoxes, and he directly associated the New Age with the constellation of Aquarius. In *Esoteric Astrology*, first published in 1913 – the year that Jung began work on *Liber Novus* – Leo declared:

> I am actuated by the primary motive of expressing what I believe to be the true Astrology, for the New Era that is now dawning upon the world.[91]

There is no mention of Aquarius in this statement. But two years earlier, Leo had declared explicitly that he believed the Age of Aquarius would begin on 21 March 1928.[92] Leo did his best to reconcile Blavatsky's idea of the Hindu Yugas with precession, but his conclusions were, in the end, closer to Jung's:

> The constellation of Taurus was in the first sign of the zodiac [i.e. Aries] at the beginning of the Kali Yuga, and consequently the Equinoctial point fell therein. At this time, also, Leo was in the summer solstice, Scorpio in the autumnal equinox, and Aquarius in the winter solstice; and these facts form the astronomical key to half the religious mysteries of the world – the Christian scheme included.[93]

In Leo's view, the great cycle of precession is concerned with spiritual evolution, and the dawning Aquarian Age will mark the turning point of the cycle: the beginning of humanity's slow ascent back to the realm of pure spirit.[94] Although Jung used psychological models and wrote about wholeness and the integration of opposites rather than a return to a perfected world of pure spirit, it seems that, in principle, he agreed.

Leo described the Aquarian Age in general terms. Max Heindel was more specific. His statement about the purpose of his Rosicrucian Fellowship, made in 1911, emphasises the Aquarian character of the New Age:

> It [the Rosicrucian Fellowship] is the herald of the Aquarian Age, when the Sun by its precessional passage through the constellation Aquarius, will bring out all the intellectual and spiritual potencies in man which are symbolized by that sign.[95]

These burgeoning 'intellectual and spiritual potencies' did not, for Heindel, involve the psychological problem of the integration of good and evil. In *The Rosicrucian Cosmo-Conception*, published in 1909, Heindel provided a detailed explanation of the precession of the equinoxes, calling the entire cycle a 'World-year'.[96] In accord with the general tendency to disagree about when the New Age would commence, Heindel declared that the Age of Aquarius would not begin for 'a few hundred years'.[97]

Heindel's *The Message of the Stars* may have been more useful to Jung, as it describes the astrological ages in relation to the polarity of each zodiacal constellation with its opposite. Heindel's view that the Age of Aquarius contains the attributes of Leo, the opposing constellation, must have been of considerable interest to Jung, who was inclined to view the workings of astrology, as well as human psychology, as a dynamic tension between opposites. Heindel had presented this theme in 1906, in *Message of the Stars*:

> There are two sets of three pairs of signs, the first being Cancer and Capricorn, Gemini and Sagittarius, Taurus and Scorpio. In these pairs of signs we may read the history of human evolution and religion . . . This is also divisible into three distinct periods, namely: THE ARYAN AGE, from Moses to Christ, which comes under Aries-Libra;[98] the PISCEAN AGE, which takes in the last two thousand years under Pisces-Virgo Catholicism; and the two thousand years which are ahead of us, called the AQUARIAN AGE, where the signs Aquarius and Leo will be illuminated and vivified by the solar precession.[99]

Heindel also discussed the religious symbolism of the astrological ages:

> In the New Testament we find another animal, the Fish, attaining great prominence, and the apostles were called to be 'Fishers of Men', for then the sun by precession was nearing the cusp of Pisces, the Fishes, and Christ spoke of the time when the Son of Man (Aquarius) shall come . . . A new ideal will be found in the Lion of Judah, Leo. Courage of conviction, strength of character and kindred virtues will then make man truly the King of Creation.[100]

Heindel's 'Son of Man', with his Leonine 'courage' and 'strength', abounds with echoes of Nietzsche's *Übermensch*. Jung, like Heindel, developed the idea that an astrological age reflects the symbolism of two opposing constellations. This is emphasised not only in Jung's discussions of the Pisces-Virgo polarity in *Aion*, but also in numerous ways through the imagery in *Liber Novus*. For example, in one of the early paintings in *Liber Primus*, the symbols of the polarity of the new Aion, Aquarius and Leo, are presented: the Lion stands at the top left of the image with a red solar disk over his head, while the Water-bearer, dressed in a blue robe, stands at the top right of the image pouring his water from a red urn, with the glyph of Saturn by his left shoulder.[101] This is only one instance of Jung's incorporation of the Aquarius-Leo polarity in *Liber Novus*. But Jung was not as optimistic as Heindel about the new Aion. Jung did not assume the union of the opposites to be a smooth passage into a higher and more loving stage of spiritual consciousness, as did the Theosophists and the 'New Age' proponents of the late twentieth century. He foresaw 'a new advance in human development',[102] but he viewed the transition into the Aquarian Aion as a dangerous time fraught with the human potential for self-destruction. In a letter to Father Victor White, written in April 1954, Jung stated that the shift into the Aion of Aquarius

> means that man will be essentially God and God man. The signs pointing in this direction consist in the fact that the cosmic power of self-destruction is given into the hands of man.[103]

With even more overt pessimism, he wrote a year later to Adolf Keller:

> And now we are moving into Aquarius, of which the Sibylline books say: *Luciferi vires accendit Aquarius acres* (Aquarius inflames the savage forces of Lucifer). And we are only at the beginning of this apocalyptic development![104]

In light of the history of the twentieth century, it seems that Jung's dark prophecy was not inaccurate.

The timing of the new aion

There has never been any accord among authors about the date for the commencement of the New Age. At the end of the eighteenth century, de l'Aulnaye believed that the Aquarian Aion had begun in 1726. At the end of the nineteenth century, Gerald Massey insisted that the Age of Pisces began in 255 BCE with the 'actual' birth of Jesus, and that the equinoctial point would move into the constellation of Aquarius in 1901.[105] Alan Leo offered the very specific date of 21 March 1928 – the day of the vernal equinox of that year – while Dane Rudhyar, writing in 1969, suggested the Aquarian Age had begun in 1905.[106] And Rudolf Steiner, in the early decades of the twentieth century, was convinced the Age of Aquarius would not start until 3573.

Jung was initially equally precise, and equally independent, about the date on which the new Aion would begin. In August 1940, he wrote to H.G. Baynes:

> This is the fateful year for which I have waited more than 25 years . . . 1940 is the year when we approach the meridian of the first star in Aquarius. It is the premonitory earthquake of the New Age.[107]

This date did not come from esoteric literature, but from a young Dutch Jewish astronomer named Rebekka Aleida Biegel (1886–1943), who had moved to Zürich in 1911 to take her doctorate in astronomy at the university.[108]

She became Jung's patient and then trained with him, giving papers at the Association for Analytical Psychology in Zürich between 1916 and 1918. One of these papers, presented in 1916, was titled 'Die Mathematische Parallele zür Psychoanalyse'; based on the observations made in her paper, Jung credited Biegel with the term 'transcendent function',[109] which he described soon afterward, in an essay written in the same year, as 'comparable in its way with a mathematical function of the same name', and which he defined as 'the union of conscious and unconscious

FIGURE 6.1 Rebekka Aleida Biegel

contents'.[110] In 1917, he further noted that he had only recently discovered 'that the idea of the transcendent function also occurs in the higher mathematics'.[111]

In 1918, while Biegel was working at the Zürich Observatory, then located in Gloriastrasse in the centre of the city, she sent Jung an envelope of materials which he marked 'Astrologie' and kept in his desk at home.[112] Biegel went to considerable trouble to prepare a lengthy list of calculations indicating when the vernal equinoctial point – the moment when the Sun enters the first degree of the zodiacal sign of Aries each year – aligned with each of the stars in the constellations of both Pisces and Aquarius. Along with these calculations, Biegel's covering letter offered three possible dates for the beginning of the Aquarian Aion: 1940 (when the equinoctial point aligned with the midpoint between the last star of Pisces and the first star of Aquarius), 2129, and 2245 (when the equinoctial point aligned with two different stars in the constellation of Aquarius, either of which might be considered the 'beginning' of the constellation).[113] What Jung called the 'premonitory earthquake' of the Aquarian Aion, according to Biegel's first suggested date of 1940, coincided with some of the worst chapters of the Second World War. Germany invaded and occupied Norway, Denmark, Belgium, the Netherlands, and France; Hitler signed his Axis pact with Mussolini; the Blitz began in London; and the largest concentration camp, Auschwitz-Birkenau, was opened in Poland, where over a million people would be murdered in the course of the next five years.

Jung later became less certain about the date of the commencement of the Aquarian Aion. In an essay titled 'The Sign of the Fishes', written in 1958,[114] he stated that the equinoctial point 'will enter Aquarius in the course of the third millennium'.[115] In a footnote to this paragraph, Jung explained that, according to the preferred starting-point, the advent of the new Aion 'falls between AD 2000 and 2200', but that 'this date is very indefinite' because 'the delimitation of the constellations is known to be somewhat arbitrary'.[116] But the 'indefinite' and 'arbitrary' nature of the date did not deter Jung from his lifelong conviction that the Aquarian Aion was coming soon, and that its initial impact would not be pleasant.

The birth chart of Jesus

Jung was as preoccupied with discovering the birth date of Jesus, whom he believed to be the avatar and chief symbol of the Piscean Aion, as he was with the date of the beginning of the aion itself. He was not alone in this quest, although his understanding of its importance in relation to archetypal patterns in the collective unconscious was unique. Jung had a wide range of references from the late eighteenth century onward which had already made an explicit link between Christ, the zodiacal image of Pisces, and the fish as a major symbol of Christian belief. These references included a work called *The Zodia* by E.M. Smith, published in 1906, in which Smith declared: 'Modern astrological speculation . . . associates the Fishes with Christ'.[117]

The search for the 'true' nativity of Jesus, although understandably not of particular interest to pagan astrologers in late antiquity, began in the Arab world in the eighth century and has continued to the present day.[118] But it has not always involved the equation of Jesus' horoscope with the advent of the Piscean Age. Arab astrologers were more interested in Jesus' birth in relation to the 'great mutation cycle' of Jupiter and Saturn. These planets are aligned in conjunction along the ecliptic roughly every twenty years, but they take 960 years to return to a conjunction in a sign of the same element. This 'great mutation cycle' of nearly a millennium was based on early Sassanian Persian astrological theories that the conjunctions of Jupiter and Saturn underpinned the great cycles of world history and the rise and fall of kings. As Jung was familiar with the work of Arab exegesists such as Abu Ma'shar, as well as with the writings of Kepler, who discussed the cycle in the early seventeenth century, the Jupiter-Saturn cycle did not escape his notice.[119]

Nor did Jung neglect the writings of the thirteenth-century astrologer and magus Albertus Magnus, who insisted that Virgo was rising when Jesus was born,[121] or the speculations of the fourteenth-century Cardinal Pierre d'Ailly, who agreed.[122] Jerome Cardanus, another of Jung's favoured early modern astrologers, also prepared a horoscope for Jesus, using the traditional date of 25 December, just after the winter solstice. Cardanus proposed a birth year of 1 BCE, with Libra rather than Virgo rising.[123] Jung compared all these 'ideal horoscopes for Christ' in *Aion*,[124] and concluded that the 'correct' birth date for Jesus was, in fact, 7 BCE, as the conjunction of Jupiter and Saturn in Pisces in that year, with Mars in opposition from Virgo, was 'exceptionally large and of an impressive brilliance'.[125] But rather than

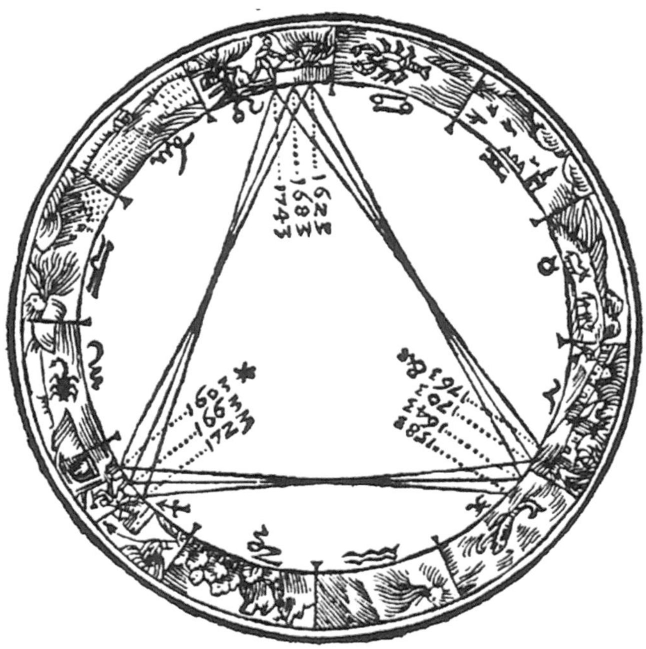

FIGURE 6.2 Kepler's diagram of the Great Mutation Cycle of Jupiter and Saturn[120]

accepting 25 December as the date of birth, Jung followed the calculations of the German astronomer Oswald Gerhardt, and proposed 29 May, the date on which the configuration of Jupiter, Saturn, and Mars had been exact.[126] This resulted in Jesus' Sun-sign as Gemini: the 'motif of the hostile brothers' that Jung believed to be one of the dominant archetypal themes of the Piscean Aion.

In Jung's discussions about the symbolism of the Fishes, he revealed a perspective on astrological images that is firmly focused on the archetypal meaning of a zodiacal symbol rather than its characterological qualities, and on its relationship with the 'God-image' – synonymous with the image of the Self – as it appears in the human psyche.

> As the highest value and supreme dominant in the psychic hierarchy, the God-image is immediately related to, or identical with, the self, and everything that happens to the God-image has an effect on the latter.[127]

The religious symbols of each zodiacal Aion thus faithfully reflect in imaginal form the 'highest value and supreme dominant' in the collective psyche for a particular epoch of history. At the beginning of *Liber Novus*, Jung emphasised the importance of this changing God-image:

> It is not the coming God himself, but his image which appears in the supreme meaning. God is an image, and those who worship him must worship him in the images of the supreme meaning.[128]

Rebekka Biegel had indicated 4 BCE as the beginning of the Piscean Aion, based on the movement of the equinoctial point. Jung's interest in the Jupiter-Saturn conjunction of 7 BCE, just three years earlier, led him to conclude that this configuration was the 'star of Bethlehem' that had appeared as the augury of Jesus' birth:

> Christ was born at the beginning of the aeon of the Fishes. It is by no means ruled out that there were educated Christians who knew of the *coniunctio maxima* of Jupiter and Saturn in Pisces in the year 7 BC, just as, according to the gospel reports, there were Chaldaeans who actually found Christ's birthplace.[129]

Jung amalgamated the image of Christ as the 'supreme meaning' of the incoming Piscean Aion with the *coniunctio maxima* of Jupiter and Saturn in the zodiacal sign of Pisces.[130] He viewed the Aquarian Aion as the epoch when individuals would interiorise the God-image; thus he did not anticipate a new avatar for the new Aion who would manifest 'out there'. He declined to adopt Steiner's belief in a 'Second Coming' of Jesus, or Annie Besant's expectation of a 'New World Teacher'.

> We now recognize that the anointed of this time is a God who does not appear in the flesh; he is no man and yet is a son of man, but in spirit and not

in flesh; hence he can be born only through the spirit of men as the conceiving womb of the God.[131]

Nor is Phanes, the new aionic god of *Liber Novus*, in any way human; he/she is androgynous and spherical, like Plato's World Soul.[132] Jung did not believe any single person would personify the spirit of the new dispensation; the Water-bearer 'seems to represent the self'.[133] He understood his own role as important, but as an individual, not an avatar, who could help to illuminate the difficult psychological process of interiorisation through his published work. Jung's understanding of the Aquarian Aion ultimately mirrors that of Alan Leo, who insisted that 'the inner nature and destiny of this sign is expressed in the one word HUMANITY'.[134]

Notes

1 Dane Rudhyar, *Astrological Timing* (New York: Harper & Row, 1969), pp. 166–67.
2 Jung, *Liber Novus*, pp. 314–15.
3 For a useful overview including references, see David John Tacey, *Jung and the New Age* (Hove: Brunner-Routledge, 2001).
4 Hammer, *Claiming Knowledge*, pp. 67–70; see also pp. 437–40 for Hammer's discussion of Jung's concept of the archetypes, which 'resembles a hermetic concept of correspondences rather than a psychological theory in the usual sense of the word'. Noll uses the word 'Jungism'; see Noll, *The Jung Cult*, pp. 7–9 and 291–94.
5 Paul Heelas, *The New Age Movement* (Oxford: Blackwell, 1996), p. 46. For Gurdjieff's own work, see G.I. Gurdjieff, *Meetings with Remarkable Men* (London: E.P. Dutton, 1964). See also P.D. Ouspensky, *In Search of the Miraculous* (New York: Harcourt, Brace, 1949).
6 Hanegraaff, *New Age Religion*, p. 497.
7 See Roderick Main, 'New Age Thinking in the Light of C.G. Jung's Theory of Synchronicity', *Journal of Alternative Spiritualities and New Age Studies* 2 (2006), pp. 8–25, p. 9; Hanegraaff, *New Age Religion*, pp. 521–22.
8 Rudhyar, *Astrological Timing*, p. 167.
9 Hanegraaff, *New Age Religion*, p. 94.
10 See Hanegraaff, *New Age Religion*, pp. 421–513; Alex Owen, 'Occultism and the "Modern Self" in Fin-de-Siècle Britain', in Martin Daunton and Bernhard Rieger (eds.), *Meanings of Modernity* (Oxford: Berg, 2001), pp. 71–96. The idea that God can be found within, and that 'God-knowledge' is 'self-knowledge', is stated explicitly in Plotinus, Ennead I:6.7 and Ennead VI:9.11.
11 Jung, CW9ii, originally published as *Aion: Untersuchungen zur Symbolgeschichte* (*Psychologische Abhandlungen* VIII, Zurich: Rascher Verlag, 1951).
12 *Aeon* is the Latin spelling of the Greek word *Aion* (Αιων). Kronos (Κρονος), as described in Hesiod's *Theogony*, is the ancient Greek Titan who became ruler of the gods after he castrated his father Ouranos. Kronos became associated with the Roman god Saturn, and it is the name used for the planet Saturn in Ptolemy's *Tetrabiblos*, which was written in Greek. *Chronos* (χρονος) is the Greek word for time. Zervan (or Zurvan) is a Persian pre-Zoroastrian deity whose name, like the Greek *chronos*, means 'time'; he is lord of the finite time of history as well as 'boundless time', the primordial light out of which everything has emanated. This deity bears many similarities with the Orphic Phanes; see Greene, *The Astrological World of Jung's 'Liber Novus'*, chapter 6.
13 Franz Cumont, *Textes et monuments figurés relatifs aux mystères de Mythra* (Brussels: Lamertin, 1896).
14 Jung, *Psychology of the Unconscious*, p. 83.

15 Franz Cumont, *The Mysteries of Mithra*, trans. Thomas J. McCormack (Chicago: Open Court, 1903), pp. 125–26.
16 David Ulansey, *The Origins of the Mithraic Mysteries* (Oxford: Oxford University Press, 1991); Roger Beck, *Planetary Gods and Planetary Orders in the Mysteries of Mithras* (Leiden: Brill, 1988); Roger Beck, *The Religion of the Mithras Cult in the Roman Empire* (Oxford: Oxford University Press, 2006).
17 See Origen, *Contra Celsum*, trans. Henry Chadwick (Cambridge: Cambridge University Press, 1953), 6:21–22; Porphyry, *De antro nympharum*, in Thomas Taylor (ed. and trans.), *Select Works of Porphyry* (London: Thomas Rodd, 1823), 5–6.
18 See Cumont, *The Mysteries of Mithra*, p. 105.
19 See Owens, 'Jung and Aion', p. 268.
20 Homer, *Iliad* 5.685, 16.453, 19.27, 22.58; Homer, *Odyssey* 5.160; Herodotus, *Histories*, 1.32. These and the following translations are available at <www.perseus.tufts.edu>.
21 Euripides, *Heracleidae*, trans. Ralph Gladstone (Chicago: University of Chicago Press, 1955), 900; *Corpus Hermeticum*, 11.
22 Aeschylus, *The Seven Against Thebes*, ed. and trans. David Grene, Richmond Lattimore, Mark Griffith, and Glenn W. Most (Chicago: University of Chicago Press, 2013), 219; Demosthenes, *On the Crown*, trans. A.W. Pickard-Cambridge, in A.W. Pickard-Cambridge (ed. and trans.), *Public Orations of Demosthenes*, 2 volumes (Oxford: Clarendon Press, 1912), 18.199.
23 Sophocles, *Trachiniae*, 34.
24 Hesiod, *Theogony*, 609.
25 Paul, *Romans*, 12.2.
26 Plato, *Timaeus*, 37d.
27 Zodiacal constellations (made up of fixed stars) and zodiacal signs (divisions of the ecliptic) are not identical; this has been known to astrologers since the second century BCE. For an explanation of the phenomenon of precession, see Patricia Viale Wuest, *Precession of the Equinoxes* (Atlanta: Georgia Southern University, 1998).
28 Mead, *Pistis Sophia,* 14.
29 See Jung, *Psychology of the Unconscious*, pp. 104–5; 110–11; 500, n. 21; 520, n. 14.
30 See Betz, *The "Mithras Liturgy"*, p. 1.
31 Mead (trans.), *A Mithraic Ritual*, II.3. See also Betz, *The "Mithras Liturgy"*, pp. 518–21, p. 51.
32 Mead (trans.), *A Mithraic Ritual*, V:3. See also Betz, *The "Mithras Liturgy"*, pp. 591–603, p. 53.
33 'This immortalization takes place three times a year': Betz, *The "Mithras Liturgy"*, p. 748, p. 57.
34 Jung, *Liber Novus*, p. 286.
35 Jung, *Psychology of the Unconscious*, pp. 313–14. Compare with Mead, *The Mysteries of Mithra*, pp. 70–71.
36 See Jung, CW9ii, ¶¶128 and 325; Jung, CW13, ¶275. Jung's remarks about the lion-headed Ialdabaoth and Saturn were first published in 1949, but the identity of the planet and the Gnostic archon is stated in Wolfgang Schultz, *Dokumente der Gnosis* (Jena: Diederichs, 1910), p. 103, where Jung would have encountered it no later than his painting of Izdubar in 1915. Jung later gave as his own references Origen's *Contra Celsum*, Bousset's *Hauptprobleme der Gnosis*, and Mead's translation of *Pistis Sophia*. As the former was cited in *Psychological Types* (1921) and the latter two in *Psychology of the Unconscious* (1911–12), Jung was already familiar with the idea of Saturn as the Deus Leontocephalus while he was working on *Liber Novus*. See above, n. 17.
37 For the Orphic Phanes as Aion in *Liber Novus*, see Greene, *The Astrological World of Jung's 'Liber Novus'*, chapter 6.
38 The image is in *Liber Primus*, folio v(r). For the text enclosed within the image, see Jung, *Liber Novus*, p. 243. For an insightful discussion of this image in relation to Jung's own horoscope, see Safron Rossi, 'Saturn in C.G. Jung's Liber Primus: An Astrological Meditation', *Jung Journal* 9:4 (2015), pp. 38–57.

39 William Butler Yeats, *The Second Coming* (1919), in *Collected Poems of William Butler Yeats* (London: Macmillan, 1933), p. 211.
40 Jung, *Liber Novus*, p. 252.
41 For the leontocephalic being as Ialdabaoth in Gnostic iconography, see M.J. Edwards, 'Gnostic Eros and Orphic Themes', *Zeitschrift für Papyrologie und Epigraphik* 88 (1991), pp. 25–40.
42 Jung, *Analytical Psychology*, p. 98.
43 For the observation that the image portrays the precession of the equinoctial point from Pisces into Aquarius, see Shamdasani, *C.G. Jung: A Biography in Books*, p. 117; Owens, 'Jung and Aion', p. 271.
44 See above, n. 28.
45 Jung, CW10, ¶585.
46 Owens, 'Jung and Aion', p. 253.
47 Jung, CW10, ¶589.
48 See Jung, CW10, ¶536.
49 For more recent works exploring this theme, see Fideler, *Jesus Christ, Sun of God*; Herbert Cutner, *Jesus* (New York: Truth Seeker, 1950), pp. 129–64.
50 See Nicholas Campion, *Astrology and Popular Religion in the Modern West* (Farnham: Ashgate, 2012), p. 22.
51 Jean Sylvain Bailly, *Histoire de l'astronomie ancienne, depuis son origine jusqu'à l'établissement de l'école d'Alexandrie* (Paris: Debure, 1775); Jean Sylvain Bailly, *Traite de l'astronomie indienne et orientale* (Paris: Debure, 1787).
52 Charles Dupuis, *Origine de tous les cultes, ou religion universelle* (Paris: H. Agasse, 1795).
53 Charles Dupuis, *Planches de l'origine de tous les cultes* (Paris: H. Agasse, 1795), p. 6.
54 François-Henri-Stanislas de L'Aulnaye, *L'histoire générale et particulière des religions et du cultes* (Paris: J.B. Fournier, 1791).
55 Campion, *Astrology and Popular Religion*, pp. 22–23. See also Godwin, *The Theosophical Enlightenment*, pp. 69 and 82.
56 See William Emmette Coleman, 'The Sources of Madame Blavatsky's Writings', in Vsevolod Sergyeevich Solovyoff, *A Modern Priestess of Isis* (London: Longmans, Green, 1895), Appendix C, pp. 353–66.
57 Godfrey Higgins, *Anacalypsis*, 2 volumes (London: Longman, Rees, Orme, Brown, Green, and Longman, 1836), II:110–11.
58 Gerald Massey, 'The Hebrew and Other Creations, Fundamentally Explained', in *Gerald Massey's Lectures* (London: Private Publication, 1887), pp. 105–40, on p. 114.
59 See Campion, *Astrology and Popular Religion*, p. 24; Hammer, *Claiming Knowledge*, pp. 248–49.
60 Gerald Massey, 'The Historical Jesus and Mythical Christ', in *Gerald Massey's Lectures* (London: Private Publication, 1887), pp. 1–26, on p. 8.
61 Jung, CW9ii, ¶149, n. 84.
62 For more on Khunrath, see Peter Forshaw, 'Curious Knowledge and Wonder-Working Wisdom in the Occult Works of Heinrich Khunrath', in R.J.W. Evans and Alexander Marr (eds.), *Curiosity and Wonder from the Renaissance to the Enlightenment* (Farnham: Ashgate, 2006), pp. 107–30.
63 Heinrich Khunrath, *Von hylealischen, das ist, pri-materialischen catholischen, oder algemeinem natürlichen Chaos, der naturgemessen Alchymiae und Alchemisten* (Magdeburg, 1597), p. 36, cited in Jung, *Modern Psychology*, Vol. 5–6, p. 156. Jung acquired Khunrath's work in the original 1597 edition.
64 Jung, *Modern Psychology*, Vol. 5–6, p. 156.
65 Horace Jeffery Hodges, 'Gnostic Liberation from Astrological Determinism', *Vigiliae Christianae* 51:4 (1997), pp. 359–73.
66 Irenaeus, *Haer.* I:29–30.
67 Irenaeus, *Haer.* I:30.12.

68 Ulansey, *The Origins of the Mithraic Mysteries,* pp. 49–51, 76–81, 82–84.
69 Jung, Letter to Sigmund Freud, 26 June 1910, in *The Freud-Jung Letters*, p. 336. See also Jung, CW5, ¶665, n. 66; Noll, 'Jung, the Leontocephalus', p. 67. Compare Jung's description of Taurus with Mead's in *The Mysteries of Mithra*, p. 63: 'The "God who steals the Bull" [Mithra] occultly signifies generation'. See also Jung, Letter to Sigmund Freud, 22 June 1910, in *The Freud-Jung Letters*, p. 334.
70 Jung, *Psychology of the Unconscious*, pp. 226–7 and p. 523, n. 60. The Tauroctony is the characteristic cult image of Mithras slaying the bull.
71 Plato, *Timaeus*, 39d.
72 Julius Firmicus Maternus, *Of the Thema Mundi,* in Taylor (trans.), *Ocellus Lucanus.*
73 For Stoic cosmology, see A.A. Long, *From Epicurus to Epictetus* (Oxford: Oxford University Press, 2006), pp. 256–84; John Sellars, *Stoicism* (Berkeley: University of California Press, 2006), pp. 99–100.
74 Macrobius proposed 15,000 years; Aristarchus proposed 2,484 years. See the discussion in J.D. North, *Stars, Mind, and Fate* (London: Continuum, 1989), pp. 96–115.
75 Jung, CW9ii, ¶286.
76 Jung, Letter to Walter Robert Corti, 12 September 1929, in *C.G. Jung Letters*, Vol. 1, pp. 69–70.
77 The other two are Gemini (the Twins), and Virgo (the Virgin). All the other constellations are represented by animals except Libra, the inanimate Balance or Scales.
78 See Friedrich Nietzsche, *Also sprach Zarathustra* (Chemnitz: Ernst Schmeitzner, 1883–84). There are various English translations of this work.
79 For Blavatsky's discussions of the 'Ages', see Blavatsky, *Isis Unveiled*, II:443, 455–56, 467–69; Blavatsky, *The Secret Doctrine*, II:198–201.
80 Blavatsky, *Isis Unveiled*, II:456.
81 <www.oocities.org/astrologyages/ageofaquarius.htm>, October 2009. This URL is now out of date but is archived.
82 Rudolph Steiner, *The Reappearance of Christ in the Etheric* (Spring Valley, NY: Anthroposophic Press, 1983), pp. 15–19.
83 See Campion, *Astrology and Cosmology in the World's Religions*, pp. 194–95.
84 Rudolph Steiner, *Friedrich Nietzsche, Ein Kaempfer Gegen Seine Zeit* (Weimar: E. Felber, 1895).
85 Rudolph Steiner, *Evil*, ed. Michael Kalisch (Forest Row: Rudolf Steiner Press, 1997; original publication, *Das Mysterium des Bösen*, Stuttgart: Verlag Freies Geitesleben, 1993), p. 56.
86 Mead, *Echoes*, I:47.
87 Jung, CW9ii, ¶142.
88 *Hair* (1967), book and lyrics by James Rado and Gerome Ragni, music by Galt MacDermot. The lyrics are from the song 'Aquarius'.
89 Jung, *MDR*, pp. 199–200.
90 Mead, *Echoes*, I:46.
91 Leo, *Esoteric Astrology*, p. v.
92 Alan Leo, 'The Age of Aquarius', *Modern Astrology* 8:7 (1911), p. 272.
93 Alan Leo, *Dictionary of Astrology*, ed. Vivian Robson (London: Modern Astrology Offices/L.N. Fowler, 1929), p. 204. This work was published posthumously.
94 For more on Leo's idea of the Aquarian Age, see Nicholas Campion, *What Do Astrologers Believe?* (London: Granta, 2006), p. 36.
95 Max Heindel, *The Rosicrucian Mysteries* (Oceanside, CA: Rosicrucian Fellowship, 1911), p. 15.
96 Heindel, *The Rosicrucian Cosmo-Conception*, pp. 159–60.
97 Heindel, *The Rosicrucian Cosmo-Conception*, p. 305.
98 Heindel's ellision of 'Aryan' with 'Arian' may reflect his own socio-religious agenda, but the former spelling has nothing to do with the zodiacal constellation of the Ram.
99 Heindel, *Message of the Stars*, p. 12.
100 Heindel, *Message of the Stars*, pp. 25–27.
101 The image is in *Liber Primus*, folio v(r). The text enclosed within the pictorial frame concludes: 'The constellation of your birth is an ill and changing star. These, Oh child

of what is to come, are the wonders that will bear testimony that you are a veritable God'. See Jung, *Liber Novus*, p. 243.

102 Jung, CW9ii, ¶141.

103 Letter to Father Victor White, 10 April 1954, in *C.G.Jung Letters*, II:167.

104 Letter to Adolf Keller, 25 February 1955, in *C.G.Jung Letters*, II:229.

105 Gerald Massey, *The Natural Genesis*, 2 volumes (London: Williams & Norgate, 1883), Vol. 2, pp. 378–503.

106 Rudhyar, *Astrological Timing*, p. 115.

107 Letter to H.G. Baynes, 12 August 1940, in *C.G.Jung Letters* I.285.

108 Biegel's dissertation on Egyptian astronomy, *Zur Astrognosie der alten Ägypter*, was published three years after her correspondence with Jung (Göttingen: Dieterichsche Universitäts-Buckdruckerei, 1921). For more on Biegel, see A.C. Rümke and Sarah de Rijcke, *Rebekka Aleida Beigel (1886–1943): Een Vrouw in de Psychologie* (Eelde: Barkhuism, 2006). Photo of Biegel, Stichting Archief Leids Studentenleven, Leiden.

109 Personal communication from Sonu Shamdasani, 28 July 2014.

110 Jung, CW8, ¶131.

111 Jung, CW7, ¶121, n. 1.

112 These materials have never been filed in any official archive. Andreas Jung kindly allowed me to examine it, and stated that it must have been of great personal importance to Jung because it had not been filed with other papers, but was kept in a special place in his desk.

113 Jung amended Biegel's calculations by the time he wrote *Aion*. In CW9ii, ¶149, n. 84, he gave the date as 2154 'if the starting-point is *Omicron* Pisces', and 1997 'if the starting-point is *Alpha* 113, which accords with the star-list in Ptolemy's *Almagest*'. Biegel also stated that the equinoctial point had arrived at the first star in the constellation of Pisces in 4 BCE, a date which Jung initially accepted as the 'true' birthdate of Christ, but which he later amended to 7 BCE.

114 Jung, CW9ii, ¶¶127–149.

115 Jung, CW9ii, ¶149, n. 88.

116 Jung, CW9ii, ¶149, n. 84.

117 E.M. Smith, *The Zodia, or The Cherubim in the Bible and the Cherubim in the Sky* (London: Elliot Stock, 1906), p. 280, cited in Jung, CW9ii, ¶149, n. 85.

118 See James H. Holden, 'Early Horoscopes of Jesus', *American Federation of Astrologers Journal of Research* 12:1 (2001).

119 For Jung's discussion of the Jupiter-Saturn cycle and Abu Ma'shar's *De magnis coniunctionibus,* see Jung, CW9ii, ¶¶130–138.

120 Johannes Kepler, *De stella nova in pede Serpentarii* (Prague: Pavel Sessius, 1606), p. 25, showing the conjunctions of Jupiter and Saturn from 1583 to 1763. Photo from Wikimedia Commons.

121 For an English translation of Albertus Magnus' *Speculum astronomiae*, which discusses Jesus' birth horoscope, see Paola Zambelli, *The Speculum astronomiae and its Enigma* (Dordrecht: Kluwer Academic, 1992). For Jung's references to Albertus Magnus, see Jung, CW9ii, ¶¶130, 133, 143, 404.

122 Pierre d'Ailly, *Tractatus de imagine mundi Petri de Aliaco* (Louvain: Johannes Paderborn de Westfalia, 1483). For d'Ailly's horoscope of Jesus, see Ornella Pompeo Faracovi, *Gli oroscopi di Cristo* (Venice: Marsilio Editori, 1999), p. 104. For Jung's references to d'Ailly, see Jung, CW9ii, ¶¶128, 130 n. 35, 136, 138, 153–54, 156.

123 Faracovi, *Gli oroscopi di Cristo*, p. 130.

124 See Jung, CW9ii, ¶130 n. 39.

125 Jung, CW9ii, ¶130.

126 Oswald Gerhardt, *Der Stern des Messias* (Leipzig: Deichert, 1922).

127 Jung, CW9ii, ¶170.

128 Jung, *Liber Novus*, p. 229. For Jung's distinction between the God-image and the ontological existence of God, see Jung, *Liber Novus*, p. 229, n. 7.

129 Jung, CW9ii, ¶172. 'Chaldaeans' is an ancient synonym for 'astrologers'; see Cicero, *De divinatione*, II:44.93.
130 Jung, CW9ii, ¶¶147 and 162.
131 Jung, *Liber Novus*, p. 299 and n. 200.
132 For the spherical nature of the World Soul, see Plato, *Timaeus*, 37d.
133 Jung, *MDR*, p. 372.
134 Leo, *Astrology for All*, p. 44.

CONCLUSION

> He [Socrates] had frequently declared in public he had received counsel from a divine voice, which he called his Daimon . . . He ought to have taken care not to pass with his friends either for a liar or a visionary; and yet how could he avoid incurring that censure if events had not justified the truth of the things he claimed were revealed to him?[1]
>
> —Xenophon

> Meaninglessness inhibits fullness of life and is therefore equivalent to illness. Meaning makes a great many things endurable – perhaps everything. No science will ever replace myth, and a myth cannot be made out of any science. For it is not that 'God' is a myth, but that myth is the revelation of a divine life in man.[2]
>
> —C.G. Jung

'The darned stuff even works after death'[3]

Based on his published statements, his letters, and the materials in his private archives, the evidence of Jung's profound and lasting commitment to astrology is inarguable. It might even be suggested that astrology was as important to him as alchemy, in terms of both a method of hermeneutics and a symbolic mapping of psychic processes, and provided him with a tool that he actively utilised in his psychotherapeutic practice throughout his adult life. However, in academic and clinical circles, Jung's commitment to astrology, and all that this might imply in terms of the development of his psychological models, has remained largely unexplored.

The lack of any reference to astrology is predictable in biographies about Jung written in the latter part of the twentieth century, and it would not be surprising if Aniele Jaffé's selective editing of *Memories, Dreams, Reflections* eradicated any mention Jung might have made about astrology's importance to him. But this lack *is* surprising in terms of the more inclusive and pluralistic approaches of twenty-first-century scholarship. An example of this tendency to utilise the old Roman practice of *damnatio memoriae* can be found in David Tacey's otherwise comprehensive work, *Jung and the New Age*. There is no reference whatsoever to Jung's astrology in this monograph, although astrology is usually considered as both a major New Age current and a central feature of the fin-de-siècle occult revival that contributed so many ideas to both contemporary New Age thought and to Jung's own developing theories.[4] Likewise, Jung's impact on modern astrologies, not least through his own astrology, has been considerable, but is not discussed in Tacey's work.

When Jung's involvement with astrology is acknowledged, the ways in which it is treated can be equally problematic. Some authors view Jung's astrological work as either an interest that waned over time, or a kind of eccentric hobby that had no significant bearing on his theories and practice, like a harmless obsession with growing giant marrows. Roderick Main's analysis of Jung's ideas about synchronicity, *The Rupture of Time*, fully acknowledges Jung's interest in astrology and his psychological interpretation of it. But Main suggests that, by the 1950s, Jung had 'replaced' astrology with other ideas about the workings of synchronicity.[5] However, it might be suggested instead that Jung simply found newer, more collectively acceptable ways of defining astrological *sumpatheia*. He certainly never ceased to seek a scientific explanation for the validity of astrology. But the idea that he had outgrown it in later life is belied not only by his lengthy statements to André Barbault, and by his recommendation to Ira Progoff that all psychotherapists should learn astrology, but also by his declaration to his daughter, made as he was dying, that 'the darned stuff even works after death'. Main seems to associate Jung's initial interest in astrology with an esoteric 'fashion' that was current in the first decades of the twentieth century, and does not discuss the extent to which Jung's immersion in the subject might have significantly helped to shape his psychological models of individuation, complexes, and typology.

Other works, while acknowledging the seriousness of Jung's commitment, use it as a justification for the insistence that his psychology is not really psychology at all, but a form of esotericism disguised as psychology, and therefore suspect within the scientific edifice of psychological and psychiatric research and practice. This response is typified by both Richard Noll and Wouter Hanegraaff. Noll suggests that Jung's interest in astrology stemmed from his Theosophical leanings, which developed through the influence of G.R.S. Mead,[6] and that these Theosophical inclinations formed an important part of Jung's 'religion-building proclivities' and served his purported efforts to create his own occult 'movement'.[7] That Jung was profoundly suspicious of movements such as Theosophy and Anthroposophy, primarily because of their lack of psychological insight, appears to have escaped Noll's notice. Hanegraaff, who seems to have based his analysis of Jung mainly on Noll's views rather than on Jung's own writings, insists that Jung 'resorted' to 'models derived from cosmology' to describe the human psyche, as though such cosmological models were somehow generated by an external source other than the psyche itself and are therefore irrelevant to psychology. Moreover, according to Hanegraaff,

Jung's work 'lends scientific legitimacy to religious beliefs', but that ultimately Jung had more in common with Blavatsky than with Freud, because he was 'a modern esotericist' who promulgated a 'cult of the Interior Sun'.[8]

If the innate assumptions and 'researcher's bias' in such perceptions are recognised, and the evidence is explored with more thoroughness and some effort to achieve greater neutrality, it becomes possible to ask more relevant questions. What kind of astrology did Jung practice? Where did he learn it? Why did he experience it as useful, and in what ways? How did he understand its longevity, and how did he incorporate its insights into his psychological work? This book has been an effort to demonstrate, not only the deep and enduring involvement with astrology that Jung pursued throughout his adult life, but also how he defined astrology, how he perceived astrological symbols within the context of the human psyche, and how astrology contributed insights and structural elements to his developing psychological models.

The more superficial aspects of astrology – such as the guessing-game of 'What is your star-sign?' – were not beneath Jung's notice.

> Sometimes people without knowing one's birthdate can make remarkable guesses as to where one's signs are. Twice it has happened to me . . . I was told that my sun was in Leo and my moon in Taurus, Aquarius rising. This made a great impression on me. How the devil did they know?[9]

This might appear a trivial comment in comparison with complex themes like the *oikodespotes*. Yet an individual who appreciates the richness of Wagner, Mozart, and Schubert may simultaneously enjoy jazz and popular music. Just as religious currents exhibit both 'learned' and 'vernacular' expressions, so too do the spheres of knowledge belonging to the liminal realms, and, being liminal, the distinctions between 'highbrow' and 'lowbrow' may be fluid or even nonexistent.[10] Jung's appreciation of both the learned and the vernacular aspects of astrology was not based on a belief in planetary or zodiacal 'influences' of a material kind, but on astrology's psychological importance as an imaginal portrayal of the cyclical qualities of time. If Sun-sign columns had existed during the early years of his astrological studies, Jung would no doubt have checked his horoscope every day in the *Neu Zürcher Zeitung*, in between translating passages from Plotinus and the *Mithras Liturgy*.

Jung related the efficacy of astrology to the innate human propensity to perceive and encapsulate the cyclical qualities of time in symbolic images, and based this idea on a synchronistic or sympathetic relationship between microcosm (the individual human being) and macrocosm (the collective unconscious). Jung's approach attributes a 'psychoid' quality to both microcosm and macrocosm – the physical and the psychic are expressions of a fundamental unity, rather than an ontological dualism of spirit and matter as described in many Gnostic treatises. This links his astrology with other symbolic frameworks and so-called mantic practices that integrate both spiritual and material domains, such as alchemy, Tarot, and the *I Ching*, all of which interested him for similar reasons. These symbolic frameworks, for Jung, reflected fundamental human psychological patterns, most important of which was the great journey through which the unconscious seeks to become conscious through utilising the symbol-making faculty of the imagination, thus generating an increasing integration and fullness of the individual personality and, ultimately, of the collective psyche itself.

Scientia and *Ars*

Astrology, like psychology, is amenable to many definitions and cannot be viewed as a single, monolithic body of knowledge or practice. Because it belongs to the liminal realms, astrology has agreeably clothed itself throughout its history in the garbs of different paradigms and different cultural contexts, envisioning itself, according to time and place, as science, art, religion, divination, psychology, philosophy, and poetic metaphor. Alexander Ruperti (1913–98), a German-born astrologer strongly influenced by both Jung's analytical psychology and Alice Bailey's Theosophical writings, observed:

> There is not one Astrology with a capital A. In each epoch, the astrology of the time was a reflection of the kind of order each culture saw in celestial motions, or the kind of relationship the culture formulated between heaven and earth.[11]

The issue of 'belief' in astrology (and whether Jung 'believed' in it) is as problematic as defining it, since many individuals who either practise astrology themselves or look to an astrologer for insights do not consider their attitude one of 'belief' or 'faith', but rather, one of experience and acquired knowledge.[12] It seems that Jung was not a 'believer', but belonged to that group of individuals who involve themselves in astrology because, for them, it 'works' – although Jung, like so many other astrologers, was never able to come up with a convincing scientific explanation of how or why this should be so. His theory of synchronicity, while acceptable to contemporary rational modes of thought, is ultimately a rewriting of the ancient idea of *sumpatheia*, couched in a language that carries no religious baggage and requires no *a priori* belief in any transcendent deity. But *sumpatheia*, as a cosmological model, is no less psychological than any model created by modern psychiatry, because it is ultimately generated by the human psyche. The sharply defined boundary between 'religion' and 'science', imposed in modern times, tends to waver and dissolve in the liminal realms of the human imagination. And attempts to 'prove' synchronicity scientifically, as Jung himself demonstrated in his astrological experiment, tend to fail because the observer, and the moment of observation, are as much part of the experiment as the observed, and the perpetually moving cyclical qualities of time will not stand still in order to please those seeking scientific validation.

Jung's approach to astrology was unique for his time, and involved a profound investigation into the interior, psychological dimensions of astrological symbolism. But within the milieu in which he worked, astrology remained, for most, a 'belief' that would have rendered his psychological theories suspect if the extent of his commitment had been widely known. Jung's correspondence with Michael Fordham, and Progoff's letter to Cary Baynes, testify to just how uncomfortable Jung felt about any publicising of his astrological work. Today, Sun-sign columns in newspapers and magazines are all that many individuals know of astrology, and the apparent frivolity of such popular writings has discouraged a more serious investigation of the subject in academic and psychotherapeutic circles. Sun-sign columns in their present form did not exist in the early twentieth century,[13] but the prejudices against astrology were already firmly in place within the burgeoning scientism of those decades.[14] Attempting to explore Jung's astrology from a scholarly, historical perspective requires an intellectual openness that many analysts, and many historians – as vulnerable to the prejudices and opinions of the collective as Jung himself was – are often not prepared to pursue.

Jung's painful conflict between *scientia* and *ars*, poignantly described in *Liber Novus* in his encounter with the giant Izdubar, was not unique to him.[15] It has existed since ancient times, evidenced in the philosophical debates between Platonists, Peripatetics, Stoics, and Sceptics, even when astrology was 'mainstream' and an integral part of the religious and philosophical currents of the cultures of the time.[16] Although *Liber Novus* is a remarkable personal testament to the depth and intensity of Jung's conflict, it reflects an endemic tension that might be viewed as fundamentally human, between the measurable evidence of the senses and the nonrational evidence of inner experience. It seems that this tension has boiled and bubbled for as long as humans have attempted to speculate on their place in the universe. Jung's psychological models might be seen as an individual effort to create a kind of neutral ground where rational thought, scientific methodology – relative, naturally, to how 'science' is defined in any given cultural context – and the experiential evidence of the liminal realms can find room for engaging in a civilised dialogue. This same effort was also being made in the world of British occultism at the turn of the twentieth century:

> The wonderful thing about the subliminal is that it provided a space for all sorts of unnatural and supernatural phenomena to occur . . . we now had a theoretical site in which they could reside. This neutrality regarding the veracity of ideas in the mind made psychology a useful no man's land in late Victorian England where scientists, clergymen and spiritualists could happily meet.[17]

Only if one is entirely wedded to the 'Spirit of This Time' – the belief that empirical science constitutes the only authoritative world-view – can the potential value of such an approach be dismissed. But even the neutral ground of the 'subliminal' has become a battlefield. Academic research into this terrain has apparently divided itself into two camps, the 'religionists' (who are often also practitioners) and the 'empiric-historical camp' (who are usually not); and warnings have been issued that the future of the study of esotericism as an academic discipline may be compromised 'if a considerable part of its representatives refuses to respect the distinction between research and the expression of personal beliefs'.[18] This statement, although apparently favouring empiricism, expresses in itself a personal belief in an ideal of pure objectivity, and the question might reasonably be raised whether it is in fact possible for any human to achieve such objectivity, devoid of any personal agenda. In his astrological experiment, Jung attempted valiantly to achieve results as free as possible from the 'expression of personal beliefs' but, as he himself acknowledged, the results of any experiment, however scientifically rigorous, are ultimately vulnerable to the psyche of the researcher. It is possible that the conflict that plagued Jung, and which continues in many circles regarding his involvement with astrology and kindred 'mantic arts', cannot be resolved, but only explored with a reasonable degree of reflexivity – an attitude on the part of the researcher that acknowledges the inevitable liability to impose personal opinions on the discussion, yet attempts to 'bracket' those opinions as much as possible. It was in this spirit that Jung declared:

> Every psychology – my own included – has the character of a subjective confession . . . Every psychology which is the work of one man is subjectively coloured.[19]

The 'spirit of this time'

A number of Jung's ideas seem to have been inspired by Plato, whose mistrust of collective opinion, in contrast to the individual capacity for knowledge acquired through reason, is evident in many of his *Dialogues*.[20]

> Right opinions are a fine thing and do all sorts of good so long as they stay in their place, but they will not stay long. They run away from a man's mind; so they are not worth much until you tether them by working out the reason . . . Once they are tied down, they become knowledge, and are stable. That is why knowledge is something more valuable than right opinion.[21]

Like Plato, Jung was suspicious of what he understood as 'mass psychology' – a perception which has sometimes been interpreted as 'elitist', but which in fact has little to do with issues of class, education, or economics.[22] 'Mass psychology', for Jung, involves the human willingness – regardless of birth, social standing, schooling, or material circumstances – to abandon individual reason, values, experience, and consciousness in order to enjoy the safety of merging with the group, which may then demand licence to vent unconscious fear, aggression, hatred, and greed without the necessity for reflection or responsibility.

> All mass movements, as one might expect, slip with the greatest ease down an inclined plane represented by large numbers. Where the many are, there is security; what the many believe must of course be true; what the many want must be worth striving for, and necessary, and therefore good. In the clamor of the many there lies the power to snatch wish-fulfillments by force . . .

> Wherever social conditions of this type develop on a large scale the road to tyranny lies open and the freedom of the individual turns into spiritual and physical slavery.[23]

Jung lived through the devastation of two world wars that were driven by mass psychology, just as Plato lived through the thirty-year-long Peloponnesian War with its successive and increasingly cynical changes of government from aristocracy to oligarchy to democracy to tyranny; and it might be argued that, given their experiences, both Jung and Plato had considerable justification for their mistrust.[24]

Also like Plato, Jung also placed enormous value on individual responsibility as the key to the welfare of the collective:[25]

> If things go wrong in the world, this is because something is wrong with the individual, because something is wrong with me. Therefore, if I am sensible, I shall put myself right first. For this I need – because outside authority no longer means anything to me – a knowledge of the innermost foundations of my being, in order that I may base myself firmly on the eternal facts of the human psyche.[26]

Although he was committed to astrology, Jung did not 'blame' the planetary configurations for life's vicissitudes, nor did he assume that fate was an external, irrevocable force imposed by an impersonal celestial order. As Shakespeare's Cassius declares: 'The fault, dear Brutus, is not in our stars, but in ourselves' – but not, in Jung's view, because humans are 'underlings'.[27] Rather, the 'fault' is the individual's reluctance to look within, resulting in those chains of unconscious choices and consequences, generated by unknown compulsions, that appear to fate not only individual lives, but also the life and history of the collective.[28]

The 'Spirit of This Time', as it gradually reveals itself in the first decades of the twenty-first century, seems to exhibit a preference for avoiding those 'big' questions that preoccupied Jung throughout his life. The nature of evil, the meaning and purpose of an individual life, the deeper motivations that drive individuals and collectives, and the enigma of human suffering, are not popular subjects for discourse in many psychological circles these days, not least because such subjects are potential minefields of politically incorrect observations. Instead, efforts are focused on finding methods – medicinal, psychotherapeutic, or social – that will dispel symptoms without investing time and expense in exploring their unconscious causes. Nor is history – whether individual or collective – perceived any longer as an essential tool in understanding the dilemmas of the present. According to the British National Health Service website, cognitive behavioural therapy

> is a type of talking therapy that can help you to manage your problems by changing the way you think and behave . . . CBT deals with your current problems, rather than focusing on issues from your past. It looks for practical ways to improve your state of mind on a daily basis.[29]

The efficacy of such an approach is, like that of all psychotherapeutic methods, the subject of ongoing debate.[30] In an effort to combine the best of both worlds, some psychotherapists and therapeutic training groups have blended cognitive and analytic techniques to produce an 'integral' model.[31] But 'CBT' is the approach presently favoured by collective authorities in Britain, and psychotherapeutic training groups of all persuasions – including Jungian groups – are currently under pressure to adopt cognitive methods if their practitioners wish to secure referrals and funding from the National Health Service.[32]

The difficulty may ultimately lie, not in the lack of usefulness of cognitive techniques, but in the amputation of a sense of continuity with the past that can sometimes result from a focus solely on present conditions and circumstances. Understanding the interior dimensions of human history – whether this is explored through the history of ideas, the history of religions, or the emotional history of a family and its story through the generations – may turn out to be the pivot on which any hope of a better future turns. This was Jung's own perspective. He described it vividly when he wrote about the multi-storeyed house that he called 'my house', which appeared in a dream he experienced while still working with Freud. The upper story of Jung's dream-house was furnished in 'rococo style'. The ground floor was much older, dating from the fifteenth or sixteenth century. A stone stairway led down to a cellar, which dated from Roman times. When Jung looked more closely at the floor of this cellar, he noticed a ring by which he could lift one of the stone slabs. Yet another staircase descended into the depths, in which he discovered 'scattered bones and broken pottery, like remains of a primitive culture'.[33] Jung interpreted the dream as 'a kind of image of the psyche'. The rococo salon, well above the ground, represented personal consciousness; the ground floor symbolised the first level of the unconscious. The deeper Jung descended, the darker the scene became, and the older and more universal the remains:

> This was my first inkling of a collective *a priori* beneath the personal psyche. This I first took to be the traces of earlier modes of functioning. With increasing experience and on the basis of more reliable knowledge, I recognised them as forms of instinct, that is, as archetypes.[34]

History, for Jung, was not a linear listing of isolated events or, as a character in one of Alan Bennett's plays puts it, 'just one f - -g thing after another'.[35] The deeper, more interior history of human creativity and destructiveness was fundamental to Jung's psychological understanding. Astrology, as he pointed out, encapsulated the psychology of the past and provided the foundations for psychology's own history. Jung, in contrast to the 'Spirit of This Time', shared Goethe's view of the central importance of history:

> Let him who fails to learn and mark
> Three thousand years, still stay,
> Void of experience, in the dark,
> And live from day to day.[36]

The 'Spirit of This Time' also appears to embrace the comfortable certainty that the individual's problems stem from a social, economic, or even climatic source rather than a psychological one, and that those problems can be 'cured' with the right government, the right legislation, and the right reassurances from a scientific establishment that too often believes itself to be, like an infallible pope, incapable of misjudgement or ignorance, even in the liminal spheres where its instruments of measurement may be inadequate or inappropriate. Jung's allegiance, in spite of himself and at the cost of considerable suffering, was ultimately and irrevocably given to what he understood as the 'Spirit of the Depths', and the older religious and philosophical currents that he studied so assiduously appeared to him as varying forms of a perpetually renewed human effort to express that Spirit – even if the prevailing collective world-view opposed it.

Invoking the 'spirit of the depths'

That Jung worked with ritual invocations of the planetary archetypes he identified in his own horoscope, and that the results of these invocations infuse many of the characters in *Liber Novus*, might seem a disturbing and even shocking suggestion to those who are unfamiliar with the historical roots of the technique Jung called active imagination. But the relationship between magic and active imagination was described by Jung himself, and the suggestion that he was unable to make his own connections between the theurgic rituals of late antiquity and the 'pursuit of the inner images' that resulted in *Liber Novus* is unconvincing. Jung also made it clear that he understood the planetary 'gods' as archetypes, and that the purpose of active imagination is to establish a dialogue between the archetypal potencies and individual human consciousness. His interest in medieval and early modern grimoires, astrologically inclined magical texts such as the *Mithras Liturgy*, and Neoplatonic theurgists such as Plotinus, Iamblichus, and Proclus, who all integrated astrology into their cosmological perceptions, underlines the likelihood that Jung made a deliberate and conscious effort to work imaginally – or, put another way, magically – with the internal conflicts that he believed were symbolically portrayed in his birth chart.

The purpose of such inner work, for Jung as for his predecessors in late antiquity, was a transformation of the personality through the integration of consciousness with the larger psychic centre that Jung understood as the Self. Although Iamblichus and his fellow theurgists variously interpreted that centre as a god or daimon, or as the Platonic One from which all else emanates, their pursuit of this process of integration through the use of symbols and images, firmly based on the underpinning of the idea of *sumpatheia*, reappears in Jung's concept of individuation and the work which he suggested might be done by the individual to facilitate an otherwise natural but unconscious, sometimes unnecessarily painful, and even unsuccessful journey. Jung was fond of citing the alchemical axiom, 'What nature leaves imperfect, the art perfects',[37] and – allowing for his preference for the idea of wholeness rather than the idea of perfection – this is the goal of the psychotherapy that he developed and practiced.

Jung understood fate in general, and astral fate in particular, as a paradox. From the astrologer's perspective, one cannot send one's horoscope back and order a new one, unless one espouses a religious conviction that promises a new horoscope coincident with a new spiritual 'rebirth', as the Christian theologian Tatian did in the second century CE.[38] Although some astrologers accept the idea that fate is concrete and fixed, more psychologically inclined astrologers understand fate as multi-levelled and negotiable. In Jung's view, horoscopic fate presents a profound conundrum. Ultimately one must 'do gladly and freely that which one must do'; but those operative adverbs, 'gladly' and 'freely', imply a voluntary conscious cooperation with the 'eternal facts' – the archetypes themselves – that cannot be coerced or eradicated through any human effort. Free will, for Jung, involved respect for, and acceptance of, the will of the daimon, while simultaneously encompassing a dialogue and potential transformation that could allow both the personality and the daimon to flower in the most creative possible way.

In Jung's context, this marriage of personality with Self does not depend on, or result in, perfection, and the suggestion that one can 'transcend', 'overcome', or 'cure' the difficult dimensions of a natal horoscope would have seemed as absurd to him as bowing one's head and accepting a fate-imposed suffering without attempting to understand why. Wholeness was the ideal toward which Jung aspired, and it requires living with the conflicts symbolised by the horoscope in ways that might sometimes involve struggle and failure, but which ultimately acknowledge meaning and teleology in those conflicts, along with loyalty to the truth of oneself. The *I Ching*, which Jung viewed as the Eastern equivalent to Western astrology, offers a similar paradoxical perception:

> They [the holy sages] put themselves in accord with tao and its power, and in conformity with this laid down the order of what is right. By thinking through the order of the outer world to the end, and by exploring the law of their nature to the deepest core, they arrived at an understanding of fate.[39]

In psychological as well as astrological realms, experience, for Jung, ultimately carried greater weight than intellectual speculation and scientific methodologies, even in the teeth of the most persuasive rational argument, and even when that argument was presented by his own scientifically trained intellect. In October 1959, toward the end of his life, Jung was interviewed by the television presenter John Freeman for a BBC programme titled *Face to Face*. Freeman asked Jung whether he still believed in God, and Jung replied:

> Now? Difficult to answer. I know. I needn't, I don't need to believe. I know.

Freeman did not ask Jung whether he 'believed' in astrology. But it is likely that the answer would have been the same.

Notes

1 Xenophon, *The Memorable Thoughts of Socrates*, trans. Edward Bysshe (London: Cassell, 1888), p. 10. Jung possessed two German translations of this work.
2 Jung, *MDR*, p. 373.
3 Jung describing astrology to his daughter Gret shortly before his death, quoted in Baumann-Jung, 'The Horoscope of C.G. Jung', p. 55.
4 For astrology as a New Age phenomenon, see William Sims Bainbridge, *The Sociology of Religious Movements* (London: Routledge, 1997), pp. 363–85.
5 Main, *The Rupture of Time*, pp. 75–77.
6 Noll, *The Jung Cult*, pp. 67–69.
7 Noll, *The Jung Cult*, p. 270.
8 Hanegraaff, *New Age Religion*, pp. 496–505.
9 Jung, *Dream Analysis*, Vol. 1, p. 405.
10 For 'vernacular' versus 'official' expressions of religion, see Leonard Norman Primiano, 'Vernacular Religion and the Search for Method in Religious Folklife', *Western Folklore* 54:1 (1995), pp. 37–56.
11 Alexander Ruperti, 'Dane Rudhyar', *The Astrological Journal* 32:2 (1986), p. 57.
12 See Campion, *What Do Astrologers Believe*, pp. 59–72. For an example of the assumption that astrology involves 'faith' or 'belief', see Bart J. Bok and Margaret W. Mayall, 'Scientists Look at Astrology', *Scientific Monthly* 52:3 (1941), pp. 233–44.
13 For the history of Sun-sign columns, see Kim Farnell, *Flirting with the Zodiac* (Bournemouth: Wessex Astrologer, 2007), pp. 123–42; Campion, *Astrology and Popular Religion*, pp. 69–84.
14 For the history of 'scientism', see Casper Hakfoort, 'Science Deified', *Annals of Science* 49:6 (1992), pp. 525–44; Gregory R. Peterson, 'Demarcation and the Scientistic Fallacy', *Zygon* 38:4 (2003) pp. 751–61.
15 See Greene, *The Astrological World of Jung's 'Liber Novus'*, chapter 2.
16 For examples of these debates, see James Allen, *Inference from Signs* (Oxford: Oxford University Press, 2001).
17 David S. Katz, *The Occult Tradition* (London: Jonathan Cape, 2005), p. 140.
18 Wouter J. Hanegraaff, 'Introduction: The Birth of a Discipline', in Antoine Faivre and Wouter J. Hanegraaff (eds.), *Western Esotericism and the Science of Religion* (Leuven: Peeters, 1998), pp. xii–xiii.
19 Jung, CW4, ¶¶774–775.
20 For the many citations from Plato in Jung's *Collected Works*, see Jung, CW20, 'Plato'. These include the Platonic Ideas as archetypes (Jung, CW8, ¶275; Jung, CW9i, ¶5) and Plato's discussions of the World Soul (Jung, CW5, ¶¶404–406, 649; Jung, CW9ii, ¶¶380, 389; Jung, CW18, ¶1361). For Plato's mistrust of the collective, see Plato, *Republic*, 6.476d–6.506c; Plato, *Meno*, 97d; Plato, *Crito*, 44–47; Plato, *Phaedrus*, 260a.
21 Plato, *Meno*, 98a.
22 For Jung's use of this term, see Jung, CW3, ¶513; Jung, CW9i, ¶¶225, 228; Jung, CW10, ¶¶453–477. For Jung as an 'elitist', see Nicholas Lewin, *Jung on War, Politics and Nazi Germany* (London: Karnac Books, 2009), pp. 145–46.
23 Jung, CW10, ¶¶538–539.
24 For Plato's discussion of political regimes and their cyclical succession, see Plato, *Republic*, 8.546–79.
25 For Plato's emphasis on the responsibility of the individual within the collective, see Plato, *Laws,* III:389b–d; Plato, *Republic*, IV:434d–e.
26 Jung, CW10, ¶329.
27 William Shakespeare, *Julius Caesar*, I.ii.140–41.
28 For Jung's impassioned plea for greater individual consciousness and responsibility, see Jung, CW10, ¶¶488–588.
29 'Cognitive Behavioural Therapy: Introduction', at <www.nhs.uk/conditions/Cognitive-behavioural-therapy/Pages/Introduction.aspx>.

30 See Andrew C. Butler, Jason E. Chapman, Evan M. Forman, and Aaron T. Beck, 'The Empirical Status of Cognitive-Behavioural Therapy', *Clinical Psychology Review* 26:1 (2006), pp. 17–31; Tullio Scrimali, *Neuroscience-Based Cognitive Therapy* (London: John Wiley & Sons, 2012).

31 This blend is sometimes referred to as 'cognitive analytic therapy'. See the Association for Cognitive Analytic Therapy at <www.acat.me.uk/page/home>, including a paper by Susie Black titled 'CAT, Jung and Neuroscience' at <www.acat.me.uk/page/acat+newsletter+4+december+2011>.

32 See Hilary Platt, 'Fighting for Professional Survival', *Psychotherapist* 48 (2011), pp. 29–32, and other relevant papers in this issue of the journal of the UK Council for Psychotherapy.

33 Jung, *MDR*, pp. 182–83.

34 Jung, *MDR*, pp. 184–85.

35 Alan Bennett, *The History Boys* (London: Faber & Faber, 2004), p. 85.

36 Johann Wolfgang von Goethe, *West-Eastern Divan*, trans. Edward Dowden (London: J.M. Dent, 1914; originally published as *West-östlicher Divan*, Stuttgart: Cotta, 1819), V:74.

37 Jung gave various paraphrases of this quote from an unknown alchemist; see Jung, CW8, ¶560; Jung, CW14, ¶422; Jung, *MDR*, p. 284.

38 For Tatian, see Lewis, *Cosmology and Fate*, p. 159.

39 Richard Wilhelm and Cary F. Baynes (trans.), *The I Ching or Book of Changes* (New York: Pantheon, 1950), p. 281.

BIBLIOGRAPHY

Cited works by C.G. Jung

Collected works

Jung, C.G., *Psychiatric Studies*, CW1, trans. R.F.C. Hull (London: Routledge & Kegan Paul, 1957)

———, *Experimental Researches*, CW2, trans. Leopold Stein (London: Routledge & Kegan Paul, 1969)

———, *The Psychogenesis of Mental Disease*, CW3, trans. R.F.C. Hull (London: Routledge & Kegan Paul, 1960)

———, *Freud and Psychoanalysis*, CW4, trans. R.F.C. Hull (London: Routledge & Kegan Paul, 1961)

———, *Symbols of Transformation*, CW5, trans. R.F.C. Hull (London: Routledge & Kegan Paul, 1956)

———, *Psychological Types*, CW6, trans. R.F.C. Hull (London: Routledge & Kegan Paul, 1971)

———, *Two Essays on Analytical Psychology*, CW7, trans. R.F.C. Hull (London: Routledge & Kegan Paul, 1972)

———, *The Structure and Dynamics of the Psyche*, CW8, trans. R.F.C. Hull (London: Routledge & Kegan Paul, 1960)

———, *The Archetypes and the Collective Unconscious*, CW9i, trans. R.F.C. Hull (London: Routledge & Kegan Paul, 1959)

———, *Aion: Researches into the Phenomenology of the Self*, CW9ii, trans. R.F.C. Hull (London: Routledge & Kegan Paul, 1959)

———, *Civilization in Transition*, CW10, trans. R.F.C. Hull (London: Routledge & Kegan Paul, 1964)

———, *Psychology and Religion*, CW11, trans. R.F.C. Hull (London: Routledge & Kegan Paul, 1958)

———, *Psychology and Alchemy*, CW12, trans. R.F.C. Hull (London: Routledge & Kegan Paul, 1953)

———, *Alchemical Studies*, CW13, trans. R.F.C. Hull (London: Routledge & Kegan Paul, 1967)
———, *Mysterium Coniunctionis*, CW14, trans. R.F.C. Hull (London: Routledge & Kegan Paul, 1963)
———, *The Spirit in Man, Art, and Literature*, CW15, trans. R.F.C. Hull (London: Routledge & Kegan Paul, 1966)
———, *The Practice of Psychotherapy*, CW16, trans. R.F.C. Hull (London: Routledge & Kegan Paul, 1954)
———, *The Development of Personality*, CW17, trans. R.F.C. Hull (London: Routledge & Kegan Paul, 1954)
———, *The Symbolic Life*, CW18, trans. R.F.C. Hull (London: Routledge & Kegan Paul, 1977)
———, *General Index to the Collected Works*, CW20 (London: Routledge & Kegan Paul, 1979)

Other cited works by Jung in English and German

Jung, C.G., *Wandlungen und Symbole der Libido*, published in two parts in *Jahrbuch für psychoanalytische und psychopathologische Forschungen* (Leipzig), III–IV (1911–12; repr. Leipzig: Dueticke Verlag, 1912)
———, 'Versuch einer Darstellung der psychoanalytischen Theorie', in *Jahrbuch für psychoanalytische und psychopathologische Forschungen* 5 (Vienna and Leipzig, 1913)
———, 'The Theory of Psychoanalysis', *Psychoanalytic Review* (New York), 1 (1913–14), pp. 1–4 and 2 (1915)
———, *Collected Papers on Analytical Psychology*, ed. and trans. Constance E. Long (London: Baillière, Tindall and Cox, 1916)
———, *Psychology of the Unconscious*, trans. Beatrice M. Hinkle (New York: Moffat, Yard, 1916)
———, *Studies in Word-Association: Experiments in the Diagnosis of Psychopathological Conditions Carried Out at the Psychiatric Clinic of the University of Zürich*, trans. M.D. Eder (London: William Heinemann, 1918)
———, 'The Psychological Foundations of Belief in Spirits', *Proceedings of the Society for Psychical Research* 31 (1920)
———, *Psychologische Typen* (Zürich: Rascher Verlag, 1921)
———, 'Die Bedeutung der schweizerischen Linie im Spektrum Europas', *Neue Schweitzer Rundschau* 24:6 (1928), pp. 1–11
———, 'Über den Archetypus mit besonderer Berücksichtigung des Animabegriffes', *Zentralblatt für Psychotherapie und ihre Grenzgebiete* 9:5 (1936), pp. 259–75
———, *The Integration of the Personality*, trans. Stanley Dell (New York: Farrar & Rinehart, 1939)
———, *Aion: Untersuchungen zur Symbolgeschichte, Psychologische Abhandlungen* VIII, (Zurich: Rascher Verlag, 1951)
———, Letters to Michael Fordham, 15 December 1954; 9 November 1954; 20 October 1954; Michael J. Fordham, Letter to C.G. Jung, 10 January 1955; Wellcome Library, London, PP/FOR/C.1/1/2:Box 7
———, 'Exercitia spiritualia of St. Ignatius of Loyola', in *Modern Psychology: Notes on Lectures Given at the Eidgenössische Technische Hochschule, Zürich by Prof. Dr. C.G. Jung, October 1933–July 1941*, 3 volumes, trans. and ed. Elizabeth Welsh and Barbara Hannah (Zürich: K. Schippert, 1959–60), Vol. 3–4, pp. 153–57

———, *Modern Psychology: Notes on Lectures Given at the Eidgenössische Technische Hochschule, Zürich by Prof. Dr. C. G. Jung, October 1933–July 1941*, 3 volumes, trans. and ed. Elizabeth Welsh and Barbara Hannah (Zürich: K. Schippert, 1959–60)

———, *Memories, Dreams, Reflections*, ed. Aniela Jaffé, trans. Richard and Clara Winston (London: Routledge & Kegan Paul, 1963), pp. 194–225

———, 'The Psychological Aspects of the Kore', in C.G. Jung and C. Kerényi, *Essays on a Science of Mythology: The Myth of the Divine Child and the Mysteries of Eleusis* (Princeton, NJ: Princeton University Press, 1963)

———, *Analytical Psychology: Its Theory and Practice* (London: Routledge & Kegan Paul, 1968)

———, *C. G. Jung Letters*, 2 volumes, ed. Gerhard Adler, trans. R.F.C. Hull (London: Routledge & Kegan Paul, 1973–76)

———, 'Letters to Oskar Schmitz, 1921–1931', trans. James Kirsch, *Psychological Perspectives* 6:1 (1975), pp. 79–95

———, *The Visions Seminars*, 2 volumes (Zürich: Spring, 1976)

———, *Septem Sermones ad Mortuos: Written by Basilides in Alexandria, the City Where East and West Meet*, trans. Stephan A. Hoeller, in Stephan A. Hoeller, *The Gnostic Jung and the Seven Sermons to the Dead* (Wheaton, IL: Theosophical Publishing House, 1982), pp. 44–58

———, *Dream Analysis: Notes of the Seminar Given in 1928–1930 by C. G. Jung*, ed. William C. McGuire (London: Routledge & Kegan Paul, 1984)

———, *Introduction to Jungian Psychology: Notes of the Seminar on Analytical Psychology Given in 1925 by C. G. Jung*, ed. William McGuire and Sonu Shamdasani (Princeton, NJ: Princeton University Press, 1989)

———, *Jung's Seminar on Nietzsche's Zarathustra*, ed. James Jarrett (Princeton, NJ: Princeton University Press, 1997)

———, *Visions: Notes of the Seminar Given in 1930–1934 by C. G. Jung*, ed. Claire Douglas, 2 volumes (Princeton, NJ: Princeton University Press, 1997)

———, *Children's Dreams: Notes from the Seminar Given in 1936–1940*, ed. Lorenz Jung and Maria Meyer-Grass, trans. Ernst Falzeder and Tony Woolfson (Princeton, NJ: Princeton University Press, 2008)

———, *The Red Book: Liber Novus*, ed. Sonu Shamdasani, trans. Mark Kyburz, John Peck, and Sonu Shamdasani (New York & London: W.W. Norton, 2009)

———, *Jung on Astrology*, selected and introduced by Keiron le Grice and Safron Rossi (Abingdon: Routledge, 2017)

Primary sources

Abraham von Worms, *Die egyptischen großen Offenbarungen, in sich begreifend die aufgefundenen Geheimnisbücher Mosis; oder des Juden Abraham von Worms Buch der wahren Praktik in der uralten göttlichen Magie und erstaunlichen Dingen, wie sie durch die heilige Kabbala und durch Elohym mitgetheilt worden. Sammt der Geister – und Wunder-Herrschaft, welche Moses in der Wüste aus dem feurigen Busch erlernet, alle Verborgenheiten der Kabbala umfassend* (Cologne: Peter Hammer, 1725)

Agrippa, Heinrich Cornelius von Nettesheim, *De occulta philosophia libri tres* (Cologne: J. Soter, 1533)

———, *De incertudine & vanitate omnium scientiarum declamatio omiectium* (Cologne: T. Baumann, 1584)

———, *De incertidome & vanitate omnium scientiarum & artium liber* (Hagae-Comitum: A. Ulacq, 1653)

———, *Die Cabbala des H.C. Agrippa von Nettesheim*, trans. Johann Scheible and Friedrich Barth (Stuttgart: Johann Scheible, 1855)

———, *Magische Werke sammt den geheimnisvollen Schriften des Petrus von Abano, Pictorius von Villingen, Gerhard von Cremona, Abt Tritheim von Spanheim, dem Buche Arbalel, der sogenannten Heil*, 3 volumes (Berlin: Hermann Bardsdorf, 1916)

———, *Magische Werke samt den geheimnisvollen Schriften des Petrus von Abano, Pictorius von Villingen, Gerhard von Cremona, Abt Tritheim von Sponheim, dem Buche Arbatel, der sogenannten Heil. Geist-Kunst und verschiedenen anderen*, 2 volumes (Vienna: Amonesta-Verlag, 1921)

Anonymous, 'Ancient Landmarks: From the Neoplatonists to H.P.B.', *Theosophy* 28:2 (1939), pp. 53–57

'Astrologers' Weekend', *Picture Post: Hulton's National Weekly*, 29 April 1939, pp. 3–4

Atwood, Mary Ann, *Hermetic Philosophy and Alchemy: A Suggestive Inquiry into 'The Hermetic Mystery' with a Dissertation on the More Celebrated of the Alchemical Philosophers* (London: Trelawney Saunders, 1850)

Bachofen, Johann Jacob, *Das Mutterrecht: Eine Untersuchung über die Gynaikokratie der alten Welt nach ihrer religiösen und rechtlichen Natur* (Stuttgart: Krais und Hoffmann, 1861)

Bailey, Alice A., *Esoteric Astrology: A Treatise on the Seven Rays, Volume III* (New York: Lucis, 1951)

Bailey, George H., 'The Descent to Birth and the Soli-Lunar Interchanges', *Modern Astrology* (1915); repr. as 'The Prenatal Epoch and the Soli-Lunar Interchanges', *Astrologer's Quarterly* 3:2 (1929)

Bailly, Jean Sylvain, *Histoire de l'astronomie ancienne, depuis son origine jusqu'à l'établissement de l'école d'Alexandrie* (Paris: Debure, 1775)

———, *Traite de l'astronomie indienne et orientale* (Paris: Debure, 1787)

Basil of Caesarea, *Hexaemeron*, trans. Blomfield Jackson (Amazon CreateSpace, 2014)

Berthelot, Marcellin, *Les origines de l'alchemie* (Paris: Georges Steinheil, 1885)

———, *Collection des anciens alchemistes grecs*, 3 volumes (Paris: Georges Steinheil, 1887–88)

Besant, Annie, *A Study in Consciousness: A Contribution to the Science of Psychology* (London: Theosophical Publishing Society, 1904)

Biegel, Rebekka Aleida, *Zur Astrognosie der alten Ägypter* (Göttingen: Dieterichsche Universitäts-Buckdruckerei, 1921)

Blavatsky, H.P., *Isis Unveiled: A Master-Key to the Mysteries of Ancient and Modern Science and Theology*, 2 volumes (London: Theosophical Publishing, 1877)

———, *The Secret Doctrine: The Synthesis of Science, Religion, and Philosophy*, 2 volumes (London: Theosophical Publishing, 1888)

———, *The Theosophical Glossary*, ed. G.R.S. Mead (London: Theosophical Publishing House, 1892)

———, *Collected Writings, 1874–1891*, 15 volumes, ed. Boris de Zirkoff (Wheaton, IL: Theosophical Publishing House, 1966)

Bouché-Leclercq, Auguste, *L'astrologie grecque* (Paris: Ernest Leroux, 1899)

Bousset, Wilhelm, *Hauptprobleme der Gnosis* (Göttingen: Vandenhoeck & Ruprecht, 1907)

Brunner, Cornelia, *Die Anima als Schicksalsproblem des Mannes* (Zürich: Rascher Verlag, 1963)

Buch Abramelin das ist Die egyptischen großen Offenbarungen. Oder des Abraham von Worms Buch der wahren Praktik in der uralten göttlichen Magie (Leipzig: Editions Araki, 2001)

Bundy, Murray Wright, *The Theory of Imagination in Classical and Medieval Thought* (Urbana: University of Illinois Press, 1927)

Cardanus, Jerome [Girolamo Cardano], *Commentarium in Ptolemaeum de astrorum iudiciis*, in Girolamo Cardano, *Opera omnia* (Lyons: Charles Sponius, 1663)

Carter, Charles E.O., *An Encyclopaedia of Psychological Astrology* (London: Theosophical Publishing House, 1924)

———, *The Astrological Aspects* (London: Theosophical Publishing House, 1930)

Coleman, William Emmette, 'The Sources of Madame Blavatsky's Writings', in Vsevolod Sergyeevich Solovyoff, *A Modern Priestess of Isis* (London: Longmans, Green, 1895), Appendix C, pp. 353–66

Cory, Isaac Preston, *Ancient Fragments of the Phoenician, Chaldean, Egyptian, Tyrian, Carthaginian, Indian, Persian, and Other Writers; With an Introductory Dissertation; And an Inquiry into the Philosophy and Trinity of the Ancients* (London: William Pickering, 1832; repr. London: Reeves and Turner, 1876)

Creuzer, Georg Friedrich, *Symbolik und Mythologie der alten Völker, besonders der Griechen* (Leipzig: K.W. Leske, 1810–12)

——— (ed.), *Plotini Enneades cum Marsilii Ficini Interpretatione Castigata; primum accedunt Porphyryii et Procli Institutiones et Prisciani Philosophi Solutiones* (Paris: Dübner, 1855)

Crowley, Aleister, *777 and Other Qabalistic Writings of Aleister Crowley*, ed. Israel Regardie (London: Ordo Templi Orientis, 1912; repr. York Beach, ME: Samuel Weiser, 1973)

Cumont, Franz, *Textes et monuments figurés relatifs aux mystères de Mythra* (Brussels: H. Lamertin, 1896)

———, *Die Mysterien des Mithra* (Leipzig: Teubner, 1903; repr. 1911)

———, *Die orientalischen Religionen im römischen Heidentum: Vorlesungen am Collège de France* (Leipzig: Teubner, 1910)

D'Ailly, Pierre, *Tractatus de imagine mundi Petri Aliaco, et varia ejusdem auctoris, et Joannis Gersonis opuscula* (Louvain: Johannes de Westphalia, 1483)

Damascius, *Dubitationes et solutiones de primis principiis in Platonis Parmenidem*, 2 volumes (Paris: Ruelle, 1889)

Delatte, Louis, *Textes latins et vieux français relatifs aux Cyranides* (Paris: Droz, 1942)

De l'Aulnaye, François-Henri-Stanislas, *L'histoire générale et particulière des religions et du cultes de tous les peuples du monde, tant anciens que modernes* (Paris: J.B. Fournier, 1791)

———, *Récapitulation de toute la maçonnerie, ou Description et explication de l'hiéroglyphe universel du maître des maîtres* (privately published, Paris, 1812)

———, *Thuileur des trente-trois degrés de l'écossisme du rit ancien, dit accepté, auquel on a joint la rectification, l'interprétation et l'étymologie des mots sacrés, de passe, d'attouchement, de reconnaissance* (privately published, Paris, 1813)

Deussen, Paul, *Allgemeine Geschichte der Philosophie*, 2 volumes (Leipzig: F.A. Brockhaus, 1894)

Dieterich, Albrecht, *Abraxas: Studien zur Religionsgechichte des spätern Alterums* (Leipzig: Teubner, 1891)

———, *Ein Mithrasliturgie* (Leipzig: Teubner, 1903)

Dionysius the Areopagite, *Was mir das Jenseits mitteilteas Der mystische Weg und innere Doktor Johannes Fausts Magia naturalis et innaturalis, oder dreifacher Höllenzwang, letztes Testament und Siegelkunst* (Stuttgart: Scheible, 1849)

Drews, Arthur C., *Plotin und der Untergang der antiken Weltanschaunng* (Jena: Diederichs, 1907)

———, *Die Christusmythe* (Jena: E. Diederichs, 1910)

Dupuis, Charles, *Origine de tous les cultes, ou religion universelle* (Paris: H. Agasse, 1795)

———, *Planches de l'origine de tous les cultes* (Paris: H. Agasse, 1795)

Eisler, Robert, *Weltenmantel und Himmelszelt: Religionsgeschichtliche Untersuchungen zur Urgeschichte des antiken Weltbildes*, 3 volumes (Munich: C.H. Beck, 1910)

———, *Orpheus the Fisher: Comparative Studies in Orphic and Early Christian Cult Symbolism* (London: J.M. Watkins, 1921); originally published as a series of articles in *The Quest* 1:1 (1909), pp. 124–39; 1:2 (1910), pp. 306–21; 1:4 (1910), pp. 625–48

———, *Orphisch-dionysische Mysteriengedanken in der christlichen Antike* (Leipzig: Teubner, 1925)

———, *L'origine babylonienne de l'alchimie: A propos de la découverte récente de recettes chimiques sur tablettes cunéiformes*, trans. Robert Bouvier (Paris: La Renaissance du Livre, 1926)

———, 'Pistis Sophia und Barbelo', *Angelos: Archiv für Neutestamentliche und Kulturkunde* 3:1–2 (1928), pp. 93–110
———, 'Nachleben dionysischer Mysterienriten?', *Archiv für Religionswissenschaft* 27 (1928), pp. 171–83
———, *Man into Wolf: An Anthropological Interpretation of Sadism, Masochism, and Lycanthropy* (London: Routledge & Kegan Paul, 1951)
Epiphanius, *Ausgewählte Schriften* (Munich: Josef Kösel, 1919)
Festugière, André-Jean, *La révélation d'Hermès Trismégiste*, 4 volumes (Paris: Bibliothèque des textes philosophiques, 1946–54)
Ficino, Marsilio, *Mercurii Trismegisti: Pimander sive de potestate et sapientia Dei* (Treviso: Gerardus de Lisa, 1471)
Flambart, Paul [Paul Choisnard], *Preuves et bases de l'astrologie scientifique* (Paris: Bibliothèque Chacornac, 1921)
Flamel, Nicolas, *Le Livre des figures hiéroglyphiques* (Paris: Veuve Guillemot, 1612)
Fliess, Wilhelm, *Der Ablauf des Lebens: Grundlegung zur Exakten Biologie* (Leipzig: F. Deuticke, 1906)
Fortune, Dion, *The Goat-Foot God* (London: Norgate, 1936)
———, 'Types of Mind Working', in Dion Fortune and Gareth Knight, *An Introduction to Ritual Magic* (Loughborough: Thoth, 1997), pp. 32–39
Frazer, James, *The Golden Bough: A Study in Magic and Religion* (New York: Macmillan, 1922)
Frey-Rohn, Liliane, Interview with Gene Nameche, C.G. Jung Biographical Archive 1968–73, Countway Library of Medicine, Harvard University, Interview 2, p. 25
Gerhardt, Oswald, *Der Stern des Messias: das Geburts- und das Todesjahr Jesu Christi nach astronomischer Berechnung* (Leipzig: Deichert, 1922)
Ginzburg, Christian D., *The Kabbalah: Its Doctrines, Development, and Literature* (London: Longmans, Green, 1863)
Heindel, Max, *The Rosicrucian Cosmo-Conception, or Mystic Christianity* (Oceanside, CA: Rosicrucian Fellowship, 1909)
———, *The Rosicrucian Mysteries* (Oceanside, CA: Rosicrucian Fellowship, 1911)
———, *The Message of the Stars: An Esoteric Exposition of Medical and Natal Astrology Explaining the Arts of Prediction and Diagnosis of Disease* (Oceanside, CA: Rosicrucian Fellowship, 1918)
———, *Simplified Scientific Astrology: A Complete Textbook on the Art of Erecting a Horoscope* (London: L.N. Fowler, 1928)
Henry, Paul and Hans-Rudolf Schwyzer (eds.), *Plotini opera. Porphyrii vita Plotini; Enneades I–III* (Paris: Desclée de Brouwer, 1951)
———, *Plotini opera. Enneades IV–VI* (Paris: Desclée de Brouwer, 1959)
Higgins, Godfrey, *Anacalypsis: An Attempt to Draw Aside the Veil of the Saitic Isis or an Inquiry into the Origin of Languages, Nations and Religions*, 2 volumes (London: Longman, Rees, Orme, Brown, Green, and Longman, 1836)
Hinkle, Beatrice, 'Jung's Libido Theory and the Bergsonian Philosophy', *New York Medical Journal* 30 (1914), pp. 1080–86
Inge, William Ralph, *Christian Mysticism, Considered in Eight Lectures Delivered Before the University of Oxford* (London: Methuen, 1899)
Irenaeus, *Irenaei episcopi lugdunensis contra omnes haereses* (Oxford: Thomas Bennett, 1702)
———, *Des heiligen Irenäus fünf Bücher gegen die Häresine*, trans. Ernst Klebba (Munich: Josef Kösel, 1912)
James, William, 'Frederic Myers's Service to Psychology', *Popular Science Monthly* (August 1901), pp. 380–89
———, *The Varieties of Religious Experience: A Study in Human Nature* (London: Longmans, Green, 1902)

Janet, Pierre, *The Major Symptoms of Hysteria: Fifteen Lectures Given in the Medical School of Harvard University* (New York: Macmillan, 1924)

Kern, Otto (ed.), *Orphicorum fragmenta* (Berlin: Weidmann, 1922)

Khunrath, Heinrich, *Von hylealischen, das ist, pri-materialischen catholischen, oder algemeinem natürlichen Chaos, der naturgemessen Alchymiae und Alchemisten* (Magdeburg: Andreas Genen, 1597)

King, Charles William, *The Gnostics and Their Remains: Ancient and Medieval* (London: Bell & Dalby, 1864)

Knorr von Rosenroth, Christian, *Kabbala denudata, seu, Doctrina Hebraeorum transcendentalis et metaphysica atque theologica: opus antiquissimae philosophiae barbaricae . . . in quo, ante ipsam translationem libri . . . cui nomen Sohar tam veteris quam recentis, ejusque tikkunim . . . praemittitur apparatus [pars 1–4]*, 3 volumes (Sulzbach/Frankfurt: Abraham Lichtenthal, 1677–84)

Krafft, Karl Ernst, *Le premier traité d'astro-biologie* (Paris: Wyckmans, 1939)

Kyranides: The Magick of Kirani, King of Persia and of Harpocration; Containing the Magical and Medicinal Vertues of Stones, Herbs, Fishes, Beasts and Birds (London: n. p., 1685; repr. as *Kyranides: On the Occult Virtues of Plants, Animals, and Stones: Hermetic and Talismanic Magic*; New York: Renaissance Astrology, 2010)

Leadbeater, C.W., *Man, Visible and Invisible* (London: Theosophical Publishing Society, 1902)

Leo, Alan, *Astrology for All, Part I: Individual and Personal Characteristics as Represented by the Sun and Moon; Part II, Casting the Horoscope* (London: Modern Astrology Office, 1899)

———, *How to Judge a Nativity* (London: Modern Astrology Office, 1903)

———, *The Progressed Horoscope* (London: Modern Astrology Office, 1905)

———, *Astrology for All* (London: Modern Astrology Office, 1910)

———, *The Key to Your Own Nativity* (London: Modern Astrology Office, 1910)

———, 'The Age of Aquarius', *Modern Astrology* 8:7 (1911), p. 272

———, *The Art of Synthesis* (London: Modern Astrology Office, 1912)

———, *Esoteric Astrology* (London: Modern Astrology Office, 1913)

———, *Mars: The War Lord* (London: Modern Astrology Office/L.N. Fowler, 1915)

———, *Saturn: The Reaper* (London: Modern Astrology Office, 1916)

———, *Dictionary of Astrology*, ed. Vivian Robson (London: Modern Astrology Office/L.N. Fowler, 1929)

Leo, Bessie, *The Life and Work of Alan Leo, Theosophist – Astrologer – Mason* (London: Modern Astrology Office/N.L. Fowler, 1919)

Longfellow, Henry Wadsworth, *The Song of Hiawatha* (Boston, MA: Ticknor and Fields, 1855)

Machen, Arthur, 'The Novel of the White Powder', in Arthur Machen, *The Three Impostors* (London: John Lane, 1895), pp. 95–111

Maier, Michael, *Symbola aureae mensae duodecim nationum* (Frankfurt: Julius Ägidius von Negelein, 1617)

Mann, Thomas, *Doktor Faustus: Das Leben des deutschen Tonsetzers Adrian Leverkühn, erzählt von einem Freunde* (Frankfurt: S. Fischer, 1947)

Marc Aurel, *Selbstbetrachtungen*, trans. Otto Kiefer (Leipzig: E. Diederichs, 1903)

Massey, Gerald, *The Natural Genesis, or Second Part of a Book of the Beginnings: Concerning an Attempt to Recover and Reconstitute the Lost Origins of the Myths and Mysteries, Types and Symbols, Religion and Language, with Egypt for the Mouthpiece and Africa as the Birthplace*, 2 volumes (London: Williams and Norgate, 1883)

———, *Gerald Massey's Lectures* (London: Private Publication, 1887)

———, 'The Hebrew and Other Creations, Fundamentally Explained', in *Gerald Massey's Lectures* (London: Private Publication, 1887), pp. 105–40

———, 'The Historical Jesus and Mythical Christ', in *Gerald Massey's Lectures* (London: Private Publication, 1887), pp. 1–26

Mead, G.R.S., '*Pistis-Sophia*', *Lucifer* 6 (March 1890–August 1890), pp. 107–13, 230–39, 315–23, 392–401, 489–99; *Lucifer* 7 (September 1890–February 1891), pp. 35–43, 139–47, 186–96, 285–95, 368–76, 456–63; *Lucifer* 8 (March 1891–August 1891), pp. 39–47, 123–29, 201–4

———, *Orpheus* (London: Theosophical Publishing Society, 1896)

———, *Pistis Sophia: A Gnostic Miscellany: Being for the Most Part Extracts from the Book of the Saviour, to Which Are Added Excerpts from a Cognate Literature* (London: Theosophical Publishing Society, 1896)

———, 'The Lives of the Later Platonists', *Lucifer* 18 (March–August 1896), pp. 185–200, 288–302, 368–80, 456–69; *Lucifer* 19 (September 1896–February 1897), pp. 16–32, 103–13, 186–95

———, 'Hermes the Thrice-Greatest According to Iamblichus an Initiate of the Egyptian Wisdom', *Theosophical Review* 25 (September 1899–February 1900), pp. 9–19

———, *Fragments of a Faith Forgotten: Some Short Sketches Among the Gnostics Mainly of the First Two Centuries* (London: Theosophical Publishing Society, 1906)

———, *Thrice-Greatest Hermes: Studies in Hellenistic Theosophy and Gnosis*, 3 volumes (London: Theosophical Publishing Society, 1906)

———, *Echoes from the Gnosis* (London: Theosophical Publishing Society, 1906–8)

———, *A Mithraic Ritual*, Volume 6 of *Echoes from the Gnosis* (London: Theosophical Publishing Society, 1907)

———, *The Mysteries of Mithra*, Volume 5 of *Echoes from the Gnosis* (London: Theosophical Publishing Society, 1907)

———, *The Chaldean Oracles*, published As Volume 8 of *Echoes from the Gnosis* (London: Theosophical Publishing Society, 1908)

———, *The Doctrine of the Subtle Body in Western Tradition: An Outline of What the Philosophers Thought and Christians Taught on the Subject* (London: J.M. Watkins, 1919)

———, *'The Quest' – Old and New: A Retrospect and Prospect* (London: John M. Watkins, 1926)

Mercurii Trismegisti: Pimandras utraque lingua restitutus, D. Francisci Flussatis Candellae industria (Bordeaux: Simon Millanges, 1574)

Meyrink, Gustav, *Der Golem* (Leipzig: Kurt Wolff, 1915)

———, *Das grüne Gesicht* (Leipzig: Kurt Wolff, 1916)

———, *Fledermäuse: Sieben Geschichten* (Leipzig: Kurt Wolff, 1916)

———, *Walpurgisnacht* (Leipzig: Kurt Wolff, 1917)

———, *Der Engel vom westlichen Fenster* (Bremen: Schünemann, 1927)

Müller, F. Max, *Lectures on the Origin and Growth of Religions as Illustrated by the Religions of India* (London: Longmans, Green, 1878)

———, *Vorlesungen über den Ursprung und die Entwickelung der Religion* (Strasbourg: Trübner, 1880)

———, *Theosophy: Or, Psychological Religion: The Gifford Lectures Delivered Before the University of Glasgow in 1892* (London: Longmans, Green, 1917)

Myers, F.H.W., *Human Personality and Its Survival of Death* (London: Longmans, 1903)

Mylius, Johann Daniel, *Philosophia reformata* (Frankfurt: Luca Jennis, 1622)

Nietzsche, Friedrich, *Also sprach Zarathustra: Ein Buch für Alle und Keinen* (Chemnitz: Ernst Schmeitzner, 1883–84)

Paracelsus, *Sâmtliche Werke: 1. Abt. Medizinische, naturwissenschaftliche und philosophische Schriften*, VIII, ed. Karl Sudhoff, 14 volumes (Munich and Berlin, 1922–33), pp. 161–70

———, *Liber de nymphis, sylphis, pygmaeis et salamandris et de caeteris spiritibus*, in *Sämtliche Werke*, 1:14.7, ed. Karl Sudhoff and Wilhelm Matthiessen (Munich: Oldenbourg, 1933)

Pearce, Alfred J., *The Weather Guide-Book: A Concise Exposition of Astronomic-Meteorology* (London: Simpkin, Marshall, 1864)

———, *The Science of the Stars* (London: Simpkin, Marshall, 1881)
——— (ed.), *The Future: A Monthly Magazine of Predictive Sciences and Events of the Day* (1892–94)
Philo Alexandrinus, *Philonis Iudaei, scriptoris eloquentissimi, ac philosophi summi, lucubrationes omnes quotquot haberi potuerunt: cuius opera uterque est integritati restitutus* (Basel: Sigmund Gelen, 1561)
———, *Opera quae supersunt*, 6 volumes, ed. Leopold Cohn and Paul Wendland (Berlin: Walter de Gruyter, 1898–1915)
Quillard, Pierre (trans.), *Le livre de Jamblique sur les mystères* (Paris: Libraire de l'art indépendant, 1875)
Raphael, *The Key to Astrology, Containing a Complete System of Genethliacal Astrology* (London: W. Foulsham, 1896)
Regardie, Israel, *The Tree of Life: A Study in Magic* (London: Rider, 1932)
———, *An Account of the Teachings, Rites, and Ceremonies of the Hermetic Order of the Golden Dawn*, 4 volumes (Chicago: Aries Press, 1937–40; repr. as one volume, St Paul, MN: Llewellyn, 1989)
———, *The Philosopher's Stone: A Modern Comparative Approach to Alchemy from the Psychological and Magical Points of View* (London: Rider, 1938)
Reitzenstein, Richard, *Poimandres: ein paganisiertes Evangelium: Studien zur griechisch-äegtischen und frühchristlichen Literatur* (Leipzig: Teubner, 1904)
———, *Die hellenistiche Mysterienreligionen* (Leipzig: Teubner, 1910)
———, *Mysterionreligionen nach ihren Grundgedanken und Wirkungen* (Leipzig: Teubner, 1910)
———, *Das iranische Erlösungsmysterium; religionsgeschichtliche Untersuchungen* (Bonn: A. Marcus and E. Weber, 1921)
Rhine, J.B., *Extra-Sensory Perception* (Boston, MA: Boston Society for Psychic Research, 1934)
———, *New Frontiers of the Mind: The Story of the Duke Experiments* (New York: Farrar & Rinehart, 1937)
Rohde, Erwin, *Seelencult und Unsterlichkeitsglaube der Griechen*, 2 volumes (Tübingen: Mohr, 1903)
Roscher, Wilhelm Heinrich, *Ausfürliches Lexikon der griechischen und römischen Mythologie Lexicon* (Leipzig: Teubner, 1884)
Rudhyar, Dane, *The Rebirth of Hindu Music* (Adyar: Theosophical Publishing House, 1928)
———, *The Astrology of Personality: A Reinterpretation of Astrological Concepts and Ideals in Terms of Contemporary Psychology and Philosophy* (New York: Lucis Trust, 1936)
———, *Astrological Timing: The Transition to the New Age* (New York: Harper & Row, 1969)
———, *The Transition to the New Age* (London: Harper & Row, 1969)
———, *The Planetarization of Consciousness* (New York: Harper, 1972)
———, *The Astrology of America's Destiny: A Birth Chart for the United States of America* (New York: Random House, 1974)
Ruland, Martin, *Lexicon alchemiae sive Dictionarium alchemisticum* (Frankfurt: Zachariah Palthenus, 1612)
Saturn Gnosis: Offizielles Publikations-Organ der deutschen Gross-Loge Fraternitas Saturni Orient Berlin
Scheible, Johann (ed.), *Das sechste und seibente Buch Mosis, das ist: Mosis magische Geisterkunst, das Geheimnis aller Geheimnisse. Sammt den verdeutschten Offenbarungen und Vorschriften wunderbarster Art der alten weisen Hebrer, aus den Mosaischen Buchern, der Kabbala und den Talmud zum leiblichen Wohl der Menschen* (Stuttgart: Scheible, 1849)
Schmitz, Oskar A.H. *Geist der Astrologie* (Munich: Müller, 1922)
Schultz, Wolfgang, *Dokumente der Gnosis* (Jena: Diederichs, 1910)

Seneca, Lucius Annaeus, *L. Annaei Senecae rhetoric opera, quae extant Integris Nicolai Fabri, Andr. Schotti, accuratissimo aucta* (Amsterdam: Elsevier, 1672)
———, *L. Annaei Senecae operum tomus secundus: in quo epistolae et quaestiones naturales* (Amsterdam: Elsevier, 1673)
Sepharial, *The New Manual of Astrology: In Four Books* (Philadelphia, PA: David McKay, 1898)
———, *Directional Astrology: To Which Is Added a Discussion of Problematic Points and a Complete Set of Tables Necessary for the Calculation of Arcs of Direction* (London: Rider, 1921)
———, *How to Read the Crystal; or Crystal and Seer* (London: Foulsham, 1922)
———, *The Solar Epoch: A New Astrological Thesis* (London: Foulsham, 1925)
Silberer, Herbert, *Probleme der Mystik und ihre Symbolik* (Vienna: Hugo Deller, 1914; published in English as *Problems of Mysticism and Its Symbolism*, trans. Ely Jelliffe Smith (New York: Moffat, Yard, 1917); repr. as *Hidden Symbolism of Alchemy and the Occult Arts*, New York: Dover, 1971)
Smith, E.M., *The Zodia, or the Cherubim in the Bible and the Cherubim in the Sky* (London: Elliot Stock, 1906)
Smith, George, 'The Chaldean Account of the Deluge', *Transactions of the Society of Biblical Archaeology* 1–2 (1872), pp. 213–34
Staudenmaier, Ludwig, *Die Magie als Experimentelle Narurwissenschaft (Magic as an Experimental Science)* (Leipzig: Akademische Verlagsgesellschaft, 1912)
Steiner, Rudolf, *Friedrich Nietzsche, Ein Kaempfer Gegen Seine Zeit* (Weimar: E. Felber, 1895)
———, *Das Mysterium des Bösen: Zehn Vorträge* (published posthumously: Stuttgart: Verlag Freies Geitesleben, 1993)
Strauss, Heinz Arthur, *Psychologie und astrologische Symbolik: eine Einführung* (Zürich: Rascher Verlag, 1953)
———, *Astrologie: Grundsätzliche Betrachtungen* (Leipzig: Kurt Wolff, 1977)
Strauss, Heinz Arthur and Sigrid Strauss-Klöbe, *Die Astrologie des Johannes Kepler: Eine Auswahl aus seinen Schriften* (Munich: Oldenbourg, 1926)
Strauss-Klöbe, Sigrid, 'Über die psychologische Bedeutung des astrologischen Symbols', in *Eranos Jahrbuch 1934, Band 2: Ostwestliche Symbolik und Seelenführung* (Zürich: Rhein-Verlag, 1935)
———, *Kosmische Bedingtheit der Psyche: Kosmische Konstellation und seelische Disposition* (Oberbayern: O.W. Barth, 1968)
———, *Das kosmopsychische Phänomen: Geburtskonstellation und Psychodynamik* (Freiburg: Walter-Verlag, 1977)
Theatrum chemicum, Praecipuous selectorum auctorum tractatus de Chemiae et Lapidis Philosophici Antiquitate, 4 volumes (Strasbourg, 1602–13)
Thierens, A.E., *The General Book of the Tarot* (London: Rider, 1930)
———, *Elements of Esoteric Astrology: Being a Philosophical Deduction of Astrological Principles* (Philadelphia, PA: David McKay, 1931)
Thorburn, James MacCaig, 'Mysticism and Art', *The Monist* 30:4 (1920), pp. 599–617
———, 'Analytical Psychology and the Concept of Individuality', *International Journal of Ethics* 35:2 (1925), pp. 125–39
———, *Art and the Unconscious* (London: Kegan Paul, Trench, Trubner, 1925)
———, 'Do the Gods Exist?', *Harvest* 6 (1959), pp. 72–87
Thorburn, J.M., A.H. Hannay, and P. Leon, 'Artistic Form and the Unconscious', *Proceedings of the Aristotelian Society* 13 (1934), pp. 119–58
Von Goethe, Johann Wolfgang, *Faust: Der Tragödie erster Teil* (Stuttgart: J.G. Cotta, 1808)
———, *West-östlicher Divan* (Stuttgart: Cotta, 1819)
———, *Faust: Der Tragödie zweiter Teil* (Stuttgart: J.G. Cotta, 1828–29)
Waite, A.E., *The Real History of the Rosicrucians: Founded on Their Own Manifestoes, and on Facts and Documents Collected from the Writings of Initiated Brethren* (London: George Redway, 1887)

———, *The Key to the Tarot: Being Fragments of a Secret Tradition Under the Veil of Divination* (London: William Rider & Son, 1909)
———, *The Secret Doctrine of Israel: A Study of the Zohar and Its Connections* (London: William Rider & Son, 1912)
———, *The Real History of the Rosicrucians and the Brotherhood of the Rosy Cross* (London: William Rider & Son, 1924)
———, *The Holy Kabbalah: A Study of the Secret Tradition in Israel* (London: Williams & Norgate, 1929)
White, William, *Emanuel Swedenborg: His Life and Writings*, 2 volumes (London: Simpkin, 1867)
Wilhelm, Richard, *Das Geheimnis der goldenen Blüte: Ein chinesisches Lebensbuch* (Munich: Dorn, 1929)
———, *The Secret of the Golden Flower* (London: Kegan Paul, Trench, Tubner, 1931)
Yeats, William Butler, *The Second Coming* (1919), in William Butler Yeats, *The Collected Poems of William Butler Yeats* (London: Macmillan, 1933), p. 211
———, *A Vision: An Explanation of Life Founded upon the Writings of Giraldus and upon Certain Doctrines Attributed to Eusta Ben Luka* (Private Publication, 1925; repr. New York: Macmillan, 1939)
———, *The Autobiography of William Butler Yeats* (New York: Macmillan, 1953)

Translated primary sources

Abraham von Worms, *The Book of the Sacred Magic of Abramelin the Mage*, trans. Samuel Liddell MacGregor Mathers (London: John M. Watkins, 1900)
———, *The Book of Abramelin*, ed. Georg Dehn, trans. Steven Guth (Lake Worth, FL: Nicolas-Hays, 2006)
Aeschylus, 'The Seven Against Thebes', in *Aeschylus 1: The Persians, the Seven Against Thebes, the Suppliant Maidens, Prometheus Bound*, ed. and trans. David Grene, Richmond Lattimore, Mark Griffith, and Glenn W. Most (Chicago: University of Chicago Press, 2013)
Agrippa, Henry Cornelius, *Three Books of Occult Philosophy (De occulta philosophia)*, ed. Donald Tyson, trans. James Freake (St. Paul, MN: Llewellyn, 2004 [1993]; first complete English translation, James Freake, London: Gregory Moule, 1651)
The Ante-Nicene Fathers, ed. and trans. Alexander Roberts, James Donaldson, and A. Cleveland Coxe, 10 volumes (Buffalo, NY: Christian Literature Publishing, 1885)
Apocryphon of John, trans. Frederik Wisse, in James M. Robinson (ed.), *The Nag Hammadi Library in English* (Leiden: Brill, 1977), pp. 98–116
Apuleius, *The Golden Ass*, trans. Thomas Taylor (Frome: Prometheus Trust, 1997)
Bachofen, Johann Jacob, *Myth, Religion and Mother Right*, trans. Ralph Manheim (Princeton, NJ: Princeton University Press, 1967)
Betegh, Gábor (ed. and trans.), *The Derveni Papyrus: Cosmology, Theology, and Interpretation* (Cambridge: Cambridge University Press, 2004)
Betz, Hans Dieter (ed. and trans.), *The Greek Magical Papyri in Translation* (Chicago: University of Chicago Press, 1986)
——— (ed. and trans.), *The "Mithras Liturgy": Text, Translation and Commentary* (Tübingen: Mohr Siebeck, 2003)
Bonatti, Guido, *Liber Astronomiae*, 4 volumes, ed. Robert Hand, trans. Robert Zoller (Berkeley Springs, WV: Golden Hind Press, 1994–96)
Charcot, Jean-Martin, *Clinical Lectures on Diseases of the Nervous System (Leçons sur les maladies du système nerveux [1886])*, trans. Thomas Savill, ed. Ruth Harris (London: Routledge, 1991)
Charles, R.H. (trans.), *The Book of Enoch, or 1 Enoch* (Oxford: Clarendon Press, 1912)

Cicero, M. Tullius, 'De divinatione', in *On Old Age, On Friendship, On Divination*, trans. W.A. Falconer (Cambridge, MA: Harvard University Press, 1970)

Clement of Alexandria, 'Stromata', in *St. Clement of Alexandria: Selected Works*, in *The Ante-Nicene Fathers: The Writings of the Fathers Down to A.D. 325*, ed. and trans. Alexander Roberts, James Donaldson, and Arthur Cleveland Cox, Vol. 2 (Buffalo, NY: Christian Literature Publishing, 1885), pp. 299–568

Copenhaver, Brian P. (ed. and trans.), *Hermetica: The Greek Corpus Hermeticum and the Latin Asclepius in a New English Translation* (Cambridge: Cambridge University Press, 1992)

Cumont, Franz, *The Mysteries of Mithra*, trans. Thomas J. McCormack (Chicago: Open Court, 1903)

Demosthenes, *On the Crown*, trans. A.W. Pickard-Cambridge, in A.W. Pickard-Cambridge (ed. and trans.), *Public Orations of Demosthenes*, 2 volumes (Oxford: Clarendon Press, 1912)

Dillon, John (ed. and trans.), *Fragments of Iamblichus' Commentary on the Timaeus* (Leiden: Brill, 1973)

Euripides, *The Heracleidae*, trans. Ralph Gladstone, in *Euripides 1: Alcestis/The Medea/The Heracleidae/Hippolytus*, ed. Richmond Lattimore and David Grene, trans. Ralph Gladstone (Chicago: University of Chicago Press, 1955)

Evans-Wentz, W.Y. (ed. and trans.), *The Tibetan Book of the Dead: Or the After-Death Experiences on the Bardo Plane, According to Lama Kazi Dawa-Samdup's English Rendering* (Oxford: Oxford University Press, 1927)

Firmicus Maternus, Julius, *Ancient Astrology, Theory and Practice: The Mathesis of Firmicus Maternus*, trans. Jean Rhys Bram (Park Ridge, NJ: Noyes Press, 1975)

Freud, Sigmund, *The Interpretation of Dreams*, SE5, trans. James Strachey (London: Hogarth Press/Institute of Psychoanalysis, 1953)

———, *Three Essays on the Theory of Sexuality and Other Works*, trans. James Strachey, SE7 (London: Hogarth Press/Institute of Psychoanalysis, 1953)

Freud, Sigmund and Joseph Breuer, *Studies on Hysteria*, SE2, trans. James Strachey (London: Hogarth Press/Institute of Psychoanalysis, 1955)

Freud, Sigmund and C.G. Jung, *The Freud-Jung Letters*, ed. William McGuire, trans. Ralph Manheim and R.F.C. Hull (London: Hogarth Press/Routledge & Kegan Paul, 1977)

Frey-Rohn, Liliane, *From Freud to Jung: A Comparative Study of the Psychology of the Unconscious*, trans. Fred E. Engreen and Evelyn K. Engreen (New York: Putnam, 1976; repr. Shambhala/Daimon Verlag, 1990)

Ganss, George E. (trans.), *The Spiritual Exercises of Saint Ignatius: A Translation and Commentary* (Chicago: Loyola Press, 1992)

Godwin, Joscelyn, *The Theosophical Enlightenment* (Albany: SUNY Press, 1994)

——— (trans.), *Hypnerotomachia Poliphili: The Strife of Love in a Dream* (London: Thames and Hudson, 1999)

Gospel of Philip, in M.R. James (ed. and trans.), *The Apocryphal New Testament: Being the Apocryphal Gospels, Acts, Epistles, and Apocalypses* (Oxford: Clarendon Press, 1924), p. 12

Gospel of Thomas, NHC II.2.50, trans. Helmut Koester and Thomas O. Lambdin, in James McConkey Robinson and Richard Smith (eds.), *The Nag Hammadi Library in English* (Leiden: Brill, 1977), pp. 117–30

Gregory of Nyssa, *On the Soul and Resurrection*, trans. Catherine P. Roth (Yonkers, NY: St.Vladimir's Seminary Press, 1993)

Herodotus, *The Histories*, trans. Robin Waterfield (Oxford: Oxford University Press, 1998)

Hesiod, *Theogony and Works and Days*, trans. M.L. West (Oxford: Oxford University Press, 1988)

Homer, *The Iliad of Homer*, trans. Richmond Lattimore (Chicago: University of Chicago Press, 1951)

———, *The Odyssey of Homer*, trans. Richmond Lattimore (New York: Harper & Row, 1967)

Iamblichus, *On the Pythagorean Life*, trans. Gillian Clark (Liverpool: Liverpool University Press, 1989)

———, *De mysteriis*, trans. Emma C. Clarke, John M. Dillon, and Jackson P. Hershbell (Leiden: Brill, 2004)

———, *Iamblichus of Chalcis: The Letters*, trans. John M. Dillon and Wolfgang Polleichtner (Atlanta, GA: Scholars Press, 2009)

Ibn Ezra, Abraham, *The Book of the World*, trans. Shlomo Sela (Leiden: Brill, 2010)

'J.K.' [Julius Kohn] (ed. and trans.), *Splendor Solis: Alchemical Treatises of Solomon Trismosin, Adept and Teacher of Paracelsus* (London: Kegan Paul, Trench, Trubner, 1920)

Kahn, Charles H. (trans.), *The Art and Thought of Heraclitus: An Edition of the Fragments with Translation and Commentary* (Cambridge: Cambridge University Press, 1981)

Kant, Immanuel, *Critique of Practical Reason*, trans. Lewis White Beck (Upper Saddle River, NJ: Prentice-Hall, 1993)

Karr, Don (ed. and trans.), *Liber Salomonis: Cephar Raziel, British Library Sloane MS 3826:2r-57r* (2007–10), at <www.digital-brilliance.com/kab/karr/Solomon/LibSal.pdf>

Kerényi, Karl, 'Kore', in C.G. Jung and Carl Kerényi, *Essays on a Science of Mythology: The Myth of the Divine Child and the Mysteries of Eleusis*, trans. R.F.C. Hull (Princeton, NJ: Princeton University Press, 1969), pp. 101–55

Lewy, Hans (ed. and trans.), *Chaldaean Oracles and Theurgy: Mysticism, Magic, and Platonism in the Later Roman Empire* (Paris: Institut d'Études Augustiniennes, 2011 [1956])

Macrobius, *The Saturnalia*, trans. Percival Vaughan Davies (New York: Columbia University Press, 1969)

———, *Commentary on the Dream of Scipio*, trans. William Harris Stahl (New York: Columbia University Press, 1990 [1952])

Marcus Aurelius, *Meditations*, trans. Martin Hammond (London: Penguin, 2006)

Marsanes, NHC X.5.24–26, trans. Birger A. Pearson, in James McConkey Robinson (ed.), *The Nag Hammadi Library in English* (Leiden: Brill, 1977), pp. 417–26

Masson, Jeffrey Moussaieff (ed and trans.), *The Complete Letters of Sigmund Freud to Wilhelm Fliess, 1887–1904* (Cambridge, MA: Harvard University Press, 1985)

Müller, Ernst (ed. and trans.), *Der Zohar: Das Heilige Buch der Kabbala* (Vienna: Heinrich Glanz, 1932)

Origen, *Contra Celsum*, trans. Henry Chadwick (Cambridge: Cambridge University Press, 1953)

Peterson, Joseph (ed. and trans.), *The Sixth and Seventh Books of Moses: Or, Moses' Magical Spirit Art Known as the Wonderful Arts of the Old Wise Hebrews, Taken from the Mosaic Books of the Kabbalah and the Talmud, for the Good of Mankind* (Lake Worth, FL: Ibis Press, 2008)

Piché, D. (ed. and trans.), *La condamnation parisienne de 1277* (Paris: Vrin, 1999)

Plato, *Plato in Twelve Volumes*, trans. W.R.M. Lamb (London: William Heinemann, 1925)

———, *The Collected Dialogues of Plato*, ed. Edith Hamilton and Huntington Cairns (Princeton, NJ: Princeton University Press, 1961)

Plotinus, *The Enneads*, trans. Stephen MacKenna, 6 volumes (London: Medici Society, 1917–30; repr. London: Faber & Faber, 1956)

———, *Enneads*, 7 volumes, trans. A.H. Armstrong (Loeb Classical Library, 1966–88)

Plutarch, *On the Daimonion of Socrates: Human Liberation, Divine Guidance and Philosophy*, ed. Heinz-Günther Nesselrath, trans. Donald Russell, George Cawkwell, Werner Deuse, John Dillon, Heinz-Günther Nesselrath, Robert Parker, Christopher Pelling, and Stephan Schröder (Tübingen: Mohr Siebeck, 2010)

Porphyry, *De antro nympharum*, trans. Thomas Taylor, in Thomas Taylor (ed. and trans.), *Select Works of Porphyry; Containing His Four Books on Abstinence from Animal Food; His Treatise*

on the Homeric Cave of the Nymphs; and His Auxiliaries to the Perception of Intelligible Natures (London: Thomas Rodd, 1823)
———, *Introduction to the Tetrabiblos*, in *Porphyry the Philosopher, Introduction to the Tetrabiblos, and Serapio of Alexandria, Astrological Definitions*, trans. James Holden (Tempe, AZ: American Federation of Astrologers, 2009)
Poseidonius, *The Fragments*, 2 volumes, ed. and trans. L. Edelstein and I.G. Kidd (Cambridge: Cambridge University Press, 1972)
Proclus, *On the Sacred Art and On the Signs of Divine Possession*, ed. Stephen Ronan, trans. Thomas Taylor and Alexander Wilder (London: Chthonios Books, 1989)
———, *Commentary on Plato's Timaeus*, ed. and trans. Harold Tarrant (Cambridge: Cambridge University Press, 2007)
———, *Commentary on Plato's Timaeus*, trans. Dirk Baltzly (Cambridge: Cambridge University Press, 2010)
Ptolemy, *Tetrabiblos*, ed. and trans. F.E. Robbins (Cambridge, MA: Harvard University Press, 1971)
Reitzenstein, Richard, *Hellenistic Mystery-Religions: Their Basic Ideas and Significance*, trans. John E. Steely (Pittsburgh, PA: Pickwick Press, 1978)
Ronan, Stephen (ed.), Thomas Taylor and Alexander Wilder (trans.), *Porphyry's Letter to Anebo and Iamblichus' On the Mysteries* (Hastings: Chthonios Books, 1989)
Ruland, Martin, *A Lexicon of Alchemy or Alchemical Dictionary, Containing a Full and Plain Explanation of All Obscure Words, Hermetic Subjects, and Arcane Phrases of Paracelsus*, trans. A.E. Waite (London: privately printed, 1892; repr. York Beach, ME: Samuel Weiser, 1984)
Savedow, Steve (ed. and trans.), *Sepher Rezial Hemelach: The Book of the Angel Rezial* (York Beach, ME: Samuel Weiser, 2000)
Schopenhauer, Arthur, *Prize Essay on the Freedom of the Will*, trans. Eric F.J. Payne, ed. Günter Zöller (Cambridge: Cambridge University Press, 1999)
Scott, Walter (ed. and trans.), *Hermetica: The Ancient Greek and Latin Writings Which Contain Religious or Philosophic Teachings Ascribed to Hermes Trismegistus*, 4 volumes (Oxford: Clarendon Press, 1924–36)
Sperling, Harry and Maurice Simon (trans.), *The Zohar*, 5 volumes (London: Soncino Press, 1931–34)
Steiner, Rudolf, *The Way of Initiation, or How to Attain Knowledge of the Higher Worlds*, trans. Max Gysi (London: Theosophical Publishing Society, 1910)
———, *An Outline of Occult Science*, trans. Max Gysi (London: Theosophical Publishing Society, 1914)
———, *Friedrich Nietzsche: Fighter for Freedom*, trans. Margaret Ingram de Ris (Englewood, NJ: Rudolf Steiner, 1960)
———, *The Reappearance of Christ in the Etheric* (Spring Valley, NY: Anthroposophic Press, 1983)
———, *Evil: Selected Lectures*, ed. and trans. Michael Kalisch (Forest Row: Rudolf Steiner Press, 1997)
———, *The Secret Stream: Christian Rosenkreutz and Rosicrucianism: Selected Lectures and Writings* (Great Barrington, MA: Anthroposophic Press, 2000)
Taylor, Thomas (trans.), *Ocellus Lucanus, on the Nature of the Universe; Taurus, the Platonic Philosopher, on the Eternity of the World; Julius Firmicus Maternus, of the Thema Mundi; Select Theorems on the Perpetuity of Time, by Proclus* (London: John Bohn, 1831)
———, *The Hymns of Orpheus: Translated from the Original Greek, With a Preliminary Dissertation on the Life and Theology of Orpheus* (London: T. Payne, 1792); repr. *The Mystical Hymns of Orpheus* (London: B. Dobell, 1896); repr. *The Mystical Hymns of Orpheus* (London: Robert Triphoon, 1824); repr. *Hymns and Initiations* (Frome: Prometheus Trust, 1994)

Thomas Aquinas, *Summa Contra Gentiles*, trans. Anton C. Pegis, James F. Anderson, Vernon J. Bourke, and Charles J. O'Neil (New York: Hanover House, 1955)
Trimorphic Protennoia (NHC XIII.1), trans. John D. Turner, in James McConkey Robinson (ed.), *The Nag Hammadi Library in English* (Leiden: Brill, 1977), pp. 461–70
Vettius Valens, *The Anthology*, trans. Robert Schmidt (Berkeley Springs, WV: Golden Hind Press, 1993–96)
Von Goethe, Johann Wolfgang, *West-Eastern Divan*, trans. Edward Dowden (London: J.M. Dent, 1914)
Von Hardenberg, Friedrich [Novalis], *Heinrich von Ofterdingen: A Romance*, trans. John Owen (Cambridge: Cambridge Press, 1842)
Walker, Alexander (trans.), *Apocryphal Gospels, Acts, and Revelations* (Edinburgh: T&T Clark, 1911)
West, M.L. (ed. and trans.), *The Orphic Poems* (Oxford: Oxford University Press, 1983)
Wilhelm, Richard and Cary F. Baynes (trans.), *The I Ching or Book of Changes* (New York: Pantheon, 1950)
Xenophon, *The Memorable Thoughts of Socrates*, trans. Edward Bysshe (London: Cassell, 1888)
Zoller, Robert (trans.), *Liber Hermetis: Book of Hermes*, 2 volumes (Golden Hind Press, 2000)

Secondary works

Addey, Crystal, 'Oracles, Dreams, and Astrology in Iamblichus' *De mysteriis*', in Patrick Curry and Angela Voss (eds.), *Seeing with Different Eyes: Essays in Astrology and Divination* (Newcastle: Cambridge Scholars Press, 2007), pp. 35–58
———, 'Oracles, Religious Practices, and Philosophy in Late Neoplatonism', *Practical Philosophy* 8:2 (2007), pp. 31–35, at <www.practical-philosophy.org.uk>
———, 'Divine Possession and Divination in the Graeco-Roman World: The Evidence from Iamblichus' *On the Mysteries*', in Bettina E. Schmidt and Lucy Huskinson (eds.), *Spirit Possession and Trance: New Interdisciplinary Perspectives* (London: Continuum, 2010), pp. 171–81
———, 'In the Light of the Sphere: The "Vehicle of the Soul" and Subtle-Body Practices in Neoplatonism', in Geoffrey Samuel and Jay Johnston (eds.), *Religion and the Subtle Body in Asia and the West* (London: Routledge, 2013), pp. 149–67
Addison, Ann, 'Jung, Vitalism, and "the Psychoid": An Historical Reconstruction', *Journal of Analytical Psychology* 54 (2009), pp. 123–42
Allen, James, *Inference from Signs: Ancient Debates About the Nature of Evidence* (Oxford: Oxford University Press, 2001)
Allen, Michael J.B., Valery Rees, and Martin Davies (eds.), *Marsilio Ficino: His Theology, His Philosophy, His Legacy* (Leiden: Brill, 2002)
Altmann, Alexander, 'Myth and Symbol', *Philosophy* 20:76 (1945), pp. 162–71
Andresen, Jensine (ed.), *Religion in Mind: Cognitive Perspectives on Religious Belief, Ritual, and Experience* (Cambridge: Cambridge University Press, 2001)
Armstrong, A.H., 'Was Plotinus a Magician?', *Phronesis* 1:1 (1955), pp. 73–79
——— (ed.), *Later Greek and Early Medieval Philosophy* (Cambridge: Cambridge University Press, 1967)
Arroyo, Stephen, *Astrology, Psychology, and the Four Elements: An Energy Approach to Astrology and Its Use in the Counseling Arts* (Davis, CA: CRCS, 1975)
Aythos, *Die Fraternitas Saturni: Eine saturn-magische Loge* (Munich: ARW, 1979)
Bain, David, 'Μελανιτις γη in the *Cyranides* and Related Texts: New Evidence for the Origins and Etymology of Alchemy', in Todd Klutz (ed.), *Magic in the Biblical World: From the Rod of Aaron to the Ring of Solomon* (Edinburgh: T&T Clark, 2003), pp. 191–213

Bainbridge, William Sims, *The Sociology of Religious Movements* (London: Routledge, 1997)
Barbault, André, *De la psychanalyse à l'Astrologie* (Paris: Seuil, 1961)
———, *From Psychoanalysis to Astrology: The Bridge Between the Soul and the Cosmos* (Munich: Hugendubel, 1991 [1961])
———, 'L'astrologia, psicologia del profondo dell'antichità', *Ricerca '90* 48 (2001), pp. 105–13
Barker, Eileen and Margit Warburg (eds.), *New Religions and New Religiosity* (Aarhus: Aarhus University Press, 1998)
Barnard, G. William, 'Diving into the Depths: Reflections on Psychology as a Religion', in Diane Jonte-Pace and William B. Parsons (eds.), *Religion and Psychology: Mapping the Terrain* (London: Routledge, 2001), pp. 297–318
Barton, Tamsyn, *Ancient Astrology* (London: Routledge, 1994)
Baumlin, James S., 'Reading/Misreading Jung: Post-Jungian Theory', *College Literature* 32:1 (2005), pp. 177–86
Beck, Roger, *Planetary Gods and Planetary Orders in the Mysteries of Mithras* (Leiden: Brill, 1988)
———, *The Religion of the Mithras Cult in the Roman Empire: Mysteries of the Unconquered Sun* (Oxford: Oxford University Press, 2006)
Becker, Ken L., *Unlikely Companions: C. G. Jung and the 'Spiritual Exercises' of Ignatius of Loyola: An Exposition and Critique Based on Jung's Lectures and Writings* (Leominster: Gracewing/Inigo, 2001)
Beebe, John, 'Can There Be a Science of the Symbolic?', in Kelly Bulkeley and Clodagh Weldon (eds.), *Teaching Jung* (Oxford: Oxford University Press, 2011), pp. 255–68
Bell, Lynn, *Cycles of Light: Exploring the Mysteries of Solar Returns* (London: CPA Press, 2005)
Bennett, Alan, *The History Boys* (London: Faber & Faber, 2004)
Benz, Ernst, *The Mystical Sources of German Romantic Philosophy*, trans. Blair R. Reynolds and Eunice M. Paul (Eugene, OR: Pickwick, 1983)
Berchman, Robert M. and John F. Finamore (eds.), *History of Platonism: Plato Redivivus* (New Orleans, LA: University Press of the South, 2005)
Bernabé, Alberto and Ana Isabel Jiménez San Cristóbal, *Instructions for the Netherworld: The Orphic Gold Tablets* (Leiden: Brill, 2008)
Bernardini, Riccardo, *Jung a Eranos* (Milan: FrancoAngeli, 2011)
Besterman, Theodore, *Crystal-Gazing* (London: Rider, 1924)
Betz, Hans Dieter, 'Hermetism and Gnosticism: The Question of the "Poimandres"', in Søren Giversen, Tage Petersen, and Podemann Sørensen, *The Nag Hammadi Texts in the History of Religions* (Copenhagen: Royal Danish Academy of Sciences and Letters, 2002), pp. 84–94
Bikerman, E., 'The Orphic Blessing', *Journal of the Warburg Institute* 2:4 (1939), pp. 370–71
Bishop, Paul, 'Thomas Mann and C.G. Jung', in Paul Bishop (ed.), *Jung in Contexts: A Reader* (London: Routledge, 1999), pp. 154–88
———, *Analytical Psychology and German Classical Aesthetics: Goethe, Schiller, and Jung* (London: Routledge, 2009)
Bishop, Paul (ed.), *Jung in Contexts: A Reader* (London: Routledge, 1999)
Black, Stephen, 'The Stephen Black Interviews', in William McGuire and R.F.C. Hull (eds.), *Jung Speaking* (Princeton, NJ: Princeton University Press, 1977)
Black, Susie, 'CAT, Jung and Neuroscience' (2011) at <www.acat.me.uk/page/acat+news letter+4+december+2011>
Bloomfield, Morton W., *The Seven Deadly Sins* (East Lansing: Michigan State College Press, 1952)
Blumenthal, Henry J. and Robert A. Markus (eds.), *Neoplatonism and Early Christian Thought* (Farnham: Ashgate, 1981)

Bok, Bart J. and Margaret W. Mayall, 'Scientists Look at Astrology', *Scientific Monthly* 52:3 (1941), pp. 233–44

Bonazzi, Mauro and Christoph Helmig (eds.), *Platonic Stoicism, Stoic Platonism: The Dialogue Between Platonism and Stoicism in Antiquity* (Leuven: Leuven University Press, 2007)

Brain, Peter, *Galen on Bloodletting: A Study of the Origins, Development, and Validity of His Opinions, with a Translation of the Three Works* (Cambridge: Cambridge University Press, 1986)

Brainard, F. Samuel, 'Defining "Mystical Experience"', *Journal of the American Academy of Religion* 64:2 (1996), pp. 359–93

Bremmer, Jan N. and Jan R. Veenstra (eds.), *The Metamorphosis of Magic: From Late Antiquity to the Early Modern Period* (Leuven: Peeters, 2002)

Brenner, E.M., 'Gnosticism and Psychology: Jung's *Septem Sermones ad Mortuos*', *Journal of Analytical Psychology* 35 (1990), pp. 397–419

Brodie-Innes, J.W., et al., *Astrology of the Golden Dawn*, ed. Darcy Küntz (Sequim, WA: Holmes Pubishing Group, 1996)

Brooke, Roger, 'Jung in the Academy: A Response to David Tacey', *Journal of Analytical Psychology* 42:2 (1997), pp. 285–96

Budiansky, Stephen, *The Character of Cats* (London: Weidenfeld and Nicolson, 2002)

Bulkeley, Kelly and Clodagh Weldon (eds.), *Teaching Jung* (Oxford: Oxford University Press, 2011)

Burckhardt, Jacob, *The Civilization of the Renaissance in Italy: An Essay (Die Kultur der Renaissance in Italien: Ein Versuch, 1860)*, trans. Samuel George Chetwynd Middlemore (New York: Doubleday, 1878)

Burnet, John, *Early Greek Philosophy* (London: A&C Black, 1920)

Burrow, John, *A History of Histories: Epics, Chronicles, Romances and Inquiries from Herodotus and Thucydides to the Twentieth Century* (London: Penguin, 2009)

Butler, Andrew C., Jason E. Chapman, Evan M. Forman, and Aaron T. Beck, 'The Empirical Status of Cognitive-Behavioural Therapy: A Review of Meta-Analyses', *Clinical Psychology Review* 26:1 (2006), pp. 17–31

Callahan, John F., 'Greek Philosophy and the Cappadocian Cosmology', *Dumbarton Oaks Papers* 12 (1958)

Campbell, Bruce F., *Ancient Wisdom Revived: A History of the Theosophical Movement* (Berkeley: University of California Press, 1980)

Campion, Nicholas, 'Sigmund Freud's Investigation of Astrology', *Culture and Cosmos* 2:1 (1998), pp. 49–53

———, *What Do Astrologers Believe?* (London: Granta, 2006)

———, *A History of Western Astrology, Vol. 2: The Medieval and Modern Worlds* (London: Continuum, 2009)

———, *Astrology and Cosmology in the World's Religions* (New York: NYU Press, 2012)

———, *Astrology and Popular Religion in the Modern West: Prophecy, Cosmology and the New Age Movement* (Farnham: Ashgate, 2012)

———, 'Is Astrology a Symbolic Language?', in Nicholas Campion and Liz Greene (eds.), *Sky and Symbol* (Lampeter: Sophia Centre Press, 2013), pp. 9–46

Campion, Nicholas and Patrick Curry (eds.), *Sky and Psyche: The Relationship Between Cosmos and Consciousness* (Edinburgh: Floris Books, 2005)

Campion, Nicholas and Liz Greene (eds.), *Astrologies: Plurality and Diversity* (Lampeter: Sophia Centre Press, 2011)

———, *Sky and Symbol* (Lampeter: Sophia Centre Press, 2013)

Campion, Nicholas and Nick Kollerstrom (eds.), *Galileo's Astrology: Culture and Cosmos* 7:1 (2003)

Carducci, Bernardo J., *The Psychology of Personality: Viewpoints, Research, and Applications* (Chichester: John Wiley & Sons, 2009)

'Carl Jung's "Red Book": The Astrology Behind the Publication of Jung's Most Personal Work' (2009), at <http://heavenlytruth.typepad.com/heavenly-truth/2009/09/carl-jungs-red-book-the-astrology-behind-the-publication-of-jungs-most-personal-work.html>.

Casement, Ann, *Carl Gustav Jung* (London: Sage, 2001)

Chapman, Graham, John Cleese, Eric Idle, Terry Jones, Michael Palin, and Terry Gilliam, 'The All-England Summarize Proust Competition', *BBC*, 16 November 1972 as Episode 5, Season 3 of *Monty Python's Flying Circus*

Charet, F.X., *Spiritualism and the Foundations of C. G. Jung's Psychology* (Albany: SUNY Press, 1993)

Childs, Gilbert, *Rudolf Steiner: His Life and Work* (Hudson, NY: Anthroposophic Press, 1996)

Chodorow, Joan (ed.), *Jung on Active Imagination* (Princeton, NJ: Princeton University Press, 1997)

Clymer, R. Swinburne, *The Rosy Cross, Its Teachings* (Quakertown, PA: Beverly Hall, 1965)

Collins, Brendan, 'Wisdom in Jung's Answer to Job', *Biblical Theology Bulletin* 21 (1991), pp. 97–101

Cooperman, Bernard Dov (ed.), *Jewish Thought in the Sixteenth Century* (Cambridge, MA: Harvard University Press, 1983)

Corbin, Henry, *Avicenna and the Visionary Recital*, trans. Willard R. Trask (New York: Pantheon, 1960)

———, 'Mundus Imaginalis, or, the Imaginary and the Imaginal', trans. Ruth Horine, *Cahiers internationaux de symbolisme* 6 (1964), pp. 3–26

Couliano, Ioan P., 'The Angels of the Nations and the Origins of Gnostic Dualism', in Roelof van den Broek and M.J. Vermaseren (eds.), *Studies in Gnosticism and Hellenistic Religions* (Leiden: Brill, 1981), pp. 78–91

———, *Psychanodia I: A Survey of the Evidence Concerning the Ascension of the Soul and Its Relevance* (Leiden: Brill, 1983)

———, *Eros and Magic in the Renaissance*, trans. Margaret Cook (Chicago: University of Chicago Press, 1987)

Crane, Joseph, *Astrological Roots: The Hellenistic Legacy* (Bournemouth: Wessex Astrologer, 2007)

Curry, Patrick, *A Confusion of Prophets: Victorian and Edwardian Astrology* (London: Collins & Brown, 1992)

———, 'Astrology', in Kelly Boyd (ed.), *The Encyclopedia of Historians and Historican Writing* (London: Fitzroy Dearborn, 1999), pp. 55–57

———, 'The Historiography of Astrology: A Diagnosis and a Prescription', in Günther Oestmann, H. Darrel Rutkin (eds.), and Kocku von Stuckrad, *Horoscopes and Public Spheres: Essays on the History of Astrology* (Berlin: Walter de Gruyter, 2005), pp. 261–74

Curry, Patrick and Angela Voss (eds.), *Seeing with Different Eyes: Essays in Astrology and Divination* (Newcastle: Cambridge Scholars Press, 2007)

Cutner, Herbert, *Jesus: God, Man, or Myth? An Examination of the Evidence* (New York: Truth Seeker, 1950)

Dan, Joseph (ed.), *The Christian Kabbalah: Jewish Mystical Books and Their Christian Interpreters* (Cambridge, MA: Harvard University Press, 1997)

———, 'Book of Raziel', *Encyclopaedia Judaica* 13 (2007), pp. 1591–93

Daunton, Martin and Bernhard Rieger (eds.), *Meanings of Modernity: Britain from the Late-Victorian Era to World War II* (Oxford: Berg, 2001)

Davies, Charlotte Aull, *Reflexive Ethnography: A Guide to Researching Selves and Others* (London: Routledge, 1999)

Davies, Owen, *Magic: A Very Short Introduction* (Oxford: Oxford University Press, 2012)

Dawson, Terence, 'Jung, Literature, and Literary Criticism', in Polly Young-Eisendrath and Terence Dawson (eds.), *The Cambridge Companion to Jung* (Cambridge: Cambridge University Press, 1997), pp. 255–80

De Mijolla, Alain (ed.), *The International Dictionary of Psychoanalysis*, 3 volumes (Farmington Hills, MI: Cengage Gale, 2004)

Dillon, John M., *The Middle Platonists* (Ithaca, NY: Cornell University Press, 1997)

———, 'Iamblichus' Defence of Theurgy: Some Reflections', *International Journal of the Platonic Tradition* 1 (2007), pp. 30–41

Dodds, E.R., 'Theurgy and Its Relationship to Neoplatonism', *Journal of Roman Studies* 37:1–2 (1947), pp. 55–69

———, *The Greeks and the Irrational* (Berkeley: University of California Press, 1957)

———, 'The Astral Body in Neoplatonism', in Proclus, *The Elements of Theology: A Revised Text with Translation, Introduction, and Commentary*, trans. E.R. Dodds (Oxford: Clarendon Press, 1963), pp. 313–21

Dourley, John P., *The Intellectual Autobiography of a Jungian Theologian* (Lampeter: Edwin Mellen Press, 2006)

Dronke, Peter (ed.), *A History of Twelfth-Century Western Philosophy* (Cambridge: Cambridge University Press, 1992)

Durand, Gilbert, 'Exploration of the Imaginal', in Benjamin Sells (ed.), *Working with Images: The Theoretical Base of Archetypal Psychology* (Woodstock, CT: Spring, 2000), pp. 53–68.

Dykes, Benjamin N., *Traditional Astrology for Today: An Introduction* (St. Paul, MN: Cazimi Press, 2011)

Eagleton, Terry, *Literary Theory: An Introduction* (London: Blackwell, 1996)

Edighoffer, Roland, 'Rosicrucianism: From the Seventeenth to the Twentieth Century', in Antoine Faivre and Jacob Needleman (eds.), *Modern Esoteric Spirituality* (New York: Crossroad, 1992), pp. 186–209

Edinger, Edward F., *Ego and Archetype* (New York: Putnam, 1972)

Edwards, M.J., 'Gnostic Eros and Orphic Themes', *Zeitschrift für Papyrologie und Epigraphik* 88 (1991), pp. 25–40

Eliade, Mircea *The Forge and the Crucible: The Origins and Structures of Alchemy* (Chicago: University of Chicago Press, 1956)

Ellenberger, Henri F., *The Discovery of the Unconscious: The History and Evolution of Dynamic Psychiatry* (New York: Basic Books, 1970)

Evans, R.J.W. and Alexander Marr (eds.), *Curiosity and Wonder from the Renaissance to the Enlightenment* (Farnham: Ashgate, 2006)

Eysenck, Hans Jurgen and David K.B. Nias, *Astrology: Science or Superstition?* (New York: St. Martin's Press, 1982)

Faivre, Antoine and Wouter J. Hanegraaff (eds.), *Western Esotericism and the Science of Religion* (Leuven: Peeters, 1998)

Faivre, Antoine and Jacob Needleman (eds.), *Modern Esoteric Spirituality* (New York: Crossroad, 1992)

Faivre, Antoine and Karen-Clare Voss, 'Western Esotericism and the Science of Religion', *Numen* 42:1 (1995), pp. 48–77

Fanger, Clare (ed.), *Invoking Angels: Theurgic Ideas and Practices, Thirteenth to Sixteenth Centuries* (University Park: Penn State University Press, 2012)

Faracovi, Ornella Pompeo, *Gli oroscopi di Cristo* (Venice: Marsilio Editori, 1999)

Faraone, Christopher and Dirk Obbink (eds.), *Magika Hiera: Ancient Greek Magic and Religion* (Oxford: Oxford University Press, 1991)

Farnell, Kim, 'A Brief Biography of Alan Leo' (2006), at <www.skyscript.co.uk/Alan_Leo.html>

———, *Flirting with the Zodiac* (Bournemouth: Wessex Astrologer, 2007)

———, 'Seven Faces of Raphael', at <www.skyscript.co.uk/raphael.html>

———, 'That Terrible Iconoclast: A Brief Biography of Sepharial', at <www.skyscript.co.uk/sepharial.html>

Fideler, David, *Jesus Christ, Sun of God: Ancient Cosmology and Early Christian Symbolism* (Wheaton, IL: Quest Books/Theosophical Publishing House, 1993)

Fields, Stanley and Mark Johnston, *Genetic Twists of Fate* (Cambridge, MA: MIT Press, 2010)

Finamore, John F., *Iamblichus and the Theory of the Vehicle of the Soul* (Chico, CA: Scholars Press, 1994)

Flowers, Stephen E., *The Fraternitas Saturni or Brotherhood of Saturn: An Introduction to Its History Philosophy and Rituals* (Smithville, TX: Rûna-Raven Press, 2006 [1990])

Fodor, Nandor, *Freud, Jung and Occultism* (New Hyde Park, NY: University Books, 1971)

Forshaw, Peter, 'Curious Knowledge and Wonder-Working Wisdom in the Occult Works of Heinrich Khunrath', in R.J.W. Evans and Alexander Marr (eds.), *Curiosity and Wonder from the Renaissance to the Enlightenment* (Farnham: Ashgate, 2006), pp. 107–30

Foster, Mary LeCron, 'Symbolism: The Foundation of Culture', in Tim Ingold (ed.), *The Companion Encyclopedia of Anthropology* (London: Routledge, 1994), pp. 366–95

Fowden, Garth, *The Egyptian Hermes: A Historical Approach to the Late Pagan Mind* (Princeton, NJ: Princeton University Press, 1993)

Frater V.D., *Die Fraternitas Saturni heute* (Büllingen: Verlag Ralph Tegtmeier Nachf, 1994)

Gersh, Stephen, *From Iamblichus to Eriugena* (Leiden: Brill, 1978)

Gerson, Lloyd P., *The Cambridge Companion to Plotinus* (Cambridge: Cambridge University Press, 1996)

Gerson, Lloyd P. (ed.), *The Cambridge History of Philosophy in Late Antiquity*, 2 volumes (Cambridge: Cambridge University Press, 2010)

Gilbert, Robert A., *A.E. Waite: Magician of Many Parts* (Wellingborough: Crucible, 1987)

———, *The Golden Dawn Scrapbook: The Rise and Fall of a Magical Order* (Slough: Quantum, 1997)

Giversen, Søren, Tage Petersen, and Podemann Sørensen (eds.), *The Nag Hammadi Texts in the History of Religions* (Copenhagen: Royal Danish Academy of Sciences and Letters, 2002), pp. 84–94

Godwin, Joscelyn, *The Theosophical Enlightenment* (Albany: SUNY Press, 1994)

Gombrich, Ernst H., 'Icones Symbolicae: The Visual Image in Neo-Platonic Thjought', *Journal of the Warburg and Courtauld Institutes* 11 (1948), pp. 163–92

Goodman, Lenn E. (ed.), *Neoplatonism and Jewish Thought* (Albany: SUNY Press, 1992)

Goodrick-Clarke, Clare and Nicholas Goodrick-Clarke, *G.R.S. Mead and the Gnostic Quest* (Berkeley, CA: North Atlantic Books, 2005)

Goodrick-Clarke, Nicholas, *The Occult Roots of Nazism* (London: Tauris Parke, 2004)

Graf-Nold, Angela, 'C.G. Jung's Position at the Swiss Federal Institute of Technology Zürich', *Jung History* 2:2, at <www.philemonfoundation.org/resources/jung_history/volume_2_issue_2>

Greenbaum, Dorian Gieseler, *Temperament: Astrology's Forgotten Key* (Bournemouth: Wessex Astrologer, 2005)

———, 'Allotment and Fate: Lots in Ancient Astrology', *Astrological Journal* 56:2 (2014), pp. 27–31

———, *The Daimon in Hellenistic Astrology: Origins and Influence* (Leiden: Brill, 2015)

Greene Liz, 'Is Astrology a Divinatory System?', *Culture and Cosmos* 12:1 (2008), pp. 3–30

———, 'Signs, Signatures, and Symbols: The Language of Heaven', in Nicholas Campion and Liz Greene (eds.), *Astrologies: Plurality and Diversity* (Lampeter: Sophia Centre Press, 2011), pp. 17–46

———, *Magi and Maggidim: The Kabbalah in British Occultism, 1860–1940* (Lampeter: Sophia Centre Press, 2012)

———, *The Astrological World of Jung's 'Liber Novus': Daimons, Gods, and the Planetary Journey* (London: Routledge, 2017)

Gurdjieff, G.I., *Meetings With Remarkable Men* (London: E.P. Dutton, 1964)

Guthrie, W.K.C., *Orpheus and Greek Religion* (Princeton, NJ: Princeton University Press, 1952)

Hair, book and lyrics by James Rado and Gerome Ragni, music by Galt MacDermot (1967)

Hakfoort, Casper, 'Science Deified: Wilhelm Osstwald's Energeticist World-View and the History of Scientism', *Annals of Science* 49:6 (1992), pp. 525–44

Hakl, Hans Thomas, *Eranos: An Alternative Intellectual History of the Twentieth Century*, trans. Christopher McIntosh (Montreal: McGill-Queens University Press, 2013)

Halbertal, Moshe, *Concealment and Revelation: Esotericism in Jewish Thought and Its Philosophical Implications* (Princeton, NJ: Princeton University Press, 2007)

Hammer, Olav, *Claiming Knowledge: Strategies of Epistemology from Theosophy to the New Age* (Leiden: Brill, 2004)

Hanegraaff, Wouter J., *New Age Religion and Western Culture: Esotericism in the Mirror of Secular Thought* (Leiden: Brill, 1996)

———, 'Introduction: The Birth of a Discipline', in Antoine Faivre and Wouter J. Hanegraaff (eds.), *Western Esotericism and the Science of Religion* (Leuven: Peeters, 1998), pp. vii–xvii

———, 'Romanticism and the Esoteric Connection', in Roelof van den Broek and Wouter J. Hanegraaff (eds.), *Gnosis and Hermeticism: From Antiquity to Modern Times* (Albany: SUNY Press, 1998), pp. 237–68

———, 'How Magic Survived the Disenchantment of the World', *Religion* 33 (2003), pp. 357–80

———, *Esotericism and the Academy: Rejected Knowledge in Western Culture* (Cambridge: Cambridge University Press, 2012)

Hart, Susan, *Brain, Attachment, Personality: An Introduction to Neuroaffective Development* (London: Karnac, 2008)

Haule, John Ryan, 'Freud and Jung: A Failure of Eros', *Harvest* 39 (1993), pp. 147–58

———, 'Personal Secrets, Ethical Questions', in Diane Jonte-Pace and William B. Parsons (eds.), *Religion and Psychology: Mapping the Terrain* (London: Routledge, 2001), pp. 151–67

Hayes, Lynn, 'The Astrology of Carl Jung and His Red Book' (2009), at <www.beliefnet.com/columnists/astrologicalmusings/2009/09/carl-jung-and-the-astrology-of.html>

Heelas, Paul, *The New Age Movement: The Celebration of the Self and the Sacralization of Modernity* (Oxford: Blackwell, 1996)

Hegedus, Tim, 'Necessity and Free Will in the Thought of Bardaisan of Edessa', *Laval théologique et philosophique* 69:2 (2003), pp. 333–44

Helleman, Wendy Elgersma, 'Plotinus and Magic', *International Journal of the Platonic Tradition* 4 (2010), pp. 114–46

Henderson, James L., *A Bridge Across Time: The Role of Myths in History* (London: Turnstone, 1975)

Hillman, James, *Loose Ends: Primary Papers in Archetypal Psychology* (Zürich: Spring, 1975)

———, 'Plotino, Ficino, and Vico as Precursors of Archetypal Psychology', in James Hillman, *Loose Ends: Primary Papers in Archetypal Psychology* (Zürich: Spring, 1975), pp. 146–69

———, 'Some Early Background to Jung's Ideas: Notes on C.G. Jung's Medium by Stephanie Zumstein-Preiswerk', *Spring* (1976), pp. 123–36

———, 'Jung's Daimonic Inheritance', *Sphinx* 1 (1988), pp. 9–19

———, *The Soul's Code: In Search of Character and Calling* (London: Bantam, 1996)

———, 'Heaven Retains in Its Sphere Half of All Bodies and Maladies', paper given at 'Cycles and Symbols III: The Return of Soul to the Cosmos' Conference, Isis Institute, San Francisco, CA, February 1997, at <www.springpub.com/astro.htm>

———, 'The Azure Vault: The Caelum as Experience', in Nicholas Campion and Patrick Curry (eds.), *Sky and Psyche: The Relationship Between Cosmos and Consciousness* (Edinburgh: Floris Books, 2006), pp. 37–58

Hillman, James and Sonu Shamdasani, *Lament of the Dead: Psychology After Jung's Red Book* (New York: W.W. Norton, 2013)

Hodges, Horace Jeffery, 'Gnostic Liberation from Astrological Determinism: Hipparchan "Trepidation" and the Breaking of Fate', *Vigiliae Christianae* 51:4 (1997), pp. 359–73

Hoeller, Stephan A., *The Gnostic Jung and the Seven Sermons to the Dead* (Wheaton, IL: Theosophical Publishing House, 1982)

———, *Gnosticism: New Light on the Ancient Tradition of Inner Knowing* (Wheaton, IL: Theosophical Publishing Society, 1982)

———, 'C.G. Jung and the Alchemical Revival', *Gnosis* 8 (1988), pp. 34–39

Hoffman, Leon, 'Varieties of Psychoanalytic Experience: Review of *The Red Book*', *Journal of the American Psychoanalytic Association* 58 (2010), pp. 781–85

Holden, James H., *A History of Horoscopic Astrology* (Tempe, AZ: American Federation of Astrologers, 1996)

———, 'Early Horoscopes of Jesus', *American Federation of Astrologers Journal of Research* 12:1 (2001)

Hone, Margaret, *The Modern Textbook of Astrology* (London: L.N. Fowler, 1950)

Hood, Ralph W., Jr., 'The Construction and Preliminary Validation of a Measure of Reported Mystical Experience', *Journal for the Scientific Study of Religion* 14 (1975), pp. 29–41

Horowitz, Asher and Terry Maley (eds.), *The Barbarism of Reason: Max Weber and the Twilight of Enlightenment* (Toronto: University of Toronto Press, 1994)

Horowitz, Maryanne Cline (ed.), *New Dictionary of the History of Ideas*, 6 volumes (Detroit, MI: Charles Scribner's Sons, 2005)

Horton, Scott, 'Inside Jung's *Red Book*: Six Questions for Sonu Shamdasani', *Harper's Magazine*, 12 July 2014, at <http://harpers.org/blog/2009/10/inside-jungs-_red-book_-six-questions-for-sonu-shamdasani/>

Howe, Ellic, *Urania's Children: The Strange World of the Astrologers* (London: William Kimber, 1967)

Hubbs, V.C., 'German Romanticism and C.G. Jung: Selective Affinities', *Journal of Evolutionary Psychology* 4:1–2 (1983), pp. 4–24

Hughes, Aaron, 'The Three Worlds of ibn Ezra's Hay ben Meqitz', *Journal of Jewish Thought and Philosophy* 11:1 (2002), pp. 1–24

Huskinson, Lucy, *Nietzsche and Jung: The Whole Self in the Union of Opposites* (London: Routledge, 2004)

Idel, Moshe, 'The Magical and Neoplatonic Interpretations of the Kabbalah in the Renaissance', in Bernard Dov Cooperman (ed.), *Jewish Thought in the Sixteenth Century* (Cambridge, MA: Harvard University Press, 1983), pp. 186–242

Iribarren, Isabel and Martin Lenz (eds.), *Angels in Medieval Philosophical Inquiry* (Aldershot: Ashgate, 2008)

Jansen, Diana Baynes, *Jung's Apprentice: A Biography of Helton Godwin Baynes* (Einsiedeln, Switzerland: Daimon Verlag, 2003)

Jensen, Ferne (ed.), *C.G. Jung, Emma Jung, and Toni Wolff: A Collection of Remembrances* (San Francisco, CA: Analytical Psychology Club of San Francisco, 1982)

Johnston, Sarah Iles, 'Introduction: Divining Divination', in Sarah Iles Johnston and Peter T. Struck (eds.), *Mantikê: Studies in Ancient Divination* (Leiden: Brill, 2005), pp. 1–28

Johnston, Sarah Iles and Peter T. Struck (eds.), *Mantikê: Studies in Ancient Divination* (Leiden: Brill, 2005)

Jonas, Hans, *The Gnostic Religion: The Message of the Alien God and the Beginnings of Christianity* (Boston, MA: Beacon Press, 1958)

Jonte-Pace, Diane and William B. Parsons (eds.), *Religion and Psychology: Mapping the Terrain* (London: Routledge, 2001)

Kassenbrock, Brian W., *Novalis and the Two Cultures: The Chiasmic Discourse of Mathematics, Philosophy, and Poetics* (unpublished PhD dissertation, Department of Germanic Languages and Literatures, New York University, 2009)

Katz, David S., *The Occult Tradition: From the Renaissance to the Present Day* (London: Jonathan Cape, 2005)

Katz, Steven T. (ed.), *Mysticism and Language* (Oxford: Oxford University Press, 1992)

Kaylo, Janet, 'Imagination and the Mundus Imaginalis', *Spring* 77 (2007), pp. 107–24

Kilcher, Andreas, 'The Moses of Sinai and the Moses of Egypt: Moses as Magician in Jewish Literature and Western Esotericism', *Aries* 4:2 (2004), pp. 148–70

Kim, J.C. and S.M. Dumecki, 'Genetic Fate-Mapping Approaches: New Means to Explore the Embryonic Origins of the Cochlear Nucleus', *Methods in Molecular Biology* 493 (2009), pp. 65–85

Kingsley, Peter, 'Poimandres: The Etymology of the Name and the Origins of the Hermetica', *Journal of the Warburg and Courtauld Institutes* 56 (1993), pp. 1–24

———, *Ancient Philosophy, Mystery, and Magic: Empedocles and Pythagorean Tradition* (Oxford: Clarendon Press, 1995)

Kirsch, Thomas B., *The Jungians: A Comparative and Historical Perspective* (London: Routledge, 2012)

Kline, Rangar, *Ancient Angels: Conceptualizing Angeloi in the Roman Empire* (Leiden: Brill, 2011)

Klutz, Todd (ed.), *Magic in the Biblical World: From the Rod of Aaron to the Ring of Solomon* (Edinburgh: T&T Clark, 2003)

Knapp, Bettina L., *A Jungian Approach to Literature* (Carbondale: Southern Illinois University Press, 1984)

Koenig, Peter-Robert, 'Did You Know Oscar R. Schlag?', at <www.parareligion.ch/sunrise/schlag1.htm>

Kontos, Alkis, 'The World Disenchanted, and the Return of Gods and Demons', in Asher Horowitz and Terry Maley (eds.), *The Barbarism of Reason: Max Weber and the Twilight of Enlightenment* (Toronto: University of Toronto Press, 1994), pp. 223–47

Kotansky, Roy, 'Incantations and Prayers for Salvation on Inscribed Greek Amulets', in Christopher A. Faraone and Dirk Obbink (eds.), *Magika Hiera: Ancient Greek Magic and Religion* (Oxford: Oxford University Press, 1991), pp. 114–16

Kugelman, Robert, 'Review of *The Red Book*', *Journal of the History of the Behavioral Sciences* 47:1 (2011), pp. 101–4

Kuhn, Thomas, *The Structure of Scientific Revolutions* (Chicago: University of Chicago Press, 1962)

Laks, André and Glenn W. Most (eds.), *Studies on the Derveni Papyrus* (Oxford: Oxford University Press, 2001)

Lehman, J. Lee, *Classical Solar Returns* (Atglen, PA: Schiffer, 2012)

Lehrich, Christopher, *The Occult Mind: Magic in Theory and Practice* (Ithaca, NY: Cornell University Press, 2007)

Lesses, Rebecca Macy, 'Speaking with Angels: Jewish and Greco-Egyptian Revelatory Adjurations', *Harvard Theological Review* 89:1 (1996), pp. 41–60

——— *Ritual Practices to Gain Power: Angels, Incantations, and Revelation in Early Jewish Mysticism* (Harrisburg, PA: Trinity Press, 1998)
Lewin, Nicholas, *Jung on War, Politics and Nazi Germany: Exploring the Theory of Archetypes and the Collective Unconscious* (London: Karnac Books, 2009)
Lewis, H. Spencer, *Rosicrucian Questions and Answers with Complete Answers* (San Jose, CA: Supreme Grand Lodge of AMORC, 1969)
Lewis, James R., *The Astrology Book: The Encyclopedia of Heavenly Influences* (Canton, MI: Visible Ink Press, 2003)
Lewis, Nicola Denzey, *Cosmology and Fate in Gnosticism and Graeco-Roman Antiquity* (Leiden: Brill, 2013)
Linden, Stanton J. (ed.), *The Alchemy Reader: From Hermes Trismegistus to Isaac Newton* (Cambridge: Cambridge University Press, 2003)
Long, A.A., *From Epicurus to Epictetus: Studies in Hellenistic and Roman Philosophy* (Oxford: Oxford University Press, 2006)
Long, A.A. and D.N. Sedley, *The Hellenistic Philosophers*, Vol. 1: *Translation of the Principle Sources with Philosophical Commentary* (Cambridge: Cambridge University Press, 1987)
Louth, Andrew, *The Origins of the Christian Mystical Tradition: From Plato to Denys* (Oxford: Oxford University Press, 1983)
Luck, Georg, *Arcana Mundi: Magic and the Occult in the Greek and Roman Worlds* (Baltimore, MD: Johns Hopkins University Press, 1985)
MacIntyre, Alasdair, 'Is Understanding Religion Compatible With Believing?', in Russell T. McCutcheon (ed.), *The Insider/Outsider Problem in the Study of Religion: A Reader* (London: Cassell, 1999), pp. 37–49
MacLennan, Bruce J., 'Evolution, Jung, and Theurgy: Their Role in Modern Neoplatonism', in Robert M. Berchman and John F. Finamore (eds.), *History of Platonism: Plato Redivivus* (New Orleans, LA: University Press of the South, 2005), pp. 305–22
Main, Roderick, *The Rupture of Time: Synchronicity and Jung's Critique of Modern Western Culture* (Hove: Brunner-Routledge, 2004)
———, 'New Age Thinking in the Light of C.G. Jung's Theory of Synchronicity', *Journal of Alternative Spiritualities and New Age Studies* 2 (2006), pp. 8–25
——— (ed.), *Jung, Synchronicity, and the Paranormal* (London: Routledge, 1997)
Marjanen, Antii and Petri Luomanen (eds.), *A Companion to Second-Century Christian 'Heretics'* (Leiden: Brill, 2008)
Martindale, Philippa, '"Against All Hushing Up and Stamping Down": The Medico-Psychological Clinic of London and the Novelist May Sinclair', *Psychoanalysis and History* 6:2 (2004), pp. 177–200
Maslow, Abraham, *Toward a Psychology of Being* (London: John Wiley & Sons, 1968)
Mayo, Jeff, *Astrology: A Key to Personality* (London: Teach Yourself Books, 1964)
Mazur, Zeke, '*Unio Magica*, Part I: On the Magical Origins of Plotinus' Mysticism', *Dionysius* 21 (2003), pp. 23–52
———, '*Unio Magica*, Part II: Plotinus, Theurgy, and the Question of Ritual', *Dionysius* 22 (2004), pp. 29–56
McCutcheon, Russell T. (ed.), *The Insider/Outsider Problem in the Study of Religion: A Reader* (London: Cassell, 1999)
McGillion, Frank, '"The Influence of Wilhelm Fliess" Cosmology on Sigmund Freud', *Culture and Cosmos* 2:1 (1998), pp. 33–48
McGuire, William and R.F.C. Hull (eds.), *C.G. Jung Speaking: Interviews and Encounters* (Princeton, NJ: Princeton University Press, 1977)
McIntosh, Christopher, *The Rosicrucians: The History, Mythology, and Rituals of an Esoteric Order* (York Beach, ME: Weiserbooks, 1998)

Merkur, Dan, *Gnosis: An Esoteric Tradition of Mystical Visions and Unions* (Albany: SUNY Press, 1993)

———, *Mystical Moments and Unitive Thinking* (Albany: SUNY Press, 1999)

———, 'Stages of Ascension in Hermetic Rebirth', *Esoterica* 1 (1999), pp. 79–96

———, *Crucified with Christ: Meditation on the Passion, Mystical Death, and the Medieval Invention of Psychotherapy* (Albany: SUNY Press, 2007)

Merlan, Philip, 'Plotinus and Magic', *Isis* 44:4 (1953), pp. 341–48

Miller, David L., 'Misprision: Pitfalls in Teaching Jung in a University Religious Studies Department', in Kelly Bulkeley and Clodagh Weldon (eds.), *Teaching Jung* (Oxford: Oxford University Press, 2011), pp. 29–50

Mulacz, W.P., 'Oscar R. Schlag', *Journal of the Society for Psychical Research* 60 (1995), pp. 263–67

Murray, Gilbert, *Four Stages of Greek Religion* (Oxford: Oxford University Press, 1912)

Myers, Isabel Briggs, *An Introduction to Type: A Guide to Understanding Your Results on the Myers-Briggs Type Indicator* (Oxford: Oxford Psychologists Press, 2000 [1990])

Neugebauer, Otto E., 'The Study of Wretched Subjects', *Isis* 42:2 (1951), p. 111

Neumann, Erich, *The Origins and History of Consciousness* (Princeton, NJ: Princeton University Press, 1954)

———, *The Great Mother* (Princeton, NJ: Princeton University Press, 1955)

Noll, Richard, *The Jung Cult: Origins of a Charismatic Movement* (Princeton, NJ: Princeton University Press, 1994)

———, 'Jung the *Leontocephalus*', in Paul Bishop (ed.), *Jung in Contexts: A Reader* (London: Routledge, 1999), pp. 51–91

North, John D., *Stars, Mind, and Fate: Essays in Ancient and Medieval Cosmology* (London: Continuum, 1989)

Oestmann, Günther and H. Darrel Rutkin (eds.), and Kocku von Stuckrad, *Horoscopes and Public Spheres: Essays on the History of Astrology* (Berlin: Walter de Gruyter, 2005)

Olyan, Saul M., *A Thousand Thousands Served Him: Exegesis and the Naming of Angels in Ancient Judaism* (Tübingen: Mohr Siebeck, 1993)

Ouspensky, P.D., *In Search of the Miraculous* (New York: Harcourt, Brace, 1949)

Owen, Alex, 'Occultism and the "Modern Self" in Fin-de-Siècle Britain', in Martin Daunton and Bernhard Rieger (eds.), *Meanings of Modernity: Britain from the Late-Victorian Era to World War II* (Oxford: Berg, 2001), pp. 71–96

———, *The Place of Enchantment: British Occultism and the Culture of the Modern* (Chicago: University of Chicago Press, 2004)

Owens, Lance S., 'Jung and Aion: Time, Vision, and a Wayfaring Man', *Psychological Perspectives: A Quarterly Journal of Jungian Thought* 54:3 (2011), pp. 253–89

Page, Sophie, 'Uplifting Souls: The *Liber de essentia spirituum* and the *Liber Razielis*', in Claire Fanger (ed.), *Invoking Angels: Theurgic Ideas and Practices, Thirteenth to Sixteenth Centuries* (University Park: Penn State University Press, 2012), pp. 79–112

Panofsky, Erwin, *Renaissance and Renascences in Western Art*, 2 volumes (Stockholm: Almqvist & Wiksell, 1960)

Patai, Raphael, *The Jewish Alchemists: A History and Sourcebook* (Princeton, NJ: Princeton University Press, 1995)

Pavlov, Ivan Petrovich, *Conditioned Reflexes: An Investigation of the Physiological Activity of the Cerebral Cortex*, trans. G.V. Anrep (Oxford: Oxford University Press, 1927)

Pearson, Birger A., *Gnosticism, Judaism, and Egyptian Christianity* (Minneapolis, MN: Fortress Press, 1980)

———, 'Jewish Elements in *Corpus Hermeticum* I (*Poimandres*)', in Roelof van den Broek and Cis van Heertum (eds.), *From Poimandres to Jacob Böhme: Hermetism, Gnosis and the Christian Tradition* (Leiden: Brill, 2000), pp. 336–48

———, 'Basilides the Gnostic', in Antii Marjanen and Petri Luomanen (eds.), *A Companion to Second-Century Christian 'Heretics'* (Leiden: Brill, 2008), pp. 1–31

Peck, M. Scott, *The Road Less Travelled: A New Psychology of Love, Traditional Values, and Spiritual Growth* (London: Hutchinson, 1983)

———, *People of the Lie: The Hope for Healing Human Evil* (London: Rider, 1988)

Peterson, Gregory R., 'Demarcation and the Scientistic Fallacy', *Zygon* 38:4 (2003), pp. 751–61

Pittinger, David J., 'Measuring the MBTI . . . And Coming Up Short', *Journal of Career Planning and Employment* 54:1 (1993), pp. 48–52

Platt, Hilary, 'Fighting for Professional Survival', *Psychotherapist* 48 (2011), pp. 29–32

Popovic, Mladen, *Reading the Human Body: Physiognomics and Astrology in the Dead Sea Scolls and Hellenistic-Early Roman Period Judaism* (Leiden: Brill, 2007)

Primiano, Leonard Norman, 'Vernacular Religion and the Search for Method in Religious Folklife', *Western Folklore* 54:1 (1995), pp. 37–56

Progoff, Ira, *The Symbolic and the Real: A New Psychological Approach to the Fuller Experience of Personal Existence* (New York: McGraw-Hill, 1973)

Quispel, Gilles, *Gnosis als Weltreligion: Die Bedeutung der Gnosis in der Antike* (Zürich: Origo Verlag, 1951)

———, *Gnostica, Judaica, Catholica: Collected Essays of Gilles Quispel*, ed. Johannes van Oort (Leiden: Brill, 2008)

Raff, Jeffrey, *Jung and the Alchemical Imagination* (York Beach, ME: Nicolas-Hays, 2000)

Raine, Kathleen, *Yeats, the Tarot, and the Golden Dawn* (Dublin: Dolmen Press, 1972)

Raitt, Suzanne, 'Early British Psychoanalysis and the Medico-Psychological Clinic', *History Workshop Journal* 58 (2004), pp. 63–85

Raman, B.V., *How to Judge a Horoscope*, 2 volumes (Columbia, MO: South Asia Books, 2000)

Reichert, Carl-Ludwig, 'Oskar Adolf Hermann Schmitz', in *New German Biography*, Vol. 23 (Berlin: Duncker and Humblot, 2007), pp. 254–55

Riffard, Pierre, *L'esoterisme* (Paris: Laffont, 1990)

Rist, John M., *The Stoics* (Berkeley: University of California Press, 1978)

———, 'Plotinus and Christian Philosophy', in Lloyd P. Gerson (ed.), *The Cambridge Companion to Plotinus* (Cambridge: Cambridge University Press, 1996), pp. 386–413

Robinson, James McConkey and Richard Smith (eds.), *The Nag Hammadi Library in English* (Leiden: Brill, 1977)

Roling, Bernd, 'The Complete Nature of Christ: Sources and Structures of a Christological Theurgy in the Works of Johannes Reuchlin', in Jan N. Bremmer and Jan R. Veenstra (eds.), *The Metamorphosis of Magic: From Late Antiquity to the Early Modern Period* (Leuven: Peeters, 2002), pp. 231–66

Rosenmeyer, Thomas G., *Senecan Drama and Stoic Cosmology* (Berkeley: University of California Press, 1989)

Rudolph, Kurt, *Gnosis: The Nature and History of Gnosticism*, trans. P.W. Coxon, K.H. Kuhn, and R. McL. Wilson (Edinburgh: T&T Clark, 1984)

Rümke, A.C. and Sarah de Rijcke, *Rebekka Aleida Beigel (1886–1943): Een Vrouw in de Psychologie* (Eelde: Barkhuism, 2006)

Ruperti, Alexander, 'Dane Rudhyar: A Seed-Man for the New Era', *Astrological Journal* 32:2 (1986), p. 57

Russell, D.A., 'Some Texts Similar to *De genio*', in Plutarch, *On the Daimonion of Socrates: Human Liberation, Divine Guidance and Philosophy*, ed. Heinz-Günther Nesselrath, trans. Donald Russell, George Cawkwell, Werner Deuse, John Dillon, Heinz-Günther Nesselrath, Robert Parker, Christopher Pelling, and Stephan Schröder (Tübingen: Mohr Siebeck, 2010), pp. 201–6

Samuel, Geoffrey and Jay Johnston (eds.), *Religion and the Subtle Body in Asia and the West* (London: Routledge, 2013)
Samuels, Andrew, *Jung and the Post-Jungians* (London: Routledge & Kegan Paul, 1985)
Sandbach, F.H., *The Stoics* (London: Duckworth, 1975)
Saunders, Barbara R., *Ivan Pavlov: Exploring the Mysteries of Behavior* (Berkeley Heights, NJ: Enslow, 2006)
Schäfer, Peter, 'Jewish Magic Literature in Late Antiquity and the Early Middle Ages', *Journal of Jewish Studies* 41:1 (1990), pp. 75–91
Scharfstein, Ben-Ami, *The Roots of Bergson's Philosophy* (New York: Columbia University Press, 1943)
Schaverien, Joy, *The Revealing Image: Analytical Art Psychotherapy in Theory and Practice* (London: Jessica Kingsley, 2009)
Schmidt, Bettina E. and Lucy Huskinson (eds.), *Spirit Possession and Trance: New Interdisciplinary Perspectives* (London: Continuum, 2010)
Scholem, Gershom, *Jewish Gnosticism, Merkabah Mysticism, and Talmudic Tradition* (New York: Jewish Theological Seminary, 1970)
———, *Kabbalah: A Definitive History of the Evolution, Ideas, Leading Figures and Extraordinary Influence of Jewish Mysticism* (New York: Meridian, 1978)
———, 'The Concept of Kavvanah in Early Kabbalah', in Alfred Jospe (ed.), *Studies in Jewish Thought: An Anthology of German Jewish Scholarship* (Detroit, MI: Wayne State University Press, 1981), pp. 162–80
———, *On the Mystical Shape of the Godhead: Basic Concepts in the Kabbalah*, trans. Joachim Neugroschel (New York: Schocken Books, 1991)
———, *Alchemy and Kabbalah*, trans. Klaus Ottman (Dallas: Spring, 2006)
Scrimali, Tullio, *Neuroscience-Based Cognitive Therapy: New Methods for Assessment, Treatment and Self-Regulation* (London: John Wiley & Sons, 2012)
Secret, François, 'Sur quelques traductions du Sefer Raziel', *Revue des Études Juives* 128 (1969), pp. 223–45
Segal, Alan F., 'Heavenly Ascent in Hellenistic Judaism, Early Christianity and Their Environment', in *Aufstieg und Niedergang der römischen Welt* (*ANRW*), Vol. 2, ed. W. Haase (Berlin: De Gruyter, 1980), pp. 1333–94
———, *Life After Death: A History of the Afterlife in Western Religion* (New York: Doubleday, 2012)
Segal, Robert A., 'Jung's Very Twentieth-Century View of Myth', *Journal of Analytical Psychology* 48:5 (2003), pp. 593–617
———, 'Jung as Psychologist of Religion and Jung as Philosopher of Religion', *Journal of Analytical Psychology* 55:3 (2010), pp. 361–84
——— (ed.), *The Gnostic Jung, Including 'Seven Sermons to the Dead'* (Princeton, NJ: Princeton University Press, 1992)
Sellars, John, *Stoicism* (Berkeley: University of California Press, 2006)
Sells, Benjamin (ed.), *Working with Images: The Theoretical Base of Archetypal Psychology* (Woodstock, CT: Spring, 2000)
Serrano, Miguel, *C. G. Jung and Hermann Hesse: A Record of Two Friendships* (Einsiedeln, Switzerland: Daimon Verlag, 1998)
Seznec, Jean, *The Survival of the Pagan Gods: The Mythological Tradition and Its Place in Renaissance Humanism and Art*, trans. Barbara F. Sessions (New York: Pantheon, 1953)
Shalit, Erel, *The Complex: Path of Transformation from Archetype to Ego* (Toronto: Inner City Books, 2002)
Shamdasani, Sonu, *Cult Fictions: C. G. Jung and the Founding of Analytical Psychology* (London: Routledge, 1998)

———, 'Memories, Dreams, Omissions', in Paul Bishop (ed.), *Jung in Contexts: A Reader* (London: Routledge, 1999), pp. 33–50

———, *Jung and the Making of Modern Psychology: The Dream of a Science* (Cambridge: Cambridge University Press, 2003)

———, *C.G. Jung: A Biography in Books* (New York: W.W. Norton, 2012)

Shamdasani, Sonu (ed.), *Jung contra Freud: The 1912 New York Lectures on the Theory of Psychoanalysis* (Princeton, NJ: Princeton University Press, 2011)

Shaw, Gregory, 'Theurgy: Rituals of Unification in the Neoplatonism of Iamblichus', *Traditio* 41 (1985), pp. 1–28

———, *Theurgy and the Soul: The Neoplatonism of Iamblichus* (University Park: Penn State University Press, 1995)

———, 'Neoplatonic Theurgy and Dionysius the Areopagate', *Journal of Early Christian Studies* 7:4 (1999), pp. 573–99

———, 'The Talisman: Magic and True Philosophers', in Angela Voss and Jean Hinson Lall (eds.), *The Imaginal Cosmos: Astrology, Divination and the Sacred* (Canterbury: University of Kent, 2007), pp. 25–34

Sheldon-Williams, I.P., 'The Greek Christian Platonist Tradition from the Cappadocians to Maximus and Eriugena', in A.H. Armstrong (ed.), *Later Greek and Early Medieval Philosophy* (Cambridge: Cambridge University Press, 1967), pp. 421–534

Sherry, Jay, *A Pictorial Guide to The Red Book* (Archive for Research in Archetypal Symbolism, ARAS Connections, 2010), at <https://aras.org/sites/default/files/docs/00033Sherry.pdf>

Silverstone, Liesel, *Art Therapy Exercises: Inspirational and Practical Ideas to Stimulate the Imagination* (London: Jessica Kingsley, 2009)

Singer, Thomas and Samuel L. Kimbles (eds.), *The Cultural Complex: Contemporary Jungian Perspectives on Psyche and Society* (London: Routledge, 2004)

Smart, Ninian, *The Science of Religion and the Sociology of Knowledge* (Princeton, NJ: Princeton University Press, 1973)

Smythe, William E. and Angelina Baydala, 'The Hermeneutic Background of C.G. Jung', *Journal of Analytical Psychology* 57 (2012), pp. 57–75

Solovyoff, Vsevolod Sergyeevich, *A Modern Priestess of Isis* (London: Longmans, Green, 1895)

Sperber, Dan, *Rethinking Symbolism*, trans. Alice L. Morton (Cambridge: Cambridge Univerity Press, 1974)

Struck, Peter T., *Birth of the Symbol: Ancient Readers at the Limits of Their Texts* (Princeton, NJ: Princeton University Press, 2004)

———, 'A World Full of Signs: Understanding Divination in Ancient Stoicism', in Patrick Curry and Angela Voss (eds.), *Seeing with Different Eyes: Essays in Astrology and Divination* (Newcastle: Cambridge Scholars, 2007), pp. 3–20

Sulloway, Frank J., *Freud, Biologist of the Mind: Beyond the Psychoanalytic Legend* (Cambridge, MA: Harvard University Press, 1992)

Swan, Wendy, 'C.G. Jung's Psychotherapeutic Technique of Active Imagination in Historical Context', *Psychoanalysis and History* 10:2 (2008), pp. 185–204

Swanson, R.N., *The 12th-Century Renaissance* (Manchester: Manchester University Press, 1999)

Swatos, William H. and Daniel V.A. Olson (eds.), *The Secularization Debate* (New York: Rowman & Littlefield, 2000)

Tacey, David John, *Jung and the New Age* (Hove: Brunner-Routledge, 2001)

———, 'The Challenge of Teaching Jung in the University', in Kelly Bulkeley and Clodagh Weldon (eds.), *Teaching Jung* (Oxford: Oxford University Press, 2011), pp. 13–27

Taylor, Anne, *Annie Besant: A Biography* (Oxford: Oxford University Press, 1991)

Thomas, Keith, *Religion and the Decline of Magic* (London: Weidenfeld & Nicolson, 1971)

Thompson, Michael, *Roots and Role of Imagination in Kant: Imagination at the Core* (unpublished PhD dissertation, University of South Florida, 2009)

Thrower, James, *Religion: The Classical Theories* (Edinburgh: Edinburgh University Press, 1999)

Torijano, Pablo A., *Solomon the Esoteric King: From King to Magus, Development of a Tradition* (Leiden: Brill, 2002)

Tsantsanoglou, K., 'The First Columns of the Derveni Papyrus and Their Religious Significance', in André Laks and Glenn W. Most (eds.), *Studies on the Derveni Papyrus* (Oxford: Oxford University Press, 2001), pp. 93–128

Ulansey, David, *The Origins of the Mithraic Mysteries: Cosmology and Salvation in the Ancient World* (Oxford: Oxford University Press, 1991)

Ulinov, Ann Bedford, 'Teaching Jung in a Theological Seminary', in Diane Jonte-Pace and William B. Parsons (eds.), *Religion and Psychology: Mapping the Terrain* (London: Routledge, 2001), pp. 51–59

Vallée, Gérard, *A Study in Anti-Gnostic Polemics: Irenaeus, Hippolytus, and Epiphanius* (Waterloo, ON: Wilfrid Laurier University Press, 1981)

Van den Broek, Roelof, 'The Creation of Adam's Psychic Body in the *Apocryphon of John*', in Roelof van den Broek and M.J. Vermaseren (eds.), *Studies in Gnosticism and Hellenistic Religions* (Leiden: Brill, 1981), pp. 38–57

———, *Studies in Gnosticism and Alexandrian Christianity* (Leiden: Brill, 1996)

———, *Gnostic Religion in Antiquity* (Cambridge: Cambridge University Press, 2013)

Van den Broek, Roelof and Wouter J. Hanegraaff (eds.), *Gnosis and Hermeticism: From Antiquity to Modern Times* (Albany: SUNY Press, 1998)

Van den Broek, Roelof and Cis van Heertum (eds.), *From Poimandres to Jacob Böhme: Hermetism, Gnosis and the Christian Tradition* (Leiden: Brill, 2000)

Van den Broek, Roelof and M.J. Vermaseren (eds.), *Studies in Gnosticism and Hellenistic Religions* (Leiden: Brill, 1981)

Van Oort, Johannes, 'Manichaeism: Its Sources and Influences on Western Christianity', in Roelof van den Broek and Wouter J. Hanegraaff (eds.), *Gnosis and Hermeticism: From Antiquity to Modern Times* (Albany: SUNY Press, 1997), pp. 37–51

Von Franz, Marie-Louise, *Alchemical Active Imagination* (Irving, TX: Spring, 1979)

———, 'On Active Imagination', in Ian Baker (ed.), *The Methods of Treatment in Analytical Psychology* (Fellbach: Verlag Adolf Bonz, 1980), pp. 88–99

Voss, Angela and Jean Hinson Lall (eds.), *The Imaginal Cosmos: Astrology, Divination and the Sacred* (Canterbury: University of Kent, 2007)

Walker, D.P., 'The Astral Body in Renaissance Medicine', *Journal of the Warburg and Courtauld Institutes* 21:1–2 (1958), pp. 119–33

———, *Spiritual and Demonic Magic: From Ficino to Campanella* (London: Warburg Institute, 1958)

Wallis, Richard T. and Jay Bregman (eds.), *Neoplatonism and Gnosticism* (Albany: SUNY Press, 1992)

Wasserstrom, Stephen, *Religion After Religion: Gershom Scholem, Mircea Eliade, and Henry Corbin at Eranos* (Princeton, NJ: Princeton University Press, 1999)

Wear, Sarah Klitenic and John M. Dillon, *Dionysius the Areopagite and the Neoplatonist Tradition: Despoiling the Hellenes* (Farnham: Ashgate, 2007)

Webb, James, *The Occult Establishment* (London: Richard Drew, 1981)

Wehr, Gerhard, *An Illustrated Biography of Jung*, trans. M. Kohn (Boston, MA: Shambhala, 1989)

———, 'C.G. Jung in the Context of Christian Esotericism and Cultural History', in Antoine Faivre and Jacob Needleman (eds.), *Modern Esoteric Spirituality* (New York: Crossroad, 1995), pp. 381–99
———, *Jung and Steiner: The Birth of a New Psychology*, trans. Magdalene Jaeckel (Great Barrington, MA: Anthroposophic Press, 2002)
Wels, Henrik, 'Late Medieval Debates on the Location of Angels After the Condemnation of 1277', in Isabel Iribarren and Martin Lenz (eds.), *Angels in Medieval Philosophical Inquiry* (Aldershot: Ashgate, 2008), pp. 113–27
Wilson, Robert McLachlan, 'Gnosis and the Mysteries', in Roelof van den Broek and M.J. Vermaseren (eds.), *Studies in Gnosticism and Hellenistic Religions* (Leiden: Brill, 1981), pp. 451–66
Wind, Edgar, *Pagan Mysteries in the Renaissance* (London: Faber & Faber, 1968)
Winnicott, D.W., 'Review of C.G. Jung, *Memories, Dreams, Reflections*', *International Journal of Psycho-analysis* 45 (1964), pp. 450–55
Wolfson, Elliot R., 'Merkavah Traditions in Philosophical Garb: Judah Halevi Reconsidered', *Proceedings of the American Academy for Jewish Research* 57 (1990–91), pp. 179–242
———, *Through a Speculum That Shines: Vision and Imagination in Medieval Jewish Mysticism* (Princeton, NJ: Princeton University Press, 1997)
———, 'Theosis, Vision, and the Astral Body in Medieval German Pietism and the Spanish Kabbalah', in Nicholas Campion and Liz Greene (eds.), *Sky and Symbol* (Lampeter: Sophia Centre Press, 2013), pp. 119–42
Wuest, Patricia Viale, *Precession of the Equinoxes* (Atlanta: Georgia Southern University, 1998)
Yates, Frances A., *Giordano Bruno and the Hermetic Tradition* (London: Routledge & Kegan Paul, 1964)
———, *The Rosicrucian Enlightenment* (London: Routledge & Kegan Paul, 1972)
Yoshida, Hiromi, *Joyce and Jung: The 'Four Stages of Eroticism' in A Portrait of the Artist as a Young Man* (New York: Peter Lang, 2007)
Young-Eisendrath, Polly and Terence Dawson (eds.), *The Cambridge Companion to Jung* (Cambridge: Cambridge University Press, 1997)
Zambelli, Paola, *The Speculum astronomiae and Its Enigma* (Dordrecht: Kluwer Academic, 1992)
Ziomkowski, Robert, 'Neoplatonism', in Maryanne Cline Horowitz (ed.), *New Dictionary of the History of Ideas*, 6 volumes (Detroit, MI: Charles Scribner's Sons, 2005), 4:1628
Zoller, Robert, *Fate, Free Will and Astrology* (New York: Ixion Press, 1992)
———, *Tools & Techniques of the Medieval Astrologer, Book One: Prenatal Concerns and the Calculation of the Length of Life* (London: New Library, 2001)

Websites

<www.capt.org/research/psychological-type-journal.htm#>
<http://wildhunt.org/blog/tag/liber-novus>
<www.fraternitas.de>
<www.oocities.org/astrologyages/ageofaquarius.htm>
<www.philemonfoundation.org/resources/jung_history/volume_1_issue_2>
<www.nhs.uk/conditions/Cognitive-behaviouraltherapy/Pages/Introduction.aspx>
<www.acat.me.uk/page/home>

INDEX

Italic page references indicate a figure.